Dear Franz,

because sound and vision
are natural compliments.

SOUND RISING FROM THE PAPER

HARVARD EAST ASIAN MONOGRAPHS 369

SOUND RISING FROM THE PAPER

*Nineteenth-Century Martial Arts Fiction
and the Chinese Acoustic Imagination*

Paize Keulemans

Published by the Harvard University Asia Center
Distributed by Harvard University Press
Cambridge (Massachusetts) and London 2014

Printed in the United States of America

The Harvard University Asia Center publishes a monograph series and, in coordination with the Fairbank Center for Chinese Studies, the Korea Institute, the Reischauer Institute of Japanese Studies, and other faculties and institutes, administers research projects designed to further scholarly understanding of China, Japan, Vietnam, Korea, and other Asian countries. The Center also sponsors projects addressing multidisciplinary and regional issues in Asia.

Publication of this book was partially underwritten by the Mr. and Mrs. Stephen C. M. King Publishing and Communications Fund, established by Stephen C. M. King to further the cause of international understanding and cooperation, especially between China and the United States, by enhancing cross-cultural education and the exchange of ideas across national boundaries through publications of the Harvard University Asia Center.

Library of Congress Cataloging-in-Publication Data

Keulemans, Paize.
  Sound Rising from the Paper : Nineteenth-Century Martial Arts Fiction and the Chinese Acoustic Imagination / Paize Keulemans.
      pages cm. — (Harvard East Asian Monographs ; 369)
  Includes bibliographical references and index.
  ISBN 978-0-674-41712-0 (hardcover : alk. paper)
  1. Martial arts fiction, Chinese—History and criticism. 2. Chinese fiction—19th century—History and criticism. 3. Sound in literature. 4. Sound—Social aspects—China. I. Title.
  PL2419.M37S68 2014
  895.13009'357—dc23

                          2014011658

Index by Jac Nelson
∞ Printed on acid-free paper

Last figure below indicates year of this printing
20 19 18 17 16 15 14

Dedicated to my parents,
Agatha Bergema and Christiaan Keulemans

Contents

List of Figures

Acknowledgments

Thanks go first and foremost to the scholars who tirelessly guided me so many years ago at the University of Chicago. I owe a huge debt to Judith Zeitlin, who prompted, supported, and motivated me for so many years as my advisor, and who has continued to question, encourage, and inspire me as a friend. I would like to thank David Roy, whose attention to accuracy in translation and annotation is only rivaled by his patience for the lack of accuracy in translating and annotating in his students. Finally I would like to thank Xiaobing Tang for teaching me to read against the grain and beyond the text to see the bigger picture.

I have been privileged to work as an assistant professor at two wonderful institutions under four very supportive chairs. I would like to thank John Treat for taking a chance to first hire me, Edward Kamens for his integrity and kindness as my mentor, Ben Elman for bringing me to Princeton and giving me the corner office, and Martin Kern for procuring me a preceptorship. I owe Sun Kang-I a tremendous debt for first inviting me to Yale University and am grateful for the countless lunches at Mory's that followed. Tina Lu has been a friend and colleague ever since she arrived at Yale; she may have been joking when she said she would be the best senior colleague ever, but she was also right. It can be daunting to be an assistant professor, and I want to thank Aaron Gerow, Chris Hill, Reggie Jackson, and Jing Tsu for being there in the trenches with me. Special thanks go to Chloe Starr for sharing her wisdom, wit, and living room. At Princeton I would like to thank all those who share food and thought at the Wednesday lunch colloquium. It has been rewarding to present my work to such a wonderful community of scholars.

Over the years, feedback at conferences has been crucial in developing this project. Among the many chairs of panels and workshops as well as audience members who prompted me to question my own thinking, the following people stand out: Sophie Volpp for being the first discussant at an AAS panel and for being a friend at every annual convention since; David Wang for bringing me to Beijing and prompting me

to think about the relationship between sound and urban space; Chris
Reed and Cynthia Brokaw for inviting me to Ohio State for a conference on print culture; Shang Wei and I-hsien Wu for including me at
a conference in New York and Lydia Liu for pushing me to think more
critically at that conference; Ellen Widmer and Dorothy Ko for bringing
balance and brilliance to a panel consisting of four men, four senses, and
four cities; Xiaofei Tian for allowing me to participate at a conference
on sound at Harvard and situating my interests in the longer history of
Chinese acoustics; Hu Siaochen and Wang Ayling for inviting me to the
Academia Sinica and Guo Yingde for sharing his incredible breadth of
knowledge while there; Margaret Wan for inviting me to Utah and introducing me to Stephen West, someone whose writing I had admired for so
long; Linda Feng for flying me to Toronto for a workshop on East Asian
Urban Spaces; and Janet Chen for keeping me grounded at Princeton
with a workshop on language, culture, and power. I also would like to
thank Wu Shengqing, Joachim Kurtz, TJ Hinrichs, and David Rolston
for being such gracious hosts and affable companions.

Various people have read my work over the years and provided
me crucial feedback. Others have shared their work with me and thus
inspired me to do better. Lam Linghon and Bao Weihong have both
shared their work with me since our graduate student days; it has been a
privilege. Wilt Idema, Maghiel van Crevel, Michel Hockx, and Christian
de Pee, who represent the very best of Dutch Sinology, have supported
me from my very first days learning Chinese. I would like to thank Chris
Hamm, Meir Shahar, and Song Weijie for sharing my enthusiasm for
martial arts literature; Elena Siu, Miao Huaiming, and Chan Kam-chiew
for their advice and insight on nineteenth-century popular performance
culture; Maram Epstein for reminding me of the importance of acoustic cliff-hangers in *The Tale of Romance and Heroism* and Madeleine
Dong for encouraging me to look at the use of dialect in the novel; Casey
Schoenberger, and Qinyuan Lei for reading parts of my manuscript
and putting up with my haphazard ways of teaching. I extend special
thanks to the two anonymous reviewers who tirelessly read through the
manuscript; their comments and insights were invaluable. Thanks go
to Kay Duffy for "volunteering" to read through the page-proofs and
Jason Stein for mapping the Huguo temple at such short notice. Finally, I
would like to thank Kristen Wanner, my editor, who guided me so skillfully through the process of publishing this book.

Parts of this book were published earlier. Parts of chapters 1 and 2 appeared first in *Twentieth Century China* (April 2004); parts of chapter 4 appeared in *Harvard Journal of Asiatic Studies* (2007); part of chapter 5 appeared in the edited volume *From Woodblocks to the Internet* (Brill, 2010). I would like to thank these publications for their permission to reprint parts of these essays, and I would like to thank the tireless editors and readers at these publications for helping me hone my thinking and writing.

Several institutions have financially supported me during the writing of this book all these years. Most notably I would like to thank the Whiting Grant and the Chiang Ching-kuo Foundation for two of those years. Columbia University's Exeas Fellowship and Society of Fellows further granted me two years of post-doctoral support, during which I began the long process of revising the manuscript. Yale University's Morse Fellowship generously provided me with a year's leave, allowing me to finish the revisions to the book. Funds from the Confucius Institute and Princeton University's Tuck Fund made research and writing in the People's Republic and Taiwan possible during the summers in between. I would like to thank Fu Gang and Liu Yucai for bringing me to Beijing University, Li Zhiyuan, Chen Zhenghong, and Wu Ge for opening the libraries at the Opera Institute and Fudan University, and Hsu Huilin for reintroducing me to the Chinese Department at Taiwan University.

I would like to thank those people in my life who make all of this scholarship worthwhile. My family in Holland and England—Mark, Ineke, Leneke, Nel, and Bert—have supported me throughout these years and across all those miles. Thanks go to Faiyaz for forty-five years of friendship (and one very handsome cover page). Inez, my daughter, I thank for being a precious gift of endless distractions. Most of all I want to thank Eugenia Lean, who has, for all these years, been both the most critical and most generous of readers. This book could not have been written without her.

P.C.A.K.

INTRODUCTION

> What is the most important object in audiovisual representation? The human body. What can the most immediate and brief meeting between two of these objects be? The physical blow. And what is the most immediate audiovisual relationship? The synchronization between a blow heard and a blow seen—or one that we believe we have seen. For, in fact, we do not really see the punch; you can confirm this by cutting the sound out of a scene. What we hear is what we haven't had time to see.
>
> —Michel Chion, *Audio-Vision*

At the end of the fifth chapter of *Ernü yingxiong zhuan* 兒女英雄傳 (Tale of romance and heroism), one of the most famous nineteenth-century Chinese martial arts novels, the hero, An Ji, a hapless young scholar from the capital, finds himself in an abandoned temple. Caught by a band of rogue priests, he is bound to a pillar, stripped of his garments, and is about to have his heart eviscerated:

> With two hands, [the evil monk] grabbed the many folds of the young scholar's lapels and, with a loud noise "KECHA," ripped them open in one single move. Pushing the lapels further back, he exposed the soft, white flesh of [the young man's] breast. Next he picked up a sharp blade from the copper alms bowl and, holding the handle with the four fingers of his right hand and steadying the blade with his thumb, he next pulled his right arm back, extended his left index finger and placed it on the young gentleman's chest, right above his heart. Our poor young scholar! His wits had already flown, and both his eyes were now pressed tightly closed! The evil monk located the exact spot and, stabbing down with his upper right arm, went straight for our young scholar's heart. You could hear a "PU," "AARGH," "GUDONG," and "DANGLANGLANG!" . . . . If you want to know whether the young scholar An survived or not, turn to the next chapter for an explanation.

EPIGRAPH: Chion, *Audio-Vision*, p. 61.

兩只手一層層的把住公子的衣衿, 喀喳一聲, 只一扯扯開, 把大衿向後又
披了一披, 露出那個白嫩嫩的胸脯兒來. 他便向銅旋子裡拿起那把尖刀,
右手四指攬定了刀靶, 大拇指按住了刀子的掩心, 先把右胳膊往後一掣,
豎起左手大指來, 按了按公子的心窩兒. 可憐公子此時早已魄散魂飛, 雙
眼緊閉! 那凶僧瞄準了地方兒, 從胳膊肘兒上往前一冒勁, 對著公子的心
窩兒刺來, 只聽噗, 「噯呀!」咕咚, 噹啷啷, 要知那安公子的性命何如, 下
回書交代. [1]

   Accustomed to the visual delights of twenty-first-century cinema, a
modern reader might expect a martial arts novel to excite through sheer
visual spectacle. Instead, the mid-nineteenth-century *Tale of Romance
and Heroism* exhilarates primarily through its suggestion of sound. To
be sure, with its emphasis on the exact position and physical trajectories of blades, arms, hands, and fingers, the book offers plenty of visual
clues to help the reader imagine the action about to take place. However,
when it comes to the actual moment the blade finds its target, when
the victim cries out and his body drops to the floor, at that moment
the text tellingly switches from sight to sound. It is the sheer noise of
the scene's climax, with its series of onomatopoeias and exclamations,
"PU," "AARGH," "GUDONG," and "DANGLANGLANG," that fills
the reader with a sense of excitement.[2] It is also these loud sounds that
compel the reader to turn the page to find out what happens next.
   A good deal of the pleasure of late nineteenth-century martial arts
fiction is located in this imaginative use of sound. As the opening quote
from *The Tale of Romance and Heroism* shows, the printed martial arts
tales of the final decades of the Qing dynasty (1644–1911) were filled
with the suggestion of aural splendor. Countless onomatopoeic phrases
enjoined the reader to imagine the martial arts scene as an acoustic
spectacle. And, as the final lines of chapter 5 of *The Tale of Romance*

---

1. Wen, *Ernü yingxiong zhuan* (Ergong 尔弓 edition, 1990 rpt.), vol. 1, chap. 5, p.
105.
2. Inspired by contemporary comic books, I have chosen to print onomatopoeia
within quotation marks and in capital letters, although late imperial novels of
course did not use such typographic conventions. Instead onomatopeia (and exclamations) were easily identifiable by their inclusion of a mouth radical. In addition,
such words were often embedded in a phrase that marks them explicitly. Both these
techniques can be observed in the first sentence of the translation offered here, "a
single sound KECHA" 喀喳一聲.

and Heroism suggest, loud onomatopoeic cliff-hangers also incited the reader to turn the page or, better yet, to spend a few more cash to buy (or rent) the next installment of a printed or handwritten tale. As if commenting on the commercial nature of the genre, textual reinventions of loud vendor calls helped to evoke the hubbub of the empire's marketplaces. Such printed reenactments of mercantile sounds called upon the reader to enjoy, albeit in tasteful fashion, his sensory consumption of commercial space and commoditized text. Finally, the mimicry of dialect accents allowed these novels to mirror the linguistic diversity of the Qing empire in terms of sound. Just as the many regional dialect sounds heard in the capital helped to lend it a sense of linguistic grandeur, so did mastering such a diverse array of dialect accents imbue the reader with a feeling of superiority. Together, these different sonic elements enabled the reader to enjoy the martial arts tale as an imagined cornucopia of sound, reading the silent text as if listening in on a loud and lively storyteller performance. The sounds of the vernacular novel may have been illusory, but many readers valued these phantasmagoric sounds precisely because, much like fiction itself, these sounds helped produce shockingly real effects. It is this remarkable affectivity of sound that provides my book with its title. As one enthusiastic commentator to the famous martial arts classic *Shuihu zhuan* 水滸傳 (Outlaws of the marsh) wrote upon facing a particularly lively, loud, if fully fictional snippet of speech, "sound rising from the paper" 紙上出聲.[3]

3. The comment is found in the Yuan Wuyai 袁無涯 edition of the text, published in 1614 with commentaries falsely ascribed to the (in)famous late Ming scholar Li Zhi 李贄 (1527–1602). The comment is inserted when the hero Wu Song loudly shouts his appreciation of wine in an inn at the bottom of Jingyang Ridge, the place where he will not much later slay a tiger with his bare hands. See *Shuihu zhuan huiping ben*, vol. 1, chap. 22, p. 419. For a description of this loud vocal moment in seventeenth-century storytelling, see chapter 2, where I discuss Zhang Dai's 張岱 (1597–1684?) anecdote about the storyteller Liu Jingting 柳敬亭 (ca. 1587–1668) performing the same episode from *The Outlaws*. Similar comments can also be found in other famous vernacular novels. For instance, when in the forty-second chapter of *San guo zhi yanyi* 三國志演義 (The romance of the three kingdoms) the hero Zhang Fei roars a load challenge to the gathered forces of Cao Cao at Changban Bridge, the commentator Mao Zonggang 毛宗崗 (1631–after 1709) adds, "It is as if on the paper you hear the sound of thunder" 紙上猶聞霹靂聲. See *San guo yanyi huiping ben*, vol. 1, chap. 42, p. 532. For an anecdote about the eighteenth-century Yangzhou storyteller Wu Tianxu 吳天緒 performing this loud

Acoustic Appreciations: Poetry and Prose

Before explaining some of the ways in which an ear for the sounds of the novel might benefit our analysis, I believe it will be useful to ask one question first: why have thus far so few scholars suggested an acoustic approach to the late-imperial vernacular novel?[4] The answer is found in part in the prominence of certain preconceptions about what a "novel" is, preconceptions that have discouraged us from taking seriously the sounds of the Chinese novel. To uncover these preconceptions, consider one genre of Chinese literature in which an acoustic approach has actually been favored by many scholars: early Chinese poetry. Conventional wisdom holds that many of the features of poetry deemed crucial to an acoustic reading do not apply to the novel. Yet I will contend that in fact certain forms of acoustic analysis prevalent in the study of early Chinese poetry can be applied fruitfully to the nineteenth-century martial arts novel.

Whereas acoustic approaches to literature have by and large been shunned in the case of the vernacular novel, such acoustic appreciations have flourished in the case of poetry, in particular the study of the songs and poems associated with *Shijing* 詩經 (The classic of poetry).[5] Two

---

literary moment, see Li Dou, *Yangzhou huafang lu, juan* 11, p. 248. This anecdote has been translated in Børdahl and Ross, *Chinese Storytellers*, p. 63. Finally it should be pointed out that the phrase "sound rising from the paper" echoes an earlier phrase by Luo Zongxin 羅宗信, who, in his preface to *Zhongyuan yinyun* 中原音韻 (A rhymebook of the Central Plain), argues that the ideal lyric should "resound loudly in one's ear and be a delight to see on the page" 耳中響聽, 紙上可觀. For a brief discussion of this quote and the relationship between imagined and performed sound in the production of Ming dynasty opera texts, see Yuming He, "Difficulties of Performance," p. 86.

4. Exceptions include an early article by Eugene Eoyang and a more recent article by Ling-hon Lam. While Eoyang's article is important because of its early date of writing, Lam's article is significant because it theorizes the important acoustic link between the novel and opera. See Eoyang, "The Immediate Audience"; Lam, "The Matriarch's Private Ear."

5. The importance of sung performance for Chinese traditional poetry of course extends beyond *The Classic of Poetry*. *The Classic of Poetry* merely represents the most famous of poetic/acoustic texts. For studies that emphasize sound (in its various forms) in other poetic genres, see, for instance, Hu Shi's 胡適 (1891–1962) *Guoyu wenxue shi* (pp. 9–36), which emphasizes the interaction of popular song

features of this research are particularly crucial to understanding the sounds of the nineteenth-century martial arts novel. First, the poems of *The Classic of Poetry* are often understood in terms of communal production and consumption epitomized in the form of the (popular) song. In these acoustic readings of *The Classic of Poetry*, formal prosodic features—rhyme, rhythm, and repetition—all function to transform silent text into an acoustic object whose very sonic features allow it to be easily shared orally.[6] In fact, as Marcel Granet makes clear, the acoustic features of sung poetry do not simply reflect their shared, communal nature, but are in fact the very features that allow the production of this community.[7] Whether we, perhaps romantically, imagine these early Chinese gatherings as groups of peasants joining in folkloric songs at communal festivals or as members of an elite hierarchy chanting sacred hymns on solemn ritual occasions, the acoustic features of poetry and song played a crucial role in producing a sense of sociability.[8]

Second, studies of *The Classic of Poetry* have further emphasized how the purely formal acoustic features of poetry had very important ideological implications in terms of the way people thought about social

---

and elite poetry in the folksongs of the Han (206 BCE–220 CE) and Six Dynasties (220–581) periods. For a study on the acoustic importance of rhapsodic *fu* 賦 poetry as sensual delight and vocal performance, see Kern, "Western Han Aesthetics," pp. 383–437. One recent study that contextualizes the emphasis on prosodic rules of tonal contrast in the practice of Six Dynasties poetry by relating it to sociopolitical changes and the growing influence of Buddhist thought is Goh's *Sound and Sight*, esp. pp. 22–39.

6. Most notably C. H. Wang drew on the work of Homer scholars Albert Lord and Milman Parry to argue for an almost exclusively oral form of composition and transmission. Scholars since then have critiqued this exclusively oral approach to *The Classic of Poetry*, pointing out that at a very early stage it was already circulating as text. As these same scholars point out, however, even when circulating as text, the oral recitation of the poems remained crucial. See C. H. Wang, *The Bell and the Drum*. For a good critique of Wang, see Kern, "*Shi jing* Songs as Performance Texts."

7. Granet, *Fêtes et chansons anciennes*.

8. See Granet, *Fêtes et chansons anciennes*, for a popular reading of the section on "guofeng" 國風 (The airs of states); for a reading of a particular poem that emphasizes ritual chanted performance in a court setting, see Kern, "*Shi jing* Songs as Performance Texts," pp. 77–111. According to some scholars, the rhythm of the songs actually allowed coordinated physical movement in court dances. See Maspero, *China in Antiquity*, pp. 274–76.

order. In early practices of poetry there was a strong sense of correlative thinking: the acoustic order of the text was thought to reflect or even create social order.[9] As Martin Kern, for example, has shown by gathering a discrete host of phonic details and imbuing these ornamental details with clearly recognizable patterns—rhyme, rhythm, stanzic repetition—hymnal songs of *The Classic of Poetry* were thought to ritually enact the collecting and ordering of the material world itself.[10] Recent studies in classical Chinese thought illustrate how this acoustic cosmological thinking was imbued with philosophical rigor. Veritable paragons of philosophy such as Zhuangzi 莊子 (369–286 BCE) and Xunzi 荀子 (ca. 312–230 BCE), indeed even the historical prose of the *Zuozhuan* 左傳, reflected the idea that by structuring the phonic features of language one could cultivate the individual body and order the social polity.[11]

When we recognize those aspects of acoustic analysis that have found most traction in the study of early poetry, it is easy to understand why, in contrast, the study of the late-imperial vernacular novel has rarely been conducted in terms of sound. First, whereas in the poetic tradition sound and orality were understood in terms of communal sociability, the late-imperial novel is often regarded as a genre of writing produced and consumed by individuals laboring and reading in private and in silence. To a degree, this image of the vernacular novel as works of individual and silent writing and reading practices is based on late-imperial Chinese aesthetics itself. Guided by the interlineal comments of seventeenth-century literati such as Jin Shengtan 金聖嘆 (1610?–1661) and Zhang Zhupo 張竹坡 (1670–98), scholars such as

9. Zheng Yuyu has expanded on these ideas of correlation in terms of *fu* poetry, showing that such ordering of the social body takes the form of acoustic healing or "harmonizing" of the individual body. See Zheng Yuyu, "Lianlei, fengsong yu shiyu tiyan de chuanyi."

10. See Kern, "*Shi jing* Songs as Performance Texts." For the way in which *fu* poetry similarly employs its acoustic form to discipline the reader, see Kern, "Western Han Aesthetics," esp. pp. 423–31.

11. For an argument not necessarily for correlative thought but instead for the idea of metaphor, see Saussy, "'Ritual Separates, Music Unites'"; for an investigation of the way sound in the writings of Zhuangzi allowed for an early form of (physical) self-cultivation, see West, "Look at the Finger"; for a discussion of the importance of musical correlative thought in the *Zuozhuan*, see Wai-yee Li, *The Readability of the Past*, pp. 118–47.

Andrew Plaks understood the Chinese vernacular novel, in particular its most famous incarnation, the six great masterworks of the late-imperial period, as texts penned by a single, genius author and consumed by an individual reader.[12] At the same time, the influence of Western notions of the novel was crucial, most notably Ian Watt's path-breaking analysis, *The Rise of the Novel*, which famously regarded the formation of the novel as a genre of writing indelibly interlinked with the formation of the modern, bourgeois individual and a realist style of prose that elided its own act of enunciation.[13]

To be sure, many of Watt's ideas have since been either nuanced or rejected.[14] For our purposes, it has been shown that although silent, interiorized modes of reading may define the consumption of the modern, Western novel, they cannot be taken to be the norm for earlier or other forms of literature or for those "novels" belonging to a non-Western tradition.[15] Similarly, the idea of an individual author whose labor is defined as

12. In the West, Plaks is the foremost champion of the idea of the "Four Masterworks" as works penned by literati authors. As he points out, it is not simply that these men composed their works as individuals, but also that they composed their works under the influence of a new, late-Ming interest in individual subjectivity as exemplified in the philosophies of Wang Yangming 王陽明 (1472–1529) and Li Zhi. See Plaks, *Four Masterworks*, esp. pp. 19–20, 25, 39, 44. The emphasis on individual authorship is most strongly worded as it relates to the most controversial novel of the four masterworks, the *Jin Ping Mei*, when Plaks refutes the notion of collective authorship and advocates the novel instead as "an astonishingly 'original' work of art, conceived, at least to some extent, within the mind of a single author." Plaks, *Four Masterworks*, p. 70. Later scholars have drawn on this work to further expand the idea of the vernacular novel as a genre of writing crucial to the formation of the individual subject. See Martin Huang, *Literati and Self-Re/Presentation*, pp. 1–44.

13. The silence of Watt's study becomes apparent in his analysis of the written epistolary form (as opposed to oral communication) of Richardson's *Clarissa* and the autobiographical journal of Defoe's *Crusoe*. See Watt, *The Rise of the Novel*, pp. 174–207 and 60–92. For a critique of the self-sufficiency of the (Western) subject from a post-colonial angle, see Lydia Liu, "Robinson Crusoe's Earthenware Pot."

14. For a review of some of the critiques of Watt and the way these critiques nevertheless incorporate many of his main tenents, see Folkenflik, "The Heirs of Watt."

15. Andrew Pettegree points out, for instance, how in the sixteenth century many forms of leisure literature, including Boccaccio's *Decameron*, remained highly suitable for reading aloud and communal discussion. See Pettegree, *The Book in the Renaissance*, pp. 155–58. For a study of a crucial seventeenth-century shift towards silent reading practices in the West and the way this shift produced a new form of

intellectual by the silence of his study has been shown to be the result of a typically nineteenth-century mode of literary production.[16] Finally, the late-imperial vernacular novel is anything but realistic and often delights in drawing attention to its own fictionality. And yet, despite some notable exceptions, Watt's ideas did leave an indelible stamp on the research of the late-imperial Chinese novel. For many, the value of the Chinese vernacular novel, in particular the most famous works in the tradition, was found in the writing and reading practices of the individual who was assumed to be silent. As a result, sound, whether real or imagined, and its associations of communal sociability had little place in the processes of writing and reading associated with these novels.

Second, the very structural and linguistic features that define the Chinese vernacular novel all too easily seemed to prohibit the kind of acoustic analysis favored by scholars of poetry. Aesthetic (and ideological) analyses of prosody make eminent sense for poetry, a form of literature that tends to be brief and is characterized by a tightly regimented use of language; they do not work as well for late-imperial vernacular novels, which are long and episodic in terms of structure and variegated, if not simply unruly, in terms of language. Linguistically and structurally speaking, the vernacular novel seems the opposite of poetic song: impossible to memorize succinctly, chant communally, transmit orally, or consume acoustically. Not surprisingly, scholars have argued for an aesthetics of the novel that is explicitly inter*textual*, an aesthetics particularly evident in studies of the sixteenth-century *Jin Ping Mei* 金瓶梅 (The plum in the golden vase). David Roy's early readings, for instance, drew on Mikhail Bahktin's notion of heteroglossia to interpret the linguistic variegation of the novel as a carefully authored interweaving of textual quotations.[17] Scholars further investigated this notion of an explicitly *textual* heteroglossia as the product of an explicitly *printed* intertextuality. Shang Wei has argued that in many ways the sixteenth-century novel most resembles a printed encyclopedia, a literary form that enthralled its

---

narration, see Jajdelska, *Silent Reading*. For a critique of some of the major twentieth-century theorists of the novel and their assumptions of a silent reader, including Wayne Booth, Mikhail Bakhtin, and Gérard Genette, see ibid., pp. 8–10.

16. See Picker, *Victorian Soundscapes*, pp. 44–81.

17. See Roy, "Introduction." Note that Bakhtin's notion of heteroglossia need not be read as inherently textual. For a discussion of the importance of orality and storytelling for Bakhtin's linguistic thought, see France, "The Speaking Author."

reader by collecting snippets of texts from other printed sources, recombining these snippets of text on a single page.[18] How can the novel, so readily defined by its intertextual features and print-cultural context, ever be understood in terms of sound, vocality, and acoustics?

Such an acoustic approach to vernacular fiction is, however, not only possible but also illuminating. Moreover, it is precisely those acoustic modes of analysis associated with the study of early poetry that allow us to read late-imperial fiction as acoustic text. In other words, even though the late-imperial novel has often been understood in terms of individual silent reading practices, it is worthwhile to borrow some of the ideas of shared poetic production and consumption championed by scholars of *The Classic of Poetry*. This is not to say that late-imperial novels were, as sometimes has been suggested, necessarily communally produced or vocally consumed in a literal sense.[19] Rather, I argue that the *suggestion* of sound allowed for *the idea* of these novels as acoustic objects that could be shared communally. First, imagining these mute texts as loud performances allowed the novels to project a sense of community even if they were in fact produced and consumed privately and silently. Second, just as the formal acoustic features of poetry imbued these texts with a sense of order, so did the imagined sounds of the novel lend structure to the text. Finally, as in the case of classical poetry, this acoustic structure of the vernacular novel was associated with a certain sense of social order: in nineteenth-century martial arts novels the imagination of a well-governed society or a disciplined subject was made possible by linking acoustic elements to the structure of the plot.

The Acoustic Structure of the Novel's Plot

Although classical poetry suggests ways in which the Chinese late-imperial novel can be read acoustically, there are crucial differences between these two very different forms of literature and their use of

18. See Shang, "'Jin Ping Mei' and Late Ming Print Culture."
19. For an argument that some of the most popular texts in fact may have been produced and consumed communally and orally, see McLaren, *Chinese Popular Culture*, pp. 32–57.

sound to provide literary structure. Most notably, whereas classical poetry primarily provides structure through prosody, the late-imperial novel primarily offers a sense of structure through plot. To uncover this acoustic order of the novel's plot, in particular the plot of the late nineteenth-century martial arts novel, I will draw on Andrew Plaks's formal analysis of the elite late-imperial novel as well as on classical poetics. Throughout my analysis, however, it remains important for the reader to differentiate the nineteenth-century martial arts novel from both ancient poetry and more elite forms of vernacular fiction. Whereas ancient poetry arose in a ritual context, the productive forces behind nineteenth-century fiction were unmistakably commercial. Plaks's reading of the vernacular masterworks of the Ming is based on the aesthetics of the literati elite, yet the nineteenth-century martial arts novel sought to engage with the politics and pleasures of the popular marketplace.

At first a focus on plot might not seem a likely way of arguing for an acoustic structure of the Chinese martial arts novel. After all, if late imperial vernacular novels are notoriously episodic and loosely structured in general, the nineteenth-century martial arts novel, a commercial and popular genre par excellence, is particularly rambling and convoluted. Seeking to please readers, the authors of these novels often introduced scores of characters whose many adventures are told through plots that promise lots of excitement but offer little in terms of structured connections. As already indicated by some of their titles— *Qun ying jie* 群英傑 (The gathered heroes; undated, early 19th c.), *Qi xia wu yi* 七俠五義 (The seven knights and the five gallants; 1889), *Xiao wu yi* 小五義 (The latter five gallants; 1890), *Qi jian shisan xia* 七劍十三俠 (The seven swordsmen and the thirteen knights; 1892)—these novels entertain by offering a huge cast of characters. Similarly, in terms of plot, even a cursory reading of a few of these novels reveals not a simple chain of events, but instead a confusing heap of multiple interconnecting and overlapping plotlines.[20]

---

20. Anyone who has ever used reference works to get a grasp of the main plot of one of these novels will quickly come to the same conclusion: there is no main plot. Rather, the novel's structure consists of a bewildering number of events that defy easy and succinct summary. For a selection of plot summaries, see Jiangsusheng shehuikexueyuan Ming Qing xiaoshuo yanjiu zhongxin wenxue yanjiusuo, *Zhongguo tongsu xiaoshuo zongmu tiyao*.

Although some early scholars have critiqued the late-imperial novel for lacking a clear structure or purposeful plot, more recently, scholars have increasingly pointed out that the multiple plotlines and myriad different characters are not necessarily the result of slipshod work.[21] Instead the abundance of characters and plotlines can also speak of a distinct, late-imperial aesthetic that prizes structural complexity over linear progression and that favors interactions among multifarious characters over the actions of an individual protagonist. As Andrew Plaks has illustrated, in the case of the famous "Masterworks of Vernacular Fiction"—*The Romance of the Three Kingdoms, The Outlaws of the Marsh, Xi you ji* 西遊記 (The journey to the west), and *Jin Ping Mei*—the superficial chaos of multiple plotlines and dozens of characters actually serves to create a highly complex, tightly structured work of art.[22] Notably, these works espoused plotlines that move through repetitive cycles of waxing and waning as they gather and disperse multiple characters and numerous events in the process. It is the repetition of these cycles that helps to structure the seemingly chaotic narrative into a single, yet still highly multifaceted, totality: the multi-chapter vernacular novel.

By focusing on sound, we find that a variety of acoustic elements contribute to the kind of structural complexity found in the late-imperial vernacular text. As the vernacular novel moves through cycles of waxing and waning, bringing together characters and events in constantly evolving constellations and juxtapositions, it employs the suggestion of sound to lend these cycles a sense of acoustic atmosphere. It is the accumulation of sounds—a plethora of onomatopoeias in action scenes, a bevy of vendor calls in urban market settings, or a diversity of dialect accents in dialogues—that helps to define the climactic moments of these tales. It is the repetition of these moments of acoustic spectacle as well as the sonic lull that follows them that creates a clear sense of rhythm in the text. Meanwhile it is the promise of ever more acoustic spectacle that lends momentum to the narrative and keeps the reader glued to the page.

21. Most notable among these early scholars is probably C. T. Hsia. Regarding the structure of *Jin Ping Mei*, for instance, Hsia has argued that the novel clearly lacks "ideological or philosophical coherence" because it manifests "obvious structural anarchy." See Hsia, *The Classic Chinese Novel*, p. 180.
22. See Plaks, *Four Masterworks*.

If these imagined sounds help to structure the ebb and flow of events in the martial arts novel, the novel's acoustic elements also help to link isolated climactic moments into longer, multi-episodic plots. As shown in the brief snippet from *The Tale of Romance and Heroism* quoted earlier, nineteenth-century martial arts novels often employ a single onomatopoeia or a series of exclamations to introduce a new character or produce a new twist in the plot. At times such acoustic elements can be understood as a sonic break that interrupts a moment of celebratory liveliness, marking a temporary climax and signaling the beginning of the inevitable cycle of dispersal. At other times, such onomatopoeia, exclamations, or vendor calls function as an acoustic bridge, linking one cycle of events to the next, enticing the reader to read on by suggesting that more sonic liveliness will soon follow.

The sounds of the vernacular novel did not merely provide a sense of aesthetic structure, in turn this structure suggested a broader sense of social order. Though some political reformers in the early twentieth century were inspired by these tales to acts of anarchism, these tales of martial men are in fact remarkably conservative in ideological outlook.[23] As Lu Xun 魯迅 (penname of Zhou Shuren 周術人, 1881–1936) has pointed out, in the end the rowdy martial men that fill the pages of these novels are brought to order under the authority of the central character, the judge, just as the rebellious potential of unbridled martial arts action is invariably legitimated by making it serve imperial power.[24] By attuning ourselves to the sounds of the novel, we can begin to discern how this sense of ideological order is not only found on the

23. In an essay titled "On the Relationship between Fiction and the Government of the People," Liang Qichao 梁啟超 (1873–1929) famously fulminated against martial arts novels, most notably *Outlaws of the Marsh* and *The Three Kingdoms*, because their descriptions of masculine brotherhood had led directly, according to Liang, to the formation of secret societies and the disaster of the Boxer Rebellion. See his "Lun xiaoshuo yu qunzhi zhi guanxi." The most famous early twentieth-century revolutionary to be inspired by tales of martial arts derring-do remains undoubtedly Qiu Jin 秋瑾 (1875–1907). For a discussion of Qiu Jin's activities as literary and revolutionary paragon, see Idema and Grant, *The Red Brush*, pp. 767–808.
24. His exact words were, "The heroes of such novels, though rough and gallant like the earlier outlaws, had to serve under some important official and considered it honorable to do so. This could happen only in an age when the people were completely subdued and subservient." In Lu Xun, *Zhongguo xiaoshuo shilue*, p. 204. Translation by Xianyi and Gladys Yang in Lu Xun, *A Brief History*, p. 371.

level of content and character, but also on the level of form. Like the heroic martial men featured in these novels, the acoustic spectacle they produce at first seems playful, liberating, perhaps even unruly. Yet inevitably, these moments of acoustic attraction are brought in line through the unfolding of a well-structured plot. Thus the acoustic seduction of vendor calls is turned into a moral lesson about disciplining one's commercial and sexual desires; the riotous liveliness of dialect accents reflects a clear hierarchy of social distinctions; the onomatopoeic sparkle of ineffable action might open up a host of undisclosed possibilities, but invariably sound is made meaningful and the teleology of plot reestablished.

Although poetry and the elite vernacular novel are instructive for understanding how imaginary sounds worked in the nineteenth-century martial arts novel, it is important to remember that the popular nineteenth-century martial arts tale also differs markedly from these two other forms. For one, the martial arts novel strategically embeds acoustic elements within prose so as to produce the progression of plot. Equally important, unlike the poetry of the ancient period, the nineteenth-century martial arts novel was produced not in a ritual context but rather in a distinctly commercial context.[25] Originally performed as popular storyteller tales staged at local markets and urban teahouses for a few coppers, these novels were eventually edited, printed, and sold by commercial book vendors who sought to cash in on the popularity of these tales. Not surprisingly, the martial arts novel is drenched not in the rarified and ritual atmosphere of the courts of the Zhou dynasty (1046–256 BCE), but rather in the aesthetics, attractions, and anxieties of the nineteenth-century urban marketplace. As a result, one of the more interesting acoustic features of these novels is found in the way they incorporate brief snippets of vendor calls into their narratives. Partially these printed and performed reenactments of the sounds of hawkers and merchants serve to evoke the attractions and atmosphere of the marketplace. Yet because these mercantile sounds are staged as

---

25. That said, as Hu Siao-chen has argued, *The Tale of Romance and Heroism*, an exceptional elite literati product, not a commercial novel, shows a strong interest in ritual form. See "Pinfan riyong yu daotong lunli." As I show in chapter 6 of this book, a focus on the acoustic aspects of the novel form reveals how this interest in ritual is not only expressed in the author's intellectual arguments, but also embedded in the very form of the novel's prose and poetic song.

crucial acoustic linkages in the unfolding of plot, they also manage to
order the wayward desires elicited by these calls into a clear and disciplined structure.

The popular, unmistakably commercial background of the nineteenth-century martial arts novel also helps to differentiate it from
the more highbrow masterworks of the late Ming dynasty (1368–1644)
favored by Plaks. The structural complexity so prized in the famous
elite novels of the late Ming most certainly influenced the aesthetics
of the commercial products of the late Qing.[26] Yet the majority of these
later novels never adhered solely to an exclusively elite, highly structured organizational scheme. Even the four elite novels discussed by
Plaks were never solely interpreted in terms of the structural complexity espoused by literati editors and commentators. As Anne McLaren
points out, the "masterworks" of the Ming dynasty were read by a variety
of audiences and for remarkably different purposes.[27] As Plaks himself
notes, the elite literati's investment in the tightly structured prose and
well-wrought plot of the masterworks of the late Ming was the result of
their often ironic reaction to the more popular source material—storyteller tales, dramatic performances, and folk legends—on which these
novels were originally based.[28]

When turning to the sounds of the nineteenth-century martial
arts novel, we must similarly keep in mind that different segments of
the population found different pleasures in the acoustic attractions
provided by these novels. While some readers read these novels with
a self-conscious ear for their acoustic aesthetics, other readers simply
appreciated the surface liveliness provided by the plethora of different sounds in the text. In fact, simply understanding that the acous-

26. Margaret Wan (*Green Peony*, esp. pp. 109–112) has argued in detail how the
earlier, literati aesthetics of the late Ming dynasty can be found in the martial arts
novels of the early nineteenth century.
27. McLaren, "Ming Audiences and Vernacular Hermeneutics."
28. In fact, Plaks notes this early on when he states, "Each [of the four great novels]
represents the culmination of a long prior and subsequent history of source materials, antecedent narratives, and alternate recensions. Yet my principal thesis here
will be that in each case the sixteenth-century text we have represents the most
significant phase of this process of evolution, the one that puts the final stamp on
the process and raises the respective narrative materials to the level of self-conscious artistic constructs." See Plaks, *Four Masterworks*, pp. 3–4.

tic elements in these novels may have been read differently by different segments of the population is not enough; it is even more important to understand how these different appreciations of the sounds of the novel may have been instrumental in the formation of different social groups. The imaginary sounds of the novel do not simply reflect sociability, they create it. In the next section I will explore the ways in which printed sound produced different modes of sociability and distinctly different imaginations of community.

Sound and Sociability

Although I draw linkages between the sounds of early Chinese poetry and those of late-imperial martial arts novels in terms of producing a sense of sociability, there remains a marked distinction between the two: unlike early Chinese poetry, the sounds of late nineteenth-century martial arts fiction are patently not real. Whereas the community engendered by the sounds of early Chinese poetry was one associated with oral and ritual performance, martial arts novels are print-cultural commodities typically consumed in silence. Rather than seeing this as an impediment to an acoustic sense of community, however, we should take the purely fictive nature of the novel's sounds as an incentive to further explore how textualized sound can produce sociability at the very heart of print culture. Specifically, I will show how the imaginary sounds of martial arts fiction were crucial in opening up paths to imagining two distinct forms of acoustic sociability. The first form, which I will call "popular," employed the sounds of the martial arts novel to produce a simulacrum of heightened sociability associated with the loud noise of popular gathering places such as temple fairs, marketplaces, and teahouses. Even when reading in silence and isolation, the individual reader was called upon by those sounds to imagine himself as part of this larger sociable experience. The second form, which I will term "elite," sought to distance itself from such vulgar and noisy gatherings and in doing so emphasized the illusory nature of sound, yet in the process produced a different, more highbrow form of sociability predicated on the appreciation of the novel's (meta)fictional technique.

Previous studies on the sociability of sound—Western and
Chinese, literary and non-literary—tend to employ sound in a concrete
sense. For historians, for example, it was the actual sound of village
bells or the genuine rhythms of the drum tower that allowed villages in
nineteenth-century France and urban sites in imperial China to establish a sense of community.[29] In literary studies, this need for sound to
be actualized in order for it to produce a sense of community is found
in the (relentless) emphasis on orality. Walter Ong, for instance, draws
a remarkably strong distinction between textual and oral culture in
terms of the production of a sense of community; according to Ong,
whereas text and, in particular, print isolate individuals, the sound of
the spoken word produces a sense of direct communication that allows
transparent accessibility and hence is eminently suitable to social interaction and communal sharing.[30] In the realm of early Chinese poetry,
the idea of *The Classic of Poetry* as a purely oral text is, of course, a
thing of the past. That said, even for those contemporary scholars who
emphasize the textual circulation of *The Classic of Poetry*, the efficacy
of these poems still depends heavily on the ritual act of chanting them
aloud.[31] In short, sound as a medium might be effective in the ways it
establishes a sense of community, but only if there is actual sound to
begin with.

To suggest, then, that the nineteenth-century martial arts novel
could likewise employ sound to produce a sense of sociability might
seem problematic. After all, these lengthy novels are eminently textual
products. Produced by well-established printing houses in Beijing
and Shanghai, clothed in a variety of para-textual wrappings that
often include calligraphic title pages and numerous illustrations, and

---

29. I am referring here respectively to Alain Corbin, who has shown how the
sound of church bells helped to define the spatial boundaries of rural communities
in nineteenth-century France, and Wu Hung, who has suggested how the rhythm
of the drum and bell tower established the temporal order of urban communities
in imperial China. See Corbin, *Village Bells*; Wu Hung, "The Hong Kong Clock."
30. Ong, *Orality and Literacy*, esp. pp. 72–75, 152–53 (where Ong coincidentally
draws on Ian Watt's earlier study).
31. See Kern, "*Shi jing* Songs as Performance Texts." For a paper that takes the
materiality of bronze inscriptions into consideration (but nevertheless keeps the
oral instantiation of such inscriptions in mind), see Schaberg, "'Virtue's Sound
Shining.'"

comprising a hundred chapters or more, there is little historical information that suggests that these works were ever intended for oral/aural consumption. Unless we imagine these novels as being read aloud, something which is always possible but for which little evidence exists, the act of reading these novels remained an act of individual and silent consumption.[32]

Yet, if the novel did not produce the kind of acoustic sociability brought to life during actual oral performance, it did offer a simulacrum of such sociability by mimicking within the text a sense of orality. Most notably, it did so through one of its more remarkable features, the rhetorical figure of the storyteller. It was the illusion of an oral presence within the text that helped to turn the silent signs on the page into a lively acoustic spectacle. Similarly, it was the storyteller figure who, as the embodiment of popular orality, lent these tales a sense of shared communal values and interpersonal intimacy. Moreover, this presence of a storyteller figure and the way in which his presence suggested a communal performance (as opposed to a solitary act of reading), grew particularly strong in nineteenth-century martial arts fiction. As I show in chapter 2, whereas in much late-imperial vernacular fiction the storyteller is merely a rhetorical figure that has little to do with actual storytelling performances, the nineteenth-century martial arts novel drew much of its material from popular storytelling cycles. Prefaces and title pages emphasized this historical link to storytelling as a way of strengthening the sense of a shared oral heritage.

In addition, nineteenth-century martial arts novels employed a host of acoustic elements associated with the storyteller figure—onomatopoeia, vendor calls, dialect accents—snippets of sound designed to draw the reader from his silent reading into the simulacrum of the "storyteller's" lively and loud performance. Sometimes acoustic elements would do so by conjuring up a sense of a shared public space. As I show in chapter 3, for instance, the insertion of simulated vendor calls in these texts recreated the text as a literary marketplace, familiar to all if still tightly segregated in terms of tasteful appreciation. Alternatively, acoustic elements projected a sense of shared linguistic community by

32. Wolfram Eberhard documents storytellers in Taipei reading novels aloud, but this form of public performance can hardly be considered a representative form of "reading aloud." See Eberhard, "Notes on Chinese Storytellers."

emphasizing the sound of the spoken voice. As I show in chapter 5, the imitation of the sounds of different dialects in these novels presents language in its most popular and easily accessible form. Together, the storyteller's voice and the myriad acoustic elements brought to life by his voice tempted the reader to enter a community defined by an imagined orality, imbuing the act of solitary reading with the aura of shared experience.

The sounds of the novel, just like the community they promised, were of course a fiction. Indeed, most readers were well aware of the illusory qualities of the acoustic spectacle, just as they were well aware that the martial arts novel, even if it presented itself as an "oral" tale, was only accessible to those who could read. This recognition could make the nineteenth-century martial arts novel particularly attractive as a "high" literary form. Although the sounds in these texts allowed the reader to imagine his act of literary consumption as part and parcel of a broadly shared oral culture, the recognition of the fictional nature of these sounds still allowed the reader to maintain a careful distance both from the illiterate masses and, more importantly, from supposedly less educated readers.

To understand how this worked, it is necessary to understand one final aspect of the acoustic pleasures of the nineteenth-century martial arts novel, its emphasis on self-conscious metafictionality. As literary critics have increasingly pointed out, there exists in the late-imperial literary tradition a strong tendency towards metafiction. Through studies of works ranging from the eighteenth-century masterwork *Hong lou meng* 紅樓夢 (Dream of the red chamber) to the Red Light fiction of the nineteenth century, scholars have shown how late-imperial fiction often presented itself in metafictional terms, delighting in fiction exposed as nothing but fiction.[33]

An acoustic approach to the novel allows us to recognize how sound played an important role in this metafictional tradition. For instance, in what undoubtedly is the prime example of self-conscious fictionality in the late-imperial vernacular tradition, *Dream of the Red Chamber*, references to the sensory experience of sound consistently draw the

---

33. See, among others, Karlitz, *The Rhetoric of the* Chin p'ing mei; Anthony Yu, *Rereading the Stone*; Starr, *Red-light Novels*.

reader's attention to the illusory nature of the text itself.[34] Of course, these sounds may be seductive, but they can never be real. Their illusion merely highlights the fictional nature of the novel and arguably even serves to call attention to the illusory and evanescent nature of life itself.

Although a sensory aesthetics of metafiction thus can be ascribed to some of the masterworks of late-imperial vernacular fiction, it cannot be ascribed to all works of premodern fiction. To be sure, strong metafictional themes can certainly be detected in the more highbrow martial arts novels such as *The Tale of Romance and Heroism*.[35] Yet in most other martial arts novels of the nineteenth century metafiction is voiced only occasionally, suggesting that much of the noise in these novels is precisely what it seems: a form of acoustic spectacle meant to delight the reader, to distract him from his everyday experience, and to immerse him in an imagined lively, communal atmosphere.

Because of this, rather than understanding the metafictional aesthetics of imagined sound as merely a reflection of the elite status of the masterworks of vernacular fiction, we should approach such acoustic metafictionality as a crucial element necessary to generate a sense of elite status. As Sai-shing Yung has recently pointed out, the sounds of late-Ming opera were often interpreted to divide neatly into elite and non-elite forms of appreciation; according to conventional readings, the raucous noise of more spectacular opera was enjoyed by more popular crowds, whereas the more muted sounds of contemplative scenes were appreciated by a more elite audience.[36] Traditional approaches to the vernacular novel and its imaginary acoustics made a similar distinction. On the one hand, readers could choose to indulge their senses in rather "vulgar" fashion, allowing themselves to be lost in the liveliness of the imagined spectacle. On the other hand, readers could tastefully recognize the evanescence of such sounds. Simply put, the recognition of the sounds of the novel as illusory became one of the

---

34. Sound is not the only sense being marshaled for the purposes of metafiction; the novel is, after all, famously visual. For a reading of the novel from a sensory and in particular olfactory "point of view," see Zhang Shijun, Hong lou meng *de kongjian xushi.*
35. For the metafictional tendencies of this novel, see Hamm, "Reading the Swordswoman's Tale." For an exploration of metafiction in earlier nineteenth-century martial arts novels, see Wan, *Green Peony*, pp. 101–29.
36. See Yung, "From Exorcism to Connoisseurship."

ways of producing an invisible dividing line between different reading practices, popular and elite, if not actual readers. [37]

This division between popular and elite tastes should be understood in light of the unprecedented print-cultural effervescence of the late-imperial age. The vernacular novel represents one of the most pre-eminent literary products of the print-cultural age.[38] Drawing on the ever-growing plethora of texts made available by the print boom of the sixteenth and seventeenth centuries, the late-imperial novel incorporated an unprecedented array of different, often heterogeneous sources and other literary forms. Similarly, in terms of language, it mixed a wild array of different registers ranging from the vernacular to the classical, including, for example, poetic diction as well as snippets of thieves' argot. Finally, the print boom of the late-imperial period also made this variegated form of literary writing readily available to a broad, diverse audience consisting of women, children, merchants, and scholars (or so prefaces often claimed).[39] In short, commercial in nature, popular in appeal, and constructed on the basis of a remarkable heteroglossic use of language and intertextual use of sources, the vernacular novel epitomized the way in which print technology allowed the culture of text to expand from a relatively small scholarly elite to a much wider audience, threatening to erase distinctions of class and cultivation in the process.

Both the excitement and the anxieties caused by these print-cultural shifts can be heard in the sounds of the novel, in particular in a term often associated with the "noise" produced by the raucous nineteenth-century martial arts novel, *renao* 熱鬧. The term, variously translated as "lively," "spectacular," "crowded," or simply "loud," is usually associated with the hustle and bustle of large crowds, the places these crowds gathered (temple fairs, marketplaces, or teahouses), and the loud atmosphere they produced.[40] Yet in the case of Chinese

37. For the way in which visual spectacle was used to produce a similar distinction in terms of taste, see Sieber, "Seeing the World."
38. See Ding Naifei, *Obscene Things*; Shang, "The Making of the Everyday World."
39. For an analysis of these different audiences and the way various paratextual materials were used to produce idealized readers, see McLaren, "Constructing New Reading Publics."
40. Not surprisingly, the term has been most theorized by scholars of anthropology. For instance, Stephan Feuchtwang, who translates the term as "spectacle," discusses *renao* as the kind of entertainment that draws crowds to temple

late-imperial literature the term can also be used to describe vernacular fiction, most notably those aspects mentioned above: its popular appeal, its appetite for spectacle, the way in which it voraciously incorporates different genres and languages into a single, exciting package. Indeed, for Chinese critics offended by the incursion of popular tastes into the sacred realm of text, *renao* signified the ways in which, amid the heady mixture of languages, genres, objects, and impressions, proper distinctions might be lost. Especially in the case of the martial arts novel, a form of fiction that could claim tremendous appeal in terms of audience and that depended quite heavily on the attraction of its loud spectacle, the concept of *renao* proved a convenient target for critics.

This is not to say that these critics were mere gainsayers of fiction or even martial arts novels per se, but rather that they embraced the notion of *renao* brought to life in these popular forms of fiction precisely to keep the distinction between high and low, elite and lower-class forms of literary consumption, intact. From the late Ming until the late Qing, critics and authors often welcomed the loud noise of vernacular forms of literature not because they identified with the vulgar pleasures brought to life by the myriad sounds of the novel, but because they thought that by recognizing such sounds as mere illusion they could differentiate themselves from the common crowd, thereby establishing their elite sense of sociability. An early twentieth-century critic such as Shi An, for instance, had little problem with the elite (literally "those belonging to the upper class" 上等社會) indulging their taste in martial arts fiction. The problem was with the lower classes and how they failed to differentiate fact from fiction. As Shi An argued, how could "these lower class kinds of people with their feeble understanding tell that these stories were mere illusory castles in the sky?" 下等社會之人類, 知識薄弱, 焉知此等書籍為空中樓閣?[41] And failing to tell the difference between fiction and reality, how could such lower-class people fail to try and imitate these martial heroes and in the process create untold social chaos, indeed cause the demise of China itself?[42]

---

festivals. More recently, Adam Chau discusses the term, or more specifically its local Shanxi variant, *honghuo* 紅火, as "red hot sociability," that is, the heightened atmosphere of social interaction found at popular religious festivals. See Feuchtwang, *Chinese Popular Religion*; Chau, *Miraculous Response*, pp. 147–68.
41. Shi An, "Chankongshi suibi," p. 443.
42. Shi An was clearly influenced by Liang Qichao, who wrote some eight years earlier, "Now everywhere among our people there are heroes of the green forests...."

The illusion of sound created by these novels lends itself beautifully to the formulation of such class distinctions. As I show in chapter
1, building on sound as the spectacular sign of illusion, the critic Jin
Shengtan applied a metafictional logic to his appreciation of one of the
more popular and rambunctious vernacular novels, the martial arts tale
Outlaws of the Marsh. In the nineteenth century, the most remarkable
product of such an acoustic aesthetics of metafiction was found in the
martial arts novel *The Tale of Romance and Heroism*. As I illustrate in
chapter 5, the writer Wen Kang 文康 (fl. 1842–51) went to remarkable
lengths to bring the sounds of the novel to life, even while keeping the
acoustic implications of those sounds firmly within the realm of the
metafictional. Indeed, his novel is unprecedented in the way it fleshes
out the storyteller figure as a fully voiced oral narrator, and yet it nevertheless tirelessly reminds the reader of the illusory nature of the sounds
produced by his voice. The novel may present itself in the guise of the
popular sociability of an oral tale, but it still allows its readers to create
a distinct, elitist sociability by reminding them of the illusory nature of
the novel's use of sound.

The Nineteenth-Century Martial Arts Novel

Though my investigation of the acoustic imagination has broader implications for the late-imperial novel, I have chosen to focus on one partic-

---

Dreams of having 'big bowls of wine, big slices of meat, sharing gold and silver and
weighing them on a scale, and putting on complete suits of clothes,' as these heroes
did, fill the minds *of the lower classes*" (emphasis mine). See Liang Qichao, "On
the Relationship between Fiction and the Government of the People," p. 80; Liang
Qichao, "Lun xiaoshuo yu qunzhi zhi guanxi," p. 18. For similar arguments that
fulminate against the illusory nature of martial arts attractions, though in this
case the lower classes have been transformed into "urban petty bourgeois" and
novels into film, see Mao Dun, "Fengjian de xiaoshimin." Mao Dun 茅盾 is the pen
name of Shen Dehong 沈德鴻, 1896–1981; most telling is his description of noisy
showings of the film *Huoshao Hongliansi* 火燒紅蓮寺 (Burning of the Red Lotus
Temple), and the effect the film has on the youthful, urban audience, for whom "the
film is no longer an illusion, it has become reality!" 影戲不復是 '戲,' 而是真實! See
Mao Dun, "Fengjian de xiaoshimin," p. 370. This passage is partially translated and
fully discussed in Fan, "Football Meets Opium," pp. 212–14.

ularly loud genre of vernacular fiction, the martial arts novel. More specifically, I limit this study to those martial arts novels produced in the late nineteenth century, a moment of interest because it represents both the end of the novel in its late-imperial form and the beginning of the martial arts tale as the most popular and financially lucrative genre of modern printed fiction. Finally, because most of these late nineteenth-century martial arts novels were first produced in the capital of the Qing empire, I have further delineated this study geographically to the martial arts novels of Beijing, which allows me to locate the acoustic aesthetics of these novels within the specific context of local storytelling performance as well as the particular late-imperial ideology of Beijing bannermen.

Although this study is not a genre study in the conventional sense, it remains nevertheless important to offer a concise outline of the nineteenth-century martial arts novel and a succinct discussion of some of the previous scholarship on this genre. The study of literary genres represents, needless to say, a modern intervention into a body of texts whose history and relationships will be mapped according to the needs and interests of the contemporary scholar. The genre that is at the heart of this study, the late nineteenth-century martial arts novel, or to be exact, "novels of chivalric justice and court cases" 俠義公案小說, is no exception.[43] Strictly speaking, the genre itself was not invented until Lu Xun devoted a single chapter to these novels in his influential study, *Zhongguo xiaoshuo shilüe* 中國小說史略 (A brief history of Chinese fiction) in 1924.[44] He defined these martial arts tales, produced between 1878 and 1900, as the confluence of two earlier genres, the knight-errantry novel and the court-case novel. According to Lu Xun, this merging of genres served an important ideological function, namely

43. As the foremost Taiwanese scholar of martial arts fiction, Ye Hongsheng, has pointed out, the Chinese term most commonly used for "martial arts fiction" 武俠小說 did not come into being until the early twentieth century, when Liang Qichao imported it from Japan. See Ye Hongsheng, *Lun jian*, pp. 8–10. See also Petrus Liu, *Stateless Subjects*, pp. 46–48; and Wan, *Green Peony*, p. 2. Even though the term "martial arts novel" is hence anachronistic when used in the context of the late nineteenth century, in this study I nevertheless use it because it is less cumbersome, enjoys broader recognition, and carries less of a connotation of outdated feudal thought implied by the term "novels of chivalric justice and court cases."
44. Lu Xun, *Zhongguo xiaoshuo shilüe*, pp. 195–204.

the containment of the potentially subversive martial hero within the imperially sanctioned framework of the official judge. Whereas the heroes of earlier martial arts novels such as *The Outlaws of the Marsh* possessed a clearly independent, indeed rebellious streak, in the case of the late nineteenth-century martial arts tale such a potential for rebellion had neatly been upended by marrying the martial arts tale to the more ideologically tame court-case novel.[45]

Since Lu Xun's first observations, many scholars have contributed to our understanding of the generic qualities and ideological implications of this particular form of fiction.[46] Margaret Wan, for instance, has sought to redefine the historical boundaries of the genre, pushing the roots of the chivalric/court-case novel back to the late eighteenth century.[47] Chen Pingyuan, arguably the most influential mainland Chinese scholar to comment on the late nineteenth-century martial arts novel, posits the relationship between the two genres of court-case fiction and chivalric justice not as a newly formed bond between two pre-existing genres, but rather as a rupture within a single genre that produced two new ones.[48] Finally, David Wang's crucial study of nineteenth-century fiction expands on the argument by directly addressing the ideologi-

---

45. Though Lu Xun does not explicitly make the point, the figure of the judge endows the novel with both ideological and formal structure, because the judge is a central figure whose presence in the novel helps organize the sometimes only loosely connected adventures of many martial men.

46. I here mention just three important scholars who have utilized Lu Xun's definition of the genre, but much of the mainland Chinese scholarship on martial arts fiction follows the logic of Lu Xun's first discussion. Cao Yibing, for instance, uses the same term, "chivalric justice and court-case novels" 俠義公案小說, but applies it to all of Chinese martial arts fiction from the Qin dynasty (221–207 BCE) to the present day. Chen Ying uses the term but reverses its order (i.e., "court-case chivalric justice novels" 公案俠義小說 instead of "chivalric justice court-case novels"). Liu Yinbo divides the chivalric justice novel 俠義小說 into different genres, one of which is the "court-case [chivalric justice] novel" 公案小說. Luo Liqun renames the "chivalric justice and legal-case novel" the "martial arts and court-case novel" 武俠公案小說, which, like Liu Yinbo, he regards as a subgenre of the Qing dynasty martial arts novel in general. See Cao Yibing, *Xiayi gongan xiaoshuo shi*, in particular pp. 176–264; Liu Yinbo, *Zhongguo wuxia xiaoshuo shi*, pp. 216–55; Chen Ying, *Zhongguo yingxiong xiayi xiaoshuo tongshi*, pp. 99–149; Luo Liqun, *Zhongguo wuxia xiaoshuo shi*, pp. 134–82.

47. Wan, *Green Peony*, pp. 21–55.

48. Chen Pingyuan, *Qiangu wenren xiake meng*, 71–95.

cal import of Lu Xun's genre definition. According to Wang, the relationship between an imperial judge and a righteous outlaw does not represent, as Lu Xun would have it, a conservative spirit of involution, but rather a radical and innovative questioning of traditional notions of justice as well as a reinvention of the literary genres and techniques associated with such justice.[49]

At the heart of the divided opinions of genre lies not simply the precise definition of a body of literary texts, but rather how we should view the existence of this particular body of texts vis-à-vis our understanding of the nineteenth century in general. Does the martial arts novel represent the last dying breath of an outdated political and literary system, as Lu Xun suggests, or the beginning of a new age, a "repressed modernity," as David Wang posits? I take up this question at various points in the book, in the first chapter where I suggest that the acoustic interests of the nineteenth-century martial arts novel are already foreshadowed in the seventeenth-century reinterpretations of *The Outlaws of the Marsh*, or in the coda, where I suggest that the sounds of the nineteenth-century martial arts novel, though divorced from the storyteller persona, have found their way into a rich variety of literary genres. It suffices to say here that the late nineteenth-century martial arts novel, thanks to earlier studies by Lu Xun and others, represents a relatively well-known body of texts whose generic boundaries and aesthetic qualities have important ideological implications.

A second reason I have chosen the nineteenth-century martial arts novel is because of its immense popularity. The martial arts novel represents a genre whose aesthetics are firmly rooted in the marketplace. As such, it is crucial to remember that beginning in the 1870s, the genre experienced an accelerated moment of commercial growth in China. Starting with the phenomenal success of two novels, Wen Kang's *Tale of Romance and Heroism* and the anonymous *San xia wu yi* 三俠五義 (The three knights and the five gallants; first published in 1879), a true tidal wave of martial arts fiction swept the country. Old and familiar tales were rewritten so as to include more martial arts mayhem, as in the case of Weng Shan's 翁山 1891 novel, *Qian Ming Zhengde Baimudan* 前明正德白牡丹 (The white peony and emperor Zhengde of the former Ming), an adaptation of the earlier 1842 work *Da Ming Zhengde you*

49. Wang, *Fin-de-Siècle Splendor*, pp. 117–82.

Jiangnan 大明正德游江南 (Emperor Zhengde of the Great Ming travels to Jiangnan). Sequels to already popular novels such as *Shi gongan* 施公案 (The cases of Judge Shi; first published in 1798; first sequel published in 1894, with a preface dated 1893) similarly included more action scenes and shifted attention from the order of the courtroom to the thrill of the green woods.[50]

To give one particular example of the late nineteenth-century martial arts novel as bestseller: after its first printing in 1879, *The Three Knights and Five Gallants* was republished at least thirteen times before the end of the nineteenth century.[51] In the process, the title changed two times, from *Zhonglie xiayi zhuan* 忠烈俠義傳 (The tale of loyalty and righteousness; its original 1879 title), to *The Three Knights and the Five Gallants* (the title most commonly used nowadays; first used in the 1883 Wenya zhai 文雅齋 edition), and *Qi xia wu yi* 七俠五義 (The seven knights and the five gallants; used for the Guangbaisong zhai 廣百宋齋 edition edited by Yu Yue in 1889). A quick search in a bibliographic database such as WorldCat reveals, moreover, that the popularity of the novel did not wane in the twentieth century. By the end of the twentieth century, *The Three Knights* had been republished in different editions and under different titles at least fifty times. By now, *The Three Knights* has been translated into six different languages (Japanese, Russian, English, Malay, Vietnamese, and French), has provided material for popular contemporary storytelling performances, most notably in the versions of Wang Shaotang 王少堂 (1889–1968) and Shan Tianfang 單田方 (1935–), has been turned into different styles of regional opera including Peking opera, and has been adapted for television and film.[52] The original novel was more-

50. For a list of martial arts novels published in the years between 1878 and 1900, see Keulemans, "Sounds of the Novel," pp. 284–89.
51. For a list of the late-nineteenth and early-twentieth-century editions of *The Three Knights and the Five Gallants* and *The Tale of Romance and Heroism*, see Keulemans, "Sounds of the Novel," pp. 312–15.
52. For the many, mostly Beijing-based operas associated with the stories of *The Three Knights* and its sequels, see Chen Tao, *Bao gong xi yanjiu*, pp. 221–28. Note that Chen slightly overstates the influence of the novel. Some of the operas Chen associates with *The Three Knights* had a genealogy that long predated the novel (or the storytelling on which the novel is based). As such, these operas may have become associated with the popular novel, but most likely were originally based on older versions of the same opera, not the more recent novel.

over soon followed by two sequels, *The Latter Five Gallants* in 1890 and *Xu xiao wu yi* 續小五義 (The continued latter five gallants) in 1891, both of which offer even more scenes of martial arts action than the original. In the years following, close to twenty additional sequels were printed, all of which show a similar fascination with heroic knights, flying heroes, and dazzling duels.[53]

As one of the most popular bodies of texts written during the late nineteenth century and as one of the genres prominently discussed by the progenitor of Chinese literary studies Lu Xun, the martial arts novel has enjoyed its fair share of scholarly attention, inspiring what can be loosely categorized as three different lines of inquiry: the generic, the philological, and the folkloric.[54] Since I have already discussed the generic approach above, let me here continue with the second line of inquiry initiated by Hu Shi 胡適 (1891–1962), who, in two seminal prefaces written in the 1920s, took a more philological approach. In his preface to *The Three Knights and the Five Gallants*, for instance, Hu Shi traced the textual genealogy of the novel, investigating issues of plot, characterization, and language from the early Song dynasty historical sources concerning the novel's main character, Judge Bao, until its eventual nineteenth-century novel form.[55] Moreover, because of his interests in the relationship between regional and national languages, Hu Shi played a crucial role in reestablishing the Beijing origins of this popular novel, a theme of geographical specificity he further elaborated upon in his preface to Wen Kang's *Tale of Romance and Heroism*, which Hu identified as "typically Beijing bannerman," both in terms of its cultural conservatism and its linguistic brilliance.[56]

---

53. For details on these editions, see Keulemans, "Sounds of the Novel," pp. 290–311.
54. The distinctions between these three lines of inquiry are of course not absolute. Moreover, the philological approach of Hu Shi, as well as the folkloric approach of Aying and others, can already be found in Lu Xun's study, albeit in brief form. Lu Xun notes, for instance, the earlier Yuan dynasty operas informing the stories of Judge Bao in *The Three Knights* just as he comments on the storyteller origins of many of these novels. See Lu Xun, *Zhongguo xiaoshuo shilüe*, pp. 198 and 203–4 respectively.
55. Hu Shi, "*San xia wu yi xu.*"
56. See Hu Shi, "*Ernü yingxiong zhuan xu.*"

Finally, we can discern a third line of inquiry that builds on Hu Shi's interest in philology, textual origins, and geographical provenance but places these concerns in the context of folk literature, in particular the specific history of nineteenth-century Beijing storytelling. As Hu Shi pointed out in his early preface, the *Three Knights and the Five Gallants* was originally authored by "a certain Shi Yukun" 石玉昆, someone Hu Shi mistakenly identified as the writer of the novel but who, as scholars such as Aying 阿英 (pen name of Qian Defu 錢德富 1900–1977) and Li Jiarui 李家瑞 (1895–1975) pointed out, was actually a popular, early nineteenth-century storyteller from Beijing.[57] This line of inquiry eventually led to the work of Susan Blader, who painstakingly compared the printed martial arts novel *The Three Knights* with earlier hand-written storyteller manuscripts located in the Fusinian library of the Institute for Historical Philology of the Academia Sinica.[58] Building on Li Jiarui's and Susan Blader's early work, scholars such as Meir Shahar, Miao Huaiming, and Margaret Wan further developed this relationship between a local storytelling manuscript culture and printed texts, each of them adding new layers to our understanding of the oral-textual interaction that led to the development of the nineteenth-century martial arts novel.[59]

This book draws on all three lines of inquiry but seeks to add a new angle by focusing on how these novels employ the suggestion of sound. If the first line of inquiry brought a strong ideological component to the study of the martial arts novel, focusing in particular on the tension between potentially rebellious and orthodox elements in terms of characters, I seek to show how such an ideological tension can also be found in the very acoustic form of the novel itself, the loud spectacle of *renao* presenting a kind of vulgar, unruly, and boisterous entertainment both exciting and potentially transgressive. From an ideological point of view the sounds of the nineteenth-century martial arts novel are interesting because they show how printed texts can simultaneously introduce and discipline the loud excitement of *renao*, producing a commodity that

57. Aying, "Guanyu Shi Yukun"; Li Jiarui, "Cong Shi Yukun de 'Longtu gongan.'"
58. Blader, "A Critical Study;" see also Blader's preface to the partial translation of *The Three Knights* ("Introduction").
59. Shahar, *Crazy Ji*; Wan, *Green Peony*. Miao Huaiming has published countless articles on nineteenth-century martial arts fiction, the most important of which is "*San xia wu* yi de chengshu guocheng."

sells because it packages—both in the sense of presenting and containing—a particularly popular form of acoustic spectacle.

The second line of inquiry introduced a philological interest in the martial arts novel and coupled this to the geographical specificity of Beijing bannerman culture. I aim to explore these issues from an acoustic angle, focusing in particular on the relationship between dialect sounds and standard vernacular pronunciation and the way the acoustic elements of speech are codified in text. Looking back at the events of the twentieth century, we might opine that the interest in bringing speech and writing together expressed in this second line of inquiry foreshadowed the vernacular language movement of the 1910s and 1920s. I prefer, however, to avoid such a teleological path pointing towards a national language movement, and instead discuss the combination of spoken and written language as expressive of typical late-imperial interests, that is, the combination of Qing dynasty evidential scholarship on the one hand and the rise of nineteenth-century regionalism on the other.

Finally, this book will add to the existing folk literature studies by showing how sound crucially mediates the relationship between oral and textual cultures. Specifically, I argue that the relationship between storyteller praxis and printed text should not simply be regarded as reflecting a straightforward evolutionary progression from primitive oral origins to sophisticated textual final product, but rather as a strategically produced association between storyteller and text promoted by the nineteenth-century printing industry. This production of storyteller liveliness within the text was not simply a matter of transcribing "sound"; rather, it involved a protracted process of textual reinvention of the storyteller voice aimed at maximizing sales while minimizing costs. By comparing handwritten storyteller manuscripts with printed texts, this book will show how authors, editors, and publishers incorporated, elided, transformed, or at times added telltale storyteller signs such as onomatopoeias, poetic song, imitation of vendor calls, or the mimicry of dialect accents, special effects that combined "storyteller" acoustic craftsmanship and printing techniques to produce a highly entertaining, highly marketable form of fiction.

The first chapter of this book begins by exploring the role of sound in the late-imperial vernacular novel by contrasting the way two important scholars—the seventeenth-century scholar Jin Shengtan and the renowned scholar Yu Yue 俞樾 (1821–1907)—imagined the voice of the popular story-teller. The writings of these two scholars, one from the beginning and one from the final years of the period in which the vernacular novel flourished as a form of writing, reveal how, despite the popular, oral connotations of the storyteller's voice, the literati employed the acoustic qualities of the storyteller figure in an elitist fashion, namely to define a realm of written textual communication shared by like-minded scholars during moments of expanding print culture.

The second chapter turns from the literati appreciation of the story-teller figure to the more local and popular realm of Beijing publish-ing in the nineteenth century. An investigation of the local roots of the martial arts novel reveals that the proliferation of this popular genre at the end of the nineteenth century should not be understood solely as the result of new printing techniques introduced from the West, but also as the revival and reinvention of certain "traditional" story-telling techniques. As the novel was transported from its original local origins to an ever-widening circle of readers, the rise of the martial arts novel remained predicated upon an older, Beijing storytelling culture that was reinvented at every reiteration of the novel as handwritten manuscript, xylographic, and eventually lithographic printed object. In emphasizing the interaction between printing technology and "tradi-tional" storytelling methods, chapter 2 shows that with technological "progress," older traditional forms of entertainment do not necessarily disappear, but rather are reinvented for the purposes of modern print. Indeed, in communities connected through the mechanics of printed text, the storyteller's voice helps to facilitate the imagination of this community by lending it an organic sense of oral intimacy.

After introducing the print-historical background of the martial arts novel in the first two chapters, in the next three chapters I focus on three specific acoustic techniques employed both by storytellers and printed texts to show how acoustic spectacle was produced in these tales. The third chapter, "Sounds That Sell," looks into the first of such techniques, the imitation of loud vendor calls. Specifically, the chap-ter explores the literary use of these acoustic advertisements in differ-ent performance texts produced in the nineteenth century, arguing that authors employed these calls to both highlight and contain the lively attractions (*renao*) of the marketplace. In doing so, these authors created a typically late-imperial literary appreciation of the marketplace, producing an implied listener/reader who approaches the literary marketplace with disciplined attention, an implied artesian storyteller/narrator whose tasteful craft allows him to transcend the vulgarity of other market attractions, and finally a narrative form that subjugates the diverse attractions of the market to the demands of a linearly unfolding plot. In the process of turning oral performance into printed text, these novels may have preserved some of the original attraction of the oral performer's mimicry of vendor calls, but they severely truncated such calls to fit the demands of the textual medium and the novel form.

If the third chapter shows how the acoustic performance of the storyteller became muted in the process of printing, the fourth chapter illustrates how, in the transformation from popular handwritten libretto to printed novel, the sound of acoustic spectacle can also become increasingly loud. In this chapter I investigate a second oral/textual technique, onomatopoeia, and show how nineteenth-century martial arts novels were increasingly filled with such acoustic sparkles of sound. Specifically, the first half of the chapter looks at the way one particularly popular martial arts series, the various novels belonging to *The Three Knights* series, uses onomatopoeia to capture the physical sensation of the martial arts action scene not on a visual but on an acoustic level. The second half places the use of this form of acoustic excitement into its print-historical context. A comparison between the early storyteller libretti on which *The Three Knights and the Five Gallants* is based and the final iteration of the novel as printed text demonstrates how the later novels employ onomatopoeia to a much greater extent than the handwritten texts, thus suggesting that onomatopoeias in such novels may well have been associated with storyteller performances, but were still repackaged for the purposes of the printing industry.

The fifth chapter shifts from these commercial aspects of acoustic spectacle to the more explicitly political uses of printed sound by investigating the storyteller's technique of mimicking regional speech. In the context of nineteenth-century regionalism, such dialect mimicry allowed martial arts novels to reaffirm Beijing's central political and linguistic status (often at the expense of the provincial periphery) in two ways. First, as a vernacular reflection of the capital, the novels brought different regional languages together, suggesting that the capital, as the center of the empire, is a place where myriad provincial languages mingle. Second, the mimicry of different dialects also functioned as a verbal form of physical slapstick; at the same time as it constructed a fictional character whose inferior, provincial nature was revealed through his linguistic incompetence, it created a cosmopolitan performer/reader whose superior Beijing identity was established precisely through his skillful imitation of "inferior" provincial speech.

The final chapter returns to the imperial city of Beijing by explicitly linking the excitement produced by the various acoustic technologies of the novel to the notion of urban space as imagined in one particularly emblematic text, Wen Kang's *Tale of Romance and Heroism*. First published in 1878, Wen Kang's novel combines many of the features I have identified as typical of the late nineteenth-century martial arts novel. Drawing both on the literati's penchant for metafictionality and the crowd's taste for sensation, the novel combines an elite aesthetics with more popular tastes. The suggestion of sound plays a crucial role in constructing a creative tension between the sheltered world of the literati on the one hand and the rowdy urban streets on the other. The novel creates this tension by employing sound and space to construct a plot in which the two male protagonists are forced out of the comfort of their home to face the loud noises of the outside world. It also draws on the tension between text and voice in the vernacular tradition so as to present itself as a constant interaction between scholarly text and street performer's voice. In the end, the novel synthesizes these tensions to suggest a view of a renewed, harmonious society (and literary genre), integrating both voice and text, bringing orality and textuality together in an acoustic vision of a single, but still clearly segregated and neatly ordered, imperial realm.

CHAPTER ONE

Acts of Ventriloquism

Literati Appropriations of the Storyteller's Voice

I have seen this book [*The Sluices of Qingfeng*], but there is nothing particularly good about it. Yet rather unexpectedly it still created a stir in those days. Perhaps it was because of the excellence of the oral telling [literally "mouth and lips"], and not because of the writing?
— Yu Yue, *Gathered Writings from the Chaxiang Studio*

I once heard him [Liu Jingting] tell the prose tale of Wu Song fighting the tiger on Jingyang Ridge. It was very different from the original text. His descriptions and delineations included the most minute of details, down to the very hairs, but his telling was still efficient and crisp and not verbose at all. The booming sound of his voice carried like an enormous bell, and when he reached a major plot twist, he would shout loudly, his roar making the room shake.
— Zhang Dai, *The Storytelling of Liu Jingting*

Yu Yue's remark is interesting not only because it directly links storyteller performance to a particular printed novel, *Qingfeng zha* 清風閘 (The sluices of Qingfeng), but also because it argues that the novel fails because it does not capture the excellence of the "oral telling" (literally "lips and mouth").[1] Remarks that explicitly differentiate between the

---

1. Much of Yu Yue's anecdote is based on Li Dou's late eighteenth-century memoir of Yangzhou life, *A Record of the Painted Boats of Yangzhou*. See Li Dou, *Yangzhou huafang lu*, pp. 195–96. For more on the novel, Pu Lin's 浦琳 storytelling performance, and the relationship between performance and novel, see Wan, "Local Fiction of the Yangzhou Region."

textual and oral version of a performance tend to be rare in the late-imperial record, in part because vernacular novels and oral storyteller performances were often conflated, and in part because storytelling was too vulgar to comment upon directly. Here, however, Yu Yue, one of the most famous late-Qing scholars, differentiates between the two. He furthermore upholds the original storytelling performance as superior, suggesting that if the author of the novel had only done a better job of translating the "lips and mouth" of the performance, the printed novel *The Sluices of Qingfeng* might have been a lot better.

During the final decades of the nineteenth century, the relationship between storyteller performance and printed vernacular novel was in flux. As I will show in more detail in chapter 2, in Beijing, popular storyteller tales were increasingly turned into novels; prefaces and title pages were increasingly drawing attention to the oral origins of the printed text. In elite Jiangnan society, too, scholars such as Yu Yue acknowledged the relationship between storyteller performance and eventual printed novel. Moreover, as can be seen in Yu Yue's remarks quoted above, there was a growing recognition that the spoken word performed by the storyteller had a quality that was to be appreciated in its own right. The idea that the spoken word per se was inferior to the written word was not necessarily thought to be true, at least not in the realm of vernacular fiction. A complete paradigm shift in the relationship between spoken voice and written text, the kind of shift that would turn voice into the medium of revolution, was still far away.[2] Yet Yu Yue's remark regarding *The Sluices of Qingfeng* shows that, in a modest way, a good storyteller was to be preferred to a bad novel, suggesting in turn that a vulgar, oral performance might at times even be better than the actual handwritten or printed product.

There are few other periods in late imperial history where the relationship between vernacular written text and storyteller performance received the same kind of interest as the late Qing, most notably the period of the late Ming.[3] Yu Yue's observation on the storytelling of Pu

2. On this paradigm shift, see Crespi, *Voices in Revolution*.
3. I am not the first to note this recurrence of a late-Ming attraction to the storyteller voice in the late Qing. Lu Decai, for instance, argues that by the late Qing, the vernacular novel in its relationship to storytelling "had come full circle, albeit on a higher level." See Lu Decai, *Lu Decai shuo Bao gongan*, pp. 210–11.

Lin 浦琳 indeed bears a striking resemblance to the second passage quoted above, which is from Zhang Dai's biography of the famous late-Ming storyteller Liu Jingting 柳敬亭.[4] Like Yu Yue, Zhang Dai explicitly remarks on the difference between oral telling and written text by relating how storyteller Liu used to tell a famous episode from the novel *Outlaws of the Marsh*. And like Yu Yue, Zhang Dai does not regard the vulgar oral version of Liu Jingting as necessarily inferior to the written original.[5] By telling how the storyteller's descriptions are "most minute in its details" yet still "not verbose," Zhang lavishes unusual praise on Liu Jingting's art. In fact, he reserves the greatest praise for the element that can never be found in the silent pages of the text itself, namely, Liu Jingting's voice, which is said to "boom like a huge bell" and physically "shake the room" in which the storyteller performs.

How do we understand the emphasis on the storyteller during these two moments of late-imperial vernacular literature? Why is it that during the rise of vernacular fiction as an elite form of literature in the late Ming, and again during its demise in the late Qing, we find this interest in oral, vocal performance versus silent, written text? Moreover, how should we interpret the print-historical context during these two periods as we seek to understand this appreciation of the storyteller and his voice? To answer these questions, I have divided this chapter into two parts. To place the late-Qing interest in the storyteller's voice as the embodiment of readerly pleasure within a broader historical context, I first trace the fascination with the sound of the storyteller back to the *Outlaws of the Marsh* commentary by the late-Ming critic

---

4. We have no exact dates for the storytellers Pu Lin and Liu Jingting. Pu Lin was a Qianlong 乾隆 era (1735–96) storyteller from Yangzhou. Based on circumstantial evidence, most scholars agree that Liu Jingting lived from roughly 1587–1668.

5. Robert Hegel argues differently, stating that this episode regarding Liu Jingting in fact proves that even an iconoclast such as Zhang Dai still regarded oral performance with a sense of "opprobrium." See Hegel, *Reading Illustrated Fiction*, pp. 67–68. As the brief snippet here shows, Zhang Dai's remark is rather ambivalent. On the one hand, he favors the expressive qualities of the storyteller's telling as superior to the novel. On the other hand, his own writing incorporates that expressiveness into yet another form of even superior writing. See also Zhang Dai's poem about Liu Jingting, in which he compares the storyteller to a "living Sima Qian" and points out that his "miraculous telling" of *The Outlaws* makes the reputed authors of the novel, Shi Nai'an and Luo Guanzhong, "bite their fingers in stunned silence." See Zhang Dai, "Liu Mazi shuoshu."

Jin Shengtan.[6] In contrast with some of the more "popular" appreciations of the storyteller figure at the time, Jin clearly differentiated
between storyteller performance and written text. Most notably, Jin
posited written authorship, rather than oral performance, as the origin
of the vernacular novel. In Jin's interpretation, the sound of the oral
performer hence became a mere metaphor for the illusion of written
fiction as text. It was this interpretation that allowed Jin to differentiate
the vulgar, newly literate reader bedazzled by such an illusion from the
elegant, literati reader capable of appreciating the illusion as a masterfully constructed fiction. Second, I turn to the elite scholar Yu Yue's
revival of the storyteller figure in the late nineteenth century to demonstrate how his renewed emphasis on the storyteller's voice allowed him
to imagine a restoration of the literati community after the ravages of
the Taiping Rebellion (1851–64). Reading the preface Yu appended to his
edition of *The Three Knights*, I will argue that for this late-Qing literatus, the storyteller's voice represented a direct link that allowed him to
reconnect with the late-Ming appreciation of the vernacular arts.

The Appropriation of the
Popular Voice in the Late Ming

At the heart of late-imperial vernacular fiction stands a dramatic
conceit—the lie that despite the written form of the text a storyteller is
speaking to the reader as if performing in front of him. For what purpose
was this conceit put to use? Depending on what author and what text
we choose to focus on, we can offer different answers to this question.
Here I focus primarily on one of the most influential commentators on
vernacular fiction of the late imperial age, Jin Shengtan, and the way he
interpreted the figure of the oral performer. In contrast to some of his
contemporaries, Jin never celebrated the storyteller's oral performance
to argue for the popular appeal of vernacular fiction. Nor did he trace the
roots of the vernacular novel back to storytelling performance. Rather,
Jin interpreted the sound associated with popular oral performance as

6. The commentary has a preface dated 1641. It was first published in 1644, the year
the Ming dynasty fell.

a metaphor for the writing of the novel. Jin's elite interest in the spoken voice of the oral performer as a metaphor for the text makes it clear that his primary goal was not promoting vernacular fiction as popular reading material, but rather defending literati domination over textual knowledge. By likening vernacular fiction to a spectacular acoustic illusion created by the storyteller's voice, Jin allowed the exalted late-Ming reader to enjoy the vernacular text while still maintaining his distance from the vulgar pleasures associated with the common crowd. Whereas a less educated reader would simply be mesmerized by the illusory verisimilitude of the text and accept it as reality, the literati reader could distinguish himself by recognizing the fundamental illusion of fiction and understanding the marvelous technique upon which this acoustic spectacle was based.

Jin's interpretation of the storyteller must be situated within the broader context of the relationship between storytelling and vernacular fiction in the late-imperial period, in particular the way vernacular fiction presented itself as if told by a storyteller figure. In the vernacular short stories published by Feng Menglong 馮夢龍 (1574–1646) and Ling Mengchu 凌濛初 (1580–1644), for instance, the longer main tale 正話 is typically preceded by one or more shorter, introductory tales 入話, a rhetorical strategy borrowed from professional storytellers who would use such introductory tales to draw an audience before beginning the main performance.[7] Many novels were larded with rhetorical storyteller phrases; chapters would usually begin with a recitation of an opening poem and then proceed with the line "the story goes" 話說 just as they would typically close with an invitation to the reader to "listen to the next episode for an explanation" 且聽下回分解.[8] Quite often the vernacular text addressed its reader directly as if he were actually attending an actual live storyteller performance, employing the purposefully ambiguous term 看官, which can be understood both as "reader" and as "audience member."[9]

---

7. For an early overview of some of the formal characteristics of the storyteller figure in *huaben* short stories, see Birch, "Some Formal Characteristics." For a more recent and full-length analysis of just the introductory tale, see Jin Mingqiu, *Song Yuan Ming huaben xiaoshuo ruhua.*

8. For a good list of the various rhetorical phrases used by the storyteller figure in vernacular fiction, see McLaren, *Chinese Popular Culture*, pp. 271–78.

9. The ambiguity of the term can be found in such phrases as 看官聽說, which can,

Given the prominence of the storyteller persona as a rhetorical figure in so many vernacular texts, it is not surprising that scholars have offered a variety of explanations for its presence. Pointing out that as early as the Song dynasty storytellers already entertained urban crowds with lively renditions of vernacular tales, earlier scholars argued that the storyteller figure in printed vernacular fiction and his host of rhetorical clichés should be understood as a remnant of those popular storytelling origins.[10] Later scholars such as Wilt Idema and Patrick Hanan rejected this link between actual storytelling and the novel to argue that the storyteller figure's voice is merely a textual technique invented by sixteenth- and seventeenth-century writers. Disagreeing with the idea that vernacular fiction is based on either storyteller performances or promptbooks, Idema and Hanan have pointed out that during the formative years of vernacular fiction in the late sixteenth and early seventeenth centuries, the storyteller figure only became more vocal as the text moved further away from its supposed oral origins.[11] A final mediating position was taken by a third group of scholars, who suggested that the storyteller figure should be regarded neither as evidence of popular oral origins nor as a purely textual invention fully divorced from actual storytelling, but rather as an elite appropriation and reinvention of popular modes of oral performance. Andrew Plaks, for instance, has pointed out that the storyteller figure in the Four Masterworks of the Ming dynasty represents an elite reinterpretation of the popular storyteller figure who serves to embody rhetorical

---

in direct address, be translated as "Gentle reader take note," but in actuality it also has a strong oral and aural connotation, i.e., "Audience, listen to what I have to say."

10. Lu Xun was one of the first to point out that most late-imperial vernacular fiction is a mere imitation of a storyteller style, but he also argued that certain texts are clear examples of actual promptbooks produced by and for storytellers. See Lu Xun, *Zhongguo xiaoshuo shilüe*, chaps. 12 and 13.

11. See Idema, *Chinese Vernacular Fiction*; Hanan, "The Making of the *Pearl-sewn Shirt*"; Hanan, "The Nature of Ling Meng-Ch'u's Fiction." For the most extensive discussion of the various rhetorical aspects of late-imperial vernacular fiction, see Hanan, *The Chinese Vernacular Story*; David Rolston neatly sums up this position by arguing (and quite rightfully so) that "whatever its original relation to actual storytelling practice, by the late Ming it was a written, literary convention, and new writers learned it from earlier models, not from trips to the marketplace or the teahouse." Rolston, *Traditional Chinese Fiction*, p. 231.

technique.[12] Similarly, Shuhui Yang has suggested that in the vernacular short stories of Feng Menglong, the folksy wisdom of the storyteller figure is accompanied by a good deal of irony, thereby allowing the elite author to voice certain morals while at the same time keeping a critical distance from these vulgar storyteller aphorisms.[13]

Here I will draw on these earlier studies of the storyteller persona but add one element that has thus far not received any attention, that is, the way the storyteller figure allowed the author to introduce the suggestion of sound into the text. In doing so, I do not mean to suggest that the acoustic cues found in the vernacular text represent direct transcriptions of storyteller performances. Nor do I mean to argue that the storyteller figure prompted actual vocalization on the part of the reader.[14] Rather, what I seek to uncover is how the storyteller persona functioned to prompt an *imagined* vocalization. In elite texts in particular, the storyteller figure could even function to highlight the *illusion* of sound. This interpretation of the storyteller figure as the embodiment of acoustic illusion was valuable because by emphasizing the illusionistic qualities of the storyteller voice, the author could draw attention to the fictional qualities of the vernacular text itself.

Recognizing the storyteller's voice as a symbol of fictional illusion reveals how the suggestion of sound in the vernacular novel allowed the literati elite to appropriate popular literary practices. As Anne McLaren has shown, in popular practice the sound of the storyteller was easily associated with liveliness, a *renao* typical of festivals, crowded teahouses, busy markets, and popular inns.[15] Indeed, when reproduced in vernacular text, the recording of such a lively storyteller voice arguably allowed the pages of the novel to convey a similar sense of liveliness to the reader. In contrast, an elite interpretation of this lively voice would present the textualized sound of the oral performer as an illusion whose function it was to remind the reader of the illusion of fiction itself. Both the vernacular novel and its loud storyteller voice represented a mirage that the sophisticated reader could appreciate not because it reproduced

12. See Plaks, *Four Great Novels*, pp. 121–22.
13. Yang, *Appropriation and Representation*, pp. 19–44 and throughout.
14. For an exploration of actual vocalization of printed texts and its link to popular storytelling, see McLaren, *Chinese Popular Culture*, pp. 32–57.
15. For a discussion of vernacular literature as a re-creation of lively festivals, see McLaren, *Chinese Popular Culture*, chap. 3.

a sense of pleasurable communal liveliness, but because it represented
an artful manipulation of the senses.

During the late Ming, a time when literati were facing an unprecedented proliferation of texts and a wave of newly educated readers, this
redefinition of vernacular fiction as an illusory spectacle ensured that
the lettered elite could remain the sole guardians of textual production.[16] As Craig Clunas has shown in the realm of visuality, in an age
when print culture allowed representational icons to circulate in ever
greater numbers, the notion of true art being "beyond representation"
came to take hold among the Chinese elite; it was a way of creating a
distinction between the elite appreciation of art and the vulgar enjoyment of lifelike representations.[17] Though Clunas applies this paradigm
to the realm of visual (print) culture, it is clear that a similar principle
can be applied to the realm of textual knowledge. In order to preserve
the elite control of textual knowledge, a group of iconoclastic literati
located true textual knowledge not in the lines of the text itself but in
between them, creating a realm of taste of which they themselves were
the final arbiters.[18] One of these areas created as the mark of good taste
was found in the medium of sound/voice personified in the figure of the
oral performer.

To illustrate this point, let me turn to a crucial text that, more than
any other, transformed the vernacular novel from a popular form of

16. For the rise of print culture during the late Ming and the various forms of elite
anxiety it produced, see, for instance, Chow, "Writing for Success"; for the most
comprehensive study of the rise of print culture until the seventeenth century, see
Chia, *Printing for Profit*.

17. See Clunas, *Pictures and Visuality*, pp. 9–24; see also his *Empire of Great
Brightness*, p. 123.

18. Ironically, these literati are usually regarded as the champions of the vernacular
text and the spoken voice of the people. In addition to Jin Shengtan, scholars such
as Xu Wei 徐渭 (1521–93) and Li Zhi 李贄 (1527–1602), as well as the three brothers most closely associated with the Gong'an school, Yuan Zongdao 袁宗道 (1560–
1600), Yuan Hongdao 袁宏道 (1568–1610), and Yuan Zhongdao 袁中道 (1570–1624),
all rebelled against certain forms of textual knowledge, which they characterized
as rote repetition. They instead embraced a form of poetic production located in
the "spoken voice" that was less amenable to facile reproduction. For a discussion
of Yuan Hongdao's appreciation of folk literature and the vernacular novel, as well
as his own use of a more colloquial language, see Chou, *Yüan Hung-tao*, pp. 68–69,
27–69; and Vallette-Hémery, *Yuan Hungdao*, pp. 128–40.

entertainment to an elite form of literary art, Jin Shengtan's commentary to *The Outlaws of the Marsh*. Though his was not the first commentary to accompany a vernacular novel or even *The Outlaws*, it undoubtedly was the most influential such commentary to be published in the late imperial age. Not only did Jin's edition of *The Outlaws* become *the* standard edition of the work until the twentieth century, even commentaries to novels Jin had never been associated with were often attributed to him so as to enhance their value. In the centuries that followed the publication of Jin's commentary to *The Outlaws*, his views on the form, function, and value of vernacular fiction became standard as his critical vocabulary, method of evaluating characters, and tools for analyzing the development of plot not only came to inform the critical commentaries appended to novels but also began to influence the writing of fiction itself.[19] As a result, Jin's views on oral performance, the sounds of such performances, and finally their relationship with vernacular fiction carry remarkable weight.

By and large Jin does not pay particular attention to storytelling and oral performance, whether in the prefaces he appended to the novel as a whole, the introductions he wrote to each chapter, or the interlineal commentaries he inserted into the text itself.[20] Unlike the prefaces to vernacular short stories penned by Feng Menglong and Ling Mengchu, prefaces that unambiguously employ the storyteller tradition as a way of celebrating the potential popular appeal of the stories published, Jin's commentaries reveal little interest in the storyteller roots of vernacular fiction.[21] In fact, Jin, in an attempt to raise the cultural credentials of the

19. For a discussion on the rise of elite appreciation for the vernacular novel and the role of textual commentary in this process, see Rolston, *Traditional Chinese Fiction*. Rolston's specific arguments about Jin Shengtan appear in chap. 1.
20. One important exception is found in the pre-chapter commentary I discuss in detail below. Another example is found in Jin's discussion of chapter 51, which features a lengthy description of a performance by the female chanteuse Bai Xiuying. For a discussion of that chapter, see Ge, *Out of the Margins*, pp. 153–56.
21. Most famous is probably the following anecdote from Feng Menglong's preface to *Jingshi tongyan* 警世通言 (Stories to caution the world): "A neighbor's boy cut his finger when helping out in the kitchen. To comments of surprise that he did not let out cries of pain, the boy replied, 'I just came back from Xuanmiao Temple, where I heard a storyteller tell how Guan Yu of *The Romance of Three Kingdoms* went on talking and laughing when a surgeon was scraping infection from a bone in his arm. Now this little pain of mine is really nothing!'" 里中兒代庖而創其指,

novel, spends remarkable time establishing the bona-fide *textual* origins of the novel.[22] In his commentary, Jin invariably employs terms such as "brush," "paper," and "ink" when elaborating on the composition of the novel. Time and again he returns to the "author" of the text, Shi Nai'an 施耐庵, when seeking to explain its "genius"; indeed, he famously forged a preface by Shi Nai'an in order to ensure that no reader could misunderstand the value of the novel as a written piece of fiction.

When oral performance enters the text of Jin's commentary, it does so neither as the potential origin of the novel, nor as the cultural context that explains the popular appeal of the novel, but rather as a metaphor. In Jin's reading the storyteller figure and his skillful acoustic performance serve solely to represent the skill of the author, Shi Nai'an. This view of oral performance and its evanescent sounds as a metaphor for the fictional qualities of the novel is most clearly represented in Jin's introductory comments to his version of chapter 65. Jin opens the chapter as follows:

> My friend Mr. Zhuoshan once praised to me a ventriloquist [literally: mouth artist] in the capital, saying: "On that day the guests were gathered for a great banquet, and in the northeast corner of the hall a tall screen was set up. The ventriloquist sat behind the screen with only a single table, a single chair, a single fan, and a single 'awakening block.'[23] After the various guests had gathered and sat down surrounding [the screen], and a bit of time had passed, they heard two slaps of the awakening block from within the screen. The entire hall fell silent, and no one dared to utter a sound.
>
> [Then they] heard from far off, in a deep alley, a dog barking. This lasted for a while, but then they suddenly heard close by the sound of a gong. Next a woman woke up with a start and yawned, shaking her husband and whispering something lewd to him. The husband mumbled,

---

不呼痛, 怪之曰: 吾傾從玄妙觀聽說《三國志》來, 關雲長刮骨療毒, 且談笑自若, 我何痛為? On the basis of this anecdote, Feng continues to argue that popular storyteller tales with real feeling are in many ways more valuable than the learned, but dry, discourses of the literati few. I am borrowing here from the translation by Yang Shuhui and Yang Yunqin. Feng Menglong, *Stories to Caution the World*, pp. 5–6; Feng Menglong, *Jingshi tongyan*, 3B–4A.

22. This has been noted by a variety of scholars; one example is Ge, *Out of the Margins*, p. 54.

23. The actual term used, *fuchi* 撫尺, is a synonym for an awakening block, *xingmu* 醒木, a small block of wood that storytellers slap on the table to get the attention of the audience, often used to frame the beginning and ending of a performance.

and at first would not respond. The woman, however, did not stop shaking him, their words mingled, and the bed began to squeak, 'GAGA.' After a bit, a child woke and cried loudly. The husband ordered his wife to nurse the child, while the child, teat in mouth, continued to cry. The woman patted [the child] and started humming to it. The husband got up and urinated. The woman, holding the child, also got up and urinated. On the bed, yet another, older, child woke up and started to whimper without end. At that point there was the sound of the wife patting the [first] child, the sound of her humming, the sound of the [first] child suckling and crying, the sound of the older child just waking up, the sound of the bed, the sound of the husband scolding the older child, the sound of urine splattering in a small receptacle, and the sound of urine splattering in a chamber pot, all issuing forth at the same time, all wondrously complete. Among the members of the audience, there was not a single one who did not stretch out his neck, peer closely, smile slightly and silently sigh in appreciation, thinking this was so wonderful it could not be surpassed.

After a while, the husband climbed back into bed, and the wife called for the older child to finish urinating; they climbed into bed to sleep, and the youngest child was also about to fall asleep. The husband started snoring, while the wife's patting of the baby gradually stopped. There was the slight sound of a mouse scurrying, 'SUOSUO,' tipping over some crockery. There was the sound of the wife coughing in her dream. The audience's attention began to drop, and they returned to a more formal posture in their seats.

All of a sudden, a man cried, 'Fire!!!' The husband woke up and yelled loudly. The wife also got up and yelled loudly. The two children together cried. All of a sudden, thousands of people were shouting, thousands of children were crying, and thousands of dogs were barking. In the middle of all this came the sound of a shed collapsing, the sound of fire bursting forth, and the wind starting up, 'WHOOSH, WHOOSH.' A myriad sounds rose up, and mixed into them were the sounds of a myriad people calling for help, the sound of buildings collapsing, 'XUXU,' the sound of people grabbing things, and the sound of water being splashed. Everything that ought to be there was there. Even if one had a hundred hands and on each hand a hundred fingers, he could not have pointed out the sources of the sounds. Even if one had a hundred mouths and in each mouth a hundred tongues, he would not have been able to name the sources of the sounds. In the face of this, there was not a single member of the audience whose face did not grow pale and who did not leave his seat. Making their sleeves fly so as to reveal their arms, their two legs shaking, it seemed as if all of them were vying to leave first. All of a sudden, the 'awakening block' sounded, and the multitude of sounds came to an abrupt halt. When the screen was removed and they [the audience] looked, there was nothing but a single man, a single desk, a single chair, a single fan, and a single 'awakening block' as before. For quite a long time the entire hall remained silent, none of the guests daring to be the first to make a noise."

吾友斫山先生,嘗向吾夸京中口技, 言: 是日賓客大宴, 於廳事之東北角, 施八尺屏障, 口技人坐屏中, 一桌、一椅、一扇、一撫尺而已. 眾賓既圍揖坐定, 少頃, 但聞屏障中撫尺二下, 滿坐寂然, 無敢嘩者. 遙遙聞深巷犬吠聲, 甚久, 忽耳畔鳴金一聲, 便有婦人驚覺欠伸, 搖其夫語猥褻事. 夫囈語, 初不甚應, 婦搖之不止, 則二人語漸間雜, 床又從中戛戛響. 既而兒醒, 大啼. 夫令婦與兒乳, 兒含乳啼, 婦拍而嗚之. 夫起溺, 婦亦抱兒起溺. 床上又一大兒醒, 猜猜不止. 當是時, 婦手拍兒聲, 口中嗚聲, 兒含乳啼聲, 大兒初醒聲, 床聲, 夫叱大兒聲, 溺瓶中聲, 溺桶中聲, 一齊湊發, 眾妙畢備. 滿座賓客無不伸頸側目, 微笑默嘆, 以為妙絕也. 既而, 夫上床寢; 婦人呼大兒溺畢, 都上床寢. 小兒亦漸欲睡. 夫齁聲起, 婦拍兒亦漸拍漸止. 微聞有鼠作作索索, 盆器傾側, 婦夢中咳嗽之聲. 賓客意少舒, 稍稍正坐. 忽一人大呼火起, 夫起大呼, 婦亦起大呼, 兩兒齊哭. 俄而百千人大呼, 百千兒哭, 百千狗吠. 中間力拉崩倒之聲, 火爆聲, 呼呼風聲, 百千齊做; 又夾百千求救聲, 曳屋許許聲, 搶奪聲, 潑水聲, 凡所應有, 無所不有. 雖人有百手, 手有百指, 不能指其一端; 人有百口, 口有百舌, 不能名其一處也. 於是賓客無不變色離席, 奮袖出臂, 兩股戰戰, 幾欲先走. 而忽然撫尺一下, 群響畢絕. 撤屏視之, 一人、一桌、一椅、一扇、一撫尺如故. 蓋久之久之, 猶滿堂寂然, 賓客無敢先嘩者也.[24]

After concluding the anecdote told by his friend, Jin continues,

At the time, when I heard his words, I thought it rather unbelievable. Laughing, I said to him, "These are merely fanciful phrases. How could such a skill really exist in the world?" But he in turn laughed and said to me, "Not only do *you* not believe it, in truth even *I* still do not believe it." Now, reading the part of this chapter where fire burns down Cuiyun Hall, I sigh appreciatively over the fact that my friend did not deceive me. There truly is such extraordinary skill."

吾當時聞其言, 意頗不信, 笑謂先生: 此自是卿粲花之論耳, 世豈真有是技? 維時先生亦笑謂吾: 豈惟卿不得信, 實惟吾猷至今不信耳! 今日讀火燒翠雲樓一篇, 而深嘆先生未嘗吾欺, 世固真有是絕異非常之技也.[25]

24. In *Shuihu zhuan huiping ben*, vol. 2, chap. 65, p. 1191. A version of this anecdote by Lin Sihuan 林嗣環 (b. 1607, *jinshi* 1649), known by the title "Kouji" 口技 (Ventriloquism), is more widely known nowadays. Lin's piece was originally named "*Qiu sheng* xu" 秋聲序 (Preface to *Autumn sounds*), and it was included in Zhang Chao's 張潮 (1650–1709) *Yu chu xin zhi* 虞初新志 (A new record of Yu Chu). See Zhang Chao, *Yu chu xin zhi*, pp. 10–11.
25. *Shuihu zhuan huiping ben*, vol. 2, chap. 65, p. 1191.

It is only after these opening remarks that Jin Shengtan allows his reader to venture into the chapter of the novel itself.

To explore the way Jin Shengtan employs this anecdote to redefine lively acoustic spectacle as an aural illusion, let us first turn to the logic of narrative accumulation that produces this sense of acoustic spectacle. In the case of the anecdote about the ventriloquist, the narrative of accumulation begins with a silent audience and is followed by a few scattered sounds—a dog barking in an alley, a woman waking up, a mother nursing a child. This process of adding more voices continues throughout the anecdote until it reaches the final climactic moment when the fire threatens to burn everything around it, and "all of a sudden, thousands of people were shouting, thousands of children were crying, and thousands of dogs were barking." The art of the ventriloquist, we are told, is one of accumulation, multiplication, and final completion, or, to quote Jin's text, "Everything that ought to be there was there. Even if one had a hundred hands and on each hand a hundred fingers, he could not have pointed out the sources of the sounds." The art of the ventriloquist undoubtedly involves acts of accomplished imitation, but what seems to define his skill as masterful is not simply imitation, but rather the ability to combine a vast number of acoustic imitations at the same time within a single coherent structure.

When we turn to chapter 65 of *The Outlaws*, we note that a similar logic of accumulation and crescendo drives the episode in which the outlaws burn Cuiyun Hall. The chapter begins with a carefully planned attack on the city, an attack that involves separate members of the band of heroes being dispatched to the city. Slowly these men gather on the night of the lantern festival, and finally they spring into action in a highly coordinated, highly spectacular moment as the band members together set fire to the city and raid the streets of the town.

Figure 1.1, the illustration from the seventeenth-century Yang Dingjian preface edition by the hand of the woodcarver Liu Junyu 劉君裕, shows how the text's appeal is found in this gathering of a rich host of different elements within a single, comprehensive frame.[26] As noted

---

26. We know relatively little about this accomplished woodblock carver from Suzhou, but he is responsible for some of the more interesting illustrations of vernacular works produced in the seventeenth century, including the *Li Zhuowu ping Xi you ji* 李卓吾評西遊記 (Journey to the west, as commentated by Li Zhi); published between 1620 and 1627).

1.1 "Shi Qian Sets Fire to Cuiyun Lou," chapter 66. (In *Zhongyi shuihu quanzhuan*, published in 1614 by Yuan Wuyai. Photo courtesy of Beijing University Library.)

by Chen Qiming, one of the first scholars to comment on the print, the illustration brings together the many narrative moments of action—the lighting of a beacon, the killing of the magistrate, the attack on the city—placing these many different elements within a single, seemingly complete but still multifaceted space.[27] The effect is a grand view that dazzles the eyes, a pleasurable suffusion of visual data that stimulates but also threatens to overwhelm the senses. The illustration, in short, calls upon the senses, giving aesthetic form to the thematics of social gathering and its potentially disastrous results told in the tale of *The Outlaws* itself.[28]

This structure of accumulation found in chapter 65 also governs the narrative of *The Outlaws* as a whole. Structurally, the novel represents a gradual sedimentation of narratives, tales of individual heroes told by storytellers, performed on stage, or found in historical sources, which only came together in a single coherent narrative in its final novel form.[29] As to its use of sources, the novel itself mirrors in its own narrative structure the historical process of accumulation. Notably, the novel revolves around two defining moments, the moment when the 108 heroes are first dispersed in chapter 1, and the moment when all the heroes are once again gathered in chapter 71 (chapter 70 of Jin Shengtan's version), at which point the names of the outlaws are once again inscribed on a ceremonial tablet.[30] In between these two moments, the tale gradually gathers the various individual heroes until finally they

27. The illustration highlights the theme of variegation not only in the way it strategically places different groups of outlaws throughout the scene, but also, for instance, in the way it distributes more than twenty lanterns of eight different kinds throughout the city. As noted by the commentators to the novel, the theme of lanterns and their relationship with the fire lit by the outlaws runs throughout the chapter. For an interpretation of the lanterns and the night of the lantern festival as a scene of carnival spirit in the novel *Xi you ji* 西遊記 (Journey to the West), see Zhou Zuyan, "Carnivalization."
28. Anne McLaren discusses this particular chapter as an example of the kind of festival spirit of masquerading and revelry that allowed for social integration as well as rebellion. See McLaren, *Chinese Popular Culture*, pp. 93–94.
29. For one of the most recent sources in English on this process of accumulation see Ge, *Out of the Margins*, pp. 36–49, and passim.
30. For a reading of these moments of inscription, see Jing Wang, *The Story of Stone*, pp. 251–54 and 260–67.

form a single band of 108 heroes.[31] With its sequential gathering of
outlaw forces leading to a spectacular moment of pyromania and
pillage, chapter 65, in short, is a miniature version of the novel's overall
narrative structure. This, in turn, was appreciated by Jin Shengtan, who
prefaced that particular chapter with an anecdote about a ventriloquist
that is constructed on a similar logic of accumulation, a careful collecting of different acoustic elements that finally coalesce in a single spectacular climax.

By including this anecdote, however, Jin does not solely point to
a narrative structure of accumulation shared by the two narratives.
He reinterprets such a gathering of multifarious elements as an act of
mimesis, making the point that the vernacular novel, like the ventriloquist's performance, functions as a spectacular illusion. This illusion,
moreover, operates directly through an appeal to the reader's senses.
Read through the lens of the opening comments to chapter 65, the
vernacular novel no longer functions as an immaterial linguistic gathering of diverse symbolic elements that calls for a disembodied moment
of quiet reflection by the reader. Nor is vernacular fiction solely a didac-
tic argument that necessitates an appropriate moral response. Rather,
the act of reading becomes an emotionally charged experience whereby
the words on the page become affectively real for the reader. When
enough elements have been gathered to overwhelm the senses of the
reader/audience, the work transmogrifies from merely a lively gathering
into a fundamentally shocking encounter with the power of mimesis.

At the same time that Jin's anecdote emphasizes the spectacular affectivity of vernacular fiction, it displaces the reader's proper
emotional response from the delight in the illusion itself to a focus on the
medium that allows the illusion to take shape and the masterful tech-

31. The notion of collecting plays a crucial role not only in the gathering of the
heroes, but also in the criticism of the Song emperor Huizong 徽宗 (1082–1135),
whose legendary aesthetic appreciation led to an empire-wide collection of objects
at the capital to the neglect of more crucial governmental tasks, most notably the
gathering of talented men to rule the empire. If the novel's gathering of heroes at
the margins of society reads as a critique of the emperor's aesthetic pursuits at
its center, this critique can also be read in light of the late-Ming obsession with
collecting. For a good essay exploring the early fictional/historical accounts of
Huizong's collection and the role of this collection in the loss of empire, see West,
"Crossing Over."

nique of the storyteller/author who controls this medium. Again, the anecdote about the ventriloquist helps Jin to illustrate how the novel's very structure reflects such masterful control. As commentators before Jin had already noted, the novel itself highlights careful planning as the heart of chapter 65. After all, if the climax of the chapter, the burning of Daming (modern-day Beijing), is found in its second half, the entire first half is taken up describing the careful arrangements made by the strategist Wu Yong in preparing for the raid. Though seemingly superfluous, the very existence of this act of careful planning in the narrative itself points to the genius of the author's own act of narrative planning. As a comment in the Rongyu tang edition (first decade, 17th c.) states, "See how he [Wu Yong] several times dispatches troops: each has its own style of writing, their marvelous and illusory permutations are each and every one different, this is truly the writing of Sima Qian" [司馬遷, 145–90 BCE] 看他幾處發兵, 各有文格, 奇錯變幻, 各各不同, 真是史遷之筆.[32] By including the anecdote about the ventriloquist at the beginning of the chapter, Jin reiterates and confirms the point identified in earlier commentaries: what truly makes *The Outlaws* a marvelous act of writing is its literary technique, the way in which the author, like the ventriloquist, has been able to accumulate so many different elements into a single complex whole and, through this act of masterful writing, create a startling illusion of verisimilitude.

If Jin argues that the novel differentiates itself from bad writing by its literary technique, even more crucial is his argument that the audience can be differentiated on the basis of its appreciation of that technique. Only a foolish reader would get up from his book screaming in horror as he reads about a city burning down. A more cultured reader would recognize the affectivity of the text and respond, perhaps, with a tasteful cry of "Excellent!" 妙.[33] Of course, such a response would follow not because the cultivated reader had been tricked by the fictional mirage, but because he delighted in the marvelous ability of the text to effect such an illusion. For Jin, in other words, the spectacle seen in the content of the tale is a reflection of the marvelous ability of the

32. *Shuihu zhuan huiping ben*, vol. 2, chap. 65, p. 1193.
33. Usually the interlineal comments instruct the reader when such a response would be appropriate by writing the term in between the lines; other such terms include the phrase "marvelous writing" 奇文, etc.

form itself. The medium of sound suggests an unmistakable appeal to the senses, yet it remains inexplicably immaterial. Sound thus comes to represent the perfect metaphor to illustrate the power of fiction. Even when a thousand acoustic elements are gathered and the volume turns deafening, it is in the end nothing but vapors and breath that animates such spectacle. Similarly, the oral performer functions as the perfect embodiment of the art of the novel. Though he may create 108 different heroes and endow each of these heroes with his own individual voice, in the end his tales of heroic outlaws are spun from nothing but thin air.[34]

   The notion that late-Ming literati were interested in the illusory affective qualities of the literary arts has long been accepted. As Wai-yee Li has demonstrated in her study of the notion of emotion 情, late-Ming literati were masters in the playful manipulation of "enchantment and disenchantment," alternatively calling for the reader's engagement with and disengagement from the text.[35] More recently, scholars have furthermore coupled these illusory affective qualities of the text with the idea that there is a self-conscious play with the senses as the vehicle to affect the reader's response. As Robert Hegel has shown in his discussion of Wu Song facing the tiger of Jingyang ridge, or Carlos Rojas has shown in his investigation of literary mirrors such as Li Ruzhen's 李汝珍 (ca. 1763–1830) *Jing hua yuan* 鏡花緣 (Flowers in the mirror), a crucial part of the act of reading involved imagining the novel as a visual spectacle, a spectacle that could only too easily beguile the reader's senses.[36]

   Yet as Jin's anecdote above suggests, the medium of sound and the sense of hearing were just as important as vision in allowing the reader to enjoy vernacular fiction as a spectacular tableau, and it took

---

34. This appreciation of fiction as a spectacular illusion composed of nothing but sound fits neatly with Jin's oft-quoted view that *The Outlaws* is superior to China's first history, Sima Qian's *Shiji* 史記 (Record of the historian), since, as Jin argues, the former "uses text to convey events, whereas in *The Outlaws* events are produced through the text" 以文運事,《水滸》是因文生事. In other words, Jin Shengtan claimed to appreciate *The Outlaws* precisely because it was fiction, not based on real events, and yet it made such fictional fantasies affectively real. See Jin Shengtan, "*Du di wu caizi shu*," p. 16. Translated by John Wang in "Jin Shengtan on *How to Read The Fifth Book of Genius*," p. 133.

35. See Wai-yee Li, *Enchantment and Disenchantment*, pp. 47–88.

36. See Hegel, *Reading Illustrated Fiction*, esp. chap. 5, "Art as Text." See also Rojas, *The Naked Gaze*.

the imagined sound of the storyteller's voice to breathe life into this acoustic mirror image. When we consider that a crucial part of any actual storyteller's act involved a spectacular manipulation of sound, it becomes clear that the rhetorical figure of the storyteller so ubiquitous in premodern fiction may well have played this role of an "acoustic mirror." Actual storytellers were masters of manipulating their vocal chords to imitate the voices of characters, a technique nowadays referred to as "performing" 演. Similarly, they excelled at the manipulation of sounds, an art referred to as ventriloquism 口技 or, alternatively, imitation 學.[37] Indeed, anyone who begins to read through premodern vernacular fiction soon discovers to what degree these texts are filled with characters who talk, curse in dialect, whisper, or shout in such a manner that the reader can almost "hear their voices."

Ironically, it was precisely by emphasizing the skill involved in the creation of the storyteller's illusion that Jin Shengtan could disassociate himself from the lowly audience the oral professional storyteller normally drew. Critics have generally recognized how Jin sought to defend *The Outlaws* as well as *Xi xiang ji* 西廂記 (The western chamber) against moral and political criticism by diverting attention from their content to their writing style and by ranking them as equal to well-recognized masterpieces in the high literary and philosophical tradition.[38] However, less attention has been paid to how Jin, in redeeming *The Outlaws*, could not simply ignore the vulgar origins of the novel and the low-class crowd associated with the vernacular text. As Jin concludes in his "Dufa" 讀法 (Methods of reading), a section of his prefatory material,

> Formerly *The Outlaws* was read even by peddlers and yamen runners. Although not a word has been added or subtracted in this version, it is not destined for petty people. Only those with refined thoughts and feelings can appreciate it.
>
> 舊時《水滸傳》, 販夫皂隸都看; 此本雖不曾增減一字, 卻是與小人沒分之書, 必要真正有錦繡心腸者, 方解說道好。[39]

37. See Wang, Wang, and Zeng, *Zhongguo pingshu yishu lun*, pp. 215–18 and 223–25 respectively. As the phrase "performing" suggests, the imitation of character relies not solely upon imitation of speech, but also on physical gesture and facial expression as well.
38. See John Wang, *Chin Sheng-t'an*, pp. 65–67.
39. Jin Shengtan, "*Du di wu caizi shu*," p. 22. Translated in John Wang, "How to Read *The Fifth Book of Genius*," p. 145.

Here, Jin Shengtan argues that his version of the novel, even though he has not changed a single character in the text, will be completely different from its more vulgar previous incarnations.[40] His argument rests on the suggestion that a single vernacular text can be read in two different manners, one that belongs to "peddlers and yamen runners" and one that belongs to those with "refined thoughts and feelings." Jin locates the "meaning" of the novel not in the text itself, but rather in the way the reader interacts with the text.[41] Whereas the vulgar reader would merely appreciate a lively spectacle, the cultured reader would recognize the emptiness hidden behind this spectacle. Whereas the common reader would be dazzled by the tales of heroism and derring-do, the sophisticated reader would notice the subtle literary technique that allowed the novelist to create such bewitching scenes.

While Jin thus employs the anecdote of the ventriloquist's performance as a metaphor to highlight the craft of writing, he also hastens to elide those physical traces that most resembled the remnants of actual storyteller practice, the standard poetic or parallel prose set-piece descriptions that the oral storyteller narrators in vernacular fiction quoted to enliven their prose narratives. In chapter 65, for instance, Jin cut several passages of parallel prose describing the splendor and liveliness of the city before the outlaws set fire to it, and he similarly elided the parallel prose poems that present images of the city once it is engulfed in flames.[42] Like his predecessors, Jin no doubt found these poetic remnants of the storyteller tradition too vulgar to leave in the text, just as he was most likely affronted by their generalized

40. Jin Shengtan in fact changed *The Outlaws* to a remarkable degree in order to fit his idea of what the novel should be like. Here he asserts that no changes have been made in order to convey the idea that the responsibility for a proper response lies fully with the reader.
41. In this sentence, Jin Shengtan conveniently places the defining quality of the sophisticated reader in his "refined thoughts and feelings," an inner heart 心腸 that locates authenticity in a realm not readily observed. The reference to the heart as the ultimate arbiter of enlightenment borrows from the heart/mind teachings of Wang Yangming and his more literary-inclined disciples, Li Zhi, Xu Wei, and the Yuan brothers (Yuan Hongdao, Yuan Zongdao, Yuan Zhongdao).
42. These descriptions are particularly nice because they juxtapose the splendor and liveliness (*renao*) of the original celebration with the chaos that descends once the town is sacked.

nature.[43] In other words, Jin's anecdote emphasizes the oral performer's voice, but the text of the novel actually omits many of the storyteller remnants; in cutting these elements, he was able to reinvent the sound associated with the storyteller's voice in terms more appropriate to literati taste.

Borrowed Voice: Restoring a Literati Tradition of Appreciation in Late-Qing Jiangnan

In 1889, Yu Yue finished editing *The Three Knights and the Five Gallants*, which had been brought to the scholar's attention by a visiting friend, Pan Zuyin 潘祖蔭 (1830–90), a prominent Jiangnan scholar, president of the Board of Works, and someone who had spent considerable time in the capital, Beijing.[44] In his preface, Yu explains how, after a careful head count, he decided that the number of knights in the novel tallied a total of seven, not three, and accordingly changed the novel's title to *Qi xia wu yi* 七俠五義 (The seven knights and the five gallants). Claiming, moreover, that the first chapter of the novel did not correspond with history, Yu Yue deleted the original content of that chapter and substituted his own musings on history instead. Finally, he wrote an influential and much-quoted preface to the novel in which he explicitly compared its writing style to a lively storyteller performance.

---

43. The commentator to the Rongyu tang edition indeed identified many such passages as despicable 可惡 or vulgar 俗, often calling for them to be deleted 刪. Although some of them were cut in the Yuan Wuyai edition, Jin is the one who eventually cut almost all of them, even when that caused problems in the logic/ progression of the narration. For more information on Jin's elision of vulgar poetry, see John Wang, *Chin Sheng-t'an*, p. 55.
44. For a biography of Pan Zuyin, see Hummel, *Eminent Chinese*, vol. 2, pp. 608–9. Pan Zuyin's style name, Boyin 伯寅, is also suggestively attached to one of the prefaces to a sequel to *The Three Knights*, the 1891 martial arts tale titled *The Continued Latter Five Gallants*. It is not clear whether this is a coincidence, or whether the publishers of *The Continued Latter Five Gallants* actually sought to cash in on Pan Zuyin's fame. In the end, it is unlikely that Pan Zuyin authored the preface because it is dated "the first month of winter of 1890" 光緒庚寅孟冬. Pan Zuyin died on December 11 of the same year. See Boyin, "*Xu xiao wu yi xu*," vol. 3, p. 1556. Pan was an avid collector of books and also owned a handwritten copy of the nineteenth-century novel *Rulin waishi* 儒林外史 (The scholars).

To understand the cultural politics behind Yu Yue's involvement in publishing a popular martial arts novel and, in particular, to explain his reference to storytelling in the context of the novel, it is necessary to take the broader historical moment into consideration. Yu Yue wrote his preface during the final decades of the nineteenth century, a period known not for its literary splendor but rather for the attempt to overcome the ravages caused by years of rebellion. In the southern regions of Jiangnan, the heyday of high Qing scholarship seemed a thing of the past. The Taiping Rebellion, with its many years of armies battling back and forth, had left an area once known for its wealth and intellectual brilliance devastated. For the literati elite in particular, the Taiping Rebellion meant, apart from horrific socioeconomic damage and personal loss of life, an alarming challenge to their central task of textual production and conservation. Literati had been displaced from their homes, academies had been closed, libraries destroyed, and valuable texts irrevocably lost.

Even though the period after the Taiping Rebellion was marked by a clear sense of loss, it still represented for many the prospect of rebuilding the culture and communities that had been destroyed during the long years of internal conflict. Known as the Tongzhi Restoration, the years following the Taiping Rebellion seemed to hold the promise of bringing back the glory days of the Qing, a promise that held true until China's ignominious defeat during the Sino-Japanese War in 1894–95.[45] Literati and officials began the arduous task of rebuilding the social structures, intellectual resources, and collections of texts that had been damaged during the war.[46] It is against this background of loss and

45. According to the classic study by Mary Wright, this period should be understood as a "last stand of Chinese Conservatism." Wright argues that conservative Confucians' rebuilding of culture that took place during these years was doomed to fail because it did not truly embrace the modernization/westernization she sees as the true solution to China's problems. See Wright, *The Last Stand of Chinese Conservatism*. Recent scholarship has begun to turn away from this narrative of failure, demonstrating how many of the reforms implemented in this period were actually quite successful. See, for instance, Elman, "Naval Warfare."

46. To get a sense of what role Yu Yue played in helping to rebuild Jiangnan culture after the Taiping Rebellion, see Rankin, *Elite Activism*, esp. p. 120. For a discussion of the ways in which Yu Yue's many editorial efforts and tireless production of carefully edited classical texts sought to recuperate the scholarly splendor of the pre-Taiping era, see Luo Xiongfei, "Lun Yu Yue."

recovery that we should understand Yu Yue's interest in publishing *The Seven Knights*.

For Yu Yue, *The Seven Knights* represents an object of sophisticated appreciation around which a literati community can be rebuilt, and he states the reason for publishing it most explicitly in his preface:

> In a previous year, Board President Pan Zuyin returned to his native home to mourn the death of a parent, and, since he lived quite close to my abode in Suzhou, we would sometimes visit one another. Conversation happened to drift to the way contemporary scholarship falls so far short of that of the past. Regardless of whether it was poetry or prose, plays or fiction, all the works produced by recent writers fall extremely far below those from before the Qianlong [1735–95] and Jiaqing [1796–1821] eras. Upon this the Board President said, "There is the book *The Three Knights and the Five Heroes*. Even though it is a product of recent years, it is still quite worth reading."
>
> 往年潘鄭盦尚書奉諱家居, 與余吳下寓廬相距甚近, 時相過從. 偶與言及今人學問遠不如希昔, 無論所作詩文, 即院本傳奇平話小說, 凡出於近時者, 皆不如乾, 嘉以前所出者遠甚. 尚書云: "有《三俠五義》一書, 雖近時所出, 而頗可觀." [47]

Yu Yue here presents the reader with a vignette of elite-literati interaction that he himself establishes as belated, namely, as occurring after the reigns of the Qianlong and Jiaqing emperors. When Yu turns to Pan's praise of *The Three Knights*, the implication is hence clear; literary production, even after the Taiping Rebellion, may at times still come close to the glories associated with the first two centuries of the Qing dynasty.

What particular quality, then, in Yu Yue's eyes, allows *Qi xia wu yi* to qualify as a novel that is "still quite worth reading"? It is here that the quality of the sound of the storyteller's voice appears as the bridge between the early Qing and the late Qing. In the preface, Yu Yue describes how, prompted by his friend, he brings the book home and is eventually overwhelmed by the sheer vivacity, brilliance, and, in particular, the "sound" of the novel:

47. Yu Yue, *"Chongbian qixia wuyi* xu," vol. 3, p. 1545.

I brought the novel back with me, and when I first looked at it, I had to laugh. "This is merely *The Cases of the Dragon Diadem*.[48] How is this worthy of even a single glance by Pan Zuyin?" However, after I had finished reading it, I came to recognize that the events described in it were new and marvelous, that the writing was intoxicating and charming, that its descriptions were drawn so minutely that even the finest of hairs were distinguished from each other, and painterly embellishments were both full of surprises and tightly connected. It was just like Pockmarked Liu [Liu Jingting] telling the episode "Wu Song Fights in the Inn." When Wu Song first enters the inn, there is no one there, so he gives a sudden roar, causing the empty jars and vats in the inn to resound, "WENGWENG." Such adding of color during a lull in the text this raises the spirit a hundredfold. Only writing of this kind can truly be called a plain-prose novel; only a plain-prose novel like this can be considered a truly unique piece of writing in the world. I then sighed in appreciation of the fact that Board President Pan's commendation of it was not without reason.

余擕歸閱之，笑曰：“此《龍圖公案》耳，何足辱鄭盦之一盼乎!” 及閱至終篇，見其事跡新奇，筆意酣姿，描寫既細如毫芒，點染又曲中筋節，正如柳麻子說武松打店，初到店內無人，驀地一吼，店中空缸空甓皆瓮瓮有聲：閒中著色，精神百倍。如此筆墨，方許作評話小說；如此評話小說，方算得天地間另是一種筆墨。乃嘆鄭盦尚書欣賞之不虛也。[49]

Whereas Yu Yue, as seen in the quote opening this chapter, criticizes the written form of *The Sluices of Qingfeng* because its writing failed to match the earlier storyteller performance, here Yu Yue says that *The Three Knights and the Five Gallants* is worthy precisely because it succeeds in capturing elements of the performance of a master storyteller such as Liu Jingting, most notably the storyteller's use of voice. It is the sound of the famous late-Ming storyteller Pockmarked Liu imitating the shout of the hero Wu Song that causes Yu Yue to remark that the novel "adds color during a lull in the text." Similarly, it is the sound of the storyteller creating the illusion of "empty vats and jars in

48. *Longtu gongan* 龍圖公案 (The cases of the Dragon diadem) refers to a popular collection of court cases involving Judge Bao that circulated as early as the late Ming but remained popular throughout the Qing dynasty. Terse in language and episodic in nature, it little resembles the much later martial arts novel. The term "Dragon diadem" references the honorable position Judge Bao once held, Scholar of the Dragon Diadem Pavilion 龍圖閣學士.
49. Ibid.

the inn resounding 'WENGWENG'" that compels Yu Yue to call the late nineteenth-century martial arts novel a truly "unique piece of writing in the world."

Though Yu Yue's lively description of Liu Jingting's performance might lead one to conclude he is referring to a performance he had personally witnessed, Yu Yue here actually draws on a much earlier description of a storyteller—that of Zhang Dai's famous early-Qing anecdote about Liu Jingting.[50] By doing so, Yu Yue creates a direct link with earlier scholars' appreciation of the sound of the storyteller's voice and their attempts to represent it in writing. Just as Zhang Dai, survivor of the fall of the Ming, had once appreciated the lowly oral arts of Pockmarked Liu, so does Yu Yue, survivor of the Taiping Rebellion, find pleasure in the oral aspects of the vernacular text. By echoing the phrases of a famous early Jiangnan scholar, Yu Yue places himself in a long textual lineage of the cultural elite's patronage of the vernacular arts, which runs uninterrupted from the late Ming to his own day.[51]

Although Yu Yue evokes a longer tradition of literati appreciation of the vernacular arts, there are of course differences in the particular ways in which late-Ming and late-Qing scholars approached the storyteller's voice. At the end of his preface, Yu Yue reminds his readers of one such difference when he criticizes another late-Ming/early-Qing literatus famous for his interest in the vernacular arts, Jin Shengtan. In particular, Yu Yue scolds Jin for falsely attributing his editorial changes to the novel to an "ancient copy."[52] Concluding his preface, Yu Yue writes, "Brandishing my brush, I just went ahead and made changes. There is no need to imitate Jin Shengtan's editing of *The Outlaws* and attribute each one of them to an 'ancient copy'" 奮筆便改, 不必如聖嘆之改《水

50. The lines are almost literally the same. The corresponding passage in Zhang Dai's text reads, "When Wu Song comes to the wine shop to buy wine, there is no one there, so he gives a sudden roar, making the empty jars and vats in the inn resound 'WENGWENG.' Adding color during a lull in the text, he [Liu Jingting] was as attentive to detail as this" 武松到店沽酒, 店內 無 人, 驀地一吼, 店中空 缸 空甏皆甕甕有聲: 閒中著色, 細微至此. Zhang Dai, "Liu Jingting shuoshu," p. 82.
51. This sense of a shared appreciation is based, at least in part, on regional identities. Zhang Dai, Yu Yue, Pan Zuyin, and Jin Shengtan were all natives of Jiangnan.
52. Jin claimed that this copy of the novel was given to him by a friend and that it represented the original version as written by Shi Nai'an.

滸傳》,處處拖之古本也.[53] Yu Yue reminds his readers that two hundred
years earlier, Jin Shengtan had similarly edited a masterpiece of martial
arts fiction, *The Outlaws*. Whereas Jin had falsely claimed to have found
an "ancient copy" with all of his changes already in it, Yu Yue frowned
at such fraudulent practices. As a late-Qing scholar, Yu Yue was writing
as the heir to two hundred years of *kaozheng* 考證 scholarship, a school
of knowledge that had specialized in helping scholars develop the critical tools that would allow them to recognize the distinction between
authentic and fraudulent texts.[54] Instead of taking Jin's approach, Yu
Yue openly authorizes himself to edit the text of the novel according to
his own lights, supposedly confident that his arguments are sufficient
justification in themselves.

    In a similar manner, Yu Yue's reference to Zhang Dai both elides
and highlights the differences between the early and late Qing. Even
though both Yu Yue and Zhang Dai use the storyteller's voice to revive
the past, the implications of this revival are significantly different.
Zhang Dai wrote after the Ming dynasty had fallen and the restitution
of the former dynasty was increasingly recognized as a dream—an
attractive illusion, but a false promise nevertheless. For Zhang Dai, who
had actually witnessed performances by Liu Jingting, the evanescent
quality of the storyteller's voice functioned to emphasize this sense of
loss by underlining how text and memory, like the voice of the storyteller, could recall the past in phantasmagoric and spectacular manner
but could never hope to recapture the reality of that moment fully.[55]
Indeed, as if to highlight this notion of illusion, Zhang Dai fills his text

---

53. Yu Yue, "*Chongbian qixia wuyi* xu," vol. 3, p. 1545.
54. Various features of Yu Yue's edition of *Qi xia wu yi*, most notably his decision
to change the title and the first chapter, display his penchant for a careful approach
to vernacular fiction based on textual criticism (*kaozheng* 考證), something very
rare before his day. For other examples of Yu Yue's literal-minded approach to
fiction, see Kang Laixin, *Wan Qing xiaoshuo lilun yanjiu*, pp. 161–82. In contrast to
Yu Yue, Jin Shengtan celebrated *Shuihu zhuan* precisely because it was fiction, and
his fraudulent claim of basing himself on an old edition may well be seen in light of
the playful late-Ming appreciation of fakes and forgeries.
55. For a more complete discussion of the relationship between the memory
of the fallen Ming and Zhang Dai's *Tao'an's Memories of a Dream*, see Owen,
Remembrances. See also Kafalas, *In Limpid Dream*. For a more historical and
broader approach to Zhang Dai's life and times, see Spence, *Return to Dragon
Mountain*.

with images of emptiness: an inn that is devoid of people, empty vats and empty jars, all desolate signs that depend on the short-lived illusion of the storyteller's voice to come to life. In contrast, Yu Yue was writing after the Taiping Rebellion had been quelled, the Restoration Movement was at its height, and the possibility of restoring the Qing dynasty to its former glory was very much regarded as real. For Yu Yue, Zhang Dai's quote represented not a doomed attempt to catch the living story-teller voice in text, but rather a successful reference to a text that had been handed down over the years and thus emphasized not the loss but rather the continuation of tradition. Not surprisingly, Yu Yue, though borrowing from Zhang Dai, ended his citation with an affirmation that negates Zhang Dai's earlier emphasis on absence: Yu Yue sighs in appreciation that Pan Zuyin's commendation of this novel is not groundless.

In short, Yu Yue's appreciation of the novel as capturing the sound of a storyteller performance may at first strike us simply as an unequivocal statement of his fondness for oral performances. On closer reading, however, Yu Yue's appreciation turns out to be a highly elite, textually informed effort. Though he employs the example of a storyteller's use of his voice to speak of the brilliance of the novel, like Jin's strategic deployment of the ventriloquist, or Zhang Dai's nostalgic memories of Liu Jingting, such references to the oral performing arts are ultimately just being borrowed to highlight the marvelous qualities of the text. For these authors, then, the oral art of the storyteller functioned as a symbol around which a community of literati scholars could be brought together precisely through their written patronage of the lowly oral performance. Stated differently, in Yu Yue's preface, Liu Jingting's art functions as an object suitable for tasteful evaluation, an object that creates a textual exchange through which scholars can "speak" to one another across time and space because of their shared appreciation. Just as Yu Yue's discussion with Pan Zuyin, the Board President recently returned from the capital, represents a moment where geographical boundaries between the north and the south are broken down through the mediation of a vernacular novel, so does Yu Yue's conversation with the earlier scholars Jin Shengtan and Zhang Dai represent the crossing of temporal boundaries. Amid the ruins of the Taiping Rebellion, Yu borrows the storyteller's voice to reconstruct a community among literati reaching from Jiangnan to Beijing, and from the nineteenth century back to the seventeenth century.

Conclusion

Yu Yue may well have directed his preface and endorsement to like-minded scholarly readers who could continue the literati traditions of the Ming and the Qing; the eventual audience of *Qi xia wu yi*, however, was in fact quite different. Writing in the first issue of the *Yangzi Fiction Journal* in 1909, the author Shi An neatly summarizes the shift from more tasteful early martial arts novels produced under the auspices of figures such as Yu Yue to martial arts novels produced in the twenty years that followed. Shi An is careful to point out how fond he is of the older, tasteful martial arts novels, especially the edition edited by the luminary Yu Yue.[56] Next, however, he continues to describe these novels' quick descent into low-class entertainment that followed only a few years later:

> From the time *The Seven Knights and the Five Gallants* appeared, not less than one hundred imitators have followed: *The Latter Five Gallants, The Continued Latter Five Gallants, The Third, The Fourth,* and *Fifth Latter Five Gallants.* There are, moreover, *The Cases of Judge Shi, The Cases of Judge Peng, The Tale of Lord Ji,* and *The Cases of Judge Hai* that are extended by sequel upon sequel, creating sequels without end. On top of this there are the so-called *Seven Swords and Thirteen Knights, The Tale of Everlasting Blessings and Peace, The Unofficial History of the Iron Immortal,* all produced from the same mold [literally: all exhaled from the same nostril]. Apart from these, particularly despicable is yet another novel, *The Continued Tale of Romance and Heroism.* Its pages are likewise filled with thieves and thief catchers: the first steals and the latter tries to nab him, and the ruckus rises up to heaven. Every time you read even a single chapter, it will cause you to throw up for three days. At first I could not understand how so much writing of this kind could suddenly appear, but later a friend told me that novels such as these are produced by

---

56. As Shi states, "[Yu Yue] only made editorial changes of some ten odd characters in each line, and yet its penmanship is completely different, displaying a craft of writing that cannot be put into words" 其刪改之處, 每行中不到十數字, 而其筆墨遂大改變, 真不以言傳哉! Shi An, "Chankongshi suibi," p. 443. *Qi xia wu yi* is of course only one of the works of fiction that Shi appreciates; other texts included for praise are such canonical works as *The Journey to the West*, *Shuihu zhuan*, and Pu Songling's 蒲松齡 (1640–1715) *Liaozhai zhiyi* 聊齋志異 (Tales of the Liaozhai studio).

Shanghai publishers who, seeking petty profits, specially hire half-educated literati to put together such books, all so as to sell them widely. Now such books as these are most suited to find favor with the lower echelons of society, so [the publishers] just change the title a bit and thus produce yet another novel, and as a result a thousand—no, ten thousand—volumes appear. These novels are like the feet of peasant women: they're both long and smelly, filling the streets and avenues, they appear everywhere.

自 《七俠五義》一書出現後，世之效顰學步者不下白十種，《小五義》也，《續小五義》也，再續，三續，四續 《小五義》也. 更有 《施公案》,《彭公案》,《濟公》,《海公案》,亦再續，重續，三續，四續之不止. 此外復有所謂《七劍十三俠》,《永慶昇平》,《鐵仙外史》,皆屬一鼻子出氣. 尤可惡者, 諸書之外有一 《續兒女英雄傳》,亦滿紙賊盜捕快, 你偷我拿, 鬧嚷宣天, 每閱一卷, 必令人作嘔三日. 余初竊不解世何忽來此許多筆墨也. 後友人告余, 凡此等書, 由海上書儈覓蠅頭之利, 特請稍識之士編成此等書籍, 以廣銷路. 蓋此等書籍最易取悅于下等社會, 稍改名字, 即又成一書, 故千卷萬卷, 同一鄉下婦人腳, 又長又臭, 堆街塞路, 到處俱是也.[57]

Blessed with twenty years of hindsight, Shi An here can voice the opprobrium Yu Yue himself might have felt had he known how his *Seven Knights* would influence the world of publishing. By the early twentieth century, martial arts novels were no longer tastefully edited, beautifully illustrated, and published in expensive, large formats. Rather, they were often hastily and shoddily produced cheap imitations, which were penned by professional but not necessarily well-educated authors and printed by Shanghai publishers whose production methods were more fully in line with capitalist modes of production. These books were then enjoyed by a middlebrow audience of readers who had little in common with Yu Yue and his select group of literati friends.

There is, then, a certain element of irony to Yu Yue's use of a popular martial arts novel and his reference to the famous late-Ming storyteller Liu Jingting as symbols of shared literati appreciation. Like so many other scholars of the late nineteenth century, Yu Yue attempted to rebuild the textual culture of the past by drawing on the printing techniques of a new age, lithography and metal type.[58] Though the aims

57. Shi An, "Chankongshi suibi," p. 443.
58. For a discussion of the interaction between the scholarly community in Jiangnan and the more commercial interests of modern printing presses in the production of collectanea, as well as the transformation of the notion of text from collected treasure to consumed commodity, see Meng Yue, "The Invention of Shanghai" pp. 111–59.

of such scholars lay in refashioning a culture founded on elite textual appreciation of classical texts, the actual effect of endorsing new print techniques turned out to be an overall popularization of print culture. By the early twentieth century, elite *kaozheng* scholars were no longer called upon to lend their textual skills to collate, edit, or otherwise sanctify the publishing efforts of Shanghai printers who now churned out a whole range of texts at lightning speed for an ever-growing audience of petit-bourgeois urban consumers.[59]

As Shi An's remark quoted above demonstrates, martial arts novels perfectly embody this movement towards a popularization of cultural production first introduced by a combination of elite scholarly authority, the appeal of lively martial arts storyteller tales, and newly imported printing techniques. Take, for instance, another early work of martial arts fiction, Wen Kang's *Tale of Romance and Heroism*. Printed with moveable wooden type and first published in 1878 by the Beijing publishing house Juzhen tang 舉珍堂, the novel found scholarly endorsement by one of the more renowned literati of the age, Dong Xun 董恂 (1807–1902). In 1888, the novel was republished in Shanghai by Feiying guan 蜚英館, the publishing house associated with the famous late-Qing illustrator Wu Youru 吳友如 (1840?–96?). Blessed by Dong Xun's literati presence and now beautifully illustrated with modern lithographic prints, the novel proved quite popular.[60] In fact, the tasteful Feiying guan edition may well have influenced Yu Yue's decision to publish his *Seven Knights* one year later with the newly established Shanghai Guangbai Songzhai 廣百宋齋 publishing house. Employing typeset metal type for the text and graced with beautiful lithographic illustrations, *The Seven Knights* became one of the major publishing hits of the late nineteenth century

59. For a discussion of the rise of a petit-bourgeois audience and the Mandarin Duck and Butterfly fiction that appealed to this particular crowd, see Link, *Mandarin Ducks and Butterflies*.
60. The transitional nature of late nineteenth-century Shanghai publishing is illustrated particularly well by one early Guangxu-era (1875–1908) edition published by the Shanghai publishing house Saoye shanfang 掃葉山房 and kept at Fudan University. This edition used lithographic printing techniques (or ordered these illustrations from a second printer) to include the Feiying guan illustrations, but reprinted the rest of the text using woodblocks, eliding most of Dong Xun's commentary. See *Huitu Ernü yingxiong zhuan*.

1.2 "Basing Himself on Orthodox History," chapter 1. (In *Qi xia wu yi*, published in 1892 by the Zhenyi shuju. Photo courtesy of Fudan University Library, Rare Book Collection.)

and spearheaded a whole line of cheaply produced martial arts novels.[61]
Soon, the audience of these novels was not necessarily limited to the
literati scholars imagined by Yu Yue; rather it consisted of a steadily
growing group of urban middle-class readers who were unfamiliar with
the name Shi Yukun and were increasingly less impressed with a name
such as Yu Yue.

An illustration from the 1892 lithographed edition of *Xiuxiang Qixia
wuyi* (The illustrated seven knights and the five gallants), published by
the Shanghai publishing house Zhenyi shuju 珍藝書局 captures the
irony of the situation.[62] The caption of figure 1.2, the illustration that
accompanies the first chapter of the novel, reads, "Basing himself on
orthodox history he overthrows *The Cases of the Dragon Diadem* 據正
史翻龍圖公安. The illustration itself shows the great Yu Yue, a cup of
tea at hand, leisurely perusing the text as a page boy carries in impres-
sive-looking volumes of what presumably is orthodox history.

Looking at the picture, the reader can identify with the great
scholar Yu Yue, taking pleasure in reading a beautifully printed volume.
Yu Yue's presence, moreover, guarantees the value of the volume as a
carefully edited work that adheres to the highest standards of scholarship. Yet despite its beautiful illustration, the Zhenyi shuju edition itself
already belonged to a different era and set of production values. Small
in size (only 9.5 by 16 cm.), its pages crammed with small characters (18
rows of 32 characters per page), but including a good number of crisp
illustrations, it was precisely this kind of cheaply produced lithographic
edition that allowed the martial arts novel to become one of the most
popular mass-produced items of the twentieth century.[63]

---

61. I have not been able to trace the link from Yu Yue to the Guangbai Songzhai
publishing house. Nor have I thus far found out who was responsible for the illustrations in this edition. Wang Qingyuan et al. list an 1887 popularized fictional
edition of the twenty-four histories as the earliest Guangbai Songzhai publication.
See Wang, Mou, and Han, *Xiaoshuo shufang lu*, p. 118.
62. *Xiuxiang Qixia wuyi.*
63. As Wilt Idema and Lloyd Haft note, "the sudden popularity of the genre of the
wuxia xiaoshuo [martial arts novel] . . . is undoubtedly tightly connected to the
introduction of the lithographic printing process." Idema and Haft, *A Guide to
Chinese Literature*, p. 241.

CHAPTER TWO

A Local Audience

Beijing Tales and the Brand-Name Recognition of Shi Yukun

> His reputation is exalted far above the common crowd,
> Crushing those idle itinerant performers.
> He has astonished high-ranking officials who praise his superb
>   tunes,
> Which circulate through the city and are widely imitated.
> His composition of the cases of Judge Bao of the Song
> Has brought fame to Shi Yukun in the present age.
> Who conferred upon him the name of "Master"
> And directly compared him to a teacher of the Classics?[1]
> —From "Shi Yukun"

This quote from the beginning of a typical Beijing bannerman song
(*zidishu* 子弟書) titled "Shi Yukun" is symbolic of a broader trend
of the nineteenth century:[2] storytellers were becoming increasingly

---

1. This latter phrase is a reference to Ma Rong 馬融 (79–166 CE) of the Eastern
Han dynasty (25–220 CE) who, according to the *Hou Hanshu* 後漢書 (*The History
of the Latter Han*), lectured on the classics in a tent of purple cloth. The original
text reads: 高抬聲價本超群, 壓倒江湖無業民. / 驚動公卿誇絕調, 流傳井市效眉
顰. / 編來宋代包公案, 成就當時石玉昆. / 是誰拜贈先生號, 直比談經絳帳人? "Shi
Yukun," vol. 2, p. 734.
2. Bannerman songs (sometimes also called "scion books") were reputedly originally performed by Manchu bannermen as they invaded China. By the eighteenth
century, the *zidishu* was generally recognized as one of the most "elegant" forms
of popular, northern Beijing songs. See Goldman, "The Nun Who Wouldn't Be";
see also Guan and Zhou, "Xu." For an English-language discussion of *zidishu*, see
Chiu, "Cultural Hybridity."

well-known celebrities who were so exalted in popular song, literati poetry, and nostalgic memoirs that they could demand hefty fees for performances.[3] Shi Yukun, the storyteller celebrated in the opening lines of the *zidishu* quoted above, is a perfect example. Even though this *zidishu* is filled with skepticism toward the legitimacy of his reputation, in particular heaping scorn on the idea of calling him "Master," in the end the piece most likely contributed to the storyteller's reputation (*shengjia* 聲價, literally "sound price").[4] Shi Yukun's fame also spread through other popular song forms such as dockworker songs (*matoudiao* 馬頭調) and reached the higher echelons of society, as evidenced by the poem *Yong Shi Yukun* 咏石玉昆 (Ode to Shi Yukun) penned by the high official Fucha Guiqing 富察貴慶 (1899 *jinshi*).[5] Shi Yukun was not the only famous nineteenth-century Beijing storyteller. Performers such as Cai Dong 彩董, De Shoushan 德壽山, Guo Dong'er 郭東兒, Suiyuanle 隨緣樂, and Zhang Sanlu 張

---

3. Laura Andrews McDaniel has illustrated how the storytelling profession, supposedly a traditional occupation outdated by the onset of modernity, actually became increasingly lucrative in the late nineteenth and early twentieth centuries. Though the time period and region of McDaniel's investigation are slightly different, the rise in visibility of early nineteenth-century storytellers suggests the same story. See McDaniel, "Jumping the Dragon Gate."

4. This *zidishu* is often used as evidence of Shi Yukun's fame and superb storytelling skills. Many scholars overlook, however, that the aim of the text is to lampoon the storyteller's fame or at least criticize those members of society who hold him in such high esteem. As in modern society, there is no such thing as bad publicity for those trying to establish themselves as stars. Indeed, the best way to establish one's own name was to denigrate someone else's name, and this led to an entire series of popular songs dedicated to defaming other popular performers as a way of establishing one's own reputation.

5. The *matoudiao* on Shi Yukun is a later rewriting of the earlier *zidishu*. For a longer discussion of *matoudiao*, see chapter 3. For a discussion of the particular *matoudiao* about Shi Yukun, see Chen Jinzhao, "Zidishu zhi ticai." Fucha Guiqing was a Manchu belonging to the bordered white banner. He passed the *jinshi* examinations in 1899 and later held the high-ranking post of President of the Board of Rites. Wu Yinghua and Wu Shaoying estimate that this particular poem on Shi Yukun was written in 1837. Because the author states that he remembers Shi Yukun's performances from twenty years ago, it is possible to assign an early date of Shi Yukun's performances to around 1817. See Wu and Wu, "You guan 'San xia wu yi' zuozhe."

三祿 all enjoyed an increased visibility that allowed them to appear in local Beijing guidebooks, memoirs, songs, and poetry.[6]

As Patrick Hanan has argued, one of the most prominent trends in nineteenth-century vernacular fiction was a shift from a rather clichéd, anonymous storyteller narrator to a more prominent, individualized narrator.[7] Did the increased visibility of storytellers in the nineteenth century contribute to this shift? How can we connect the growing prominence of storytellers in society, as evidenced by popular song and literati poetry, to broader print-cultural trends? And does the interest in storytelling, both in actual performance and in writing, shed light on who read these novels, how they read them, and why? In this chapter, I will argue that the spreading fame of nineteenth-century storytellers led to their increased presence in prefatory material to vernacular martial arts novels and to a more prominent role for the storyteller in the texts of the novels themselves.[8] The increased presence of the storyteller figure reveals that long before Yu Yue decided to edit *The Three Knights and the Five Gallants* and change its name to *The Seven Knights*, local Beijing publishers and authors were drawing on the brand-name recognition of famous storytellers such as Shi Yukun to recreate an acoustic environment that allowed local, often bannerman, readers to imagine their capital during the height of Qing power.

6. Especially useful in this regard is the *matoudiao* "Kuo daye zhui Ding" 闊大爺追丁 (Big master chases [his wife] to [Ximen]ding), which tells of a wealthy man scolding his wife for constantly inviting entertainers into the house. Since the tirade takes the form of listing every performer ever invited, the song provides us with a convenient overview of famous mid-nineteenth-century performers. See "Kuo daye zhui Ding." See also Chong, *Dao Xian yilai chaoye zaji*, pp. 7–9, 12, and 20 respectively. Finally, see the *zidishu* "Guo Dong'er" 郭棟兒 and "Suiyuanle" 隨緣樂. The most famous of nineteenth-century guidebooks is Yang Jingting's 楊靜亭 *Dumen jilüe* 都門紀略 (A short account of the capital), which offers poetic depictions of various performers.
7. For Hanan's discussion of the nineteenth-century narrator, see his *Chinese Fiction*, pp. 9–32.
8. For more on this, see in particular chap. 6, where I discuss the way the novelist Wen Kang created a singularly loquacious and individualized narrator in *The Tale of Romance and Heroism*.

Local Tales of Imperial Power

> This city of Beijing is the grand capital at the emperor's feet. It's
> filled with hidden dragons and crouching tigers; all kinds of
> heroes can here be found.
> —Guo Guangrui 郭光瑞, *The Tale of Everlasting*
> *Blessings and Peace, Part 1*

Whereas readers in the South may have had their own reasons for
enjoying *The Three Knights*, in Beijing the martial arts novels were
popular because they allowed readers to imagine their local community as it had been a century ago in times of splendor. Bannermen were
often involved in the telling and editing of these tales, suggesting that
they may well have been attracted to the stories as readers, too. Many of
these novels tell tales of strong-minded martial heroes living during the
two reigns that represent the apex of Qing dynastic power, the reigns of
Kangxi (1661–1722) and Qianlong (1735–96). Plots inevitably involve a
series of adventures that allow these heroes to employ their martial (and
sometimes storytelling) talents to vanquish heterodox sects and pacify
regional rebellions.[9] As the heroes rise from rags to riches, they steadily
move up in rank; the plots often culminate in a grand finale in which
the emperor himself benevolently looks on as the martial men display
their talents at court. The heroes are then rewarded generously and with
elaborate ritual for their meritorious service.[10]

9. One of the heroes of *The Tale of Everlasting Blessings and Peace, Part 1* is in fact
both a talented martial artist and a silken-voiced singer of popular Beijing ballads.
It is the combination of these two talents that allows the hero, Zhang Guangtai, to
make a remarkable rise in fortune. Though martial skills are crucial to these novels,
it should be noted that the martial arts practiced in them rarely belong to the typical bannerman skills of equestrianism and archery. Rather, these novels feature a
brand of "kung-fu" skills associated with different schools of Han Chinese martial
arts and hand-to-hand combat.
10. See, for instance, *San xia wu yi* (1996), chaps. 22 and 49; *Xu xiao wu yi*, chaps. 19
and 20; *Shi gong quan an*, chaps. 184 and 185; Tanmeng daoren, *Peng gongan*, chap.
28; Guo Guangrui, *Yongqing shengping qianzhuan*, chap. 7. The last two examples represent a variation on the theme. In chap. 28 of *The Cases of Judge Peng*,
for instance, the hero Huang Tianba subdues a wild tiger in front of the Kangxi
emperor during the spring hunt and is subsequently rewarded an imperial yellow
robe. There is no elaborate court setting nor a bestowing of titles.

In the preface he appended to the 1892 martial arts tale *Yongqing shengping quanzhuan* 永慶昇平前傳 (The tale of everlasting blessings and peace, part 1), Guo Guangrui puts this kind of wish fulfillment typical of the late nineteenth-century martial arts novel into words:[11]

> *The Tale of Everlasting Blessings and Peace* is a true story that tells how our dynasty the Great Qing rewarded the loyal and punished the sycophants while rooting out rebellious thieves and heterodox sects. In it, the loyal and righteous knights and the straightforward and heroic men loyally defend the dynasty and protect the people with devotion. The writing is straightforward, and truly there are old sources that support the story. This is not just some drum-song or fictional history.[12] These facts have been transmitted since the beginning of our dynasty.
>
> [永慶昇平]一書, 乃我國大清襃忠貶佞, 剿滅亂賊邪教之事實. 內有忠義俠烈之人, 慷慨豪杰之士, 忠心護國, 赤膽佑民. 書理直爽, 實有古蹟可憑, 並非古詞野史. 國初以來, 有此實事傳留.[13]

Anyone can appreciate a good swashbuckling tale of heroic men finding their fortune. An audience of primarily Beijing bannermen hoping to revive the good old days, however, must have attached special significance to the "loyal and righteous knights" who were so generously "rewarded" by sage emperors of the none-too-distant past.

It is easy to overlook to what degree these late nineteenth-century novels were typically local Beijing products. When May Fourth scholars began writing the history of vernacular fiction in the early twentieth

11. Little is known about Guo Guangrui. Based on his style name, Xiaoting 筱亭, it is likely that he also wrote another popular late nineteenth-century martial arts novel, *Yanping Jigong zhuan* 演評濟公傳 (The storyteller tale of Jigong), first published in 1898. Guo signs his preface as the "Retired Scholar of Yannan" 燕南居士. He lived in Qingluhe 清潞河, a small town in the vicinity of Beijing.

12. The characters are 古詞, "old lyrics," but this might very well be a typographical error and actually refer to 鼓詞, that is, "drum-song." Drum-songs are a predominantly northern popular form of prosimetric literature that alternates verse and prose, song and recitation to the accompaniment of a drum. In the nineteenth century, drum-songs were wildly popular not only as performance but also as text. For more on drum-songs, see Li et al., "*Zhongguo guci zongmu.*" The standard work in English is presently Stevens, "Peking Drumsinging."

13. Guo Guangrui, "*Yongqing shengping xu,*" vol. 3, p. 1561. Also translated by Meir Shahar in *Crazy Ji*, pp. 121–22. My translation is slightly more literal.

century, most of the late nineteenth-century martial arts novels were no longer local products and, in fact, were quite often not readily available in their original Beijing imprints.[14] Moreover, these May Fourth writers were so invested in the project of constructing a national history of vernacular literature that they had little consideration for the regional, and sometimes ethnic, origins of works they saw as representing the voice of the downtrodden masses of the entire Chinese nation. Even more recent scholars have generally tended to share Lu Xun's preoccupation with the class origins and political viewpoint of the texts, agreeing that Wen Kang's novel *The Tale of Romance and Heroism* should be classified as an elite example of "knight-errant court-case fiction" and *The Three Knights and Five Gallants* represents a popular example of the same genre. Rarely do these scholars explore the texts' regional originals; and furthermore, they tend to downplay the fact that despite their very different "class origins," both novels had in fact been published first by the same Beijing publishing house, the Juzhen tang on Longfu Temple Street, an establishment specializing in bilingual Manchu/Chinese texts.[15]

To be sure, after the publication of *The Seven Knights* in 1890, Shanghai publishers may have flooded the market with reprints of martial arts novels. However, in the early years many of these novels were first produced as local Beijing tales.[16] For instance, the first two sequels to *The Three Knights*, that is, *The Latter Five Gallants* and *The Continued Latter Five Gallants*, were both published by Shi Duo 石鐸

14. Hu Shi was one of the few early scholars to identify these novels as typically northern and part of bannerman culture. As he investigates the shift of these works from their northern, Beijing origins to their eventual Shanghai production in his preface to *The Three Knights*, he laments that even northerners nowadays do not recall the Beijing origins of the tale. The relationship between martial arts novels and Beijing bannerman culture is explored most fully in his preface to *The Tale of Romance and Heroism*. See Hu Shi, "*San xia wu yi* xu," esp. p. 314; Hu Shi, "*Ernü yingxiong zhuan* xu."

15. For more information on the publishing house Juzhen tang, see Widmer, "*Honglou meng ying.*"

16. For instance, *The Continued Latter Five Gallants* was first printed in 1891 by the Beijing publishing house Wenguang lou 文光樓. During the last decade of the nineteenth century, it was reprinted nine times, one time in Beijing, one time in Chongqing, and seven times in Shanghai. See Keulemans, "Sounds of the Novel," appendix C.

of the Wenguang lou 文光樓.[17] Most likely, the same Shi Duo was also responsible for publishing the sequel to another famous Qing martial arts novel, *The Cases of Judge Shi*, namely, *Shi gongan houzhuan* 施公案後傳 (The continued cases of Judge Shi; 1893 preface, 1894 first edition).[18] *The Tale of Everlasting Blessings and Peace, Part 1* (1891 preface, 1892 first edition) was published by yet another Beijing publisher, the Baowen tang 寶文堂. The novel's sequel, *Yongqing shengping houzhuan* 永慶昇平後傳 (The tale of everlasting blessings and peace, part 2), was published in 1894 by Benli tang 本立堂, located in Beijing at the western gate of Liulichang. This publishing house was also responsible for printing *Peng gongan* 彭公案 (The cases of Judge Peng; 1892), another famous late-Qing martial arts novel. Not all late nineteenth-century martial arts novels were first published in Beijing, yet a remarkable number of them originated in the capital.[19]

Moreover, a closer look at the provenance of the two most famous of these novels, *The Three Knights* and *The Tale of Romance and Heroism*, reveals that this production was not simply local to Beijing, but at times could be specifically attributed to bannermen. In his memoirs of the capital, *Dao Xian yilai chaoye zaji* 道咸以來朝野雜記 (Random notes of the court and the people since the Daoguang and Xianfeng reigns),

17. For more information on Shi Duo, the owner of the Wenguang lou, see Miao, "*Xiao wu yi, Xu xiao wu yi* de kanxingzhe."
18. Since the first edition of *The Continued Cases of Judge Shi* is lost, we cannot be sure that Shi Duo was indeed the publisher; however, a few facts suggest as much. First, the preface to *The Continued Cases* is signed by Wenguang zhuren 文光主人 (The Master of Wenguang), which is strikingly similar to Wenguanglou zhuren 文光樓主人 (The Master of the Wenguang Establishment). Second, the style in which the preface to *The Continued Cases* is written reminds us of the prefaces of *The Latter Five Gallants* by Shi Duo. Both, for instance, emphasize the precise number of volumes and pages associated with the project. Third, both projects use an unfinished older novel, *The Three Knights* in one case and *The Cases of Judge Shi* in another, to introduce a new series of books. Finally, the timing of the projects makes sense; *The Continued Cases* was first printed in 1893, two years after the publication of *The Continued Latter Five Gallants*, a period sufficient for Shi Duo to begin this new project. See also Miao, "*Xiao wu yi, Xu xiao wu yi* de kanxingzhe."
19. For instance, *Qianlong xunxing jiangnan ji* 乾隆巡幸江南記 (The tale of Qianlong touring Jiangnan; also known as *Shengchao dingsheng wannian qing* 聖朝鼎盛萬年青 (Our everlasting blessed dynasty) was most likely first published in the south. See Sun Kaidi, *Zhongguo xiaoshuo shumu*, pp. 85–86.

Chong Yi 崇彝, a Beijing bannerman belonging to the Plain Red Banner, writes,

> On the south side of the east end of Longfu Temple Street, there was the bookshop Juzhen tang (now out of business). This was originally the old address of the Tianhui ge. In the Tongzhi years [1862–74], it was taken over by a bannerman from the Household Department by the name of Zhang, who changed the name to Juzhen. . . . Among the books printed by the Juzhen tang, the most famous is *The Cases of Judge Bao* (this is *The Three Knights and the Five Gallants*). Because there was no original manuscript for this tale, in those days several of my old friends (the two gentlemen Xiang Leting 祥樂亭 and Wen Ye'an 文冶庵 [Wen Liang 文良] among them) would every day go and listen to the telling of the story and after returning home together write it down comparing notes. This is how the book came about. The characters in this novel all had lyric encomiums (the current edition does not have these). There were a lot of interesting bits in it, and the tale was both humorous and elegant. This was the story that was handed down by Shi Yukun in the Daoguang years. *The Tale of Romance and Heroism* was written by Wen Tiexian [Wen Kang]. In the process, Mister Ye'an and Mister Ti'nan 俶南 [Wen Shuo 文碩] offered a lot of support. But the Juzhen tang editions for these two books are now extremely hard to obtain.
>
> 隆福寺街東口路南聚珍堂書肆(今歇業). 本天繪閣舊址, 同治中, 為一內務府旗人張姓接收, 改名聚珍. . . 所印之包公案(即三俠五義)最有名. 因此書本無底本, 當年故舊數友(有祥樂亭, 文冶庵二公在內), 每日聽評書, 歸而彼此互記, 因湊成此書. 其中人物, 各有讚語(今本無). 多趣語, 諧而雅. 此道光間石玉昆所傳也. 兒女英雄傳為文鐵仙先生所傳. 其間冶庵, 俶南兩先生多所讚助. 然此二書聚珍本極難得. [20]

In Chong Yi's account, the sense of a local, Beijing bannerman community is palpable.[21] Of the six individuals mentioned in his brief

20. Chong Yi, *Dao Xian yilai chaoye zaji*, p. 19. Notes within parentheses are found in the original; information within brackets is provided by me. Ellen Widmer also translates this passage in Widmer, "*Honglou meng ying*," pp. 37–38.

21. Chong Yi is writing a memoir of Beijing, and the sense of community that is found in his description may reflect fond memories rather than historical accuracy. Moreover, as Ellen Widmer points out, Chong Yi is not always completely reliable. For instance, he claims that the Juzhen tang set out to print *The Dream of the Red Chamber* but did not finish the project. We know, however, that the Juzhen tang did publish *The Dream* in 1876. More importantly, Widmer points out that the owner

account, four can be identified as bannermen: the publisher Zhang; Wen Liang, one of the transcribers of the storyteller performance; Wen Kang, cousin of Wen Liang and author of *The Tale of Romance and Heroism*; and Wen Shuo, a patron of Wen Kang and similarly a family member of the Wen clan.[22] To this crowd should be added another figure not mentioned by Chong Yi, Wen Lin 文琳, a Chinese banner-man belonging to the Plain Yellow Banner who was one of the authors of a preface to the first edition of *The Three Knights* and most likely one of its principal writers/editors.[23] Again, authors, publishers, and editors were not exclusively Beijing bannermen, but it is striking to what degree bannermen were involved in the production of the two most famous examples of these tales.[24]

Once we take the point of local Beijing production into consideration, it becomes clear that various aspects of the martial arts novels produced during the last two decades of the nineteenth century provided Beijing readers with a clear sense of a shared community. For

---

of the Juzhen tang may well have been named Liu and not Zhang. See Widmer, "*Honglou meng ying*," p. 38. In the case of the identities of Wen Kang, Wen Liang, and Wen Shuo, Chong Yi is probably reliable, since he was directly related to them through his maternal grandmother. See Yu Shengting, "Shi Yukun ji qi zhushu." For more on the background of the clan to which Wen Kang belonged, see Zhang Bing, *Wen Kang yu 'Ernü yingxiong zhuan.'* It is not clear whether Wen Shuo, Wen Kang, and Wen Liang were brothers or cousins.

22. It has been suggested that Shi Yukun himself might have been a Manchu as well. The surname Shi is quite common among Manchus, but more importantly Shi Yukun's telling was interlaced with *zidishu*-style songs, a form of song considered typical for bannermen. Shi Yukun's identity remains shrouded in mystery, however, and the idea that he was a Manchu must remain a suggestion. See Blader, "Introduction." I have not been able to identify Xiang Leting.

23. As Yu Shengting has demonstrated, Rumidaoren 入迷道人, one of the authors of a preface to *The Three Knights*, can be identified as Wen Lin on the basis of his remark that he held the post of commissioner in Huai'an in the year 1875. Yu Shengting, "Shi Yukun ji qi zhushu," p. 152.

24. A second, clearly identifiable group of authors, editors, and publishers consisted of sojourning scholars, men who claimed to have come to the capital for the imperial examinations and found they had the right skills needed to edit these tales. The most famous example of such a sojourning scholar associated with martial arts fiction is Dong Xun, mentioned in chapter 1. For more on the sojourners (from high officials to examination candidates) and the way they patronized opera (as opposed to vernacular tales), see Goldman, *Opera and the City*, pp. 17–60.

instance, many late-Qing martial arts novels frequently refer to local geographical sites a Beijing audience would immediately recognize. Indeed, even when the historical record does not support reference to Beijing sites, tales still foreground the capital's topography. The story of *The Three Knights*, for instance, takes place during the Northern Song dynasty and consequently is set in the capital of the Northern Song, Bianliang (modern Kaifeng), and not Beijing. From descriptions in the novel, however, it becomes clear that in the reader's and author's mind the Song and Qing capitals could be conflated.[25] Other novels change the historical record not only to emphasize a Beijing background, but at the same time play up a Manchu bannerman identity in the process. For instance, *The Cases of Judge Peng* is based on a historical figure, Peng Peng 彭鵬 (1637–1704), a commoner from Fujian province who eventually rose to the rank of governor of Guangdong.[26] The novel changes this Fujianese man into a Manchu bannerman belonging to the fifth regiment of the Red-Bordered Banner 鑲紅旗滿洲五甲喇, and opens its tale with the man living in a typical Beijing alleyway 胡同 located close to the first ceremonial arch of Dongdan 東單, just inside Beijing's Chongwen Gate 崇文門.[27]

Geographical references not only serve as anchors which a local community can use to define itself, they also provide the opportunity to transform the familiar everyday locale, Beijing, into the grand imperial center of the vast Qing empire. In *The Three Knights*, for instance, we find a curious interruption of the tale by the narrator, who feels obliged to remind his audience of the splendor of Beijing. As the narrator tells us,

---

25. For instance, in chap. 79, the text mentions the "Yellow Pavilion," which it locates behind the Drum Tower. The *Dictionary of Beijing Place Names* tells us that in Beijing there indeed was a famous Yellow Pavilion, located by the Drum Tower. See *San xia wu yi* (1996), vol. 2, chap. 79, p. 463. Wang and Xu, *Beijing diming cidian*, pp. 483–84. Similarly, some of the sites of the Forbidden City described in this episode refer to the imperial palace in Beijing, not Bianliang. For instance, in the next chapter, Zhi Hua is said to cross "Gold Water Bridge," which is found in the Forbidden City in Beijing, not Kaifeng. Chen Qiaoyi, *Zhongguo ducheng cidian*, p. 276.
26. On the historical Peng Peng, see Hummel, *Eminent Chinese*, vol. 2, pp. 613–14.
27. *Zhengxu Peng gongan*, vol. 1, p. 1. For more on the life of the historical Judge Peng, see Li Yonghu, "Jiaodian houji."

Take the case of the Yudong Jin'ao Bridge in the capital: truly it is a
gorgeous site made by heaven and earth.[28] Each season—spring, summer,
autumn, and fall—offers its own beautiful scene. How could a few simple
words ever tell its beauty in full? . . . However, if you walk by it every day
and see it day in and day out, you become accustomed to its beauty and
don't notice it anymore.

即如京師玉蝀金鰲, 真是天造地設的美景, 四時春夏秋冬, 各有佳景, 豈是
三言兩語說得盡的呢? . . . 然而, 每日走着, 時常看着, 習以為常, 也就不理
會了.[29]

Here the narrator directly addresses his audience, assumes an everyday familiarity with the Yudong Jin'ao Bridge, and, most importantly,
re-endows such local spots with a sense of splendor.

In a similar manner, many martial arts novels seek to add a sense of
excitement to everyday life by turning familiar Beijing sites into scenes of
action and coupling such action to the munificent presence of imperial
power itself. It is not merely that heroes race through *hutongs* or sneak
through windows, turning everyday architecture into the site of extraordinary spectacle. Rather, by actually having Qing emperors walk these
familiar routes, these narratives transform everyday locales into sites
blessed by the imperial presence.[30] *The Tale of Everlasting Blessings and
Peace, Part 1*, for instance, opens with the Kangxi emperor sneaking out
of the palace through the Donghua gate, following the wall of the forbidden city to the Zhengyang gate, then moving west following the moat

28. This bridge is located between the Zhonghai and the Nanhai and is named
"Jade Toad and Golden Fish" after the two ceremonial arches that used to be
located at its east and west ends. See Chen Wenliang, *Beijing chuantong wenhua
bianlan*, p. 562.
29. *San xia wu yi* (1996), vol. 2, chap. 65, p. 380. The scene is strategically placed
during a sightseeing trip made by the Northern Knight who seeks out a famous
ancient site, Dragon Slaughter Bridge, and ends up completely disappointed. It is at
this point that the narrator interrupts with his ode to Beijing.
30. These tales of emperors' escapades were most likely inspired by the various
imperial tours south by the Kangxi and Qianlong emperors. The most obvious
example is the novel *The Qianlong Emperor Tours the South*, which features the
emperor sneaking out of the palace in order to enjoy the beauty/ies of Jiangnan.
The manner and particular path chosen by the emperor in these fictional fantasies of course bore little resemblance to the pomp and splendor of actual imperial
outings.

until he reaches the grand avenue at Shunzhi gate.[31] Beijing audiences must have been delighted to see the places they knew so well featured as the background to the heroic martial adventures and secret escapades of the Kangxi emperor. By juxtaposing Beijing as imperial seat of government with Beijing as everyday urban locale, these novels allowed local readers to recognize the city they knew so well, while still imagining these familiar places basking in the light of a blessed imperial presence.

The food enjoyed by various heroes in these novels similarly is often unique to Beijing and, in some of the earlier storyteller tales, is even designated explicitly as a way of allowing the reader/listener to identify with local culture. In the novel *The Tale of Everlasting Blessings and Peace*, for instance, characters not only gorge on mutton outside the Fucheng Gate, but enjoy cut cake 切糕[32] and corn-flour buns 黃窩窩,[33] and are found eating at "two-dish restaurants" 二葷舖.[34] In fact, in *The Tale of Everlasting Blessings and Peace*, the usual, rather clichéd description of a hero becomes a wonderfully inventive pastiche when it compares the physique of the man to local Beijing food items: "A face as sweet as sweet porridge, a nose dotted like sugared pretzels, and two eyebrows and big eyes matching two big sugar-bowl ears" 甜醬粥的臉蛋, 垂糖麻花的鼻子, 兩道揚眉, 一雙馬眼, 配著兩個糖耳朵.[35]

31. The Shunzhi Gate is the popular name for the Xuanwu Gate. See Chen Wenliang, *Beijing chuantong wenhua bianlan*, p. 202. Throughout, *The Tale of Everlasting Blessing and Peace* employs the gates' popular names, such as Zhangyi Gate instead of Guangning Gate, Pingze Gate instead of Fucheng Gate, etc.

32. Cut cake is a typical Beijing delicacy containing dates. Yu Yue dedicated a poem to the subject, "Yi jingdu ci" 憶京都詞 (Remembering the capital), in which he writes, "How I remember the capital's snacks made with care / The sliced cake from the plate both sweet and soft / Fried oily buns both crisp and flaky / Not like the northern cakes that you eat down here / So hard that for your last few teeth you fear" 憶京都, 小食更精工. 盤內切糕甜又軟. 油中炸果脆而松. 不似此間吃胡餅, 零落殘牙殊怕硬." Quoted in Chen Wenliang, *Beijing chuantong wenhua bianlan*, p. 545. Fried oily buns, more popularly referred to as fried oily ghosts 油炸鬼, are also a northern delicacy. See, for instance, *Liu gongan*, section 24, chap. 2, p. 371. For the typical Beijing pronunciation of "gui," see chap. 5, p. 000 of this study.

33. Corn-flour buns are a kind of bun made with corn or sorghum flour.

34. "Two-dish restaurants" are cheap eateries that serve only two dishes. See Guo Guangrui, *Yongqing shengping qianzhuan* (1995), chap. 6, p. 20; Gao and Fu, *Beijinghua ciyu*, p. 252. All of the dishes mentioned above are "popular," everyday kinds of food, not grand imperial banquet-style dishes.

35. Guo Guangrui, *Yongqing shengping qianzhuan* (1995), chap. 1, pp. 2–3.

The emphasis on a shared diet is even stronger in handwritten texts that stand closer to the local performance tradition. In the late eighteenth- and early nineteenth-century drum-song (*guci* 鼓詞) titled *Liu gongan* 劉公案 (The cases of Judge Liu), for instance, the eponymous hero is said to enjoy his own local Shandong dishes, but also some typical Beijing fare. What kind of food does the judge enjoy? The narrator tells us:

> What kind of food was this? It was two plain *bobo* buns, which he had brought with him from our Beijing, as well as fork-fried fritters that he had not finished while on the road.
> 甚麼東西? 還有咱這京裡帶去吃剩下的兩個硬面餑餑, 還有道兒上吃不了的叉子火燒.[36]

Judge Liu was originally from Shandong and the fact that he eats fork-fried fritters 叉子火燒, a typical Shandong dish, should not surprise us.[37] What is interesting, however, is that the narrator here also has the Judge enjoying some typical Beijing buns 硬面餑餑 and turns this plain, local fare into a site of familiarity shared by narrator and audience. As the narrator states quite explicitly, the Judge had brought these buns "from *our* Beijing."[38]

Linguistically, as well, these novels are larded with Beijing phrases and local expressions often comprehensible only to Beijing insiders.[39] Even martial arts novels set in the distant south, such as *The Storyteller Tale of Ji Gong*, betray their northern origins through their particular

36. *Liu gongan*, section 1, chap. 1, p. 3. *Bobo* buns are a typical Beijing, originally Manchu, term for plain buns without meat or vegetable filling. See Chen Wenliang, *Beijing chuantong wenhua bianlan*, p. 549.
37. Fork-fried fritters are a typical Shandong dish from the Yantai region. The word "fried" is probably not entirely correct since the dish does not involve frying, but rather baking layers of batter dipped in sesame seeds and sesame oil. See Zhang Lianming, "Chazi huoshao."
38. *Bobo* buns do not strike me as necessarily a Beijing dish, but clearly the narrator seems to suggest as much.
39. For a longer discussion of the use of regional language in these novels, especially the mimicry of different regional dialects, see chap. 5 of this study.

brand of colloquial language.[40] Some of the novels include the occasional, transcribed Manchu phrase. A novel such as *The Cases of Judge Shi*, for instance, will emphasize that its main character, Judge Shi, is a banner-man who speaks Manchu and chooses to converse at times with other officials in this shared language.[41] More telling is when, in the mid-nine-teenth-century novel *The Tale of Romance and Heroism*, a brief Manchu dialogue is transcribed phonetically.[42] Though the linguistic sophistica-tion displayed by *The Tale of Romance and Heroism* is unique, the novel's interest in using a language that readers would consider typically Beijing (or Manchu) is not.[43]

On a temporal level, moreover, these tales are set in the bannermen's "own" dynasty, something that allowed late nineteenth-century Beijing readers to identify even more strongly with the heroic adventures of both the judges and the martial men portrayed.[44] *The Cases of Judge Shi* and its sequels, as well as *The Cases of Judge Peng* and its sequels, all focus on the adventures of martial men serving famous historical figures from the Kangxi period, the righteous Judge Shi and the incor-

40. For a fuller discussion of the use of Beijing dialect in this novel as well as the earlier drum-song, see Shahar, *Crazy Ji*, pp. 116 and 128. As Shahar notes, due to their closer relationship to storytelling performance practices, the handwritten manuscripts of drum-songs tend to contain considerably more dialect phrases than the later printed novels.
41. For Manchu phrases used in *The Tale of Everlasting Blessings and Peace, Part 1*, see especially the edition edited and annotated by Ergong 尔弓 and published by the Jing Chu shushe in Ji'nan in 1990. As to the Manchu phrases in *The Cases of Judge Shi*, they are often limited to basic words, such as *anda* for "brother," *beilei* for "nobleman," *gusai* for "banner," etc. In the one case where a fairly specific word, *nisiha* (meaning "name-card"), is used, the editor of the modern Baowen tang edition suggests the word is used incorrectly. See *Shi gongan*, chap. 69, vol. 1, p. 156.
42. See Wen Kang, *Ernü yingxiong zhuan* (Shanghai edition, 1990 rpt.), vol. 107, chap. 40, p. 2166.
43. The publishing house responsible for first publishing *The Tale of Romance and Heroism*, the Juzhen tang, specialized in bilingual, Manchu-Chinese texts. The particular use and precision of its transcription of Manchu hence not only reflects the bannerman author's interests, but also those of the publisher.
44. Some of the handwritten drum-songs on which many of these novels were based, most notably *Peng gongan guci* 彭公案鼓詞 (The cases of Judge Peng drum-song) can actually be dated to the reign of the emperors in which the tale is set. See Cui, "Cong shuochang dao xiaoshuo."

ruptible Judge Peng.[45] *The Tale of Everlasting Blessings and Peace* refers specifically to the campaigns against the White Lotus Rebellion (Bai lian jiao 白蓮教) and the Heaven and Earth Society (Tian di hui 天地 會), even if, despite protestations found in the preface, the novel gets many of the historical facts wrong. The drum-song *The Cases of Judge Liu* alerts us to this interest in "current" affairs, by stating, "This tale is not like ancient novels where people just say whatever they want. This is a tale that takes place before our very eyes, during the Great Qing" 這書不像古書, 由着人要怎麼說就怎麼說. 這都是眼前的故事, 出在大 清.[46] Before the nineteenth century, vernacular novels, with some notable exceptions, tended to be set in past dynasties, even if such ancient times served as thinly veiled allegories of the writers' own times.[47] As such, the nineteenth-century shift to printing tales concerning one's own dynasty, especially the glorious days of Kangxi and Qianlong, is indeed marked.

Taken separately, none of the elements mentioned above may seem significant. For most contemporary readers, references to "sliced-cake" or Manchu phrases such as *geger* 格格兒 (meaning "Ms.") mean little and are best left to footnotes.[48] Taken together, however, these constant references to local Beijing food, geographical sites, linguistic practices, or temporal frameworks give a sense of a vibrant, lively, and tellingly local Beijing culture. Given that these local elements were featured as part of grand and heroic narratives that focused on the establishment of Qing imperial order in troubled times, it is likely that for a local Beijing audience, the nineteenth-century martial arts novel functioned to reaffirm the central position of dynastic power after a long period of internal rebellion and political chaos.

45. Judge Shi was an actual historical figure from the Kangxi period; his full name was Shi Shilun 施世綸 (1659–1722). His biography can be found in *Qing shi gao* 清史 稿 (The draft of the Qing dynastic history), *juan* 27. The biography identifies Judge Shi as a Chinese bannerman who belonged to the Bordered Yellow Banner.
46. Quoted in Qiu, "Che wangfu quben," p. 59.
47. The major exception to this rule is the genre of "contemporary novels" 時事小 說 published for a brief period during the late Ming and early Qing. For more on this genre, see Han Li, "News, history, and 'Fiction on Current Events.'"
48. This is a Manchu term used to refer to daughters from a well-to-do household. See Wen Kang, *Ernü yingxiong zhuan* (Ergong edition, 1990 rpt.), vol. 1, chap. 7, p. 132; explanation of the term by Ergong is found on p. 141.

Does this mean that only Beijing bannermen could enjoy these late-Qing tales? Clearly not. Though martial arts novels produced in the last two decades of the nineteenth century were most often first printed in Beijing, they usually were reprinted without much delay in other cities, sometimes even within the same year. The two most famous men involved in the appreciation and production of these texts were in fact not Beijing men, let alone bannermen. As shown in chapter 1, the Beijing novel *Three Knights* found a ready patron in the Jiangnan scholar Yu Yue. Similarly, the bannerman novel *Tale of Romance and Heroism* found its most famous reader in Dong Xun, who wrote a popular commentary to the novel. Though Dong spent considerable time in Beijing holding various prominent positions as an official, he nevertheless hailed from southern Suzhou.[49]

The point is that these novels projected an image of the capital that may have begun on a local level, on street corners and in teahouses, in popular handwritten tales such as the drum-song *The Cases of Judge Liu*. However, because of the power of print, this image soon spread throughout the empire and was popularized not only through guidebooks, literati poetry, and elite memoirs, but also through the mass reprinting of popular martial arts tales. As such, the mechanisms that allowed Beijing martial arts novels to disseminate the image of Beijing as the center of the Qing empire and home to the Manchu emperor are in many ways similar to the methods that allowed the equally famous late-Qing Shanghai novels to spread the image of Shanghai as a modern cosmopolis throughout China.[50] One telling difference between these two kinds of tales, however, was not simply that one drew on Beijing and one drew on Shanghai for inspiration, or that one promoted muscular tales of martial men while the other seduced its readers with the lure of red-light

49. This particular, annotated edition containing Dong Xun's commentary was first published by the Juzhen tang in 1880, four years after the novel's first printing. Since reprints of this edition were already circulating in the south, at least as early as 1888, it may well have been that this novel inspired Yu Yue to attach his name to a similar exercise of elite patronage of a popular Beijing novel. A biography of Dong Xun can be found in Hummel, *Eminent Chinese*, vol. 2, pp. 789–91.
50. For a discussion of how modern printing techniques allowed Shanghai to be spread as image, see des Forges, *Mediasphere Shanghai*. See also Catherine Yeh's *Shanghai Love* on the notion of splendor and its association with the urban site of Shanghai.

dalliance, but more importantly that the central voice associated with the Beijing martial arts novel was located in the storyteller figure.

From Local Storyteller Tale to Printed Novel

In the first chapter, I discussed the importance of the storyteller figure for elite southern authors such as Jin Shengtan and Yu Yue, but what role did the storyteller figure play in the local imagination of a Beijing-centered restoration? In this section I will show that in late nineteenth-century martial arts tales, the storyteller first developed from an anonymous teller of tales to a marketable figure with brand-name recognition and finally to an abstract symbol defining a literary community and its idealized reading practices. To prove this point, I will focus briefly on the actual, oral origins of many of these popular martial arts tales; in particular I will pay attention to the question of how, during the transformation of the martial arts tale from local, handwritten tale to inter-regionally produced product, the storyteller took on symbolic importance in the prefaces and title pages of printed novels. It is in these prefaces that the storyteller comes to represent a form of reading that is defined as lively and "full of flavor," a sociable and pleasurable form of entertainment associated with the public spaces of Beijing, even if the reader is partaking of such pleasures in the privacy of his own home in Shanghai.

To start, it should be stated that even though a storyteller narrator plays a crucial role in most late-imperial fiction, prefaces to such fiction did not often remind the reader of his presence.[51] This is not only true

51. Given the long history of vernacular fiction, exceptions can, of course, be found, most notably in prefaces of the late Ming, such as the famous prefaces to Feng Menglong's collections of short stories. Note, however, that such prefaces as well ascribed to a generalized notion of the storyteller and do not mention specific storytellers by name. To my knowledge the only exception to this rule is found in an early-Qing contemporary novel 時事小說, *Jiaochuang xiaoshuo* 剿闖小說 (Eradication of the rebel prince), which attributes its tale to a storyteller from Suzhou who goes by the name Landaoren 懶道人. Unfortunately we know nothing about this Landaoren and the style of the novel itself betrays none of the hallmarks we associate with oral storytelling.

of prestigious eighteenth-century vernacular works such as *The Dream of the Red Chamber* and *Rulin waishi* 儒林外史 (The scholars) that were penned by the literati elite and indeed had little to do with actual storytellers. It is also true of novels published during the publishing boom that followed the reign of the Qianlong emperor, novels that could actually lay explicit claim to storyteller origins. Margaret Wan, for instance, has analyzed ten martial arts tales of the late eighteenth and early nineteenth centuries and proved the oral provenance of many of them.[52] Yet even though these novels undoubtedly drew on the audience's familiarity with the tales from either storytelling or opera performance, their prefaces avoid the topic of oral performance itself. Even the two novels that nowadays can be positively determined as having been originally told by storytellers identifiable by name, *The Sluices of Qingfeng* (original storyteller Pu Lin 浦琳) and *Fei tuo quan zhuan* 飛跎全傳 (The tale of the flying cripple) (original storyteller Zou Bixian 鄒必顯), do not mention the performers' names in either title or preface. We only know of the performer's involvement with these novels from other sources such as Li Dou's *Record of the Painted Boats of Yangzhou*.[53]

This tendency to elide the connections between oral storytelling and printed fiction in prefatory material comes to an end with the first printing of *The Three Knights* in 1879. Its title page includes four characters that alert the reader to the storyteller origins of the tale: "Told by Shi Yukun" 石玉昆述.[54] The term "told by" 述 carries some ambivalence. It implies that the original oral tale by Shi Yukun needed to be edited in order to make it fit for publication, something further emphasized in the prefaces. That said, by placing the name of the storyteller on the title page, the novel pays unprecedented attention to the storyteller originally associated with telling the tale, Shi Yukun.

This appearance of the storyteller's name on the cover can partially be explained by the fact that the novel is probably based, if indirectly,

52. Wan, *Green Peony*.
53. Li Dou, *Yangzhou huafang lu*, p. 190. See also chap. 1, note 3 in this book. The earliest extant edition of *The Sluices of Qingfeng* dates from 1819. *The Tale of the Flying Cripple* has a preface dated 1817.
54. The preface does refer to the tale as originally having been a "performance" 演藝. However, by the late Qing, the term no longer referred necessarily to storyteller performances, just as the term *xiaoshuo* 小說, now most often translated as "fiction" or "novel," did not necessarily mean that the tale was actually spoken.

on the famous story cycle once told by Shi Yukun. As early twentieth-century scholars have already established, Shi Yukun was a Beijing
storyteller who lived during the early years of the nineteenth century.[55]
Circumstantial evidence, most notably the eponymous *zidishu* quoted
at the beginning of this chapter, tells how Shi Yukun was most famous
for a tale about Judge Bao and his valiant martial helpers entitled either
Bao gongan 包公案 (The cases of Judge Bao) or *Longtu gongan* 龍圖公案
(The cases of the Dragon diadem). As more recent scholarship has shown,
moreover, the 1879 novel can be traced back to an earlier handwritten
manuscript, *Longtu erlu* 龍圖耳錄 (The aural record of the Dragon
diadem) that contains only prose and, in turn, to an even earlier prosimetric version, *The Cases of Judge Bao* or *The Cases of the Dragon Diadem*.[56]
Internal evidence from this manuscript itself clearly emphasizes the association between this manuscript and Shi Yukun's storytelling, even if it
also establishes that the manuscript is not a transcription of an actual
performance by Shi Yukun, but rather a performance by someone of a
later generation cashing in on Shi Yukun's reputation in Beijing.[57]

55. See Li Jiarui, "Cong Shi Yukun de 'Longtu gongan' shuodao 'San xia wu yi.'"
For a more recent and lengthy study, see Hou, *San xia wu yi xilie xiaoshuo*. Shi
Yukun is often believed to have been a native of Tianjin, but as Yu Shengting points
out, this is a mistake most likely based on the confusion between Shi Yukun and
the publisher of the first sequel to *The Three Knights*, who was also named Shi. See
Yu Shengting, "Shi Yukun ji qi zhushu chengshu," p. 147.
56. The title of the prose manuscript, *Aural Record*, suggests that the text was a
transcription of storyteller performances. Indeed, as shown earlier in this chapter, Chong Yi claims that the text was purely a transcription because no text was
available. However, as pointed out by Susan Blader and Lu Decai, the relationship
between the earliest manuscript, *The Cases of Judge Bao*, and the later versions is
unmistakable. For more on the relationship between the libretto *The Cases of Judge
Bao*, the handwritten *Aural Record of the Dragon Diadem*, and the final printed
product *The Three Knights and the Five Gallants*, see Blader, "A Critical Study." See
also Lu Decai, *Lu Decai shuo Bao gongan*, pp. 75–100.
57. *The Cases of Judge Bao* at various points refers to Shi Yukun in the third
person, making it very clear that the manuscript is *not* an actual transcription of a
performance by Shi Yukun. For instance, in one episode of *The Cases of Judge Bao*,
"Nanqing gong qing shou" 南清宮慶壽 (The birthday celebration in the Nanqing
Palace), there is the following storyteller aside: "Let's just take Third Master Shi
Yukun as an example. No matter what, I cannot outdo him in storytelling. At present he no longer makes appearances. But when he would go to that storytelling
hall, he would tell three chapters of a story in one day and collect many tens of

The presence of Shi Yukun's name on the title page shows that publishers of printed fiction were beginning to recognize an audience of potential readers to whom the name would be an incitement to purchase the novel. For readers in Beijing, the name of Shi Yukun indeed elicited a form of brand-name recognition that could be easily transformed into monetary value. During his lifetime material about Shi Yukun had not always been completely positive, but by the time of the first printing of *The Three Knights*, Shi Yukun had probably already died or the patina of age had made his name synonymous with quality storytelling performances.[58] Sellers of hand-copied opera and storytelling libretti such as Hundred Volumes Zhang (Baiben Zhang 百本張) and Leshan tang 樂山堂, for instance, actively sought out "authentic" transcriptions of Shi Yukun's storytelling performances. A catalogue from the Leshan Tang, for instance, notes the following:

> This establishment copies and sells *zidishu* and also new Shi-style tales with accompanying paeans. They have been corrected by persons of consequence. The plots are sensible, their meanings exquisite; they are not idle ramblings. Other shops may have some, but they merely aim to tack on that label to make their profit; the lines are mostly different from Shi-style tales. For several years this establishment has made great effort to find [these tales], and we were fortunate to obtain several original manuscripts that match the Shi-style tales.
>
> 本堂抄賣子弟書詞並有石派帶讚新書. 授自名人校正. 情理符合, 書義精微, 非等閒之論也. 別家或有是書, 希惟應明獲利. 書中章句大備均與石書相反. 本堂數年來精工採訪, 遂得數底幸與石書相合." [59]

---

strings of cash. Now today his name resounds in the nine cities, and there is no one who has not heard of him. I, myself, collect only one or two strings of cash a day for my storytelling" 就拿玉昆石三爺他說吧, 怎麼就該說不過他? 他如今是不出來咧。他到那個書館兒, 一天只說三回書就串好了幾十吊錢, 如今名動九城, 誰不知道石三爺呢? 我如今說書, 一天才不過一兩吊錢. "Nanqing gong qing shou," vol. 407, pp. 53–54. Translated in Blader, "A Critical Study," pp. 102–3.

58. The long *zidishu* "Shi Yukun" quoted at the beginning of this chapter is probably the first and undoubtedly the most ambivalent of the popular nineteenth-century sources on Shi Yukun. The earliest known version of the piece dates between 1843 and 1845. See Aying, "Guanyu Shi Yukun."

59. Originally translated by Meir Shahar with some minor changes. Shahar, *Crazy Ji*, p. 125. For the original text, see "[Leshan tang] Zidi, dagu shu mulu," p. 1A–B. For the history of the "Hundred Volumes Zhang" and other sellers of handwritten popular libretti, see Fu Xihua, "Baiben Zhang"; Chen Jinzhao, "Shipai shu de tizhi."

Clearly the publishers at Leshan tang thought that it was worth-while to claim they had spent time and money to gain possession of authentic Shi-style storytelling tales. The prices charged reflect this assertion; the first two volumes (or six chapters) of the tale that was to become *The Three Knights*, "Jiu zhu pan he" 救主盤盒 (Saving the emperor by carrying him in a box), sold for three strings and 600 cash.[60]

In popular texts associated with storytelling performances, Shi Yukun had similarly become a paragon of storytelling virtue. One particular example, for instance, the *zidishu* "Guo Dong'er," upholds Shi Yukun's "marvelous tunes" (*qiao qiangr* 巧腔兒) and "excellent phrases" (*miaoju* 妙句) as models for the hopelessly inferior storyteller Guo Dong'er.[61] Another example, the *zidishu* "Guang Huguosi" 逛護國寺 (Strolling through the Huguo Temple), tells of an affluent gentleman who orders a handwritten libretto of the martial arts tale *Lü mudan* 綠牡丹 (The Green Peony) as well as *The Cases of Judge Shi*, saying, "I'll order a copy of *The Cases of Judge Shi* / And moreover a copy of *The Green Peony to* rival [a performance by] Shi Yukun" 我定抄一部[施公案] / 還抄一部[綠牡丹]亞賽石玉昆.[62] Here the term "to rival" 亞賽 makes it clear that in order for a popular martial arts tale such as *The Green Peony* to qualify as excellent, it had better capture the qualities associated with the famous storyteller Shi Yukun.[63]

The publication history of *The Three Knights* and the interest in reading novels that are self-identified "storyteller" novels show that in the late nineteenth century, indigenous sources and imported print-ing techniques, popular interests and elite tastes began to coalesce in a new form of fiction addressed to a steadily growing audience of urban readers. Margaret Wan has shown that as early as the late eighteenth

60. "[Leshan tang] Zidi, dagu shu mulu," p. 14B.
61. See "Guo Dong'er," p. 338. The particular line reads, "The excellent tune and marvelous phrases of Shi Yukun demonstrate his skill" 石玉昆的巧腔兒妙句兒有功夫. The piece tells of a storyteller whose art is considered below par. Shi Yukun's name appears in the first few lines as an example of a master storyteller from the past.
62. Helüshi, "Guang Huguo si," p. 329. For more on the author Helüshi, which is the pen name for Yigeng 奕賡, a prince belonging to the Aisinjoro clan, see Kang Baocheng, "Zidishu zuozhe 'Helüshi.'" For a partial translation of the song in ques-tion, see chap. 3, pp. 170–72 and 177–78.
63. For the term "*yasai*," see Gao and Fu, *Beijinghua ciyu*, p. 919.

century, local publishers had drawn on the popularity of long-familiar storyteller tales and begun a process of translating handwritten libretti into print. In the late nineteenth century, this indigenous process of printing local tales received further impetus from newly established, foreign printing houses. As Ellen Widmer has argued, the publication of fiction by the Juzhen tang, the publisher responsible for the 1879 *Three Knights*, may well have been inspired by the success of the Shenbao guan 申報館 in Shanghai, a printing house established by Ernest Major that drew on the latest printing techniques to publish a variety of popular materials, including fiction.[64] Such materials, moreover, may well have appealed originally to a low-brow audience, but their eventual printed form undoubtedly involved the labor of well-educated men of letters. As Chong Yi's anecdote regarding the publishing of *The Three Knights* articulates, though the story was based on popular oral performances, its transcribers were not semi-literate nobodies but rather were prestigious elite members of the local Beijing community.[65] The printing of *The Three Knights*, then, can be seen as the culmination of both indigenous and imported printing practices, popular and elite tastes, the combination of which led publishers to recognize the value of the storyteller's name and reach out to an urban audience they thought would be familiar with the performances of Shi Yukun.

The Three Knights was only the first novel to draw attention to the original storyteller's name. *The Latter Five Gallants*, the 1890 sequel to *The Three Knights*, makes an even more explicit reference to Shi Yukun. In his prefatory remarks, the publisher Shi Duo goes into considerable detail about the impeccable storyteller origins of the novel:

> Why am I publishing *The Latter Five Gallants*? It is because I had sought to gather the draft of *The Cases of the Dragon Diadem* for many years but had been unable to get hold of it. It so happened there was a friend of mine who had been long acquainted with the disciples of the storyteller

64. See Widmer, "*Honglou meng ying*," p. 46. For more on the Shenbao guan's printing of popular fiction, see Wagner, "The Early Publishing Activities of the Shenbaoguan."
65. Even though Chong Yi regards the publishing of popular novels with the usual modicum of scorn, he also notes that one of the transcribers, Wen Ye'an, was one of the biggest book collectors in nineteenth-century Beijing. See Chong Yi, *Dao Xian yilai chaoye zaji*, pp. 19 and 57 respectively.

school of Shi Yukun, and, as we were just sitting in my shop chatting, we came to discuss this book and I asked my friend to look for it. Just a few days later after my friend left, he came back carrying the original draft by Master Shi. It came to over three hundred chapters, was bound in seventy or eighty volumes, contained over three thousand episodes in three major parts, and had the name *The Tale of Loyalty and Righteousness*.

《小五義》一書何為而刻也? 只以採訪《龍圖公案》底稿, 歷數年之久, 未曾到手, 適有友人與石玉昆門徒素相往來, 偶在舖中閑談, 言及此書, 余即拖之搜尋. 友人去不多日, 即將石先生原稿攜來, 共三百餘回, 計七八十本, 三千多篇, 分上中下三部.[66]

Shi Duo's preface draws on a variety of discourses to justify his publishing of a popular, commercially lucrative, and hence slightly inappropriate text. Like many publishers in the post-Taiping era, Shi employs the term "gather" 採訪, a term associated with the preservation of popular materials after the devastation wrought by the Taiping rebels.[67] Similarly, Shi couches his preface in the language of friendship and leisure, so typical of late-imperial literati activity, introducing his contact with the Shi Yukun school of storytelling as a "friend" and emphasizing that their shared interest was discussed in a "leisurely chat" 閑談. Most notably, however, Shi draws on the authority of the storyteller's name Shi Yukun and his famous *Cases of the Dragon Diadem* to legitimize his sequel to the popular *Three Knights* novel. Shi claims not only to have spent many years searching for an original manuscript, but also to have put forward considerable capital; at the end of his preface, he mentions how he bought the manuscript "without begrudging the great cost" 不惜重資.[68]

66. Shi Duo, "*Xiao wu yi* xu," vol. 3, pp. 1552–53.
67. For a full discussion of the term *caifang*, see Meyer-Fong, "Gathering in a Ruined City," pp. 52–54.
68. Shi Duo, "*Xiao wu yi* xu," vol. 3, p. 1553. In fact, the editor of *The Latter Five Gallants*, Fengmi Taoist 風迷道人 (probably a name that is supposed to call to mind the Rumi Taoist 入迷道人, one of the editors of the first novel), claims that *The Latter Five Gallants* represents the true Shi Yukun tale, suggesting that the original *Three Knights* must have been a fake. As stated in the preface, "The previous *Tale of Loyal Knights and Gallant Heroes* is not exactly the same as the original draft of Shi Yukun that I received, and the names of people in it are slightly different. Therefore one knows that these texts were not produced by a single hand" 前套《忠烈俠義傳》與余所得石玉昆原摘, 詳略不同, 人名稍異, 知非出于一人之手.

Like Yu Yue, Shi Duo uses the preface to the novel to elevate the
figure of the storyteller. Yet it is clear that the storyteller referred to and
the reason for referring to a storyteller in the first place are completely
different. Shi Duo was writing for a middlebrow and typically local
Beijing audience, and he expected his readers to appreciate that the original material came from a particular Beijing storyteller whom some of
them might remember from performances they had heard themselves. In
contrast, for a Jiangnan literatus, the name of the storyteller in question,
Shi Yukun, was of little value. His name still appears on the title page
of the first edition of *The Seven Knights and the Five Gallants*. However,
the particular phrase used, "Previously ascribed to Shi Yukun" 舊題石
玉昆述, suggests that the publishers were not entirely sure who this Shi
Yukun was.[69] Not surprisingly, when Yu Yue in his preface decides to
associate the novel with storytelling, he does so by choosing a famous
storyteller more amenable to elite Jiangnan tastes, Liu Jingting.

Shi Yukun was not the only storyteller to become explicitly linked
with a novel. Undoubtedly inspired by the success of *The Three Knights*
and its sequels, other publishers began in a similar manner to produce
martial arts novels that drew on well-known storyteller names as a
marketing device.[70] The author Guo Guangrui, for instance, introduces
his novel *The Tale of Everlasting Blessings and Peace, Part 1* by explicitly
referring to not one, but two, famous storytellers:

When I was young, I traveled throughout the empire, and when in the
capital I would listen to the story of *Everlasting Blessings and Peace*. . . .
During the Xianfeng reign [1851–62], there was a Master Jiang Zhenming,
who used to tell of things ancient and new and would perform this tale,

Fengmi daoren, "*Xiao wu yi* ban" 小五義辨. For more on the Rumi Taoist, see Song
Kefu, "Zheng xu *Xiao wu yi* zuozhe kaolun."
69. The phrase "previously ascribed to" 舊題 is often used when editors think the
ascription might be erroneous. In this particular case, I find it more likely that the
publisher conscientiously decided to preserve the name "Shi Yukun" on the title
page, as in earlier editions, but was not entirely sure who this Shi Yukun was. As a
result, the name was preserved, but the publisher phrased it in such a way that he
need not take responsibility for the ascription. See *Qi xia wu yi* (1990), vol. 1, p. i.
70. The similarities between the prefaces of this 1892 martial arts novel and the
prefaces of the 1879 *Three Knights and the Five Gallants* confirm that the editors
and publishers of *The Tale of Everlasting Blessings and Peace* were writing their
prefaces with the older novel in front of them.

but there was no one who put it into print so it could circulate in the world. I often heard the storyteller Master Hafuyuan perform the tale; I memorized it and in leisurely moments recorded it in four *juan* to dispel boredom.

余少游四海, 在都嘗聽評詞《永慶升平》一書 . . . 咸豐年間, 有姜振名先生, 乃評談今古之人, 嘗演說此書, 未能有人刊刻傳流於世. 余長聽哈輔源先生演說, 熟記在心, 閑暇之時, 錄成四卷, 以為遣悶.[71]

The names of the two storytellers Guo evokes to sell his tale are Jiang Zhenming, a storyteller from Shandong province who had invented the tale of *Everlasting Blessings and Peace* after coming to Beijing, and his disciple Hafuyuan, a Mongolian bannerman who, in order to make ends meet, had turned to performing on street corners and at temple fairs and who, at the time this preface was written, was still performing in the capital.[72] By mentioning two storytellers, Guo Guangrui ups Shi Duo's ante. He draws on the patina of a famous older storyteller, appeals to contemporary tastes by referring to a storyteller who is still performing, and creates a lineage in the process.

Later martial arts novels followed this model, not only imitating *The Three Knights* in their matter of content or choice of title, but also in their emphasis on popular storytelling. Novels such as *The Cases of Judge Peng*, however, began to show a marked difference in the way the storyteller figure was used. Whereas *The Three Knights*, *The Latter Five Gallants*, and *The Tale of Everlasting Blessings and Peace, Part 1* had drawn on readers' familiarity with a particular storyteller, the reference to the storyteller origins of *The Cases of Judge Peng* does not employ a specific name, instead simply referring to a generic, unnamed story-

71. Guo Guangrui, "*Yongqing shengping* xu," p. 1559.
72. Apart from this preface, I have not found any contemporary sources on these two men. Additional information on the two comes from one of the most interesting (but perhaps not completely reliable) sources on Qing dynasty storytelling, Yunyouke's 雲游客 *Jianghu congtan* 江湖叢談 (Gathered tales of the *jianghu*); Zhang Cixi also mentions the two storytellers and moreover provides us with the names of the other students of Jiang Zhenming. See Zhang Cixi, *Renmin shoudu de Tianqiao*, pp. 122–23. Even though Yunyouke is not entirely reliable, as a famous storyteller himself (Yunyouke is a pseudonym for the Manchu storyteller Lian Kuoru 連闊如 [1903–71], whom Yunyouke just happens to praise in his own book), Yunyouke does provide us with a lot of inside information into the storytelling world.

teller "from the capital" who performs the story. The preface to the novel written by Sun Shoupeng 孫壽彭 opens as follows:

> *The Cases of Judge Peng* is copied all over the capital. In broad streets and shallow alleys, it is narrated everywhere as an extraordinary tale appetizing to all. Therefore there are countless storytellers performing this tale at temple fairs, with audiences packed so thickly that they form a solid wall and the listeners forget that they are tired. In my leisure hours after study, I would sometimes listen to a few phrases and find them full of flavor.
> [彭公案]一書, 京都鈔寫殆遍, 大街小巷, 侈為異談, 皆以為膾炙人口. 故會廟場中談是書者, 不計其數, 一時觀者如堵, 聽者忘倦. 予課暇亦少聽幾句, 津津有味 . . . [73]

In this preface, the oral telling of *The Cases of Judge Peng* is represented as taking place at the center of a Beijing community of listeners. Though careful to point out that he is well educated and only had time to listen to a few phrases, Sun, coincidentally not a native of Beijing himself, still emphasizes that he is one of these listeners, appreciating the sentences he finds "full of flavor." By buying and reading the printed novel himself, the reader in turn can enjoy imagining himself a part of this listening community.[74]

In fact, for a novel such as *The Cases of Judge Peng*, the oral nature of the original telling allows the author to suggest the kind of organic, oral community that is replaced by the printed tale this novel represents. For instance, after introducing it as a tale told by storytellers at the temple fairs of the capital, Sun Shoupeng continues his preface by imagining the way this story will spread after having been printed as a novel:

> I think that once this book comes out, not only will people in urban and country streets and markets be delighted to pass it on by chanting it out

---

73. Sun Shoupeng, *"Peng gongan xu,"* vol. 3, p. 1616.
74. Hu Siao-chen has argued how various features of nineteenth-century *tanci* allow the construction of an "imagined reading community" of female listeners. Hu Siao-chen, *Cainü cheye wei mian*, pp. 24–25. Whereas this "imagined reading community" of female listeners is private, intimate, and addressed by a feminine voice, here the references to a male storyteller allow the construction of an "imagined reading community" that is male, public, and imagined as participating in the liveliness of Beijing storytelling.

loud, scholars, peasants, artisans, and merchants will all rejoice in hearing it. Truly it will be sufficient to help cultivate the morals of the world, to enlighten the human heart, and be an aid toward transforming the people and improving customs.

思此書一出, 非特城鄉街市樂於傳誦, 士農工商欣于聽聞, 實亦足以培植世道, 感發人心, 而為化民成俗之一助云尔.[75]

Contrary to the picture presented here, it is likely that most consumers would take the numerous volumes of the printed tale home to read in isolation. Yet by highlighting the original storyteller context in which the tale was first told, Sun was able to suggest a much more intimately connected reading community that could share the tale orally.

As martial arts novels with close connections to oral storytelling gained in popularity, this way of using the oral storyteller as the symbol of local origins and the center of an intimate crowd can be readily imagined as a locus of folkloric authenticity in an increasingly modernizing world. A preface to the first edition of *The Storyteller Tale of Ji Gong*, a Buddhist martial arts tale first published in 1898, for instance, nicely juxtaposes oral origins with appeals to scholarly erudition and modern printing and marketing techniques.[76] The preface, written by Lou Jiangde 婁江得, borrows heavily from earlier martial arts novel prefaces and reads as follows:[77]

---

75. Sun Shoupeng, "*Peng gongan* xu," vol. 3, p. 1616.

76. Like *The Three Knights*, *The Cases of Judge Peng*, and *The Tale of Everlasting Blessings and Peace*, this particular novel is most likely based on a storytelling cycle. Apart from openly declaring its storytelling origins in the title, certain features in the novel betray its popular, oral origins, most notably its use of local expressions, its inclusion of certain rhythmic linguistic patterns and performance clichés, and its references to episodes that do not actually appear in the novel itself. See Gu, "Qianyan." Meir Shahar compares the novel with an older drum-song manuscript and concludes that the tale must be based on a storyteller performance that drew on the drum-song and in turn inspired the book. Gu Qiyin suggests that the particular storyteller may well have been Zhang Tairan 張泰然. Zhang Cixi mentions how Zhang Tairan was famous for telling the tale of Jigong in two parts (note that the printed novel eventually appeared in two parts as well, but this may be coincidence) and in his day was as famous as Shi Yukun. Zhang Cixi, *Renmin de shoudu Tianqiao*, p. 125.

77. The preface is signed 婁江得古歡室主人, the most likely translation of which is "The Master of The Gaining Pleasure from Antiquities Studio from Loujiang."

My friend the provincial graduate Zhang Wenhai is a renowned scholar
from Qiantang [Hangzhou]. For the purposes of his studies, he traveled
to the capital [Beijing], where, during his spare hours, he happened to
come to a place filled with a huge crowd. They were all listening to a storyteller narrating episodes from this novel. The stories were so captivating
that the audience did not grow weary of listening to them. [My friend]
searched the bookstores but could not find this novel. Just then, his friend
Yan Huaxuan brought him [a version of] this novel written by Mr. Guo
Xiaoting. Zhang leafed through it once. He found the portrayal of both
monks and layman so vivid that he felt he was going through the experience himself and seeing the characters with his own eyes . . . Thus he
sighed in appraisal and clapped his hands and would not think of keeping it as his own secret. So he negotiated with the owner of the Zhuzi
shanfang in Tianjin, Wei Daipo, who, not shrinking from the cost of the
investment, had it printed by means of lithography and asked me to write
a preface. I think that once this book comes out, not only will people in
the city and countryside delight in passing it on by reading it aloud, but
it will also help to some degree in improving morality and in opening
up people's hearts, and be an aid toward transforming the people and
improving customs.

余友張孝廉文海, 本錢塘名士, 以游學京師, 公餘之暇, 偶于稠人眾多之
區, 見有談是書之事者, 一時膾炙人口, 聽者忘倦; 及購, 諸坊本皆無. 適有
友人閻君華軒, 攜郭小亭先生所著是書來, 張君翻閱一過, 覺文言道[通]
俗, 如歷其境, 如見其人 ... 因擊節嘆賞, 不敢自秘, 遂商于津門煮字山房主
人魏君岱坡, 不惜重資, 付之石印, 索余為弁言. 余思此書一出, 非特城隅閭
巷樂於傳誦之, 意聊以培植世道, 感發人心, 而為化民成俗之一助云尔.[78]

As would have been true also for *The Cases of Judge Peng*, the
production and distribution of *The Storyteller Tale of Jigong* relied on
a sophisticated system of middlemen, editors, investors, and publishers

---

Alternatively, the Zhonghua shuju edition may have misprinted a "de" 得 for a
"shi," 是 in which case the name might be Lou Jiangshi, as Shahar suggests, in
which case the studio name would be "Pleasure in Antiquities." Shahar, *Crazy Ji*,
p. 116.

78. Loujiang deguhuanshi zhuren, "*Pingyan Jigong zhuan* xu," vol. 1, p. 11.
Translated (with some minor modifications) in Shahar, *Crazy Ji*, pp. 116–17. The
preface is here dated to 1898. Ding Xigen reprints the same preface but gives the
author as Yao Pinhou 姚聘侯 from Qinyang 芹陽, and the date is now given as
1906. See Ding Xigen, *Zhongguo lidai xu ba ji*, vol. 3, pp. 1421–22. Meir Shahar offers
some theories regarding the various authors mentioned in *Crazy Ji*, pp. 268–69,
notes 6 and 12.

who sold their products through a network of booksellers to a growing crowd of urban consumers. Yet despite this reliance on a developing trade in printed popular reading material that now was beginning to employ lithography, and despite the fact that the last novel mentioned was printed not in Beijing but in Tianjin, the emphasis on the story-teller's persona still allowed publishers to try and conjure up a reading public that spontaneously gathered to share these tales by chanting them out loud and passing them on orally. In Lou Jiangde's preface, southern erudition, Tianjin lithography, and of course the popular Beijing story-teller's oral tale come together to project an image of a folksy community loudly sharing in the telling of a local popular tale.[79]

Conclusion

The choice to publish *The Storyteller Tale of Jigong* in Tianjin using modern lithography may signal a broader shift that was taking place in China's printing industry. During the last decade of the nineteenth century and the first decade of the twentieth century, modern printing techniques became the backbone of the Chinese printing industry, and as a result the commercial book center of China was shifting from the alleys of Liulichang in Beijing to the concession area of Qipanjie in Shanghai.[80] Tellingly, when Hu Shi wrote a preface to a reedited edition of *The Three Knights* in 1925, he found that many readers were no longer aware that this martial arts tale had originally been a local Beijing product. As Hu Shi points out, in recent years Shanghai editions had simply replaced the older, original Beijing versions of the novel, leading to a

79. I have not yet been able to track down any of the individuals mentioned in the preface. Zhang Wenhai may well have been in the capital to study for the examinations. Then again, he may simply have wanted to project the image of such famous Jiangnan literati as Yu Yue and Dong Xun. Note that in his preface to *The Cases of Judge Peng*, Sun Shoupeng similarly suggests he is a sojourner in Beijing studying for the examinations.
80. For the rise of modern printing in Shanghai, see Reed, *Gutenberg in Shanghai* (2004). On the importance of Liulichang as a printing center in the eighteenth and nineteenth centuries, see the first chapter of Reed's dissertation, "Gutenberg in Shanghai" (1996).

loss of memory regarding the local Beijing tradition.[81] Ironically, Hu
Shi himself was not fully aware that the Shi Yukun mentioned on the
title page of the older Beijing editions was not the editor or author of
the novel, but rather the famous storyteller originally associated with
telling the tale. It took the work of slightly later scholars more informed
about the history of Beijing performance art, scholars such as Li Jiarui,
Aying, and Sun Kaidi, to uncover that particular piece of information.

Hu Shi's partial recovery of the Beijing origins of *The Three Knights*
may thus serve as a reminder of the Beijing roots of the novel; at the
same time, it also highlights how the storyteller voice, so central to the
martial arts novels produced in the early Beijing days, was disappearing. The success of the original *Three Knights* and its editing by Yu Yue
had carried the novel from a local Beijing audience to an elite Jiangnan
audience, and, with this shift, the name of the storyteller associated with
it changed from the local Shi Yukun to the more universally recognizable figure Liu Jingting. In turn, mass-produced martial arts novels,
no longer printed by xylography or moveable wood type in Beijing, but
rather by lithography and metal type in Shanghai, did not call as much
attention to supposed connections to storytellers. Looking for producers who could better guarantee a steady supply of material, Shanghai
publishing houses turned from the handwritten storyteller manuscripts
that had been the basis of the Beijing novels to professional writers.[82]
Finally, by the beginning of the twentieth century, the storyteller had
disappeared from the prefaces of most popular martial arts novels.[83]

81. As Hu Shi writes, "In recent years, the old editions of *The Three Knights* are not
easily bought anymore, and the edited, southern edition, *The Seven Knights,* has
already begun to encroach on book markets in Beijing and Tianjin. I am afraid that
in the future, even northerners will no longer know of *The Three Knights.*" See Hu
Shi, "*San xia wu yi* xu," p. 314.
82. For the professionalization of the writer of vernacular fiction, see Yuan, *Jindai
wenxue de tupo,* pp. 38–39. Recall also the remark by Shi An quoted in chapter
1: "Novels such as these are produced by Shanghai publishers who, seeking petty
profits, ask scholars with limited knowledge to write such books, all so as to sell
them broadly." Shi An, "Chankongshi suibi," p. 443.
83. Martial arts novels based on storyteller tales continue to be written, but they
are increasingly outnumbered by novels authored by non-storyteller professionals.
In the Republican Period, two storyteller/novelists in particular were prominent.
The first is Chang Jiemiao 常杰淼 (1875–1929), a storyteller from Tianjin whose tale,
Yongzheng jianxia tu 雍正劍俠圖 (Pictures of the sword knights of the Yongzheng

Does this mean that the storyteller figure became irrelevant in the twentieth century? Drawing on David Wang's notion of "repressed modernities," I would argue that this is not the case. As Wang has shown, following the univocal paradigm put forth by the May Fourth generation, scholars have been too hasty in writing off the late nineteenth century as a period lacking literary interest. The late nineteenth century was particularly rich in a variety of "modernities" whose unorthodox elements are valuable precisely because they fail to live up to the now-familiar May Fourth notions of what modern literature should be.[84] In the next few chapters, I will aim to demonstrate how the notion of "repressed modernities" holds true not only on a thematic level but also on a fundamental linguistic and material level. Turning from the prefaces of late nineteenth-century martial arts novels to the tales themselves, I will show how their language and the mechanical and human techniques used to reproduce this language still call on us to hear the often-forgotten voice of the storyteller.

reign), first was serialized in the New Tianjin Evening Post 新天津晚報 and was eventually published in forty-one volumes in 1928. The second is Zhang Jiexin 張杰鑫 (1862–1927), a storyteller who had studied with the same teacher as Chang. Zhang's most famous tale, *San xia jian* 三俠劍 (The three knightly swords), was roughly based on *The Cases of Judge Shi* and ran simultaneously in Shanghai and Tianjin newspapers in the late 1920s. Storytellers such as Shan Tianfang are still drawing on their fame as performers to publish martial arts novels.
84. Wang, *Fin-de-Siècle Splendor*.

CHAPTER THREE

Sounds That Sell

Vendor Calls and the Acoustic Aesthetics of the Marketplace

Let me begin my investigation into the role sound played in imagining the late-imperial marketplace with a brief snippet from a nineteenth-century Beijing folksong entitled "Kuo danainai zhen guang Xiding" 闊大奶奶真逛西頂 (The grand dame truly tours Xiding).[1] As the title intimates, the song describes how a young woman of a wealthy household, the eponymous Grand Dame, visits one of Beijing's most

---

1. Xiding was one of the popular religious sites close to Beijing, which, as is made clear in this song and other popular songs in the same series, was an active space of commercial exchange and popular performance. See Naquin, *Peking*, pp. 244, 277, 430–31, 518–20, 526, 560, 561. The song quoted here exists in a variety of versions, all with the same title. I am here quoting the Hundred Volumes Zhang version kept at the Fu Sinian Library at the Institute of Historical Philology at the Academia Sinica. The folksong in question is a *matoudiao* 碼頭調. This type of song, found throughout China, traces its history back to as early as the Song dynasty. In Beijing the local variant was particularly popular in the eighteenth and nineteenth centuries. Many of these songs were included in two of the most famous collections of late-imperial folksongs, Yan Zide's 顏自德 (fl. ca. 1795–ca. 1828) *Nishang xu pu* 霓裳續譜 (Supplementary formulary of the rainbow skirts; 1795) and Hua Guangsheng's 華廣生 *Bai xue yi yin* 白雪遺音 (Bequeathed songs from the white snows; 1828). Hundred Volumes Zhang, one of the Beijing purveyors of written copies of these texts, includes some 250 titles of *matoudiao* in its catalogue. *Matoudiao* consist of uneven lines of characters in a single rhyme scheme and combine singing with chanting, the last line of a sung part being printed in small characters, the last line of chanting marked by an exclamatory phrase. For more information as well as a musical score of one of these songs, see Li Jiarui, *Beiping suqu lue*, pp. 77–80.

famous temple fairs, the fair at Xiding.[2] Told from the perspective of a woman who was normally expected to stay within the confines of the boudoir, the song hints at the transgressive nature of such a visit. Yet at the same time the song clearly relishes listing the various entertainments and attractions found at the Xiding fair as seen and heard through her eyes and ears. Here, I merely offer the few lines that mark the lady's arrival at the fair:

大奶奶,花枝招展,	Gorgeously decked out, the Grand Dame
進了西頂仔細觀瞧.	Enters Xiding and carefully looks around.
這座廟場許多的,	At this fair, there's
作買作賣吆喝聲張.	Lots of buying, lots of selling,
吆喝聲張.	Loudly spread the vendors' sounds.
又听浮(sic.),	She also hears
絲絃笛管,鑼鼓叮咣.	Strings, and flutes, and gongs, DINGDANG.
趕廟的頑藝兒有多少擋.	Accumulated at this fair, how many attractions can be found?[3]

Next follows a line written in smaller characters, marking the end of the sung part and the beginning of the declamatory part, which neatly sums up the scene, "Truly this is very lively" (*renao*) 真個的熱鬧非常.

Although we have grown accustomed to thinking of the marketplace and its potentially dangerous lures in terms of visuality, the opening lines of this popular song suggest its attractions in terms not of sight, but of sound.[4] To be sure, the song states that when the Grand

---

2. Susan Naquin provides a succinct yet complete summary of the use of temple fairs as markets during the Qing. The fair at Xiding receives only limited attention from Naquin who, in her discussion of this particular place, is most interested in the organizational politics of religious processions and only focuses on the seventeenth and early eighteenth centuries. For a summary of temple fairs as marketplace and sites of entertainment, see Naquin, *Peking*, pp. 623–38. The first song in the series on the Grand Dame offers the date of the outing as the eighth day of the fourth month, which would mark it as the birthday of The Original Princess of the Vesper Mist 碧霞元君, an important Taoist goddess whose following was predominantly female. Her primary temple in the Beijing area was located west of the city at Xiding, at Mount Miaofeng 妙峰山.

3. "Kuo danainai zhen guang Xiding," p. 1A.

4. The importance of a visual framework for understanding the marketplace is found, for instance, in a literal understanding of the term "spectacle." Within

Dame arrives at the fair she "looks carefully," but the lines that follow
emphasize not a visual but an acoustic experience. First, the song notes
how the Grand Dame "listens." Next, the song provides an enumeration
of the various kinds of instruments she hears, the end of the line enact-
ing the sound of instruments itself through the onomatopoeia "DING
DANG." This sense of acoustic enticement not only involves the musical
entertainments at the fair, but crucially also extends to the activity of
trade itself. The song states that there are many merchants at the fair,
but it impresses the volume of trade upon its listener by commenting on
the merchants' voices with the declaration, "loudly spread the vendors'
sounds." Sound, in short, promises excitement, a spectacle just beyond
vision's reach, an acoustic suggestion of a lively, potentially transgressive experience that draws in the Grand Dame as well as the reader, who
is equally curious to find out just how many lively entertainments can
be found.

In this text, sound is particularly suited to sing the siren's song of
the marketplace because it at once holds out the promise of profuse
excitement as well as the containment of such potentially transgressive pleasures. Thus, on the one hand, the plentiful references to sound
and acts of listening draw the reader into the space of commoditized
popular entertainment by constructing it as a place that overflows with
commodities and services for purchase. When we are told, for instance,
that the Grand Dame listens, the text suggests an acoustic experience
that is attractive in its volume and variegation: the Grand Dame is
affected by the strings *and* woodwinds, drums *and* gongs, terms whose
aim is not descriptive exactitude but categorical amplitude, evoking
infinity and variety by combining different instruments of the same
category within a single term to denote the range found between these
two terms, i.e., flute 笛 and reed pipe 管, gong 鑼 and drum 鼓, as well as
every other instrument that falls within these categories. Similarly, the
second line states that the fair is filled with "*lots of* buying, *lots of* sell-

---

critical theory the term is mostly associated with Guy Debord, who employs it to
theorize the way social relationships in late-capitalist societies have been increasingly mediated through the prism of commodity exchange. See Debord, *Society of
the Spectacle*. For a more historically grounded application of Debord's framework
that situates the notion of spectacle in a context (late nineteenth-century Paris)
that nicely mirrors the setting of this study (late nineteenth-century Beijing), see
Schwartz, *Spectacular Realities*.

ing," a point the same sentence stresses acoustically by concluding with
the idea that the vendor calls spread as well. In fact, in purely linguistic terms this line itself produces amplitude, indeed hints at excess,
reduplicating the verb in *zuo mai, zuo mai* 作買作賣 instead of the
simple, more economic *zuo maimai*. Thus the text fills up the sentence
with seemingly superfluous sounds, the repetition and variegation of
homophonic words suggesting the way in which the market attracts
its customers with vendors of all kinds. Hence, when the final line of
the section translated above invites the reader further into the fair by
asking how many entertainments can be found at the market, it does
so not simply by promising a concrete answer (the rest of the song that
follows has eighteen different entertainments, to be exact). Rather, the
question tempts the reader to imagine a countless infinitude.

If, on the one hand, the textually imagined sounds promise the
profusion of marketplace attractions, on the other hand they also
manage to contain these very attractions. Most notably, the sounds of
the words are controlled by a disciplinary regime: the representations of
pleasures are ordered by the formal features of the song: rhyme, rhythm
(opposition between stressed and unstressed beat or feet), organization
into couplets, and tune.[5] As hinted at in the final line of the section
translated above, the attractions of the marketplace may be variegated
and "countless," but each of the eighteen different entertainments
described next is clearly separated in sections 落, and throughout all
of these sections a strict rhyme scheme is upheld; all the multifarious
entertainments are described in lines that end with the same "ang"
rhyme seen in lines 2–4 of the translated section.[6] Similarly, the riot

5. Even though this distinction between order and profusion seems to follow the
lines of a clear-cut distinction between content and form, in reality such is not the
case. For instance, if the line that emphasizes the loud sound of the vendors creates
unnecessary and amplitudinous sounds through the repetitive use of *zuo mai, zuo
mai*, such uneconomical repetition also emphasizes structure by forcing the line to
follow the appropriate number of beats and creating poetic structure through repetition. Similarly, the onomatopoeia in line 3, *DING DANG*, is excessive in terms of
content, but it is a crucial element in the way it allows the line to obey the rhyme
scheme. Indeed, the single rhyme scheme "ang" adds to the order of the text, but
the accumulative power of the constant variation and repetition of final "angs"
clearly adds to the volume of sound.
6. Or, using the rhyme categories of the age itself, the song employs the *jiangyang*
rhyme scheme 江洋轍.

of entertainers at the market may be diverse, but the rhythm in which these entertainments are represented, though undoubtedly lively, also follows a clear and strict regimen. Finally, the lengthy section that lists the "countless" (eighteen) entertainments is labeled as musically separate from the rest of the song since this particular part of the overall song is set to its own tune, the tune of the pass (*bianguan diao* 邊關調).[7] Thus, just as the ceremonial arch of the temple creates a spatial barrier that separates the festive space of the fair inside the temple from the rest of the world outside, the shift in tune separates the introductory, more narrative elements of the song from the multifarious collection of entertainments listed at its heart. If the ceremonial arch orders the temple as a single space by differentiating it from the outside world, the tune of *bianguan* similarly constructs an acoustic order for its presentation, containing the numerous attractions of the fair within a clear narrative and formal frame.[8]

The Chinese term used to describe this alluring play between copious abandon and regimented order is perfectly captured in the final line quoted above, "Truly this is very lively" (*renao*) 真個的熱鬧非常. The term *renao*, often translated as "lively," "loud," or "bustling," is readily and often unselfconsciously used to describe the excitement of a crowded marketplace (or a well-executed literary performance), precisely because it captures the ambiguity of the marketplace and its variegated attractions. After all, if *renao* on the one hand promises liveliness, excitement, and the intermingling of so many different sights and sounds, bodies and objects, it also calls for structures to contain a potential threat of chaos, of liveliness turning riotous, of bodies intermingling without proper order or distinction. Or, to use the Chinese terms, *renao* always carries the threat of variegation 雜 devolving into

7. Li Jiarui explains that the term "tune of the pass" was originally derived from the meaning of the original song which told of a woman sending off her husband who was leaving for the frontier. As Li points out, the tune of the pass song consists of a series of sections 落, in this case consisting of the eighteen different forms of entertainment, in the case of Li Jiarui's example, the twelve months of the year. See Li Jiarui, *Beiping suqu lue*, pp. 87-90.

8. For the importance of the ceremonial arch as a spatial boundary that separates inside from outside, see Meyer, "Rural Villages and Buddhist Monasteries." For more on the importance of walls, gates, and sounds representing the threat and promise of crossing such boundaries, see chap. 6 in this book.

chaos 亂. By both offering and disciplining the acoustic attractions of the marketplace, the martial arts novels, drum-songs, and popular tunes that "sung" the liveliness of temple fairs became themselves exciting commodities that could be sold on the basis of their packaging, in the sense of both presenting and containing, the *renao* of festive occasions and mercantile prosperity.

To analyze the way late nineteenth-century popular texts employed sound to create an aesthetics of *renao* and in turn theorize the way such *renao* both evoked and disciplined the attractions of the marketplace, I will explore one acoustic phenomenon that appeared with remarkable regularity in martial arts tales: lively and loud vendor calls. To begin, I investigate the nineteenth-century market for popular martial arts tales by focusing on the way authors and publishers drew on the notion of *renao* to advertise their tales. Second, I focus on one literary technique popular performance texts use to highlight as well as discipline the sensory experience of the marketplace, the inclusion of a disciplined observer who provides a model for regimented consumption. Next, I turn to the way these texts employ vendor calls to draw attention to the way the storyteller himself manipulates language to sell his act while showcasing his art, thereby turning an incitement to purchase into an invitation to appreciate. Finally, I end by looking at the way printed martial arts novels based on performance texts also include the vendor call as a sign of marketplace attractions. By heavily truncating such calls yet highlighting their importance in terms of narrative structure, however, these novels shift the reader's attention from artesian performance of diverse attractions to the notion of the linear progression of the plot.

The Sounds of the Market in Popular Performance Texts

The martial arts tales that became so popular at the end of the Qing dynasty were ultimately commercial in nature; they were performed, copied by hand, and printed in order to make money. While chapter 2 emphasized how the storyteller's reputation was employed to add value to a text, this chapter pays attention in particular to the way these texts employed the notion of liveliness or *renao* to market themselves.

The *matoudiao* that opens this chapter, "The Grand Dame Truly Tours Xiding," presents a good example of a popular song sold as a commodity using the promise of excitement as a way of enticing readers to keep purchasing one book after another. As attested by catalogues issued by the primary seller of performance texts in nineteenth-century Beijing, Hundred Volumes Zhang, the song sold for 300 cash.[9] The song, moreover, was merely the fifth of a six-part series of Grand Dame texts, each text capitalizing on the brand-name recognition of the "Grand Dame franchise": "Kuo danainai yao guang Xiding" 闊大奶奶要逛西頂 (The grand dame wants to tour Xiding) sold for 400 cash; and the remaining four texts, "Lao gu taitai quan shan zu xing" 老姑太太勸善阻行 (The old mother-in-law urges [the grand dame] to be good and prevents the outing), "Kuo danainai gua daojin" 闊大奶奶挂倒勁 (The grand dame blows a gasket), "Kuo danainai guang Wanshou si" 闊大奶奶逛萬壽寺 (The grand dame visits the Wanshou Temple), and the concluding story, "Danainai gaixie guizheng" 大奶奶改邪歸正 (The dame mends her wicked ways), each sold for 300 cash.[10] Each

9. For the various prices of these songs, see Fu Xihua, *Beijing chuantong quyi zonglu*, pp. 613–15. An anonymous catalogue composed in Guangxu 12 (1887) located in the Opera Library of the National Academy for the Arts offers a slightly different series, which includes three additional songs on the Grand Dame, namely "Kuo danainai qiao da gui pao che" 闊大奶奶瞧打鬼跑車 (The grand dame watches the beating of the ghosts and the running of the carts), "Kuo danainai chu shanhui" 闊大奶奶出善會 (The grand dame goes out to a religious celebration), and "Kuo danainai shang Miaofeng shan" 闊大奶奶上妙峰山 (The grand dame ascends Mount Miaofeng). This catalogue also places one of the songs associated with the Grand Dame's husband, "Daye zhui Ding" 大爺追頂 (The master chases [the grand dame] to [Xi]ding), before the final song of the series, where the Grand Dame finally mends her ways. See *Ganban paizi kuaishu*, p. 8A–B. For an article that lists the major catalogues of popular songs, see Chen Jinzhao, "Shipaishu de tizhi."

10. In addition to these popular *matoudiao* series, there are other *matoudiao* on the Grand Dame that do not strictly speaking belong in the series, but clearly cash in on its popularity by employing the same central character. Some of these I have already mentioned in the preceding footnote. In addition there are "Kuo danainai fuxi" 闊大奶奶赴席 (The grand dame attends a banquet), "Kuo danainai guang Heisi" 闊大奶奶逛黑寺 (The grand dame tours the black temple), as well as a second series that focuses on the Grand Dame's husband, *The Master of the*

song places the Grand Dame in a different, lively setting, ending with a promise to the reader of additional excitement in the next episode. The song quoted at the beginning of this chapter, "The Grand Dame Truly Tours Xiding," in fact ends with two such statements. The first holds out the prospect of closure: "Continued by [the Grand Dame] Mends Her Wicked Ways" 下接改邪歸正. This promise of mending one's ways apparently was not exciting enough. Consequently a second line was added suggesting an alternative sequel, "Continued by the Master of the House is about to Chase the Grand Dame" 接大爺要趕大奶奶.[11] Not only does the prospect of a chase sound more spectacular, but the term "about to" in the title also suggests that the Master of the House does not actually give chase quite just yet. For the actual chase, the reader presumably has to buy yet another sequel in the series.[12]

In the process of serialization, *renao* played an important role, because the promise of future acoustic liveliness tempted the reader to explore further.[13] In the various serial martial arts tales that begin to

---

House Chases Her to (Xi)ding, and "Kuo daye guang longfu si" 闊大爺逛隆福寺 (The master of the house tours the Longfu Temple). There are also two *zidishu* on the same theme, "Kuo danainai ting shanhui xi" 闊大奶奶聽善會戲 (The grand dame listens to opera at a religious festival) and "Kuo danainai guang Erzha" 闊大奶奶逛二閘 (The grand dame tours the Two Sluices), as well as a *paizi qu* "Kuo danainai guang shi yiyuan" 闊大奶奶逛施醫院 (The grand dame visits the hospital). For a discussion of *paizi qu* (basically a popular song form that links different tunes together), see Li Jiarui, *Beiping suqu lue*, pp. 99–101. The Grand Dame series also inspired songs that are a clear variation of the theme, such as "Qiong danainai guang Baiyunsi" 窮大奶奶逛白雲觀 (A poor old dame visits the Baiyun Taoist Temple). For an overview of the titles, the various publishing houses that sold these titles, and the prices these houses asked for each copy, see Fu Xihua, *Beijing chuantong quyi zonglu*, pp. 285 and 613–15. There exists an interesting Shanghai variant of Beijing's Grand Dame titled "Shanghai de shao nainai" 上海的劭奶奶 (The beautiful lady from Shanghai). As Laura Andrews McDaniel has pointed out, Shanghai's Beautiful Lady (and her wayward consumption habits) were crucial to the formulation of a distinctly urban, Shanghai identity. See McDaniel, "Jumping the Dragon Gate," pp. 212–14.

11. "The Grand Dame Truly Tours Xiding," p. 12B.

12. In the sequel, *The Master of the House Chases Her to (Xi)ding*, the grand dame's husband never actually chases her, but merely launches a long and spectacular tirade that promises he will track her down, in the next sequel.

13. This technique of interrupting a tale at the most lively point had, of course, long been used by oral performers. A good example of a nineteenth-century text

flood the market by the late nineteenth century, this use of *renao* turns explicitly commercial as publishers begin to end installments with the promise of more liveliness in the next installment. The publisher of the 1879 novel *The Three Knights and the Five Gallants*, for instance, introduced the idea of a sequel by listing the adventures that still remained to be told. Piling up one adventure after another, the publisher employed the final page of the novel as the printed counterpart of a vendor call, a long and lively list that uses the attraction of *renao* to sell the next installment:

> If you want to know how the various heroes laid siege on Xiangyang, how the numerous "tigers" were foiled by witchcraft, how the latter knight delivered hasty messages to Pittrap Island, Jasmine Village, and the Liu Family Compound, how the Five Tigers from the Liu Family rushed to Xiangyang, how Aihu crossed the mountains to subdue the Three Robbers, how Liu Long hurried to befriend the Two Heroes, how Lu Zhen single-handedly escaped from being surrounded, how Ding Yao and Ding Feng together found the mountain, how the band of brothers all came together in Xiangyang, and how they laid a plan to rescue the numerous heroes, all these many exciting (*renao*) plots cannot all be told [here]. But close to a hundred chapters can all be found in *The Latter Five Gallants*. Read it and all will become clear.
>
> 要知群雄戰襄陽, 眾虎遭魔難, 小俠到陷空島茉花村柳家莊三處飛報信, 柳家五虎奔襄陽, 艾虎過山收服三寇, 柳龍趕路結拜雙雄, 盧珍單刀獨闖陣, 丁蛟丁鳳雙探山, 小弟兄襄陽大聚會, 設計救群雄; 直到眾虎豪傑脫難, 大家共義破襄陽, 設圈套捉拿奸王, 施妙計掃除眾寇, 押解奸王, 夜趕開封府, 肅清襄陽郡, 又敘鍘斬襄陽王, 包公保眾虎, 小英雄金殿同封官, 顏查散奏事封五鼠, 眾英雄開封大聚首, 群俠義公廳同結拜; 多少熱鬧節目, 不能一一儘述. 也有不足百回, 具在 "小五義" 書上, 便見分明.[14]

The list is a jumble of episodes, each individual episode sounding more exciting than the last, each promising a seemingly ever-increasing

---

describing such an interruption is found in the *zidishu* titled *Fengliu cike* 風流詞客 (The cosmopolitan teller of tales) by Helüshi. The three-chapter ballad is an extensive description of a storyteller performance and tells how the storyteller cuts his tale short to collect money "right when he's come to the most exciting (*renao*) part, the most crucial part of the plot" 他說到那熱鬧中間, 緊關節要. Helüshi, "Fengliu cike," p. 348.

14. *Zhonglie xia'yi zhuan*, vol. 2, chap. 120, p. 694.

number of heroes brought together in a variety of spectacular settings. Actual comprehension of the exact meaning of their descriptions is unimportant. Indeed, the descriptions are arguably designed specifically to prevent full understanding.[15] After all, the author does not want the reader to know exactly what happens until he has actually bought and read the next installment of the series. In short, the author here does not merely promise more liveliness in the next volume, *The Latter Five Gallants*, he actually produces such *renao* to conclude his own text. Stacking one episode on top of the next, heaping up exciting plotline after exciting plotline, the breathless way in which the novel concludes enacts precisely that which it is trying to sell in the next installment, variegated liveliness.[16]

Though literary *renao* may have thus been appreciated by audiences for its lively attractions and by publishers and performers for the way it allowed them to sell their tales, not everyone was quite as sanguine about the qualities of such spectacle. Take, for instance, the following observation made by the author Jin Liankai 金連凱 in an early nineteenth-century work, the *Lingtai xiaobu* 靈臺小補 (A brief supplement to Lingtai), a guide to opera performance in the capital. Jin writes in no uncertain terms regarding the pernicious effects of popular [drum-song] performance:

> These stories are full of prodigies, feats of strength, chaotic events, and gods. Since they are just to make people laugh, they seem to cause no harm. But in the modulation of their lyrics, they seek only *renao* and on the whole they uphold as virtuous such things as studying magic

15. Alternatively, such endings might refer to plotlines that were already widely known to readers from other media. Miao Huaiming has rightfully pointed out that none of the plotlines mentioned at the end of the first novel in the series match the plotlines actually found in the first sequel, and that hence it is clear that the two texts were not only produced by different publishers, but also come from different storyteller material. See Miao, "*San xia wu yi* cheng shu xin kao," pp. 209–24, in particular p. 214.
16. The first sequel to *The Cases of Judge Shi*, the 1894 novel *The Continued Cases of Judge Shi*, similarly ends with the promise of many "exciting" (*renao*) plotlines. See *Shi gongan quan an*, vol. 1, chap. 100, p. 692. For a list of martial arts novels series published in the late nineteenth century and the way these novels end with a moment of suspense and a promise of *renao*, see Keulemans, "Sounds of the Novel," appendix B.

with one's master, exorcising demons and employing deities, gathering [outlaws] in mountain forests, or raiding execution grounds.

此書多演怪力亂神, 供人捧腹, 似乎無害, 然辭氣抑揚之間, 但圖熱鬧, 總以拜師學法, 驅役鬼神, 嘯聚山林, 劫奪法場等為賢.[17]

Jin Liankai here typifies the popular drum-song through the concept of *renao*. Yet for him this *renao* is solely negative, associated with the kinds of things the Master did not speak of, prodigies, feats of strength, chaotic events, and spirits.[18]

Given the potential negative connotations of *renao*, publishers and performers may have appreciated liveliness because it made for a lucratively exciting tale, but they also needed to defend its potential merits, contain its potential for vulgarity and disorder. In an aside in the drum-song *The Cases of Judge Liu*, the storyteller hedges his bets by promising both fictional liveliness and orthodox history. When caught telling an obviously fabricated tale about a historical figure, the narrator once again turns directly to his audience:

> This tale is not like those old stories, where people just say whatever they want to say. It is not as if someone from history would actually show up to give counter evidence, right? This tale today, however, does not dare stray from the facts: as for what office so and so occupied, what was witnessed, and how Judge Liu apprehended [the suspects], these must be true. As for the prosecution of this case, I guess it's seven-tenths true; I added three-tenths of embellishments so as to make it *renao*. If not, how would it still resemble a [real] story?
>
> 此書不像古書, 由着人要怎麼說就怎麼說, 難道還有古時之人來對証嗎? 那才是無可考查! 今書不敢離了, 某人何官, 看甚麼事情, 劉大人怎麼拿問, 必是真事. 審問此案, 想來還有七成真事, 愚下添出三成枝葉, 圖其熱鬧. 不然怎麼像書呢?[19]

---

17. Quoted in Li Jiarui, *Beiping suqu lue*, pp. 1–2.
18. The reference is to the famous phrase from *Analects* 7:21 in which Confucius is said not to have spoken of these things.
19. *Liu gongan*, section 26, chap. 4, p. 410. The phrase "seven-tenths truth, three-tenths embellishment" recalls Zhang Xuecheng's 章學誠 (1738–1801) dictum about *The Romance of the Three Kingdoms* being "seven parts true, three parts fiction, thus misleading its reader" 三國演義七實三虛, 惑亂觀者.

Sounds That Sell   107

The narrator here engages his audience in a sales pitch that promises liveliness to excite his audience, while at the same time containing this liveliness within a framework he asserts to be true to the facts. Liveliness is a crucial component of the value of his tale. Indeed, without liveliness, how would a story still qualify as a story worth telling? At the same time, the author defends his use of liveliness by stating that his story is not just made up but based on factual history. Orthodox history and factuality are called upon to contain liveliness, but in fact both *renao* and history are needed to make the perfect product. After all, if the vulgar fictional liveliness makes up "three-tenths" of his product, it is precisely the appeal to the seventy percent of history that allows the storyteller to differentiate his product from all those other tales out there on the market, tales told by "people just saying whatever they want to say."[20]

Literary liveliness, in short, carried in many ways the same connotations as the liveliness imagined to be typical of the temple fair; it was deemed attractive and marketable but also suspicious and potentially vulgar. That said, the liveliness present in a text is not the same as the actual liveliness of temple fairs. Obviously, the fiction of many heroic figures coming together in a grand spectacular finale is not the same as the physical friction produced by actual live bodies mingling at the temple fair. Even within the realm of fiction, the promise of many exciting plotlines at the end of a novel is not the same as the use of many different acoustic elements in a song such as "The Grand Dame Truly Tours Xiding." The question we might want to focus on next, then, is what different literary techniques did the various commercial tales of

20. As Jiang Kun and Ni Zhongzhi argue, during the late imperial and early Republican periods, drum-songs developed along a clear trajectory from countryside to city. The defensive pose by the drum-song in this particular instance is perhaps due to the recognition of this perceived countryside vulgarity of the genre and represents an attempt to raise the genre's standing among a more "discerning" crowd. See Jiang and Ni, *Zhongguo quyi tongshi*, pp. 420–28. The preface to *The Tale of Everlasting Blessings and Peace* is a good example of a printed novel that seeks to differentiate itself from the vulgar genre of the drum-song by making a similar appeal to historical fact: "This is a tale of true events that can be relied on, unlike those drum-songs or wild histories. Indeed, these true events have been handed down since the founding of Our Dynasty." See Guo Guangrui, "*Yongqing shengping xu*," p. 1559. See also chap. 2 of this book.

the late nineteenth century employ to create the illusion of a sense of (acoustic) liveliness in the text? Similarly, having conjured up both the attractions and negative potentialities of *renao*, what techniques did texts use to contain such *renao*?

Disciplined Observation and the Creation of an Economic Subject

One of the distinct literary techniques prevalent in popular performance texts is the focalization of the sensory experience of the market through the ears and eyes of a single protagonist who moves through city streets and temple fairs. Though the purpose of this technique is to bring the reader into the experience, the focused movement of the protagonist and the constant emphasis on his disciplined observation also serves to order this dazzling sensory experience. The result is not simply a lively simulacrum of the variegated sensory attractions of the market, but rather a lengthy process of aesthetic disciplining. The result is an economic subject that is capable of both appreciating and in turn ordering the manifold attractions of the marketplace.

To get a sense of the way popular texts employ a central protagonist seeing, hearing, and moving through the market, let us turn to the late nineteenth-century drum-song, *Bao gongan* 包公案 (The cases of Judge Bao). A scene depicting a temple fair occurs when two of Judge Bao's helpers, the heroes Ma Han and Wang Chao, find their way to a fair held to celebrate the birthday of the flower god and arrive at the temple:

On the road they saw a [crowd] endlessly circulating, boisterous and chaotic, with men and women mixed together, so pressed together that it was hard to move. They saw how before the temple there was a ceremonial arch with four pillars and three gates. The people who had come to see the fair were like a ten-thousand-headed Buddha, a veritable mountain, no, a sea of people that could not even get past the arch, let alone make it into the temple. Wang Chao and Ma Han as well had to squeeze in with the crowd and looked to either side carefully:

只見路上來往不斷, 亂亂烘烘, 男男女女, 擁擠不動. 只見廟前有坐四柱三門的牌樓, 那看会的人千佛頭一般, 是人山人海, 连牌樓都過不去, 莫說近廟. 王朝馬汗二人也只得擠在那人群之內, 往兩旁仔細的观看.

二英公	The two heroes
一齐迈步往前走	Together stepped forward,
举目抬頭看分明.	Lifted their eyes, raised their heads, and saw clearly.
有些個	There were
作買賣作夾近廟	People selling, people buying, people who'd come to the temple;
道旁一溜是席棚.	All along the central path there were rows of stalls,
賣的是	Where were sold
青巾代子青白布	White cloth sacks and dark and white fabric,
緞絹沙罗与細綾.	Satin, gauze, and fine silk.
还有那	There were as well
珠翠首飾靴鞋店	Shops with pearl and kingfisher feather jewelry, shoes and boots;
设擺几坐估衣棚.	Several secondhand clothing stalls had also been set up.
一个个	One after another,
大声吆喝嗓子亮	Loudly calling out with voices clear,
脸憨皮后[sic]庄女人	Were shameless peasant women.
口中說	Mouthing loudly,
该賣该賣價不大	"Must sell, must sell, really cheap.
这件只要五子銅.	This one only five coppers! "
生意人	Commercial performers:
男扮女庄无休恥	Men dressed like women, without shame,
扭扭攝攝穿着群.	Swaying as if on bound feet, pressing through the throng.
也有那	And there was also
賣茶賣酒葷素菜	The selling of tea, selling of wine, selling of meat and vegetable dishes,
猜拳行令說笑声.	The playing of guess fingers and drinking games, the sound of talking and laughing.
又听得	And they hear as well
一声喊叫賣毡貨	Someone's voice calling as he sells felt:
避冷遮寒不透風.	"Keeps out the cold, protects against chill, lets no wind through!"
那边是	Over there
有人吆喝賣絲代	There are people hawking ribbons:
稍些家去与子孫.	"Take some home and give 'em to your children and grandchildren."
也有賣	There are also those selling
磁器茶中与飯碗	Porcelain, tea-cups and rice bowls,
中碗大碗磁花瓶.	Medium bowls, large bowls, porcelain vases.
那一边	Over there

尽是一溜果子市	The whole place, a fruit market,
干鮮各樣俱現成.	Dried or fresh, all kinds fully provided.
又見那	And they moreover see
把式廠內耍拳棒	In the wrestling ring the flourishing of fists and clubs,
說書唱曲是美耳中聽.	Storytelling and singing songs, all so sweet to the ear.
他二人	The two men
看把[sic]又往前边看	After finishing looking [at these], went forward to look.
來到那,	And came to
戲館根前細留祥.	The foot of the opera stage and paid careful attention.[21]

Like a lengthy list, the song enumerates the many attractions of the market.[22] Unlike an orderly list, however, the song seems to emphasize the diversity of objects and people, sights and sounds, to the point of confusion. Old clothing and precious silk, expensive jewelry and cheap boots are found right next to one another. Moreover, it is not just objects that are thrown into a single variegated and exhilarating heap; people mingle in a similar manner. The prose introduction to the poem emphasizes that "men and women" were pushing themselves past the gate without much differentiation, producing a loud and chaotic hubbub, the various bodies melding together into a single "thousand-headed Buddha." In the song itself this "sea of human bodies" becomes an even more deliberate mingling of the sexes as "professional performers, men dressed like women, shamelessly . . . press through the throng." The temple fair, in short, is not simply crowded, nor are its manifold objects merely variegated. The song suggests that the density of objects and people, sights and sounds creates an atmosphere that is borderline chaotic.

Yet even though the song enacts the profusion of people and objects, sights and sounds so as to highlight the potential for confu-

---

21. *Bao gongan guci*, roll 33, p. 0021. The text contains a good amount of non-standard characters and homophonic substitutions. The use of these characters in the original manuscript not only signals the "vulgar" origins of the text, but also shows that the text emphasized an acoustic form of reading in which homophonic characters can be easily substituted for one another.

22. For a discussion of the notion of lists in late-imperial culture, see Clunas, *Empire of Great Brightness*, chap. 4.

sion, it also includes mechanisms that help the text to provide a sense of order. One such device is particularly important: the presence of a protagonist whose movement is purposeful and whose mode of observation is disciplined. Though much of the drum-song's depiction of the market consists of an enumeration of objects, these countless objects are framed within and continuously connected through a breathless staccato of short, three-syllable phrases that emphasize the perception of these objects by the song's two protagonists as they move through the temple grounds. To be sure, there are phrases that merely function to give the reader a sense of enumeration ("there were moreover those" or "there were as well"). Yet these phrases are constantly matched with lines that highlight the sensorial plenitude of the experience ("moreover they heard" or "and then they saw"). Indeed, the beginning and the ending of the vendor fair song are bounded by a few crucial lines that emphasize the entire fair as placed within a framework of observation constructed along a vector of movement. At the beginning we read, "The two heroes / together stepped forth / raised their eyes and carefully looked." These opening lines are then echoed in the final phrases, "The two men / after watching, went forward and watched some more / when they came / to the opera stage and carefully observed."

This emphasis on the personal observation and constant movement of the two protagonists deepens the immersive potential of the song, yet it also creates a framework that clearly orders the potential chaos of the marketplace. The song does this by emphasizing a disciplined form of observation and coupling this disciplined observation with a focused forward momentum. Again, note the various phrases at the beginning and end of the song depicting the temple fair. If the brief phrases in the middle merely stress "continued observation" ("again they saw" and "as well they heard"), the phrases at the beginning and end inevitably call for a more regimented gaze/ear. The last line of prose before the song, for instance, tells how the two heroes squeeze in with the crowd, but "watch both sides *carefully*." The first line of the song states that the heroes "raise their eyes, lift their heads, and look *clearly*." Again, the final line concludes with the two men reaching the opera stage and "observing with *detail*." Stated differently, the song time and again emphasizes that the two men are not at the fair to simply see the sights; they are, following the larger plot of the story, two heroic men on a mission to find clues in a mysterious

crime and are, as a result, constantly on the lookout to prevent even
further chaos.

This sense of a careful, disciplined gaze is further strengthened
when it is coupled with a focused physical movement on the part of the
protagonists. Like the sensory immersion that marks the description of
the temple fair, the movement of the heroes through the temple seeks
to evoke the street-level experience of the fair, a physical presence that
actually moves among the crowd and in between the manifold attractions of the crowd.[23] Yet the song never suggests a random or faltering
movement for the two heroes; instead it repeatedly offers decisive and
progressive movements. To be sure, the two men need to squeeze in with
the crowd. Yet unlike the crowd, which is said to "not even get beyond the
ceremonial arch," the two protagonists relentlessly move ahead. In the
song lines, "The two heroes / together they stepped forward / they lifted
their eyes, raised their head, and saw clearly," there is a palpable sense
of coordination ("together") and direction ("forward"). This clearly
directed movement is then carried into the next phrase, connecting it
with the controlled gaze of the heroes: "lifting their eyes and raising
their head, they looked carefully." Here the gaze is constructed through
active physical movement, a lifting of eyes and raising of heads, which
in turn results in the production of visual order. In the Chinese text,
which consists of a sharp and short, four-character verb-object verb-
object phrase (舉目抬頭), active and attentive action is stressed.
Followed directly by a verb expressing "seeing clearly," a decisive link
is established between active observation and, through such careful
observation, the ordering of the potentially chaotic temple fair.

As hinted at above, the qualities of strict observation and purposeful movement are not limited to the two heroes, but are constructed to
include the reader as well. By leaving the grammatical subject of the
various verbs of observation open to interpretation, the song creates a
blank subject position.[24] In the song lines, for instance, "And then [they]

23. This kind of street-level immersion becomes particularly clear in songs that
express a limited point of view followed by the sudden intrusion and hence shocking experience of a spectacular sight or sound, usually preceded by the phrase
"suddenly he hears/sees" 互見.
24. I borrow the term "subject position" from Bronwyn Davies and Rom Harre;
see their "Positioning." I would, however, add two elements to their discussion of
the way speakers and listeners position themselves strategically in discourse and

furthermore see," or in the prose passage describing how "on the road [they] saw a boisterous and chaotic crowd," there is no explicit subject. Indeed, we might think of this as a direct address and the verb as an exhortation. In the song lines, "And [they] hear as well / Someone's voice calling as he sells felt: 'Keeps out the cold, protects against chill, lets no wind through,'" does the sentence tell the reader that the two heroes heard a vendor of felt loudly hawking his wares, or is the reader enjoined to listen himself to the sounds of the market?[25] Andrea Goldman, commenting on the lack of a clearly defined subject in such sentences, has rightfully pointed out that this grammatical feature leads to an increased identification between protagonist and reader.[26] Building on Goldman's argument, I would argue that this sense of identification, created both by the lack of a subject *and* by the consistent emphasis on a verb of observation, should not be understood solely as identification, that is, the equation of two "subjects," but rather as a continued process of discipline that produces a reader/listener by placing him in the position of observer.

The order imposed through the act of observation and purposeful movement organizes the experience of the text on a variety of levels, ranging from the spatial layout of the imagined space to the poetic order of the text itself. Take, for instance, another song that depends on the movement of its protagonist to both evoke and order the lively jumble of a temple fair, the late nineteenth-century *zidishu* by Helüshi 鶴侶氏

---

hence produce a sense of self. First, the notion of positioning emphasizes a concept of locating oneself spatially, crucial in these performance texts both in the sense of grammatical construction (the subject precedes the verb in a sentence), as well as the content of these texts in terms of the marketplace. Second, the spatial emphasis of the term highlights the notion that the position is initially open or empty, to be filled by a reader who is constructed as a result of entering this space. The connotation of emptiness that space carries is better captured in the Chinese word for space, *kongjian* 空間.

25. Sometimes this shift to the reader/listener is made explicit through the use of the second-person pronoun. This is the case in the drum-song *The Cases of Judge Liu*, for instance. Amid a lengthy sequence that tells how the Judge enters the capital and observes one street performance after another, the song unexpectedly cuts in with a direct address to the reader, "You look!" 你瞧. *Liu gongan*, section 23, chap. 3, p. 362. For a translation of this sequence and for more on the background of the drum-song in question, see Wan, "The Drum Ballad *Cases of Judge Liu*."
26. See Goldman, "The Nun Who Wouldn't Be."

(early 19th c.) entitled "Strolling through the Huguo Temple."[27] The song, which is basically a long list of commodities and commercial entertainments as observed and enjoyed by the protagonist as he strolls through the temple grounds, describes the young man's arrival at the temple:

> When he gets to the gate, he sees a person standing in front, his face all smiles.
> It's someone who is charitably distributing well-known special prescriptions and sutras that urge one to do good,
> He takes a sheet, reads it, and says, "Not worth the trouble, you're wasting paper and ink bothering people here."
> When he gets to the Yonghe Hall, he first drinks a bowl of sour plum juice,
> Then he follows the central walkway, paying special attention to the heaps of jade objects.
> Those who know him get up and vie to offer him a seat,
> He clearly rattles off a list of orders, wildly stretching out his hands.
> He says, "I've been asked to find a pair of jadeite stepping stones for mounting horses.
> And I also need a six-foot-long coral dragon-head cane,
> And in addition a pair of pearls, like melons so big.
> Old man Li, please make special effort to find them for me."
> When he gets to the Matreya Buddha Hall, he sees that Zhang the Featherman has set up shop inside,
> And says, "I want a six-eyed feather with a long central shaft and vanes neatly equal on both sides."
> Then he sees a stand selling swords, and he wants to chat:
> "I want a top-notch European Khitan blade, broad and braided so I can place it round my waist."[28]
> The rusty-red eyes of the dagger seller shoot him a piercing glance,
> And he lowers his head and down the steps he goes scurrying towards the back.
> 至門前,見一人當門而立面含春.[29]
> 原來是施捨鄉經驗的偏方兒合勸人的經典,

27. For more on this prolific *zidishu* author, see chap. 2, note 62. For an English introduction to this song, the temple in question, and Hundred Volumes Zhang, one of the manuscript merchants at the fair, see Chiu, "Cultural Hybridity," pp. 253–69.
28. The meaning of this phrase puzzles me; the character 倭 suggests a Japanese blade, but in the context of the line, I am not sure.
29. In the original text, the poetic lines include half-size characters written next to one another in a double column within the line. Here, these characters are printed in a smaller font but they are not printed above one another. Susan Blader suggests that in manuscripts belonging to the Shi school of storytelling, characters are simi-

接一張看說: "何苦來, 費紙費墨在這裡冤人!"
來至永和齋, 先將梅湯喝一碗,
順甬路, 玉器堆上細留神.
相熟的站起忙讓坐,
他分明打落亂把手伸
說: "有人托我尋翡翠的馬臺石一對,
還用六尺長珊瑚子,龍頭拐杖一根, 西瓜大的真珠用一對,
屬老大, 你著意留留替我尋."
上了彌勒殿, 見翎子張在門內擺,
說: "我要一枝六眼花翎, 要線兒長長邊翅兒勻."
又見那腰刀攤子, 他也想打落:
"我要頭路兒金塔子紅毛刀, 單倭單放可繞身."
那寬刀的用那通紅的爛眼睛將他一瞪,
他一低頭下了臺階往後奔. 30

As in the temple fair song, the presence of the young man plays a double role. While bringing the reader into the temple fair as if he himself were there, it also orders the multifarious objects found at the temple in a clear spatial/poetic order. In terms of space, the text is suffused with brief phrases like "when he arrives at the gate," "when he gets to the Yonghe Hall," "as he follows the central thoroughfare," and "as he climbs the Matreya Buddha Hall." Though ostensibly functioning to describe the movement of the protagonist, these phrases are better understood as a device that provides a spatial framework for the multifarious shopping experiences of our "hero." Read from beginning to end, these cues would have made it possible for a contemporary reader to draw a map of the temple's spatial and purchasing layout, each gate, hall, and courtyard described in a few lines that carefully position each commodity in its own discrete area.[31] A twenty-first-century scholar can at best hope to arrive at an approximation; see figure 3.1 and its accompanying legend.[32]

larly written in small font in order to make the line lengths an even three or seven characters. See Blader, "*San-hsia wu-i*," p. 16.
30. Helüshi, "Guang Huguo si," vol. 2, pp. 327–30.
31. For an actual map (as well as a brief description) of the by now long-destroyed Huguo Temple, see Li Luke et al., *Beijing gu jianzhu ditu*, pp. 302–3.
32. To produce this image I have combined data from the bannerman song with the *Qing Neiwufu cang Jingcheng quan tu* 清內務府藏京城全圖 (The Qing Imperial Household Agency's complete map of the capital), originally produced in 1750, here scanned from the 1940 Kōain Kahoku Renrakubu Seimukyoku Chōsajo reproduction.

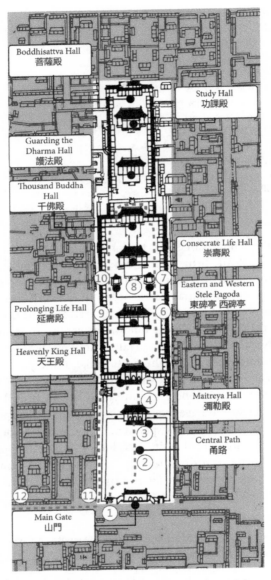

Boddhisattva Hall
菩薩殿

Study Hall
功課殿

Guarding the
Dharma Hall
護法殿

Thousand Buddha
Hall
千佛殿

Consecrate Life Hall
崇壽殿

Eastern and Western
Stele Pagoda
東碑亭 西碑亭

Prolonging Life Hall
延壽殿

Heavenly King Hall
天王殿

Maitreya Hall
彌勒殿

Central Path
甬路

Main Gate
山門

3.1 A Map of Commercial Activity at the Huguo Temple, with legend. (Adapted from *Qing Neiwufu cang Jingcheng quan tu* 清內務府藏京城全圖 [The Qing Imperial Household Agency's complete map of the capital], originally produced 1750, here scanned from the 1940 Kōain Kahoku Renrakubu Seimukyoku Chōsajo reproduction.)

LEGEND TO FIGURE 3.1
(vendor calls are printed in bold)

1. charitable tracts

2. sour plum juice
   jade trinkets

3. feathers
   swords

4. antique wooden curios

5. jade

6. steamed buns
   fans
   jewelry

7. opera libretti
   clay figurines

8. southern paper
   Western-style paintings
   sesame candy
   longzhua **ginger**
   eye medicine
   beggar song performers
   stick fighter
   fortune teller
   physiognomist
   character riddles
   medicine
   noodles
   juggling
   cross-talking
   "dry-boat" performance
   cross-talking
   sword swallowing
   mice performance
   opera performance
   seal performance
   fiddle playing
   peepshow

9. jade
   old books
   old paintings
   smoke paraphernalia
   ducks
   pipes
   rat poison
   jewelry
   wound medicine
   tobacco pouch seller
   dentist
   lotus root
   steel scissors
   embroidery needles
   medical ointment

10. opera libretti
    carved gourds
    old books
    damask fabric
    fish

11. old clothing
    porcelain
    carved wood
    book seller

12. dog market

If the brief, descriptive phrases clearly position the various objects in terms of the floor plan of the temple, they also guide the reader's experience of the text. Each phrase of spatial location such as "when he arrives at the gate" or "when he gets to the Yonghe zhai" is strategically located at the beginning of a new sentence and the beginning of a discrete commodity experience. Placed, like gates, at important junctures in the text, they provide cues that are crucial for an orderly understanding by the listener, clearly signaling that a new experience is about to unfold. Especially in a performance text, a text experienced unilinearly through time that leaves no room for re-orientation by reading back a few lines or jumping ahead a few sections, these phrases crucially orient the reader/listener. In short, by including a protagonist who moves through the temple, the text constructs a clear architectural as well as poetic experience out of discrete moments of commercial exchange and sensory plenitude.

The constant tension between marketplace attractions and the gaze and movement of the protagonist represents more than simply a playful example of having one's cake and eating it too. By consistently contrasting the delights of the market with the disciplined behavior that contains these attractions (or, as is the case in "Strolling through the Huguo Temple," the lack of such discipline), songs such as these help to imagine a broader economic order and prescribe the kind of appreciative but disciplined subject suitable for this order. In a different context and with a focus on visual material, this constant play between distraction and focus has been theorized as the result of nineteenth-century industrialized capitalism and the precondition to modern consumer society.[33] The grounds of the Huguo Temple as depicted by the bannerman Aisinjoro Yigeng are, of course, not the boulevards of Paris as painted by the likes of Seurat. Nor should a comparison between the two be used to argue that late-imperial China possessed the same markers of industrial modernity as the West or was somehow progressing towards such a modernity. Rather, the point is that the seemingly playful attractions of these performance texts had larger implications and that by listening to the sounds of these songs, we can begin to discern the contours of the mechanisms that allowed the construction of a uniquely late-imperial economic subject within a larger imperial socioeconomic order.

33. Crary, *Suspension of Perceptions*, esp. the introduction.

Indeed, it is hard to ignore that a song such as "Strolling through the Huguo Temple" helps to "educate" its reading public in the proper economic behavior within such an order. Most certainly, the song tells readers with great precision where to buy feathers, daggers, and jade (apparently the Maitreya Buddha Hall and the thoroughfare of the Huguo Temple) and with what particular vendor one should do business (Old Man Li and Feather-man Zhang, to name but a few of the people identified).[34] More importantly, a song such as this instructs its readers/listeners to engage with the market while at the same time disciplining their potentially wayward desires. Consumption, the text tells us, might be allowable, but it needs to be done with disciplined movement and focus.

Some texts, for instance the above-quoted Judge Bao drum-song, establish this discipline by providing positive role models, guiding the reader with heroic, always forward-moving men. Other songs, such as "Strolling through the Huguo Temple," conversely do so by presenting the reader/listener with a perfect example of a purposeless, undisciplined consumer and lampooning him. To a degree, such a lack of consumerist savvy is betrayed by the sometimes erratic movements of the protagonist. For instance, though the protagonist enumerates objects "in orderly fashion," he is said to do so while waving his arms "chaotically." Similarly, after he has disgraced himself at the sword seller's booth, the protagonist beats a decidedly unheroic and hasty retreat, "sallying to the back." Most notably, however, the protagonist's failure as a consumer is told through the list of objects he orders when faced by the bevy of jade sellers, each of the items carefully designed to betray an excess of boorish self-aggrandizement and a deficiency of taste. Horse-stepping stones, for instance, were crucial markers of social status in late-imperial Beijing, but the idea that these large objects can be made of "jadeite" is ridiculous.[35] Similarly, one-, two-, and three-eyed

34. In this sense, the lengthy song resembles texts that are more easily categorized as guidebooks, such as Yang Jingting's *Dumen jilue*, which similarly highlights the multifarious, indeed chaotic, pleasures of Beijing's attractions yet also promises its readers, supposedly traveling merchants and visiting scholars, that it will provide order to this maze. For more on Yang Jingting and his guidebook, see Naquin, *Peking*, pp. 465–66.
35. Older texts had long established the horse-stepping stone as a potentially self-aggrandizing sign of prestige. We find, for instance, that Ximen Qing, the

feathers were bestowed by the emperor on fourth-level officials, lower
nobles, and the highest of nobles respectively and hence represented
a clear system of social distinction. By ordering a "six-eyed feather,"
the protagonist betrays his lack of consumer savoir-faire; the object
sounds grandiose, but it simply does not exist.[36] Each of these items,
in short, illustrates an order of prestige that mixes the imperial with
the commercial, betraying a society caught between the emoluments of
officialdom and rank bestowed by the emperor on the one hand, and the
consumerist demands of taste and the keen observation of the connoisseur on the other.[37] The interaction of the protagonist with these items
shows how, within this order, our shopper is fully unaware that true
status is conferred not through unchecked consumption, but through
disciplined and tasteful restraint.

Though "Strolling through the Huguo Temple" spends much
time on appreciating a variety of objects, it crucially extends the tasteful consumption of objects to literary works by including a variety of
performance texts as objects of the protagonist's unbridled interest.[38]

---

boorish merchant of the sixteenth-century novel *Jin ping mei*, has a set of these
stones in front of his compound's gate. Given the importance of horse riding in
Manchu culture, the significance of horse-stepping stones seems even greater in
this song. For a photograph of such a stone, as well as an early-Republican ordi-
nance that bans such stones from public spaces to "facilitate traffic" (but of course
also to eradicate a system of social distinctions belonging to the old order), see Liu
Xiaomeng, *Qingdai Beijing qiren shehui*, pp. 799–801. For an important discussion
of things, objects, and material culture in *Jin Ping Mei*, see Volpp, "The Gift of a
Python Robe."

36. One joke nowadays only funny for scholars of late-imperial literature would
be the last item in the *zidishu* ordered at the Gathering Text Bookshop 聚文書
坊, "The Six Character Primer, first edition, imperial imprint, with commentaries
by Jin Shengtan, fully illustrated" 殿板金批出刻繡像《六言雜字本》. See Helüshi,
"Guang Huguo si," vol. 2, p. 330.

37. The author's own social position reflects this tension between the demands of
consumerist taste on the one hand and officially (and hereditary) bestowed rank
on the other. After all, Helüshi, though famous for his poetry, was also a member
of the imperial Aisinjoro Clan with a commensurate sinecure as imperial guard.
Pamela Crossley notes how Yigeng was a connoisseur of Manchu history, in particular the complex system of Manchu sartorial symbolism and other material forms
of rank. See Crossley, *Orphan Warriors*, pp. 94–95.

38. The text also includes a long list of live performances, the liveliest and loud-
est part of the text. For a list of these performances, see figure 3.1 and its legend,
number 8.

By doing so, the song first of all signals its own status as a commodity traded on Beijing's lively market. More importantly, by presenting the text through the protagonist's eyes and by including his commentary, the song also provides the reader/listener with a clear aesthetic order that allows the perusal and purchase of such potentially vulgar and lively performance texts. The song describes the moment as follows:

> He sees the Tongyue Hall[39] at the Western Stele Pavilion has spread out storytelling and opera libretti,
>   Lately they have added small painting scrolls in the hope of getting rich.
>   Ma the Sixth gets up and hurriedly asks him to sit down,
>   And says, "Please have another look at this new two-chapter story; it is really funny.
>   It's Helüshi's two-chapter "A Fashionable Bloke Strolls through the Huguo Temple."

見同樂堂在西碑亭,下擺著書戲本,
近日他新添小畫想發財.
馬六站起忙讓坐,
說:「再請看,這兩回新書倒詼諧.
這是鶴侶氏的兩回《時道人逛護國寺》」.

After including the author's own pen name, Helüshi, and a fuller (and surely more ironic) version of its own title, "A Fashionable Bloke Strolls through the Huguo Temple," the text then humorously continues to disparage its own value through the words of the protagonist, the fashionable young bloke.

> He says, "Give them to me, I'll take a look," and sitting down receives them.
>   He reads the two chapters, shakes his head emphatically and says, "It's merely words strung into phrases,
>   And the meter is wrong, it's just like *shulaibao*, why bother? "[40]

39. The name of the establishment is a reference to Mencius's famous line about "enjoying music together" where the term 樂 puns as enjoyment (*le*) and music (*yue*). For the original text, see *Mencius* 1B.
40. Unlike *zidishu*, which were regarded as the most elegant of lyrical songs in Beijing, *shulaibao* were a form of popular, fast-paced song associated with beggars. See Li Jiarui, *Beiping suqu lue*, pp. 163–64.

他說:「拿來我看看.」坐下將書接過來.
看了兩篇, 搖頭晃腦說:「成句而已,
未必勾板, 數來保一樣, 這是何苦來? [41]

The protagonist then proceeds to give a brief lecture on the history
and aesthetics of the genre of *zidishu*, consistently drawing a negative
comparison between this recent one by this Helüshi and the true *zidi-shu* masters of old, Songchuang 松窗, Yunchuang 芸窗, and others.[42]

The protagonist may disparage the accomplishments of the song,
deriding it as a vulgar market entertainment not worth bothering with,
but it is precisely by including this critique that the text educates its
reader on how to listen with care for the aesthetics of the performance
text. By mimicking the kind of learned phrases used to critique the song,
it reminds the reader that there are clear aesthetics, indeed cultural prestige, associated with the genre of the *zidishu*. At the same time it enjoins
the reader/listener to pay attention to those aesthetic rules through an
act of careful listening, by moving beyond the surface critique of the
ill-educated protagonist, and hearing how the song puts these aesthetics
in practice. If the protagonist calls the song's lines hardly worth the trouble, the listener discovers that the lines are actually, to quote from the
song itself, "detailed and balanced" 詳而穩, like the "method of phrasing
by Sir Zhuxuan" 竹軒氏句法.[43] Though critiqued as hardly better than
a beggar's song, "Strolling through the Huguo Temple" in fact more
closely resembles the writing of Sir Xiyuan 西園氏, which "adds a bit
of humor to the spirit of the text" 將文意帶詼諧.[44] Indeed, the song is a
perfect example of a text that "allows one to enjoy at the same time the

41. Helüshi, "Guang Huguo si," p. 329.
42. For more on these famous *zidishu* authors, see Cui, *Shuzhai yu shufang zhi jian*, pp. 25–31. Cui also discusses point of view, but her analysis is more encyclo-
pedic and formalist than geared towards uncovering the disciplinary importance
of the act of observation. See also Huang Shizhong, "Chewangfu chaocang zidishu
zuozhe kao," pp. 413–57; and Chiu, "Cultural Hybridity," pp. 58–59, which includes
a partial translation.
43. Helüshi, "Guang Huguo si," p. 329. For more on Sir Zhuxuan, see Huang
Shizhong, "Chewangfu chaocang zidishu zuozhe kao," pp. 444–45.
44. Sir Xiyuan was the penname of Wang Zhihan 王志翰, a *zidishu* author
known for his humorous style. Little is known about his life. See Huang Shizhong,
"Chewangfu chaocang zidishu zuozhe kao," pp. 436–39.

vulgar and the elegant, obeying the rhymes and following the rhythm" 亦須要雅俗共賞, 合轍勾板, which, according to the protagonist, places one among the exalted genealogy of "lords of composition, who can be called masters of old" 編書的國主,可稱元老.[45] The song may locate itself among the many commodities of the marketplace, indeed, it may feature a protagonist who boorishly derides its accomplishments, but through the lengthy self-referential act of critical appraisal, it actually manages to place itself within a higher aesthetic order that can only be found if the reader listens to its text carefully. The song offers a careful, yet lively, enumeration that includes the rules one needs to consume the text as part of a disciplined, aestheticized reading/listening practice.

To sum up, like so many other late nineteenth-century performance songs depicting the multifarious attractions of the market, the song disciplines its reader/listener to partake in the liveliness of the marketplace in an orderly fashion. This order, as I have argued, crucially depends on placing the reader/listener in the position of the protagonist. If the protagonist is heroically moving without being distracted by the marketplace's attractions, the reader/listener can emulate the regimented observation of its protagonist. Alternatively, if the song's protagonist fails to control himself, the reader/listener can differentiate himself from such a lack of self-controlled sophistication. Either way, the song manages to incorporate the variegated attractions within a carefully constructed aesthetic arrangement that emphasizes active and disciplined engagement with the market. At first blush, this engagement may seem purely visual. Yet when it comes to the consumption of the text, such careful discipline inevitably calls upon the reader's ear, his ability to discern the prosodic features of the text that distinguish its carefully constructed acoustic formal order from the chaos of commodities it describes. Finally, such songs feature the lively attractions of the market to advertise their own brand name.[46] It is hard to miss how Helüshi's song, ironically precisely by critiquing its status as a commodity, in fact ends up adding to its own value, both as

45. Ibid.

46. Cui Yunhua argues that the various ways in which *zidishu* authors playfully include their own name represents "a literary game" (*Shuzhai yu shufang zhi jian*, p. 25). I would add that the purpose of this playful game of hiding, yet revealing, one's signature is the same as praising one's own text through the guise of a critique: it disavows self-interest but still manages to promote the author's name.

a commodity and as an object of artistic creation. To investigate further
how popular texts managed to use moments of acoustic appreciation to
increase their value within a competitive market filled with attractions,
I now turn from the issue of consumption to the issue of production,
from the appreciative discipline of the marketplace protagonist to the
artesian mastery of the popular storyteller.

The Artesian Arts of the Performer

The previous section focused on the idea of regimented consumption.
This section moves from the issue of consumption to the topic of production, from a subject position created through the act of observation to
a subject position created through the act of speaking. In particular,
I return exclusively to the idea of sound, specifically the sound of the
vendor call, to argue that by employing vendor calls, popular performance texts call our attention to the masterful way in which the seemingly chaotic atmosphere of the temple fair is the creation of a highly
skilled artisan, the storyteller.

　　To see how vendor calls highlight the verbal artistry of the storyteller, let us briefly turn back to the drum-song *The Cases of Judge Bao*.
Here I would like to emphasize how, as a piece to be performed, the text
does not merely depict variegated liveliness or hint at the possibility of
chaos, but in fact recreates this sense of material plenitude and sensory
confusion in its use of language. Like the *matoudiao* describing the fair
at Xiding that opens this chapter, both prose introduction and poem
are overflowing with the prosodic use of sound. Unlike the *zidishu* with
its lines of variable length, the verse in this kind of drum-song consists
of couplets of seven-character lines preceded by a short three-character line, with the final line of one couplet rhyming with the final line
of the next. In addition, within the lines themselves there are alliterative reduplications (*luanluan honghong* 乱乱烘烘, *nannan nünü* 男男女
女, or *niuniu nienie* 扭扭攝攝), playful chiasmatic juxtapositions (*zuo
mai mai zuo* 作買賣作), and rhythmic repetitions and variations (*mai
cha mai jiu* 賣茶賣酒, *ren shan ren hai* 人山人海), all of which employ
rhythm and rhyme to fill the text with acoustic density.

　　This alliterative throng of people, objects, and words does not
simply provide the song a sense of density, it pushes the reader's sense

of plenitude to the point of distraction and confusion. With its syntactically diffuse lines, its lengthy, often only marginally connected strings of nouns, its lines lacking clear grammatical subjects, its interpenetration of direct and indirect speech, as well as the occasional pun—for instance, [crossdressers] "penetrating through the throng" (*chuanzhe qun* 穿着群) puns with [crossdressers] "wearing skirts" (*chuanche qun* 穿着裙)—the song does not merely depict the confusion of variegated liveliness, but in fact recreates this sensory disorientation in the language it employs. In the poem, in short, words are arranged so as to evoke the seemingly random array of objects. Stacked one on top of another, mingling in profuse density, they dazzle the eyes and the ears with a pleasurable liveliness that borders on the chaotic.

If the song mimics the potentially confusing experience of the marketplace in its very linguistic structure, it is of course through the act of creating (or appreciating) such a seemingly chaotic but in fact highly ordered and complex piece of verbal art that the song returns to a sense of order. Especially in oral performance, it is the act of skillfully vocalizing the attractions of the market and then placing them within the appropriate poetic order that turns an average storyteller into a master of his craft. The dense proliferation and variegation of seemingly similar but crucially different sounds lets the storyteller showcase his verbal dexterity. With their unremitting juxtapositions, repetitions, and alliterations, the lines of the song require one to twist one's tongue. Lines such as *zhu cui shou shi xue xie dian* 珠翠首飾靴鞋店 or *cai quan xing ling shuo xiao sheng* 猜拳行令說笑声 constantly juxtapose palatal sounds with retroflexes, giving the speaker's tongue an acrobatic workout. Similarly, tonal repetitions and juxtapositions, such as "zuo4 mai3 mai4 zuo4" 作買賣作" or "bi4 leng3 bi4 han2" 避冷遮寒 require great precision in flexing one's throat. Stated differently, the rich and variegated acoustic structure of the piece makes for a wonderful tongue twister (*raokou ling* 繞口令 or *jikou ling* 急口令), an open invitation for verbal mix-ups.[47] Yet it is precisely this possibility of verbal confusion that allows the oral performer to display his technical accomplishment.

---

47. For a good example of a tongue twister used in an early novel, see chap. 60 of *Jin Ping Mei*, where the character Ying Bojue performs a *jikouling* amid the lively merriment of drinking games at a party. See Lanling xiaoxiaosheng, *Meng Mei Guan jiaoben Jin Ping Mei*, vol. 2, chap. 60, p. 942.

Within this seemingly chaotic but in fact highly ordered sequence
of verbal acrobatics, the vendor calls play a particularly important
role. On the one hand, these snippets suggest the direct importation
of the market's loud attractions into the song. As such they add to the
market's sense of variegation, shifting linguistic register from indirect
to direct speech, moving from descriptive prose to theatrically enacted
words, thus adding to the color of the piece and symbolizing the various
distractions and enticements one would encounter at a fair. On the other
hand, the inclusion of vendor calls provides a stage for the performer to
showcase his art. For one, the performer is given the opportunity to
mimic the different voices of the people who loudly hawk the different
wares, from the peasant women who sell old clothes to the men vending
felt hats. As is the case with the dialect mimicry I discuss in chapter 5,
this constant shifting of personae enacted through the storyteller's voice
was one significant way in which storytellers distinguished themselves
in their craft, "mimicry" representing one of the crucial components of
the storyteller's art.[48]

To this I should add that in the context of a poetic song, the storyteller not only has to act out these different voices—he has to fit these
lively acoustic snippets into the prosodic and melodic rules of the song in
question. The tonal juxtapositions found in the song quoted above would
have been difficult to produce even when read aloud, but to perform
those sounds in the context of a song was even more challenging. The
first lines from a popular bannerman song (*chaqu* 岔曲) titled *Having
a Laugh* remind us of the importance of performing tones correctly:
"Really exciting is the big drum's [sound], / the diction is precise, the
singing smooth" 大鼓真帶勁, 字正腔圓.[49] Though presented as mere
entertainment (the song's title is, after all, "making someone laugh"
in Beijing colloquial language),[50] the performer's adage, "the diction is
precise, the singing smooth," illustrates the serious complexity of juxtaposing tones in performance. Not only does the phrase emphasize that
one is not allowed to mispronounce words 倒字 or mangle the melody

48. See Wang, Wang, and Zeng, *Zhongguo yishu pingshu lun*, p. 83.
49. "Dou gen" 逗哏 (Having a laugh), p. 37.
50. As the *Dictionary of Beijing Dialect* explains, the term refers to telling a joke or
performing slapstick and can be used to describe specifically the oral performance
art of cross-talking (*xiangsheng* 相生). See Xu Shirong, *Beijing tuyu cidian*, p. 113.
For more on the art of cross-talking, see chap. 5.

飄音, it also prescribes the complex relationship between the tone of the word and the pitch of the melody, where the "'melody should be based on the words,' not 'the words on the melody'" 因字而設腔, 不能因腔而填字.[51] In the case of performing vendor calls within the context of the drum-song, obeying the complex rules of performance becomes even more challenging. Like a collage, the fragments of sound have to be presented as supposedly gathered snippets of popular speech. And yet these fragments nevertheless have to fit seamlessly within the artful creation of the song as a whole.

If the tension between distracting sound and masterfully performed song already exists in these brief snippets of vendor calls, such a tension becomes particularly tangible when the vendor call is elongated, becoming a single lengthy performance piece. After all, by sustaining a vendor call over an extended number of lines and taking on the persona of a vendor, the storyteller draws attention to the fact that what is being sold at that moment is not just any other object at a temple fair, but in fact the linguistic performance itself. Take, for instance, an example from the drum-song referenced earlier, *The Cases of Judge Bao*. The scene occurs when a young examination candidate, Fan Zhongyu, first comes to the capital and takes in its magnificent sights as he moves from the outskirts into the city; soon he is waylaid by a young inn-boy with an enticing sales pitch:

After walking for two or three days, he [Fan] reached the walls of Bianliang and saw how the landscape was not the same as other places but extremely lively (*renao*):

走了兩三天的工夫, 就到了汴梁城外. 只見風景不同, 十分热闹:

Fan Zhongyu
Came close to the city wall of Bianliang,
And taking note opened wide his eyes and saw clearly.
He saw
The defense towers rising up, piercing the sky,
Propitious clouds draped like dragons over a cosmos like brocade.
Next to the hanging bridge
Covering the moat by the wall were gold-threaded willows,
It was the time of mid-winter so they had not opened yet.
On the bridge

51. Jin and Zhang, *Beijing qiren yishu*, pp. 9–10.

The jade and stone balustrade was carved with running animals,
And unicorns sleeping on the top of Mount Kunlun.
The soldiers guarding the city wall
Are each and every one fierce as tigers,
The entire city is full of prosperous people doing business.
Fan Zhongyu
After leisurely observing the scenery outside the Eastern Capital's walls,
Entered the city of Bianliang itself.
There he saw
Every kind of trade in small little alleys,
The shops, all shiny and bright, lining the boulevard.
And he heard
Stringed instruments sounding in the pleasure quarters,
And the sound of singing coming from the brothels and sing-song houses.
In addition he saw
People from all walks of life, the smoke from cooking fires thick.
Scholars, farmers, artisans, and merchants going back and forth.
Truly it was
A splendid place under heaven that is blessed with wealth,
A splendid imperial capital right here on Earth.
Fan Zhongyu
While still appreciating the scenery walked forward,
But a lad from an inn came up and blocked his way.
He said:
"The rooms in our inn are very spacious,
Inside they've been swept clean as clean can be.
If you want
Sumptuous dishes, vegetarian or meat, we have them all,
Fine wine from Jinhua and 'Top Candidate' wine.
And we have as well
Fresh and dried fruit all nicely peeled,
Fried or cooked, steamed or boiled, each and every one delightful.
Our
Innkeeper treats people so well.
Welcoming you when you come and seeing you off when you go.
At this place of ours
The prices are fair, no unexpected charges.
As long as what you give is close, we will not haggle.
Dear Sir,
If you do stay at our 'Rising Prosperity' Inn,
You'll be the one to take first place in the examinations."
Fan Zhongyu,
Tongue tied, could not help but be pleased at heart.

He
Parted his teeth, started to speak, and said some words.

范仲羽 来近汴梁城一坐,留神闪目为分明.
只見那 敵楼高聳沖霄汗 (sic), 祥云尨罩錦乾坤.
吊橋傍 滿城河边金線柳. 時值隆冬尚未清.
橋上边 玉石欄杆凋走獸. 崑崙頂上臥其(sic)犐(sic).
守城的 軍兵个个如猛虎. 滿城经商龍秀民.
范仲羽 懶观東京城外景, 近(sic)了汴梁一坐城.
但只見 各行生义在小巷 臨街甫(sic)甚鮮明.
只听得 柳巷花街絲線响. 楚館秦楼歌唱声.
又見那 三教九流人烟廣. 士農工商來往行.
真乃是 天下繁華有福地. 人间錦繡帝王京.
范仲羽 正然观景往前走,店小兒前來把路横.
說道是: "我家店房甚寬廠, 裡边打掃甚干淨.
若要用 葷素餚饌全都有, 金華美酒狀元紅.
还有那 干鮮果品都皮修, 煎炒烹炸件件精.
我家的 店家待人多和氣, 來足接風去送行.
我这里 店價公平无期外, 或多或少不掙競.
相公你 若要住此興隆店, 獨占鰲頭第一名."
范仲羽闇然不由心內喜. 相公他
啟齒開言把话云 ... [52]

Here the inn-boy's lengthy sales pitch beautifully captures the commercial lures of the city, capturing its many sights and sounds but also cutting short the hero's leisured appreciation of such sights. More specifically, the lengthy sung passage is best understood as a gradual, three-part movement from a tasteful and distanced appreciation of splendor, to a more detailed observation of *renao*, until finally ending with an enticing sales pitch. Thus, as the hero comes close to the city, he first appreciates the various sights, as the poem states, in "leisurely fashion" 懶观. The prose introduction describes the scene as *renao*, but a better term is actually suggested later under the notion of *fanhua* 繁華, a sense of architectural splendor that bespeaks prosperity befitting the capital and is here neatly given form through cloud-piercing towers and mythical metaphors of sleeping unicorns.[53] Next, as the hero enters the city's walls, the observational intensity and the many different

52. *Bao gongan guci*, roll 32, pp. 916–17.
53. For more on the term *fanhua*, see Meng Yue, *Shanghai and the Edges of Empire*, esp. chap. 3.

impressions grow denser as, slowly, the song moves from splendor to liveliness. At this point, the poem highlights a more dazzling mix of people, sounds, and sights, and increasingly features acts of observation. Finally, even this moment of observing liveliness is cut short as our hero is accosted by the animated patter of an inn-boy. The act of tasteful appreciation 观景 is disrupted right in the middle 正然; the hero's progress 往前走 is waylaid 把路横. Indeed, Fan Zhongyu is not mentioned again until some good twenty lines later, when it is remarked that he is speechless, rooted to the ground, unable to move further. In short, unlike the previous temple fair song where the brief snippets of vendor calls were easily contained within an overall structure of disciplined observation and physical progress, here the song fully emphasizes the disruptive attraction of the city's acoustic enticements.

This sense of disruption is further marked by a shift in subject position, a shift from the observing hero Fan Zhongyu to the speaking inn-boy, something that alerts us that the song's true interest no longer lies in the act of observation, but instead in the act of speech. In the first two-thirds of the song, as in the previously quoted song of the temple fair, the brief three-character phrases orienting the reader emphasize the observing subject, in this case Fan Zhongyu, who observes the various sounds, sights, and objects presented to him as external representations. In contrast, the final third of the song shifts the three-beat sentence openings to the inn-boy and his words: "our inn here," "we also have," and "then he said." The lines do not only suggest the inn-boy as the speaking subject, they similarly highlight the verbal performance, suggesting that what is represented is not an external reality observed, but a host of different delicacies presented orally though the words of the inn-boy. What the reader/listener appreciates is not the idea of various dishes "fried, cooked, steamed, and boiled," but rather the way in which the young boy manages to pack his sentences tight with these different delicacies, his words "each and every one delightful."

Moreover, while in the case of the observing protagonist the subject position is shared by the reader/listener, in the case of the speaking protagonist the subject position is shared with the storyteller. As a result, the lengthy vendor call represents a double-edged sword. On the one hand, the attention paid to the seductive and disruptive powers of language can be said to reflect negatively on the commercial art of the storyteller himself. After all, if the inn-boy's eloquent vendor call represents a way of selling the manifold luxurious features of the inn, for the storyteller it becomes a way of selling his own manifold abilities as a storyteller. If, for instance, we imagine the song as performed at the marketplace, the song functions as an invitation to stay and listen some more. Indeed, even though in the written text the song does not fall at the end of a section, the direct invitation to the listener is very much phrased like a cliff-hanger.[54] We can only imagine what the stunned Fan Zhongyu would say after the verbal assault of the inn-boy/storyteller. As a result, the storyteller would be in a perfect place to ask his audience for a few cash so they can find out what Fan Zhongyu (or the storyteller himself) was going to say next.

On the other hand, even though the song functions like a vendor call in that it captures the attention of a crowd and seduces it with its spectacular nature, the vendor call still allows the storyteller to differentiate himself from the other vulgar and commercial sounds of the marketplace. Most notably this is done by staging the commercial attractions of the market as an aesthetic object, by turning what is an invitation to purchase into an invitation to appreciate. Whereas within the diegetic frame of the song, the inn-boy's call represents an invitation to rent a room, in the storyteller's masterful performance of the song, this becomes an invitation to appreciate the delightful way in which the performer constructs an edifice of carefully arranged words. Indeed, in the articulated aesthetics of storytelling, there exists a rich host of phrases that emphasize the kind of verbal dexterity we see on display in the lengthy vendor call just quoted. In her work on twentieth-century Yangzhou storytellers, for instance, Vibeke Børdahl offers

54. Disrupting a character in the middle of his speech or, alternatively, ending an episode right as a character is about to answer was a standard way of creating a cliff-hanger in drum-songs in print up until at least the 1920s. See, for instance, the drum-song "Lincheng da jie'an" 臨城大劫案 (The great Lincheng [train] robbery), which ends one of its chapters, "Guo Qicai got up from the banquet table and hurriedly replied . . . . If you want to know what Master Guo said, in the next chapter we will delineate in detail what was here first sown." Quoted in Li et al., *Zhongguo guci zongmu*, pp. 7–8. As this example makes clear, even in printed text interrupted speech was still used for the commercial purpose of bringing the reader back for more. Vernacular fiction often employs a similar use of interrupted speech to create a cliff-hanger.

a variety of terms that emphasize the ability to pile up lengthy strings of words in an orderly fashion and at breakneck speed. For instance, Børdahl offers the term *pokou* 潑口, which she defines as "accelerating speed and special breathing . . . used for emphasis, for example in linked passages where the last words of one sentence are repeated at the beginning of the following sentence." In a similar manner, Børdahl defines *duikou* 對口 as "telling a long passage of several sentences all in one breath, accelerating the pace, but keeping every syllable distinct." In turn, both of these fall under the general storyteller maxim "[speaking] fast but not confused" 快而不亂.[55] The point here is not simply that storytellers recognized the orderly presentation of potentially difficult passages as part of their craft but rather that, through this articulation of the rules of the craft, distinction could be bestowed on performer and listener alike. As Børdahl writes, emphasizing the importance of disciplined sensory appreciation, "Customers who sit near the stage, however, often listen with closed eyes, paying little attention to the mimicry and gesticulation of the storyteller. They are insiders of the profession and so they truly 'listen to storytelling' (*tingshu*)." Similarly, she argues that master storytellers should be referred to with the honorific title of "master" 先生, something which differentiates their art from more "humble professions."[56]

In short, the vendor calls performed in popular drum-songs should be understood as a device that highlights not just the dangers of the market, but the dangers of market language. Vendor calls draw the reader's attention to the storyteller's own use of the lure of language, but at the same time they also foreground language as a disciplined, artesian craft. These calls not only managed to sell an audience a simulacrum of the acoustic liveliness of the market, but they disciplined such liveliness by turning a self-conscious aesthetic gaze to their own artesian practice. As I will explain further in the next section, the vendor call also

55. See Børdahl and Ross, *Chinese Storytellers*, p. 94. The dictum is part of a two-line phrase, but the second half, "slow but not disjointed" 慢而不散, is less applicable to this particular situation.
56. Børdahl and Ross, *Chinese Storytellers*, pp. 58 and 59 respectively. As Natasha Korda points out in "Gender at Work," in English early-modern theatrical performance the vendor call plays an increasingly important role in differentiating the well-crafted words of the ever-more professional actor from the disorderly and clumsily performed words of vendors outside the theater.

transcends the marketplace by including a moral lesson, redirecting the manifold attractions within the unilinear framework of punishing transgressive desire. Though this feature is found in the drum-songs, it becomes particularly important in novels that have little use for the performative aesthetics of the storyteller song and instead employ the more cost-effective printing of an exciting plotline.

Emplotting Marketplace Desires

The attractions the vendor call evoked should not solely be thought of in terms of a singular desire for many different objects, all located in the marketplace. Rather, in literature the attraction of the vendor call was found in the way it gave voice to the diversification of desire itself, coupling commodity desire to various other desires, ranging from the physical desire of sex to the more abstract lure of literary delight, from the bodily craving for food to the immaterial wish for social advancement. One of the lures of nineteenth-century martial arts tales lay in the way they employed the vendor call to stage these desires only to subsequently contain them, doing so specifically by drawing the reader into an exciting plot which inevitably ends with the punishing of wayward behavior.

There are many examples of the way late-imperial vernacular literature employs the vendor call to evoke a plethora of different desires.[57] Here, let me choose a vendor call associated with the seller of sundry articles to demonstrate how different media, ranging from printed illustrations to four-line poems, make use of this particular call to link material and sexual desire.

57. Stephen West has offered a variety of such narratives from literary sources of the Song through Ming dynasties, most notably a telling example from the *zaju* opera *Cheng fengliu Wang Huan Baihuating* 逞風流王煥百花亭 (Wang Huan shows off his brilliance at the Baihua Pavilion). In this opera, a young man contacts a courtesan by skillfully performing a vendor call outside her window. As the example shows, the economic seduction here is turned into sexual seduction, while sexual penetration is staged as spatial crossing of boundaries. At the same time, the song itself is so lusciously scripted that it cannot help but seduce the reader/listener. See West, "Playing with Food."

Figure 3.2 nicely combines economic with sexual desires to portray the seduction of the vendor call as a complex visual game. Drawn by Zhou Quan 周權 (courtesy name Muqiao 慕橋; 1868–1922), one of the illustrators of the famous late nineteenth-century pictorial *Dianshizhai huabao* 點石齋畫報, the illustration presents the viewer with an exchange of gazes that stage nested, visual narratives of sexual, economic, and narrative seduction. To begin with, the product sold by the itinerant peddler consists of an assortment of cosmetic articles whose sole function, or so men would like to believe, is to make women more attractive in the eyes of men. In the illustration, the tables in the game of seduction have naturally been turned: it is not the makeup being worn by a woman that seduces a man; instead it is the assortment of products with their promise of beauty that seduces a woman. And, finally, the whole unwholesome narrative sold in the picture itself seduces the viewer, whose eyes, guided by the unseen gaze of the male peddler, are drawn into the frame of the illustration and the woman's window to uncover an affair that reaffirms a moral order based on an equation of economic seduction, sexual transgression, spatial crossing of boundaries, and, of course, female culpability.

In many ways the illustration is a harbinger of the visual emphasis typical of the commodity culture of the twentieth century, employing an exchange of gazes to frame its narratives of desire even while hiding the construction of these narratives (and their producer) behind the veil of realism.[58] Yet it should be noted that even in this early twentieth-century illustration the complex labor of seduction is also conceptualized through sound, the by now well-familiar acoustic cue of the vendor. Indeed, the illustration combines sexual and economic lures on the

58. The artist, Zhou Quan, was one of the most famous illustrators of calendar girl advertisements 月份派, colorful posters of alluring beauties whose early twentieth-century visual narratives helped establish the economic order of commodities such as cigarettes, toiletries, and pharmaceuticals as part of everyday life. For a biography of Zhou Quan and a short narrative of his work, see Laing, *Selling Happiness*, pp. 95–113. Even though the text in the illustration alerts the viewer to the hand of the author (Zhou Quan, *zi* Muqiao, of Ancient Wu), the illustration itself does not call attention to the act of composition. For a good contrast, compare this illustration of a peddler with the various Song-dynasty illustrations of peddlers by famous artists such as Li Song 李嵩 (ca. 1130–1230), paintings in which intricacy plays a crucial role in emphasizing the mastery of the painter.

3.2 Zhou Muqiao, *The Lady Caller*. (In Zhou Muqiao, *Da ya lou hua bao*, juan 4, page 50. Reprinted in 1923 by Bi wu shan zhuang, Shanghai. Photo courtesy of the Harvard-Yenching Library.)

basis of an instrument whose name suggestively combines erotic and material desires, "The Lady Caller" 唤娇娘. The text accompanying the illustration explains:

> The "hoop chest" is also called "The Lady Caller." In his chest he packs things like makeup, hair ribbons, silk thread, or soap. In his hand he holds a small brass drum with two ears on the side. Holding the handle, he shakes it, and when women hear this, they vie to come out and buy his wares. This is how it got to have such a beautiful name. The chest, however, should be carried on one's back, which is why it is called a hoop chest. Nowadays in Shanghai there are those who have switched this for a carrying pole, and hence it has lost its original meaning. Produced in jest by Zhou Quan, *zi* Muqiao, of Ancient Wu.

環箱子一名喚嬌娘,箱中儲花粉, 頭繩,絲線, 肥皂之屬, 手握小銅鉦,兩旁
有耳,持其柄而搖之, 婦女聞之, 爭出購取, 故得此美名. 然其箱必環於背,
故曰環箱子. 今滬上有易之以擔者, 則已失其本旨矣. 古吳慕喬周權戲作.[59]

Though merely a detail in the illustration, Zhou Muqiao's text
offers fuller reference to the acoustic play at the heart of the sexual and
economic exchange being described therein. Though in the text the
term "The Lady Caller" 喚嬌娘 is used to refer to the chest the vendor
uses to carry around his wares, clearly it is the sound of this drum that
alerts the young woman inside to the presence of the makeup seller
outside. It is this distinctive call of the drum that demands a response,
prompting the lady in question to open her window and "vie to go out
and buy his wares."

The power of the vendor's sound lies precisely in the fact that it can
layer different desires like a palimpsest, the vendor call becoming an
overdetermined sign of economic as well as sexual attraction, of spatial
transgression and aesthetic pleasure. Take, for instance, a mid-nineteenth-century poem by Shi Qu 石渠 (zi Meisun 枚孫; 1803–ca. 1873), a
little-known literatus from the town of Suzhou, that explores the same
topic as the illustration by Zhou Quan, namely the "Lady Caller" drum:

喚嬌娘
The Lady Caller

綠窗檢點女兒箱,	By her boudoir window she is picking through her maiden's chest:
採線斷絨針斷芒.	Colorful strings, their thread unraveled, needles with a broken point.
繡罷鴛鴦方卻坐,	Just as she has finished embroidering a pair of ducks and is sitting silently,
慢聲遠遠喚嬌娘.	When from far, far away comes the distinct sound: The Lady Caller."[60]

59. Reproduced in Wang Jiaju, *Sanbai liushi hang*, vol. 1, p. 234.
60. Shi Qu, *Kuiqingju shilu*, pp. 58–59. The poem is one of six devoted to vendor
calls, each employing the instrument of the vendor as title and each closing with
a repetition of those words. Moreover, each name is suggestive of different themes
of desire and seduction. For instance, the small gong used by the candy seller is
called "Yin haier" 引孩兒 (Enticing the children), while the wooden castanets of
the snack vendor are known as "Cui ji" 催飢 (Urging hunger).

As in Zhou Quan's illustration, Shi Qu's poem elicits desire by inscribing it on the female subject in her boudoir. Yet whereas in Zhou Quan's illustration all agency is ascribed to the vendor's call, here that call, though creating an opening for the expression of desire, is merely an answer to the pent-up longing of the girl. After all, even if the subject matter and the title of the poem focus on the vendor's call, the narrative still begins with the image of the young girl's boudoir window, an image that neatly illustrates a state of unfulfilled female desire. Similarly, like Zhou Quan's image, Shi Qu's poem suggests a complex interaction of productive and consuming economic energies. Whereas Zhou Quan's illustration depicts cosmetics (something consumed passively), the needles and thread in Shi Qu's poem signify sanctified female labor, the productive work of chaste embroidery. Indeed, from a moral point of view, the desire that underscores the entire poem is strikingly ambiguous, presenting the reader with an image of what might be fruitfully called promiscuous chastity. On the one hand, the girl embroidering the mandarin ducks has clearly bought into the exclusive politics of monogamy, having promised herself to a single mate for the rest of her life. On the other hand, since the role of the husband is not yet fulfilled, the mandarin ducks are also a way of advertising an open-ended form of yearning since, at this point, *any* man can still be that man.

In short, in Shi Qu's poem the vendor call opens up a whole range of ambiguous desires. It is not surprising that the poem, though ending definitively with the exclamatory three-character 喚嬌娘, leaves the narrative conclusion open. Perhaps the vendor will only supply the young girl with needle and thread so she can return to the confines of her boudoir, dreaming her solitary spring dreams while patiently continuing her embroidery. Alternatively, the vendor (or more likely, the male protagonist disguised as a vendor) himself might enter the girl's boudoir and become the man she has been waiting for. Either way, the vendor's long, drawn-out sound presents, but still keeps at bay, the promise of a connection that will complete the unfulfilled desire symbolized by the broken needles and frazzled threads first found in the young girl's maiden chest. The song, like the maiden's heart, may be tightly scripted in its acoustic form, but its ending has yet to be determined, the vendor call promiscuously conjuring a whole range of multifarious, previously hidden desires—male and female, private and public, economically productive and consuming.

In contrast to the suggestive, open-ended nature of the vendor call in the "Lady Caller" and in the illustration by Zhou Quan, in the tightly scripted martial arts tales that are the subject of this study, what makes the vendor call attractive is the way it can regiment these desires through the workings of plot. To understand this disciplinary effect of the plot, let us turn to an example from a performance text entitled *The Cases of the Dragon Diadem*, the handwritten set of libretti associated with the storyteller Shi Yukun and the basis for the later novel *The Three Knights and the Five Gallants*. The scene revolves around a mysterious murder that puzzles the imperial official Judge Bao, who decides to use the case as a way of testing someone who has been newly recommended to him, the learned Gongsun Ce. Faced with the difficult challenge of solving the case, Gongsun Ce decides to go undercover and disguises himself as a medicine peddler. At first, Gongsun Ce is unable to find any information on the streets, but then he decides to use a vendor call. In the handwritten libretto, the moment is described as follows:

[Gongsun Ce] thought to himself, "Yesterday I labored all for nothing, but now I have figured out a plan. Instead of not saying a word [like yesterday], let me call out publicly. Who knows but that it might produce a clue."

心中暗想，"昨日空勞而今到想出個主意來，且不要一語不發，待我公喝公喝，萬一有些來歷也未可見得.

思想已畢,	After figuring this out,
他將那串鈴搖動,	He started shaking his medicine bell,
前行已至七里村中.	And before he knew it had reached Seven Mile Village.
見有人家他便說話.	Whenever he would meet someone, he would do his spiel,
雖無腔調卻可聽.	Even though there was no melody, it was still pleasant to hear.
嘩楞楞響,	*HUALENGLENG* goes the sound
是串鈴.	Made by the bell.
好喉嚨,	In a fine voice
說: 學術靜.	He said, "Truly learned that I am.
專能治,	I am a specialist in
疑難病.	Difficult diseases that are hard to treat.
管保能,	I guarantee that I can
應手活人見效見功.	Immediately bring results.

爆發眼,	Swollen eyes,
把火清.	I'll clear up the infection.
還能止,	I can also stop
風火牙痛.	Painful toothache.
那怕那,	No need to fear
偏正頭風.	Any kind of headache.
理內外,	I take care of inside and out,
五臟六腑調味和榮.	The five organs and six receptacles I'll put in line.
要扎針,	If you need acupuncture,
我也能.	I can do that too.
有膏藥,	I've got potions,
真正靈.	Truly effective.
治癬疾,	I cure scabies
四六風.	And newborn inflictions.
更能治,	I can also cure
多年庤漏化管無雙	Persistent hemorrhoids, without
還能夠不癢不疼.	itching or any pain.
會決疑,	I can resolve doubts
又禳星.	And exorcise misfortune.
講周易,	I am versed in the *Book of Changes*
論子平.	And Xu Ziping's [school of fortunetelling].
觀風水,	I can form geomantic configurations,
敗與興.	Tell what will fail and what will prosper.
還會那,	And I can, as well,
陰宅陽宅點穴尋龍.	Find just the right spots for dwellings for both the quick and the dead."
此頓間,	Right at that moment,
先生言語猶未畢,	Though he had not yet finished speaking,
早聞得,	He already heard
有人開門喚的分明.	That there was someone who had opened her door and was calling to him clearly.[61]

Like the illustration and poems devoted to the Lady Caller, the song from the storyteller libretto evokes a variety of desires. In terms of content, the song promises long life, health, and prosperity. At the same time, and perhaps more subtly, it voices Gongsun Ce's own desire. He hopes that the song will allow him to find the clues he needs to solve the case, impress Judge Bao, and thereby gain steady employment. In

61. "Qi li cun," vol. 405, pp. 135–37.

addition, the song serves to seduce the reader/listener with the literary delight of its fanciful rhymes and its humorous and hyperbolic claims. Like the other songs we have read throughout this chapter, the song piles one brief line on top of another, which, when performed with a lively and increasingly rapid beat, wonderfully and humorously showcases the talents of the performer.[62] Finally, and most notably, the final lines show us yet another powerful desire, that is, the reader's own desire to know what happens next. Who is the person who calls to the disguised Gongsun Ce, and what will this undercover agent learn after he speaks to her?

It is this desire to know what happens next that illustrates how the plot can rein in the various desires elicited by the vendor call, both in a spatial sense and in a narrative sense. Spatially, the vendor call marks a sense of spatial progression, opening up and connecting places that previously lay outside the supposed boundaries of imperial power/knowledge. First, the vendor call is part of the disguise that helps Gongsun Ce hide his identity as an assistant to an imperial official, thus allowing him to enter the popular space of the street incognito. Then, after crossing the boundary between the official space of the *yamen* and the popular space of the streets, Gongsun Ce uses the vendor call to gain access to a third space, the inner chambers of a woman's residence. Spatially, then, the vendor call creates a sense of exchange, a crossing between inner and outer spaces, and a mimicry that allows a loss of distinction between official and unofficial, popular and elevated modes of language, an expansion of invisible imperial power into the realm of everyday life and the inner chambers of women.

---

62. Though the actual music of Shi Yukun's performances is lost, it is possible to garner some clues from the related genre of Beijing drum-singing 京韻大鼓. In this particular case, the most notable feature of the song is the extended use of three-character lines, or "hats" 帽子. As Kate Stevens points out, in drum-singing such three-character lines can be piled up 垛句 when performed to a particularly fast rhythm 快版, whose tempo moreover accelerates throughout the performance. Stevens notes that these phrases, by being set to a separate tune, delay the musical progression of the piece. The result, I would argue, is a playful contrast between an increasingly rapid beat and a delay of actual musical progress. This contrast mirrors the way in which the song's narrative content is filled with illustrative detail but withholds the unfolding of the plot. Stevens, "Peking Drumsinging," pp. 118 and 152.

The storyteller tale maps this spatial progression associated with the use of the vendor call onto narrative progression, carefully constructing a plot that leads backwards to the crime at the same time as it inexorably leads forward to the eventual meting out of justice. By using a vendor call, Gongsun Ce does not merely trick the woman into allowing him into her rooms, he also seduces her into revealing her secrets. Through her confession we find out that her husband has been involved in a case of adultery, bribery, and murder. With this knowledge in hand, Gongsun Ce returns to Judge Bao, who in turn immediately punishes the wicked, re-establishing imperial order, economic propriety, and sexual morality. The vendor call in this tale activates a vengeful narrative of righting wrongs by inverting the call's usual seductive power. If, as we have seen above, the sound of "Calling the Maiden" is the acoustic cue that triggers economic desires and links those desires to sexual attractions, setting into motion a series of spatially transgressive acts, in the Judge Bao adventure it is precisely the vendor call that allows the punishing of such desires.[63] The storyteller tale absorbs the excitement created by the vendor call into the unfolding of plot, seducing the reader in two ways: first, as part of an exciting murder mystery, the vendor call is one of the mechanisms that delays but also facilitates the gradual unveiling of the culprit. Second, as part of a larger moral narrative, the spectacle of the vendor call illustrates how imperial power and universal morality extend into spaces that often seem out of reach for the official secluded in his *yamen*.

63. In nineteenth-century martial arts fiction, the use of a vendor call as a disguise to uncover crimes is a bit of a cliché. To name but a few examples: in *The Cases of Judge Liu Drum song*, for instance, Judge Liu himself ventures out, once as a prognosticator (part III, chap. 3, and part IV, chap. 1) and once as an itinerant doctor (part VI, chap. 1); in *The Cases of Judge Peng*, Judge Peng disguises himself as a physiognomist in chapter 3 and as a seller of candy in chapter 84. In *The Three Knights and the Five Gallants* the vendor call ploy is used three times. In addition to the story of Gongsun Ce, there is the story of Zhao Hu, who, inspired by Gongsun Ce's previous success, disguises himself as a beggar and makes a horrible mess of his peddler song (chap. 10). Finally, there is the sequence where Long Tao disguises himself as a hot-bun peddler at a temple fair (chap. 65).

Conclusion

> [The storyteller's] instinctive grasp of alliterations and asso-
> nances is sharpened. One word begins to suggest another by its
> very sound; one phrase suggests another not only by reason of
> idea or by a special ordering of ideas, but also by acoustic value.
> —Albert B. Lord, *The Singer of Tales*[64]

In this chapter, I have argued that in a range of performance texts, including popular songs such as "The Grand Dame Truly Tours Xiding," drum-songs such as *The Cases of Judge Bao*, and storyteller tales such as *The Cases of the Dragon Diadem*, the vendor call is used both to evoke and to discipline the attractions of the marketplace. Yet what happens when we turn from texts closely connected to oral performance to a form of literature that seems, by definition, to be silent, the novel? There is no single answer to this question. Here, I merely want to sketch one possible answer through a brief comparison of *The Cases of the Dragon Diadem* storyteller libretto and the novel based on it, *The Three Knights and the Five Gallants*. The printed novel from 1879 describes the moment Gongsun Ce goes undercover as a medicine peddler as follows:

As it turns out, Gongsun Ce had only been paying attention to his thoughts and had forgotten to shake his bell. Now that he remembered, he hurriedly started shaking his bell while saying,

原來公孫策只顧思索, 忘了搖串鈴了. 這時想起, 連忙將鈴兒搖起, 口中說
道:

有病早來治, 莫要多延遲.	"If you're ill come quickly to be cured, Do not tarry too long.
養病如養虎, 虎大傷人的.	Nursing an ailment is like nursing a tiger, Once the tiger is full grown, it will bite you.
凡有疑難大症,	Whatever puzzling or difficult-to-cure disease you might have,
管保手到病除.	I guarantee that as soon as I set to work it will disappear.
貧不計利.	Poor people can pay later without interest."

As he was chanting, it so happened that an old woman called him over, saying "Doctor, Doctor, come over here." . . . The old woman led him into

---

64. Lord, *The Singer of Tales*, p. 33.

her thatched door, lifted the curtain of woven reed stalks, and asked the doctor to enter.

正在念詠, 可巧那一邊一個老婆子喚道, "先生, 這裡來, 這裡來." . . . 那婆子引進柴扉, 掀起了蔑子柑的帘子, 將先生請進.[65]

Little is left of the lengthy and lively call we first saw in the story-teller libretto. Not only is that call several times as long, but it is also much more vulgar, variegated, rhythmic, and livelier than its printed counterpart. The acoustic attraction of the performance text, in short, has been seriously diminished.

We can think of various reasons, ranging from the aesthetic to the economic, why the publisher chose to truncate the vendor call. For one, novels use song much more sparingly than their drum-song counter-parts. Indeed, as we have seen in chapter 1, as late-Ming editors and commentators such as Jin Shengtan began making fiction suitable for elite consumption, one of the first things they did was elide much of the previous poetry and parallel prose that was considered "too vulgar." The elision of lengthy vendor calls from the storyteller's libretto follows this pattern. Usually taking the form of song, the poetic rules and lively rhythms of the lyrics make them eminently suitable as performance pieces, a way for the storyteller to establish himself as a masterful oral artisan. The novel, however, possessing little patience for such oral poetics, inevitably omits these traces of marketplace liveliness from its pages. As a perfomer, the storyteller Shi Yukun had been famous for his singularly strong voice and the way he shaped his beautifully rhymed passages, so much so that the storyteller libretti carrying his name advertised themselves on the basis of "including the original Shi Yukun encomia." In the novel, as well as in its prose predecessor, *The Aural Record of the Dragon Diadem*, all of these poetic passages have been cut.

Another reason may be purely economic. As pointed out above, storytellers employed these lengthy vendor calls for good economic reasons. The lively and tongue-twisting poetics of these pieces allowed storytellers to showcase their skill at manipulating sound and language, and undoubtedly helped them attract an audience, while at the same time transforming the business of telling stories into the art of a master-ful oral craftsman. To this long list of profitable reasons for storytellers

65. *San xia wu yi* (1996), vol. 1, chap. 8, p. 55.

to perform vendor calls we should add another: as a series of only loosely
connected objects and impressions, the vendor call can be lengthened or
shortened at will. As long as the performer brings the call to an appropriate end, he can decide to sing as long as he feels is necessary for the
particular occasion. Going the rounds with his hat, a storyteller could
easily add a few more commodities to his list of marketplace attractions
or a few more diseases to the list of things to be cured if he needed more
time, just as he could shorten the list if he wanted to wrap up his performance or move back to the main storyline. In terms of production, this
kind of expandable or contractable list-song works perfectly within the
mode of production described by Albert B. Lord and Milman Parry
in their analysis of the improvisational skills of the singer of tales. By
combining a set of rhythmic and rhymed formulas, the storyteller could
undoubtedly make up a marketplace song on the spot, employing the
aesthetics of the song as a convenient device for ordering the list into an
extremely flexible piece of lucrative art.[66]

In contrast, printers would have had much less economic incentive
to produce these songs. In written form they may still be lively, but they
are hardly the evidence of masterful storytelling skill that they are in
live performance. Indeed, the printed form inevitably calls for different
and often purely visual forms of attraction to seduce a buyer, ranging
from an alluring title page or nicely calligraphed prefaces to splendid
illustrations. Yet the attractions the novel used to entice its readers were
not solely limited to the visual realm. The martial arts novels of the
late nineteenth century excelled in marketing themselves on the basis
of the acoustic spectacles they sold, particularly, as we shall see in chapter 4, the loud noise of the martial arts action scene and the carefully
constructed use of an acoustic cliff-hanger.

66. Though I am clearly indebted to Lord and Parry for their notion of the formula
and the way it allows for improvisatory composition, I regard the work of the nineteenth-century Beijing storyteller as rather more mercenary.

CHAPTER FOUR

Listening to the Martial Arts Scene

Onomatopoeia in *The Three Knights* Series

> In language, as the metacode of sounds, the most complete
> identification is obviously that which simultaneously desig-
> nates the sound and its source ("rumble of thunder"). But if
> one of the two indicators has to be suppressed, it is curious
> to note that it's the aural indicator that can most easily be
> suppressed with the least loss of recognizability. If I perceive
> a "rumble" without further specification, some mystery or
> suspense remains.
> —Christian Metz, "Aural Objects"

Living in the twenty-first century, when martial arts films have become
a household staple and cinematic special effects enable martial artists
to fly right before our eyes, it is easy for us to imagine the premodern
martial arts novel as visual spectacle.[1] Take, for instance, the following
scene from *The Latter Five Gallants.*

> Let's tell how Xu Liang took aim at the back of his [Zhou Rui's] hand.
> As soon as he [Xu?] lowered his head, the arrow left the crossbow, which
> hit precisely the back of [Zhou Rui's] hand. Xu Liang jumped to his feet,
> sweeping his leg up in a "carp move." His hand happened to be resting on
> a stone. As soon as Xu Liang let out a curse Zhou Rui shot him a glance,
> and with a loud "BA," the rock hit Zhou Rui squarely on the forehead.
> Things happened much faster than can be told. Xu Liang had already

EPIGRAPH: Metz, "Aural Objects," p. 155.

1. On the importance of special effects and the flying body in early twentieth-
century martial arts movies, see Zhang Zhen, *An Amorous History,* chap. 6.

leapt past him and placed his foot on the sword. Shaking his hand, Zhou Rui took off. One of the others, thinking he could deftly sneak a move in, tried to grab the sword, but with a loud "TANG," he was kicked by Xu Liang quite a distance. He scrambled up and took off. Xu Liang said, "After him!" "TENG TENG TENG TENG." [Xu] did not take a single step to chase after him but only stamped his feet in place.

且說徐良對準了他的手背, 一低頭, 弩箭出去, 正中手背上. 用了個鯉魚打挺, 往起一躥, 可巧手按著一塊石頭子兒. 徐良一罵, 周瑞一瞧, 他吧的一聲, 正中周瑞面門之上. 說時遲, 那時快, 徐良早就縱過去, 把刀就踹住了. 周瑞把手甩著就跑了. 有一個手快的貪偏宜, 他打算要撿刀去, 早被徐良鐙的一聲, 一腳踢出多遠去了, 爬起來就跑, 徐良說, "追!" 騰騰騰騰, 一步也沒追, 淨是斡踩腳.[2]

The scene, a typical action scene from one of the more popular martial arts novels of the late nineteenth century, overflows with visual clues and physical movements that trigger the reader's visual imagination. The reader sees the hero Xu Liang aim at his enemy Zhou Rui's hand, and, as Xu lowers his head, a crossbow bolt soars off to hit Zhou Rui's hand precisely where targeted. The reader then sees the hero jumping to his feet, using a spectacular "carp move," and witnesses how one villain is kicked so hard that he flies several paces back. With all these specific physical positions and target trajectories, the scene easily fulfills the reader's desire for visual excitement.[3]

Yet, amid the visual onslaught, the scene is also filled with numerous acoustic details that enable the reader to imagine a fully auditory experience. First, onomatopoeia abounds. When Xu Liang hits Zhou Rui, the impact is underscored with a loud "BA," while his later kick is echoed with a resounding "TANG." Second, bursts of dramatic speech add acoustic life to the scene. When Zhou Rui takes off, for instance, Xu Liang interrupts the action with a brief and forceful shout: "After him!" In Chinese the shout is conveyed in a single, explosive "ZHUI!," and its effect can be readily imagined. Third, in a striking metafictional move, Xu Liang runs in place to recreate the sound of sprinting feet in

2. *Xiao wu yi* (1993), chap. 81, p. 312.
3. A "carp move" involves getting to your feet from a position lying down without using your hands by relying solely on the momentum of your feet (i.e., the tail) as you sweep them upwards.

pursuit of an opponent: "TENG, TENG, TENG, TENG."[4] Along with the visual spectacle of flying projectiles, kicks, and "carp moves," the novel adds bangs and clangs, shouts and curses—acoustic fireworks to keep the reader amused.

How do we begin to understand this incessant noise of the action scene shown above? What implications do these different sounds have for our understanding of the late-Qing martial arts novel? And is it possible to draw on the acoustic spectacle found in these brief snippets of martial mayhem to shed light on the broader cultural practices of reading, writing, and printing during the late nineteenth century? This chapter pursues these questions in two ways. First, by reading a few of the most representative late nineteenth-century martial arts texts, in particular those novels belonging to the *Three Knights* series, I seek to unpack the linguistic mechanics involved in their use of onomatopoeia and demonstrate how it affected the process of reading. It is the very acoustic material from which the onomatopoeic sign is constructed, I argue, that allows the reader to experience the physical action on the page as an exciting acoustic spectacle. The resulting reading experience is best understood as lively (*renao*).

Second, I place this creation of a lively reading experience of *renao* in its historical context by focusing on the way *The Three Knights* and its sequel, *The Latter Five Gallants,* "invent" the use of onomatopoeia in the martial arts text. Even though both novels claim to be based on old storyteller tales, a comparison with commercially produced story- teller libretti shows that the spectacular use of acoustic elements is not necessarily a remnant of previous live performances. At times, publish- ers and authors could also insert these acoustic elements in places where they were not found in the original. This assertive insertion of sound becomes particularly striking in the case of the first sequel of *The Three Knights*, the 1890 novel *The Latter Five Gallants*. In this case, the publisher Shi Duo employed the acoustic excitement created by the storyteller's voice to market his wares to an ever-broader middlebrow reading public. Shi Duo, in other words, reinvented the spectacle of the

---

4. Another onomatopoeic expression, "PUCHI," is found on the previous page when the projectile is first seen colliding with Zhou Rui's hand. It is common for chapters to end at an acoustic high point of the plot. *Xiao wu yi* (1993), chap. 80, p. 311.

storyteller's voice as a promise of ever more excitement, the fulfillment
of which he strategically deferred by ending his novel on an acoustic
cliff-hanger designed to entice the reader to purchase the next installment of the series.

Print Culture and the Recovery of the Voice

Inspired by studies of the history and culture of print in Europe and
America, scholars of Chinese premodern literature have recently begun
to pay attention to the material conditions of the late imperial novel,
focusing in particular on the previously ignored visual aspects of these
texts. Robert Hegel's work, *Reading Illustrated Fiction in Late Imperial
China*, exemplifies this interest by exploring in great detail the size and
form of various late imperial works of vernacular fiction. He shows,
among other things, that much of the pleasure of reading vernacular
fiction lies in visualizing the action described on the page.[5]

In ascribing value to these visual aspects of the text, it becomes easy
for us to overlook the dimension of sound. As Walter Ong has argued,
modern cultures tend to reduce their conceptualization of the sign to a
purely visual level. In less visually oriented cultures, he claims, written
signs may well have had oral, even acoustic, qualities to which modern
readers are no longer attuned.[6] The modern emphasis on the visual may
have overshadowed another aspect — the sound of the text coming to
life as it is read aloud or simply imagined as being spoken aloud.

This acoustic dimension of the premodern vernacular text becomes
apparent when we read the commentaries appended by Jin Shengtan to
the famous episode in chapter 22 of *The Outlaws of the Marsh*, where the
hero Wu Song battles a tiger on Jingyang Ridge. Robert Hegel has shown
how Jin's commentaries prompt the reader to visualize the action on
the page. A second look reveals that, in addition to the visual elements
Hegel notes, Jin's commentaries also emphasize the acoustic experience
of the text. For instance, on entering the inn at the bottom of Jingyang
Ridge, Wu Song loudly shouts, "Innkeeper, quickly bring me some

5. Hegel, *Reading Illustrated Fiction*.
6. Ong, *Orality and Literacy*, p. 76.

wine" 主人家, 快把酒來吃! Here Jin's commentary reads, "To Wu the Younger, good wine is like life itself. Just this single opening sentence is like hearing his voice and seeing his person" 好酒是武二生平, 只此開場 第一句, 便如聞其聲, 如見其人.[7] Jin's comment encourages the reader not only to "see" the hero but also to "hear" his voice. Similarly, after Wu Song scolds the innkeeper for trying to keep him from crossing the ridge, a different commentator interjects, "This passage really brings out the shape and sound" 此一段寫得形聲俱出.[8] Again, when Wu Song exclaims, "Good wine!" 好酒, another commentary found in the early seventeenth-century Yuan Wuyai 袁無涯 edition responds: "The sound rises from the paper" 紙上出聲.[9]

The episode where Wu Song crosses the Jingyang Ridge similarly conveys acoustic phenomena, employing three loud climactic exclamations at the beginning, middle, and end to provide structural unity. The first exclamation, "AIYA" 哎呀, interrupts the narrative as Wu Song first comes eye-to-eye with the tiger. The second exclamation punctuates the text when the hero, halfway down Jingyang Ridge, is surprised by a group of hunters disguised as tigers. The final exclamation, made as Wu Song cries out in astonishment upon recognizing a man who approaches him from behind, brings the chapter to a close.[10] Jin clearly understands the structural importance of these three exclamations. The third "AIYA," he comments, "Is the sound of a shocked heart and shaken innards" 哎呀者, 驚心動膽之聲. He also rewrites the different graphs representing this sound in earlier editions into an identical "AIYA."[11] The anti-climactic descent from Jingyang Ridge is underscored by an acoustic diminuendo, in the form of three exclamations, exclamations Jin links by using the same graph for each. Whereas previously the three

7. *Shuihu zhuan huiping ben*, vol. 1, chap. 22, p. 419.
8. Ibid., p. 422, citing the commentary from the Yuan Wuyai edition with commentaries attributed to Li Zhi 李贄 (1527–1602). David Rolston rejects the authenticity of the Li Zhi commentaries in this and the Rongyu tang 容與堂 editions of *The Outlaws*; see Rolston, *How to Read*, pp. 356–63.
9. *Shuihu zhuan huiping ben*, vol. 1, chap. 22, p. 419.
10. Ibid., vol. 1, pp. 423, 426, and 429 respectively.
11. In the earlier Rongyu tang edition, the exclamations are written differently, as "AIYA," "AIYA," and "AYE" 阿也. For the Rongyu tang and other editions, see Zheng Zhenduo, *Shuihu quan zhuan*, vol. 1, pp. 346, 347, 350 and the notes on vol. 1, pp. 352 and 354 respectively.

exclamations were separate climactic moments, Jin's revision prompts the reader to relate these moments to one another. Can it be that the final, rather unheroic cry retroactively divulges the lack of heroism in Wu Song's earlier outcry when he faced the tiger at the top of Jingyang Ridge?

At these moments, the reader is not simply supposed to *hear* the hero's exclamations. Exhilarated by the sudden twists in the narrative and the enthusiastic prompts of the commentaries, he may well cry out in shock himself, the three voices of hero, commentator, and reader melding in a single outburst. Such a moment of affective communion is explicitly described in Yang Dingjian's 楊定見 introduction to *Outlaws of the Marsh*:

> We made tea and, sipping it together, took out the text of Li Zhuowu's [Li Zhi] preface to *The Loyal and Righteous Outlaws of the Marsh* and read it aloud together with one voice.[12] Angry waves rose up over the vast river as if in response. I forgot Wuyai, and Wuyai forgot me, and we were conscious only of Li Zhuowu.
> 煮茶共啜, 取桌吾先生敘《忠義水滸傳》文同聲讀之, 胥江怒濤, 若或應答. 吾忘無涯矣, 無涯忘吾矣, 知有桌吾先生而已矣.[13]

Here Yang Dingjian and Yuan Wuyai share tea and text, dissolving the boundary between self and other in a moment of bonding that arises from the act of vocally bringing the text to life. The sound of the text creates a communion that erases the boundaries between past and present, as the voices of Yang and Yuan become one with that of the deceased commentator. If for these gentlemen-scholars an acoustic appreciation of the text created a mutual engagement and sense of elite

12. Often the term used for reading a novel can be translated as "reading aloud" (*du* 讀). Because recitation was often the first step in learning how to read in China, this term evokes careful and painstaking attention to the text. Yet the term also has strong acoustic connotations, as seen in anecdotes about scholars locating a school by following the loud voices of students emanating from its windows. For a variety of such anecdotes and the importance of vocal recitation in late-imperial China, see Li Yu, "Learning to Read." For an exhaustive investigation of the different connotations of Chinese verbs meaning "to read," see Behr and Führer, "Einführende Notizen."
13. Yang Dingjian, "*Shuihu zhuan* xiaoyin."

companionship, for less highbrow readers the sounds of the novel could create an equally appealing, if less exalted, mode of interaction. To understand this more popular form of acoustic reading, I now turn to the use of onomatopoeia in *The Three Knights* series and the way these texts produced the sense of *renao* for readers.

Acoustic Excitement and Physical Action

Onomatopoeia is crucial to the understanding of an acoustic dimension, epitomized in the term *renao,* in the experience of reading late imperial vernacular literature. This *renao* mode of reading is best understood when contrasted with the highly visual mode of reading characteristic of nineteenth-century European realist fiction. Whereas realist novels are invested in establishing semantic meaning and the creation of a hierarchical subject-object relationship, the loudly vocal *renao* of the vernacular novel emphasizes sensory immersion and the dissolution of the boundary between reading subject and textual object. Below I illustrate how countless onomatopoeias create *renao* in the *Three Knights* series by entertaining the reader with the noisy process of the body's material destruction.

Onomatopoeia appears in many Chinese literary genres, from the opening lines of the first poem of the *Classic of Poetry* to the Ming-Qing vernacular tale,[14] yet few genres seem to favor these sparkles of sound as much as the late nineteenth-century martial arts novel. The association between martial arts action and the use of acoustic elements is so strong that martial arts novels often self-consciously comment on their use in metafictional fashion. For instance, when in *The Three Knights* a hero battles three villains underwater, the narrator explicitly mentions that there will be no sound since it is impossible to hear anything below the waves: "Underwater battles are not like battles on ships in that, even when blades parry back and forth, there is no sound" 原來水內交戰不比船上交戰, 就是兵刃來往也無聲息.[15] In the following chase sequence

14. Few scholars have remarked on the abundance of onomatopoeia in Chinese literature. An exception is found in Johnson, *A Glossary,* esp. pp. xiii–xiv.
15. *San xia wu yi* (1996), vol. 2, chap. 85, p. 598.

from *The Latter Five Gallants*, the implied narrator plays with the reader's expectations by commenting on the difference between various onomatopoeic sounds in martial arts action:

> Yao Meng cursed him, "You hill bandit! You son of a bitch! I knew you'd use hidden weapons! You just look out for Second Master's darts!" After speaking, he shot some at Peng Yu, "TANGLANGLANG," but didn't hit him. When you hit a person, it doesn't make that noise. "TANGLANGLANG" was the sound of the darts hitting the rocks.
> 姚猛罵道, "山賊! 狗娘養的! 打算著就是你會暗器. 你瞧瞧二太爺的這個鏨子! 說畢, 衝著朋玉鏢嘟嘟打將出來, 沒打著. 打著人就不是這個聲音了, 這鏢嘟嘟是在山石上頭出來的聲音.[16]

Here the narrator points out that the reader should know that the darts missed. As any self-respecting reader of martial arts fiction knows, darts hitting a body go "PUCHI," not "TANGLANGLANG."

In these situations, onomatopoeias achieve their effect by recreating the "sensation" of the action while remaining literally meaningless. Try reading the following scene from *The Latter Five Gallants* twice, once with the onomatopoeias found in the original, and once without.

> Cui Long drew a sword and chopped. Xu Liang brought his sword up to parry and, "QIANGLANG," Cui Long's sword was cut in two. Once again, "TANGLANGLANG," the point of the sword fell to the ground, scaring [Cui Long] so that his courage dissipated and his wits were shocked. Already a thrust from Ai Hu was bearing down on him. Cui Long ducked his head and bent his waist like a prawn so that the blade missed his neck. But he could not save his bandana. "CHI," half of his bandana was cut off.
> 崔龍拔刀就剁, 徐良用刀往上一迎, 嗆嘟一聲, 削為兩端. 仍是鏢嘟嘟, 刀頭墜地, 嚇了個膽裂魂驚. 早被艾虎一刀剁將下來. 崔龍縮頸藏頭, 大蝦腰躲過了脖頸, 躲不過頭巾, 只聽見哧的一聲, 把頭巾砍去了一半.[17]

If sound words are omitted from this brief episode, the meaning of the passage remains exactly the same. Yet, without the onomatopoeias, the passage conveys a completely different feeling.

16. *Xiao wu yi* (1993), chap. 100, pp. 397–98.
17. Ibid., chap. 84, p. 325.

The difference in affect arising from the use of onomatopoeia is a result of the acoustic materiality of these signs. This is best explained by applying the distinction that Jean Francois Lyotard draws between the semantic content of the sign and the physical shape of the sign to the realm of sound. Lyotard, thinking in primarily visual terms, argues that signs inevitably have a material form, a "line" whose physicality inevitably exceeds the mere semantic meaning of the "letter" itself. As he puts it, "We can say that the tree is green, but this does not put the color into the sentence."[18] Lyotard emphasizes the visual form of the sign, presenting his study as "a defense of the eye." Yet this materiality can be found on an acoustic level as well. The sound of a word spoken quickly registers differently from the sound of the same word spoken slowly; a word whispered affects the listener differently from one that is shouted. Even though the late nineteenth-century martial arts novel is a written text rather than an oral performance, its copious use of onomatopoeia illustrates Lyotard's thesis in acoustic terms. The semantic meaning of the onomatopoeias in the martial arts novel is negligible; yet the way they draw the reader's attention to the acoustic qualities of language itself cannot be denied.[19]

For the reader, the absence of meaning in onomatopoeia works in concert with the emphasis on materiality to engender a "reality effect" such as that defined by Roland Barthes when he examined the concrete but superfluous visual details offered in nineteenth-century French realist writing. These details—a door in Michelet or a barometer in Flaubert—have no discernible relevancy to the narrative and therefore function at a level beyond semantic meaning. Unlike signs, these details do not point to a concrete referent. Rather, they signify more broadly the notion of "the real." As Barthes puts it, "Flaubert's barometer, Michelet's little door, say, in the last analysis, only this: *we are the real.*"[20] As with the visual detail of the mid-nineteenth-century French realist novel, the sounds of late nineteenth-century Chinese martial arts

18. Lyotard, *Discours/Figure*, p. 52.
19. Obviously, once a text is written down, it continues to exist only at the level of visual materiality. However, visual form can still remind us of certain acoustic expectations. See, for instance, Susan Blader's partial translation of *The Three Heroes*, in which onomatopoeias (when translated) are printed in italics with an exclamation mark. Blader, *Tales of Magistrate Bao.*
20. Barthes, "The Reality Effect," p. 16.

fiction have little meaning. But by introducing the acoustic qualities of physical action directly into the text, their lack of meaning adds a layer of excitement.

In their effect on readers, therefore, acoustic details in the vernacular tale resemble the visual details of nineteenth-century French realist fiction. Yet, visual and vocal effects differ in terms of the kinds of relationships they produce between reading subject and material object. The reality effect described by Barthes results in a commanding gaze, a mode of detached observation based on a strictly hierarchical subject-object relationship. In this relationship, the silent passivity of the observed object reconfirms the superior identity of the detached observer. In contrast, the sounds in the late nineteenth-century martial arts novel overwhelm the reader with a sense of physical spectacle. Far from registering a host of immobile objects patiently awaiting discovery by the reader, they actively call the reader's attention to the blinding speed of bodies and objects in the midst of physical action and the process of destruction. Onomatopoeia does not function to construct a stable identity of a subject masterfully surveying his surroundings; rather, it triggers a pleasurable dissolution of cognitive boundaries as the reader becomes immersed in the barrage of sounds.

Onomatopoeia promotes the dissolution of boundaries in two distinct ways. First, at the level of the depiction of the human body and other physical objects, onomatopeia loudly traces a trajectory of noise that registers first a sense of speed, then the moment of impact, and finally damage to the physical body. To achieve this effect, many acoustic details project a striking sense of kinetic movement and speed. Swords whoosh ("SHUA" 刷), arrows buzz ("MING" 鳴), and darts whistle ("SOU" 嗖). Equally importantly, human bodies are constantly moving at breakneck speeds ("SOU" 嗖) over walls and across rooftops. The sheer speed of these bodies, represented as acoustic "special effects," is mesmerizing in that it pushes the boundaries of what is physically possible. However, the boundaries are quickly reestablished when onomatopoeic words project the sound of impact as two objects crash into each other. Swords clang ("TANGLANG" 鐺朗), bodies collide ("PENGPENG" 弁弁),[21] and darts strike their target ("BENG" 弁) or hit

21. This is the sound of two bulls butting their heads. See *Xiao wu yi* (1993), chap. 103, p. 408.

rocks ("TANGLANGLANG" 鏜嘡嘡).[22] Swords may move at amazing speed, but when they clash the sound reminds us that the two colliding objects are solidly real. This sense of reality hits home when the material impact is destructive, as when bodies fall from high places ("PUTONG" 噗唪),[23] tables are kicked over ("HUALA" 嘩啦),[24] people are cut down ("CHICHAKECHA, like slicing a melon" 叱哎磕哎 仿佛削瓜),[25] compounds are burned down ("KECHACHA" 磕哎哎),[26] or skulls are broken by rocks ("BACHA" 吧哎").[27] In short, onomatopoeic sound, in intimating dazzling speed and movement as well as evoking shocking consequences, enables readers to experience the thrill of action. It establishes the boundaries defining objects and bodies by allowing the reader to hear them being physically destroyed.

If onomatopeias mark the presence of the physical body, the conspicuous lack of sound marks the transcendence of physical form. Ghosts, for instance, float above the ground without making any noise. Thus, in the *Continued Latter Five Gallants,* when Xu Liang hears the footsteps of a "ghost" chasing him, he can only conclude that this is a flesh-and-blood villain disguised as an immaterial spirit.[28] Similarly, silence marks the physical transcendence of the principal heroes in *The Three Knights* series, Zhan Zhao, Ouyang Chun, and the two Ding brothers. Physically, the superiority of these true knights is illustrated by their absolute control of their bodies, which move at a remarkable speed without producing any sound. In this scene from *The Latter Five Gallants,* two of these knights engage in a duel:

> The two men displayed all the martial skills they had learned in their lives. Their hands, eyes, bodies, techniques, and foot movements, their hearts, their souls, their wills, and their thoughts were all developed to perfection. They lept forward and jumped back; they twisted and dodged and quickly moved out of the way. They were nimble like a cat or a rat, swift like a

22. Ibid., chap. 100, pp. 397–98.
23. Ibid., chap. 107, p. 427. This is actually the sound of two bodies falling into the water.
24. Ibid., chap. 98, p. 389.
25. Ibid., chap. 98, p. 396.
26. Ibid., chap. 99, p. 393.
27. Ibid., chap. 84, p. 324.
28. *Xu xiao wu yi*, chap. 47, p. 247.

monkey or an ape. Their bodies would turn round dazzlingly fast, leaping high and crouching low, *but underneath their feet there was not a single sound*, as they went round and round like a merry-go-round lantern.[29] All their movements belonged to the six marvelous skills of jumping like a cat, dodging like a dog, scurrying like a rabbit, swooping like an eagle, flitting like a swallow, and hanging like a painted scroll. Even though it was a match like this, *there was not a single sound of their breathing*. You only heard a "SOU, SOU, SOU" and a "POU, POU, POU." "SOU, SOU, SOU" was the sound of the blades cutting the air. "POU, POU, POU" was the sound of their jackets flapping in the wind. [italics mine]

二人施展平生的武藝, 手、 眼、 身、 法、 步, 心、 神、 意、 念足, 躥迸跳躍, 閃輾騰挪, 輕若貓鼠, 捷恰猿猴, 滴溜溜身軀亂轉, 躥高縱矮, 足下一點聲音皆無, 類若走馬燈兒相仿. 全講的是貓躥、 狗閃、 兔滾、 鷹拿、 燕飛、 掛畫六巧之能. 雖然這般的比試, 鼻息口氣的聲音皆無, 就聽見颼、 颼、 颼, 剖、 剖、 剖. 颼、 颼、 颼, 是劍刀劈風的聲音; 剖、 剖、剖, 是衣襟刮風的聲音.[30]

The two knights demonstrate their transcendence of material reality by producing not a single sound as their bodies perform magnificent feats, transcending all physical constraints and leaving no material trace.

Second, onomatopoeia further creates acoustic spectacle by loudly introducing unlikely and unexpected events into the plot, thus causing a breach within the text through which a startling moment of "action" is glimpsed. In order for the reader to perceive this action as pure sensation, the author must use language completely devoid of semantic content to capture the extra-linguistic experience. As long as the sensory experience of sound is coupled with a clearly comprehensible semantic meaning, this use of onomatopoeia merely provides an acoustic gloss to the action described on the page. Whereas the description *tells* us what happens, onomatopoeia *shows* us, and the combination produces a pleasurable effect for the reader who can "hear" what is going on. However, it is also possible for the novel to defer the moment in which the meaning is unveiled; in this way, it uses onomatopoeia to heighten suspense.

29. A merry-go-round lantern (also known as a zoetrope) has pictures that turn as they are propelled by the hot air produced by the lantern's flame. In late nineteenth-century martial arts fiction, it comes to symbolize rapid physical movement.
30. *Xiao wu yi* (1993), chap. 36, p. 132.

A scene from *The Cases of Judge Liu,* a nineteenth-century hand-written drum-song, illustrates the distinction between experiencing an acoustic moment as sensation and apprehending its meaning as sense. In this scene a lascivious monk dies at the hands of two heroic knights-errant:

> It must have been that the monk's evil deeds had finally caught up with him. Right in the corner there happened to be a chair, and Jingkong, failing to pay attention, tripped over it and almost fell. Seeing this, Zhu Wen was not about to be merciful. He rushed forward, aimed for the back of the monk's head, and "TANG," swung his metal bar. A barrage of noises ensued: "BACHA," "GUDONG," "KECHA," "HUALA."
>
> "There's someone in the audience saying, "Stop your story right there! How come your mouth is just one twist of the tongue after the other? Is it 'GUDONG' or 'BACHA,' 'KECHA' or 'HUALA'? You're turning the entire affair into 'an old fellow from Shanxi pulling a camel train—a whole string of humps in a row!' "
>
> Gentlemen, please, don't get all excited. Listen as I explain it all at a leisurely pace. When the monk Jingkong was hit by Zhu Wen's metal bar, did that sound like "BACHA" or not? When the monk Jingkong fell forward and hit the ground, wouldn't that be "GUDONG"? And when he pulled the table down and all those bowls, teaware, and porcelein vases dropped on the floor, would that not sound like "HUALA"? That's how we ended up with this barrage of noise. Now the story's all cleared up.
>
> 也是和尚的惡貫滿盈, 可可兒的那邊攔着一張椅子, 淨空和尚不妨, 被椅子一絆, 險些栽倒. 朱文一見, 那肯容情? 趕上前去, 照着他的腦後噹是一尺, 只聽吧叉, 咕咚, 喀嚓, 嘩啦, 這一路亂響.
>
> 有人說, 你這書可不用說了, 怎麼滿嘴裡都是舌頭? 到底是 咕咚, 是吧叉 是喀嚓, 是嘩啦? 你鬧了個老西兒拉駱駝—擺了這麼一大溜!
>
> 眾位明公, 別心急, 聽在下的慢慢破解明白: 淨空和尚中了朱文鐵尺, 是「吧叉」的一聲不是? 淨和尚往前一撲, 栽倒在地, 是「咕咚」的一聲不是? 兩隻手又一板地下的高桌, 把那些個蓋碗咧、茶盤咧、瓷瓶咧這些東西都掉在地下咧, 是「嘩啦」的一聲不是? 所以, 才這麼一路亂響. 書裡講明.[31]

This passage pushes to its limit the boundary between the sensory appreciation of the sounds of action and the cognitive recognition of those sounds. The text opens the physical action in the usual manner, using a

31. *Liu gongan,* chap. 77, p. 356.

loud "TANG" to represent the sound of the metal bar making contact with
the skull of the monk. After this, however, the text continues with a series
of onomatopoeias ("BACHA, GUDONG, KECHA, HUALA"), piling
them up without explanation, thus turning them into literally meaningless sounds. Not surprisingly, a "member of the audience" interrupts the
"storyteller" to demand an explanation. Clearly, there is a limit to which
one can push the use of onomatopoeia. If semantic content is indefinitely
deferred, onomatopoeia threatens to destabilize the process through
which meaning is established, and the "audience" will rise up in protest.

Most late-Qing martial arts texts do not exploit the tension between
sound and meaning to this extent. Instead, they introduce onomatopoeia to mark a startling and exciting development that takes the reader
by surprise, suspending meaning only for a brief second to allow the
reader to imagine what will happen next. As a result, onomatopoeias
invariably appear to create a moment of shock before a description of
events; once meaning has been provided, the shock is alleviated. In the
following scene from *The Latter Five Gallants* (chap. 101), several characters are sitting together amiably, when "all of a sudden they heard someone come rushing in from outside. 'PUDONG,' he fell to the ground.
Looking at him, everybody was completely amazed" 忽聽打外面蹌近一
人, 扑咚摔倒在地. 眾人一看, 好不詫異.[32] Here, as a new figure enters the
story and is about to dramatically change its course, a sudden auditory
interruption disrupts the text. The reader, like all the other witnesses of
the scene, is stunned and at the same time eager to know what happens
next. Who entered all of a sudden and why did he fall?

An acoustic shock followed by suspense is a recurrent feature of
martial arts novels. Most frequently, it is found at the end of a chapter,
or, as I will show, at the end of a novel that is part of a longer series.
At those points, the reader is no less surprised than the character in
the novel. A typical cliff-hanger ending would read: "Yunsheng came
down from the roof and fell, 'PUDONG,' into a pit. If you want to know
whether he lived or died, listen to the next section" 芸生下房, 噗咚墜落
坑中. 若要知生死如何, 且聽下回.[33] Or: "He pulled his sword and struck.
'BENG,' a flash of red sprang forth. If you were to ask whether Master
Liu lived or died, listen to the exposition in the next chapter" 擺刀就剎,

32. *Xiao wu yi* (1993), chap. 101, p. 403.
33. Ibid., chap. 88, p. 344.

崩的一聲, 紅光崩現. 若問柳爺生死如何, 且聽下回分解.[34] Even though he knows that everything will be all right and that Master Liu will not die, the reader is, for a few tense but pleasurable seconds, suspended in midair much like the sword and the fate of Master Liu.

To sum up, onomatopoeia turns the reading of fiction into a lively and suspenseful experience, constantly drawing the reader into the story through a barrage of sounds that establishes a sensory experience of lively spectacle. This experience results in disorientation, both in the reader's shocking awareness of the limits of physicality where he is constantly confronted with the "scene" of physical destruction, and in a pleasurable immersion which compels the reader to continue reading to know what happens next. Or, to phrase it more precisely, the use of onomatopoeia creates in the reader a desire to understand the event that has already taken place and to make sense of the sensory illusion created by the text.[35] Given the close relationship between martial arts fiction and popular storytelling, we might think that in these popular novels this acoustic spectacle might merely represent the transcription of a storyteller's voice. Yet the relationship between the sound of the storyteller's voice and the acoustic spectacle produced by the page of the printed novel is more complicated than at first might seem to be the case. To explore this complex relationship more fully, I turn in the next section to a comparison between the printed novel *The Three Knights* and the handwritten libretto of storyteller performance.

Reinventing Storyteller Sounds: From Storyteller Libretto to Novel

The most likely source for the variegated sounds of the novel and, in particular, the use of onomatopoeia in nineteenth-century martial arts fiction is found in the storyteller figure. As pointed out in chapters 1 and 2, elite

34. Ibid., chap. 106, p. 420.
35. This desire to understand what already has happened is in the West most often found in detective fiction, where the reader follows in the footsteps of the detective to solve the crime. For the way this desire to know translates into an ineluctable plot-drive, see Brooks, *Reading for the Plot*.

authors and editors had posited the storyteller as the narrative personification of loud and lively entertainment, while local Beijing publishers had been quick to cash in on the growing brandname recognition of increasingly famous storytellers such as Shi Yukun. Contemporary Beijing storytellers still make abundant use of such snippets of sound; and Vibeke Børdahl and Jette Ross have shown that storytellers from Yangzhou similarly employ onomatopoeia to enliven their tales.[36] Writing in the 1950s, when the memory of late-Qing and early Republican-era storytelling was still fresh, Zhang Cixi confirms that storytellers from every province of China would employ onomatopoeia:

> This is the reason why storytellers are found in each province, and even though their accents are different, their movements when they perform are all about the same. When they imitate wind, they always say, "MING MING MING, a violent wind rose up." When they imitate rain, they must say, "HUA HUA HUA, rain fell as if poured from a gourd dipper." When they do a cannon shot, they must say, "GUANG, GUANG, GUANG, three cannon shots rang out." When they imitate thunder, they must say, "GULULU, the heavy thunder rocked the heavenly bureacrats." "CANGLANGLANG, the gongs sound": that must be the signal for the troops to retire from the battlefield. "KECHACHA, one blade cut!" It's bound to be that someone was cut down from his horse. "BA, a single sound": if that is not the sound of a pebble thrown to gauge the distance, then it must be a hidden projectile. When it comes to making the sound of a cudgel, then it's "SHUASHUA," which always means arrows flying like a swarm of locusts. [sic] As for falling snow, they might well open their mouth, but there would be no way of actually doing it.
>
> 所以此項評書家, 各省皆有, 口音雖不同, 而表演時一舉一動, 大致全都差不多. 學風時必要說: '嗚嗚嗚, 狂風大作.' 學雨時必說: '嘩嘩嘩, 大雨猶如瓢潑的一般.' 發炮時必說: "光光光, 三聲炮響." 學雷時必說: "咕嚕嚕, 沉雷震東天曹." 倉啷啷一聲鑼響, 必是鳴金收兵; 喀叉叉一刀, 勢必劈於馬下; 叭的一聲, 非探路石, 即是暗器. 說到一聲棒子響, 便刷刷, 必是箭似飛蝗. 就怕趕上說下雪, 干張着大嘴沒法兒辦.[37]

Zhang may dislike the clichéd manner in which storytellers employed onomatopoeia, yet his testimony underscores that acoustic snippets were part and parcel of every storytelling performance.

---

36. Børdahl and Ross, *Chinese Storytellers*, p. 90.
37. Zhang Cixi, *Renmin shoudu de Tianqiao*, p. 93.

Given that the device of onomatopoeia was widely used in story-telling and that many printed novels were closely associated with the work of Shi Yukun and other professional storytellers, we might be tempted to trace the onomatopoeias dotting the printed text of the *The Three Knights* series back to storyteller libretti and to see them both as surviving remnants of the original oral performances. We might further expect these snippets of sound to be more prominent in written texts more closely connected to performance. In the last chapter, for instance, we saw an example in which a lengthy vendor call in a storyteller libretto was abbreviated and muted when that text was transformed into a printed novel. In the case of onomatopoeia, however, we sometimes find the opposite. Whereas the printed novels of *The Three Knights* series employ onomotopoeia with gusto, the earliest storyteller version on which the first of the printed novels is based, the handwritten libretto entitled *The Cases of Judge Bao*, actually uses such snippets of sound sparingly.

The widespread use of onomatopoeia therefore represents the novelist's invention, something that becomes clear when we compare one of the most famous action sequences from *The Three Knights* with the same scene in the storyteller libretto.[38] Here the fifth hero, the rebellious Jade-Pelted Rat, Bai Yutang, comes to the capital to challenge the Southern Knight, Zhan Zhao, nicknamed the Imperial Cat. As the sequence begins, the martial men loyal to Judge Bao are sitting around in the yamen, drinking as they discuss recent events. One of them, the buffoon Zhao Hu, loudly proclaims that Bai Yutang had better not show up, for Zhao will surely teach him a lesson if he does. He is interrupted in the middle of boasting:

> No sooner had he spoken these words when they heard a sound, "PAI," and from the outside an object came flying in, which, wavering neither to the left nor to the right, hit the wine cup Master Zhao was holding smack in the middle. All they heard was "DANGLANGLANG" as the wine cup shattered. Zhao Hu was startled, and all the others were stunned. See how Master Zhan had already left his seat, closed the door, turned round, and blown out the lamp. He then took off his outer garment, underneath

38. This is the scene Lu Xun chose to quote extensively in his *Short History of Chinese Fiction* as exemplary of the nineteenth-century chivalric court-case fiction. See Lu Xun, *Zhongguo xiaoshuo shilue*, pp. 199–200.

which he was already completely dressed for combat. Silently taking up his sword in his hand, he made as if he was going to open the door. There was a single sound, "PAI," as once again an object hit the screen. Only then did Master Zhan open the door and, with a single movement, slipped out. All he felt was a cold wind rushing toward him as, with a "WHOOSH," there came the thrust of a blade. Master Zhan met the blade with the flat of his sword, parrying and blocking. Under the light of the stars Zhan Zhao had a good look. He saw a person wearing a dark silk night-stalker outfit. The movements of the man's feet were nimble, and he vaguely resembled the figure Master Zhan had met before at the Miao home.

剛說至此, 只聽拍的一聲, 從外面飛進一物, 不偏不歪, 正打在趙虎擎的那個酒杯之上, 只聽噹啷啷一聲將酒杯打了個粉碎. 趙爺嚇了一跳 眾人 無不驚駭. 只見展爺早已出席將隔扇掩, 回身復又將燈吹滅. 便把外衣脫下, 里面卻是早已結束停當的. 暗暗的將寶劍拿在手中, 卻把隔扇假作一開, 只聽拍的一聲, 又是一物打在隔扇上. 展爺這才把隔扇一開, 隨著勁一伏身竄將出去, 只覺得迎面一股寒風, 嗖的就是一刀. 展爺將劍扁著往上一迎, 隨招隨架. 用目在星光之下仔細觀瞧, 見來人穿著簇青的夜行衣靠, 腳步伶俐, 依稀是前在苗家集見的那人.[39]

The action continues with a heated exchange of sword thrusts and, after Zhan Zhao breaks Bai Yutang's blade and the Jade-Pelted Rat takes off over the rooftops, culminates in a chase.

In the printed novel, acoustic details are, above all, crucial to the introduction of new and unexpected shifts in the plot. In this episode, the scene abruptly changes from dialogue to physical action with the sound of a single stone shattering a cup of wine. The cup shatters, "DANGLANGLANG," and within seconds the amiable conversation of friends is cut off and the knight Zhan Zhao is standing outside exchanging blows with his nemesis Bai Yutang. I have quoted only part of the action sequence, but the full text reveals that onomatopoeia is also used to bring the duel with swords to an end, as Zhan Zhao cuts Bai Yutang's blade in half with a single "CENG" 噌.[40] At this point the scene changes from an exchange of blows to a rooftop chase. The entire action sequence then concludes with a third sound, "GULULU" 咕嚕嚕, as a rock rolls down the roof after having missed Zhan Zhao.[41]

39. *San xia wu yi* (1996), vol. 1, chap. 39, pp. 232–33.
40. Ibid., p. 233.
41. Ibid.

By conveying a sense of striking speed, acoustic details generate much excitement. The object that opens the action sequence moves so fast that its physical effect registers first as the sounds "PAI" and "DANGLANGLANG" before it is seen and recognized. Then, as Zhan Zhao faces his opponent, the first impact of the sudden onrush of blows is registered as haptic and aural. Only after Zhan Zhao and Bai Yutang have exchanged a series of blows does the narratorial lens pull back to allow Zhan Zhao (and the reader) a good look at his mysterious opponent and finally identify him as the Fifth Rat Bai Yutang.

In contrast with the printed novel, the storyteller libretto offers the same scene without any onomatopoeic representations of sound.[42] The disruption of the conversation between the friends, for instance, is introduced in the following manner:

一句話,	This single phrase
尚未說完一聲響亮,	He had not yet finished speaking when a sound rang out
把個酒杯打在埃塵.	And the wine cup fell to the floor.

Zhao Hu was speaking excitedly as suddenly from the outside a stone was thrown in, shattering his wine cup and splattering wine all over. Zhao Hu had had a few cups too many to drink and said, "Brother, why did you snatch my cup? Do you mean that you want me to stop drinking? I'm not drunk at all. Quick, get me a cup for me to drink, or else I'll take yours. What do you think you're up to?" All the others were stunned and did not know what was going on. The Southern Knight said with a smile, "Fourth Brother, don't mistakenly blame Brother Wang. Someone has arrived outside."

趙虎正然說得高興, 忽然從外面一個石子打將進來, 把他的酒杯打碎. 酒是洒了一事家. 趙虎也搭着多喝了幾盅兒了, 說, "大哥, 你為何搶我的盅子? 難道不叫我喝了麼? 兄弟沒醉呀. 你快挐來我喝. 不佳, 我挐你的盅子. 這是怎麼話說呢?" 別人是全都愣了, 不知道是怎麼件事情. 南俠代笑說道, "四弟, 不必錯怪王大哥. 外邊有人到了."

---

42. These popular, handwritten libretti are hard to date. Internal evidence in the libretti, *The Aural Record*, and *The Three Knights* makes it clear the novel is based on the handwritten *Aural Record* and that the *Aural Record* is in turn based on the libretti kept at the Academia Sinica. Since the oldest manuscript of the *Aural Record* dates from 1867, the libretto must date from no later than the late 1850s or early 1860s. The extant manuscript may itself be a copy of a later date. See Miao, "*San xia wu yi* de chengshu guocheng"; Miao, "*Longtu erlu* banben kaoshu."

真俠客,	A true knight,
一見酒杯被石子打落,	As soon as he saw that the wine cup had been knocked down by a rock,
就知道,	He immediately knew that
外邊廂有來拜訪玉貓的人.	Outside the room someone had come to pay a call on the Jade Cat.
代笑開言呼眾位,	Smiling, he said, "Everyone,
他來了.	He's here.
待小弟前去好把他拎.	So wait nearby while I go out and catch him."
說著話,	As he spoke,
站起身,	He stood up,
挽挽袍袖,	Rolled up his sleeves,
披披衣衿,	Tucked in his shirt, and
取寶劍,	Grabbed his sword,
鋒銳甚.	Sharp as a razor.

As soon as the Southern Knight saw Bai Yutang rushing over with nimble steps and agile body, he silently admired him, thinking.
展南俠一見白玉堂奔將過來, 步法玲瓏、身體輕巧, 暗暗的夸獎道.[43]

Both sound and the particular way the storyteller is said to employ his voice play an important role in the libretto. However, unlike the sequence in the novel, the same scene in the libretto does not register abrupt narrative shifts through onomatopoeic markers, nor does it present the spectacle of physical action by inserting onomatopoeic highlights. True, the conversation ends with a sound, but the phrase "a sound echoed" involves the descriptive use of signs rather than the iconic use of onomatopoeia. Where the combat between Zhan Zhao and Bai Yutang is punctuated by continuous bursts of onomatopoeic sound in the novel, the same moments remain silent in the storyteller libretto. No swords whistle, no blades clang, and no rocks come barreling down the roof as they almost hit the Southern Knight.[44]

Instead, the libretto marks transitions in the narrative by shifting from prose to song and from song back to prose. When the rock is thrown in, the singing ends and a few lines of comic prose follow that

43. "Zha Junheng," pp. 16B–17B.
44. The phrase "all of a sudden a sound echoed" in the libretto appears only at the beginning of this section. There is no suggestion of such a sound anywhere after that in this scene.

show the drunken reaction of Zhao Hu to the sudden turn of events. At the phrase "a true knight," the storyteller switches back to song, signaling a shift in focus from Zhao Hu to the Southern Knight Zhan Zhao. Then, when Zhan Zhao shifts from speech to action, the sung part changes from long seven-beat lines to rapid three-beat lines set to a presumably quick-paced tune: "As he spoke / he stood up / rolled up his sleeves / took off his coat." Again, after Zhan Zhao has rushed outside and observed Bai Yutang's appearance, the songbook shifts from song to prose as Bai Yutang rushes into combat. Verse and prose alternate back and forth as the tale unfolds, yet not a single onomatopoeia is to be found.

As I have shown in chapter 3, the lengthy poetic songs employed by the storyteller were crucial to the performer's ability to portray himself as a masterful craftsman, draw an audience, and sell his art. Extant descriptions of the performances by Shi Yukun confirm that for him as well, rhymed song was central to his genre of oral performance. Recall the bannerman song "Shi Yukun" discussed in more detail in chapter 2:

> See him strike the three-stringed lute as if issuing a command.
> In the entire hall, all is silent, neither crow nor sparrow heard.
> Just see how his fingering is nimble, his voice loud and clear,
> His expression elegant, his phrases clear and fresh.
> He causes all the gentlemen to praise each sentence, to compliment
>   each word.
> All hearts rejoice together, all mouths speak in harmony.[45]

Unlike storytellers working in the plain narrative (評書) tradition, which employs no musical accompaniment or song, Shi Yukun does not open his performance with a wooden clapper.[46] Instead, he uses another acoustic marker—a sudden strike on the three-stringed lute, which carries an authoritative ring. Next, the performer adopts his "loud and clear" voice, which is accompanied by "fingering" that is "nimble." With its emphasis on the storyteller's instrument and his remarkable

---

45. "Shi Yukun," p. 735.
46. The sound of the "awakening wood" serves to call the audience to attention, either by formally marking the beginning of a storytelling session or by emphasizing certain pivotal moments within the narrative itself. For more on the awakening wood in Yangzhou storytelling, see Børdahl and Ross, *Chinese Storytellers*, p. 106.

use of voice, the description suggests that Shi Yukun's performance may
belong to a tradition of storytelling that, unlike the now more familiar tradition of *pingshu* storytelling, emphasizes poetic song, not prose
narrative.

Later sources similarly establish Shi Yukun as a paragon of elegant
and poetic lyrics and tunes, rather than a storyteller celebrated for his
clever plots or lively depictions of martial arts action. A song about
another popular performer, the *zidishu* titled "Guo Dong'er" 郭棟
兒, for instance, tells how "the strong melodies of Shi Yukun and his
excellent phrases show his skill." [47] The line itself is brief and offers little
information. However, in that it contrasts Shi Yukun's particular merits
with the diverting plot lines of a storyteller called "Wang the *Shuihu*
King" 水滸王 and the lowbrow humor of Guo Dong'er himself, the line
makes clear that at some point in the nineteenth century Shi Yukun had
become known as an accomplished and elegant lyricist. Writing much
later at the turn of the twentieth century and primarily on the basis
of hearsay, the bannerman Chong Yi also briefly mentions Shi Yukun,
noting how this man was most renowned for telling *The Three Knights*
and was considered the originator of the art of singing to the accompaniment of the single-stringed lute. [48] Song, in short, was what allowed
Shi Yukun to differentiate himself from the other vulgar performers of
the market and create a name for himself. [49]

When we turn to the libretti that are based on, or at least sold as,
the transcriptions of Shi Yukun's performances, the libretti that bear
Shi Yukun's name prominently on their title pages, we find a similar
abundance of lyrical songs. Roughly half of the text of the libretto
consists of rhymed and rhythmic passages, which range from descriptions of scenery during the different seasons and depictions of heroes
that are almost photographic in their eye to detail, to long, emotive
soliloquies voiced by a broad range of characters. The value of these
lyrical elements is affirmed by the fact that certain Shi Yukun lyrics (
贊) circulated separately from the libretto. The collection of the

---

47. "Guo Dong'er," p. 338.
48. Chong, *Dao Xian yilai chaoye zaji*, p. 9.
49. It is difficult to tell whether this use of song actually describes the praxis of
Shi Yukun or whether it is an aestheticization of his art ascribed to him by later
generations.

Academia Sinica, for instance, includes encomia belonging to the Shi school of storytelling that sing the praises of summer scenery ("Xia jing zan" 夏景讚 [In praise of summer scenery]), a precious sword ("Bao jian zan" 寶劍讚 [In praise of a priceless blade]), or the character Chen Lin, an upright eunuch who plays an important role in the Judge Bao tale, "Chen Lin zan" 陳林讚 (In praise of Chen Lin).[50] Similarly, some merchants specializing in manuscripts of storyteller tales emphasized as an advertising tactic that these eulogistic passages were included with their Judge Bao libretti. The Leshan tang catalog, for instance, highlights the announcement: "new Shi-style libretti with encomia" (*shipai daizan xinshu* 石派帶讚新書).[51] In short, it was the lyrical qualities of Shi Yukun's songs, not his ability to use onomatopoeia, that made the man famous and libretti based on his storytelling marketable. As relatively inconsequential parts of the text, onomatopoeia could simply be omitted.

In contrast, when the tale of Judge Bao was finally printed as a novel, onomatopoeic words and phrases were clearly accepted as signs that should be included in the martial arts text. Perhaps half a century separates the original libretto from the printed novel and, as Margaret Wan has shown, it was during this period that the martial arts novel grew to maturity and established itself as a printed genre of text with its own conventions of plot, character, and style.[52] In the case of *The Three Knights*, this development can be readily seen in the increasingly important role of the martial hero. Whereas the first forty chapters, those chapters based on the libretto, give Judge Bao the central role, the next eighty chapters, presumably composed at a later date, focus much more centrally on the adventures of his martial helpers. The different titles used as the tale transformed from handwritten manuscript to printed novel illustrate the growing importance of martial arts as well. The oldest titles, *The Cases of Judge Bao*

50. Zhongyang yanjiuyuan yuyan yanjiusuo suwenxue congkan bianji xiaozu, "Shuochang lei Shipai shu zongmu."
51. "[Leshantang] zidi, dagu shu mulu," p. 1A. The catalog furthermore refers to the Shi-style manuscripts as "tales [using] Shi-style rhymes" 石韻書, suggesting that it was the lyrics and their rhyme schemes that were considered to be unique to the Shi Yukun school of storytelling. Ibid, p. 2A. For more on the *zan*, see Chen Jinzhao, "Shipai shu de tizhi."
52. Wan, *Green Peony*.

and *The Cases of the Dragon Diadem*, all emphasize the civil persona of Judge Bao. *The Tale of Loyalty and Righteousness*, the title of the first printed edition of the novel, already highlights the actions of righteous martial artists to a greater degree. This becomes even more explicit in the title first appended to the 1883 edition, *The Three Knights and the Five Gallants*, which does not mention Judge Bao at all.[53] In short, by the time the first of the *Three Knights* novels was published in 1879, the editor was inserting these snippets of sound into the text to be printed even when they were not to be found in the libretto in front of him. By the final decades of the century, onomatopeia, sound, and martial arts action had become firmly linked as scriptural devices.

To summarize, the insertion of onomatopoeia into the printed text suggests that the historical trajectory from oral performance to handwritten text and from handwritten text to printed manuscript is not always a linear progression from acoustic orality to silent visuality. For sure, storytelling presents a form of entertainment that employs the spoken word and hence the materiality of sound to delight its listener. Similarly, any text, whether handwritten or printed, will inevitably need to use visual signs in order to communicate with its reader. And yet, as any storyteller will argue, the challenge for the performer is not simply using the sound of his voice, but rather using it in such a fashion that the listener can "see" the action described.[54] Similarly, when martial arts novels increasingly employ onomatopoeia, the effect should not simply be understood as either increased visualization or acousmatization, but rather as a suggestive synesthesia of sight and sound, the visual sign on the page calling for the acoustic imagination of the reader who "hears" the liveliness of the text, a liveliness which in turn allows him to envision the flying fists and startling leaps which, in reality, never took place.

53. See St. André, "Getting Down Off a Tiger Isn't Easy."
54. This is the way Wang Jingshou describes the art of using sound in storytelling: "The key [of storytelling] lies in using language which has sound but no shape in such a way as to trigger the imagination of the audience, and within this kind of particular context and set limits, to create an artistic image that has form and color, flesh and blood." In Wang, Wang, and Zeng, *Zhongguo pingshu yishu lun*, p. 83.

Onomatopoeia and the Spectacle of Commercial Publishing

> The word cliché "initially described a ready-made unit of type, a metal plate from which issued unending, standardized reproduction of print or design. The word was derived from the onomatopoeic French verb *clicher*, a variant of *cliquer* (to click) and mimicked the sound of typesetting machines.
> —Zamora Parkinson, *The Usable Past*

By the time *The Latter Five Gallants*, the first sequel to *Three Knights and Five Gallants*, was published in 1890, the incorporation of onomatopoeia had become a commercially motivated practice. Seeking to reproduce the commercial success of *Three Knights and Five Gallants*, the entrepreneur Shi Duo issued a sequel that in turn ended *in medias res*, thereby leaving the possibility open for printing yet another sequel. To entice the reader to return for the next sequel, Shi Duo ended *The Latter Five Gallants* with a loud cliff-hanger, thereby reproducing the storyteller technique of employing onomatopoeia in the practice of late nineteenth-century commercial printing, ending an installment on a high note while promising even greater spectacle in the next installment. The cooptation of storyteller technique by the commercially printed novel marks the beginning of the vogue for printing seemingly endless series of martial arts novels in the late nineteenth and early twentieth century.

Just as *The Three Knights and the Five Gallants* introduces onomatopoeia where its handwritten predecessor uses almost none, so its sequel, *The Latter Five Gallants*, incorporates many more onomatopoeic words and phrases than appear in the first novel. Most notably, in order to create cliff-hangers at the ends of chapters, *The Latter Five Gallants* employs onomatopoeia to greater dramatic effect and more strategically than the first novel. In contrast to *The Three Knights and the Five Gallants*, which only uses onomatopoeia once at the end of a chapter, *The Latter Five Gallants* uses it sixteen times to conclude chapters.[55] For instance, a typical chapter ending in *The Latter Five Gallants* reads:

---

55. The number of chapters in the two novels is roughly the same. *The Three Knights* runs to 120 chapters; *The Latter Five Gallants* runs to 124. Onomatopoeias in *The Latter Five Gallants* appear at the end of chaps. 9, 12, 14, 57, 74, 87, 88, 89, 100, 102, 104, 105, 109, 111, 113, and 124.

It was just the third watch of the night when, all of a sudden, "HULA" the
shutter to the window opened and someone came rushing in, brandishing a sword and slashing down. If you want to know whether these two
lived or died, listen to the explanation in the next chapter.

正打三更, 忽然間唿刺一聲, 隔扇一開,闖進一人, 擺刀就砍. 不知二人生死
如何, 且聽下回分解.[56]

Here the highly dramatic onomatopoeia signals the sudden entrance
of a newcomer and thus the beginning of new and potentially lethal
action.

What truly sets *The Latter Five Gallants* apart, however, is the way
in which it applies this use of an acoustic cliff-hanger to the final chapter of the entire novel. At this point, the use of onomatopoeia to create
acoustic excitement has passed beyond a merely playful narrative ploy
to become a mechanism to spur consumption, enticing the reader to
purchase the next volume in the series. When *The Latter Five Gallants*
comes to a close, the reader has patiently been waiting for more than one
hundred chapters for the various heroes to gather in a grand reunion
so that they can destroy, once and for all, the "Copper Net Trap" that
killed their sworn brother Bai Yutang at the beginning of the novel. But,
rather than revealing how the heroes finally destroy the trap, the novel
ends on a moment of suspense, as three separate groups of heroes are
caught in the trap without any hope of escape. Meanwhile, the actual
climax of the plot is deferred to the next installment in the series, leaving the reader with a pressing desire to read on.

For two of the three trapped groups, a sudden plot twist leads to
a final moment of suspense that is captured with the dramatic use of
onomatopoeia.[57] The first of these denouements involves the heroes
Jiang Ping and Liu Qing:

This is why Master Jiang fell for the trap. As "HULALA" sounded underneath his feet, he took a quick step back, but already he had stepped on the
trapdoor. "PUTONG PUTONG," down the two men fell. At the bottom,
four guards of the Prince were lying in wait and trussed up their hands

56. *Xiao wu yi* (1993), chap. 12, p. 40.
57. The third group is trapped underground amid raging flames. Suspense here,
however, does not hinge on the use of onomatopoeia.

> and feet. Furious with Jiang Ping, Liu Qing closed his eyes, waiting for death. The guards drew their swords, poised to make the kill, but we will not tell of that for now.
>
> 故此蔣爺上當. 腳底下呼喇喇一響, 趕著撤身回來, 早就登的翻板上了, 噗嗵, 噗嗵, 兩個人墜落下去. 原來底下有四個王官, 把他們四馬攢體捆上. 柳青怨恨蔣平, 閉目合睛等死. 王官拉刀要殺. 暫且不表.[58]

Two other heroes face death in a moment similarly encapsulated by onomatopoeia. As one of them, the wily Zhi Hua, is about to reach out for the grand prize, the list of names involved in the conspiracy of the Prince of Xiangyang,

> "CHI," a knife with a curved edge came falling from above. "DANG," it struck master Zhi straight in the middle. Master Zhi closed both eyes. The fate of Master Zhi, the dismantling of the Copper Net Trap, all of these episodes, in more than one hundred chapters, will later be printed in a sequel that will appear before too long.
>
> 哧的一聲, 從上面掉下一把月牙式的刀來, 正在智爺的腰上噹的一聲. 智爺把雙睛一閉. 智爺生死, 破銅网陣, 一切節目, 仍有一百余回, 隨後刊刻續套嗣出.[59]

In both these moments, the reader is left with heroes on the brink of death, an impending spectacle of physical destruction that, richly suggested through onomatopoeia, seems inescapable. The reader is left with no recourse but to wait with bated breath until the next installment is available for purchase.[60]

Publishers and authors had, of course, long before this drawn on the fame of an earlier novel.[61] However, up until this time, most sequels had been discrete units penned by literati authors. Sequels to *The Outlaws of the Marsh* exemplify this type. Over the years,

58. *Xiao wu yi* (1993), chap. 124, p. 499.
59. Ibid., p. 500.
60. Even though *The Three Knights and the Five Gallants* has an open ending that lends itself to this kind of serialization, it does not end with the kind of noisy cliffhanger that we find in *The Latter Five Gallants*. For a discussion of the list of plot events suggested at the end of *The Three Knights and the Five Gallants* and the way that list reads like a "vendor call," see chapter 3.
61. For a collection of essays on sequels to vernacular novels, see Martin Huang, *Snakes' Legs*.

the popularity of the original novel spurred the production of
many rewritings and sequels, the most famous of which is the *Jin
Ping Mei*, which draws on a ten-chapter segment from the original *Outlaws* to construct a full-fledged erotic novel of a hundred
chapters. Other sequels, though less famous, followed the original
more closely. The *Shuihu hou zhuan* 水滸後傳 (Continuation of the
Outlaws of the marsh), by Chen Chen 陳忱 (1613–after 1663), extends
the plot of the original novel in order to present a hidden message of
loyalty to the fallen Ming dynasty.[62] Another sequel to *Outlaws* is Yu
Wanchun's 余萬春 (1794–1849) *Dang kou zhi* 蕩寇志 (Suppression of
the bandits), also known as *Jie shuihu quan zhuan* 結水滸全傳 (The
complete conclusion to the Outlaws of the marsh). Like the *Jin Ping
Mei* and Chen Chen's sequel, this work is by a literati author who was
motivated by a moral and political agenda rather than thoughts of
commercial success (of course, some of these sequels came to enjoy
huge commercial success regardless).

In the nineteenth century, the production of sequels took a decidedly more commercial turn. As Ellen Widmer has shown, the unprecedented popularity of *Dream of the Red Chamber* led to a boom in the
publishing of sequels.[63] Among the more than ten sequels Widmer
discusses as examples of this trend, one pair of novels, *Bu hong lou meng*
補紅樓夢 (Supplement to the Dream of the red chamber) and *Zeng bu
hong lou meng* 增補紅樓夢 (Another supplement to the Dream of the
red chamber), both by Langhuan shanqiao 嫏嬛山樵, are among the
first to explore the potential of a series. The 1814 preface to the first of
these two supplements clearly prepares readers for future sequels: "Here
I first publish forty-eight chapters to give the reader a taste of the whole
thing, but there is a further supplement of thirty-two chapters, which
will shortly be published for the reader's perusal" 茲者先刻四十八回,
請為嘗鼎一臠, 尚有增補三十二回, 不日嗣出, 讀者鑑之.[64] Despite this
early example of serialization, most *Dream of the Red Chamber* sequels
remained discrete works produced by different authors and published
by different publishing houses.[65]

62. For a discussion of this novel, see Widmer, *The Margins of Utopia*.
63. Widmer, *The Beauty and the Book*, pp. 217–47.
64. Quoted in Cheng Junbao, "Bu *Hong lou meng*," p. 20.
65. Widmer summarizes the sequel phenomenon as follows: "The sequels to

Inspired by the narrative possibilities of serialization, Shi Duo recognized the profit that could be made by publishing a series of sequels. A brief note appended to the last chapter of the first edition of *The Latter Five Knights* makes this clear:

> The next hundred plus chapters have not been published yet. Why do we stop at this point of excitement (*renao*)? It is all because the costs of publishing this second installment were over two thousand silver and we have no way of printing the last installment. . . . If there is a generous person who wishes us to continue printing, we ask him to come to this publishing house for deliberation. This publisher will be willing to work on his behalf and within a year will return not only the original sum, but also an interest of three to five hundred in silver. To gain both fame and fortune, is that not a wonderful thing?
>
> 下餘一百餘回尚未刊刻．刻到此熱鬧節目為何住手？皆因中部所費不下二千餘金，無力再刻下部 . . . 如有慷慨富厚之士願為續刻者，請到本鋪商酌本坊主人情願效勞計一年中除繳還資本外尚可得利三五百金．名實兼收，豈非快事？[66]

If Shi Duo was promising three to five hundred in silver as interest on a loan of two thousand, he must have expected his investment to be highly profitable. Shi Duo did manage to find an investor, a certain Boyin 伯寅, who in one of the prefaces to the second sequel, the 1891 *Continued Latter Five Gallants*, claims to have parted with thirty pieces of silver to expedite the publishing of the novel.[67] Shi Duo's expectations were most certainly met, and the novel proved to be a hot commodity. It was reprinted three times in the same year by different publishing companies in Shanghai. In *The Continued Latter Five Gallants*, Shi Duo appends a personal anecdote that illustrates the success of the first two novels in the series:

Honglou meng emerged out of a wave of interest set in motion by the parent novel, yet each was an independent creative act with its own agenda, purposes, and intended readership." See Widmer, *The Beauty and the Book*, p. 220.

66. Found in the 1890 Wenguang lou edition of *The Latter Five Heroes*. See *Zhonglie xiao wu yi zhuan*, chap. 124, p. 8B. See also Miao, "*Xiao wu yi, Xu xiao wu yi* de kanxingzhe."

67. Boyin, "*Xu xiao wu yi* xu," vol. 3, pp. 1556–57.

Because the previous volume, *The Five Latter Gallants*, ends before the
Copper Net Trap was disarmed, readers have been discussing the matter
avidly, and no fewer than several hundred of them have been coming on
and off to my shop to buy the next installment.
因上部《小五義》未破銅网陣，看書之人紛紛議論，屢續到本鋪購買下部
者，不下數百人.[68]

Shi Duo also seems to have been outraged that competing entre-
preneurs were cutting into his lucrative business by offering similar
sequels, some even fully illustrated.

Recently certain shameless crooks have been putting up advertisements
in the streets and marketplaces to claim, without basis, that they possess
editions with complete illustrations in which the puzzle of the Copper
Trap has been solved. . . . This deludes and confuses the hearts of men.
For this reason, this publishing house has hastened to produce the sequel
to delight people's hearts.
近有無恥之徒，街市粘單，膽敢憑空添破銅网增補全圖之說. . . . 是乃惑亂
人心之意也. 故此本坊急續刊刻，以快人心.[69]

Shi Duo was not alone in having been awakened to the idea of
making money by producing sequel after sequel. After he sparked this
trend in producing sequels to action adventures, one novel series after
another rapidly appeared. Some of these series, for instance *The Tale of
Everlasting Blessings and Peace, Part 1* (first published in 1892) and *The
Tale of Everlasting Blessings and Peace, Part 2* (first published in 1894),
discreetly finished their tales with the second or third installment.[70]
Pretty soon, however, novel series such as the ones based on *The Cases of
Judge Shi* were running to ten installments.[71] By the Republican period

68. *Xu xiao wu yi*, chap. 1, p. 1.
69. Ibid.
70. Other examples are *Seven Swords and Thirteen Knights* (earliest extant edition
in 1897, with a preface dated 1892; and two sequels that followed in 1901) and *Da ba
yi* 大八義 (The original eight gallants; first extant edition of the novel, published
together with its sequel in 1899).
71. The first Judge Shi novel has a preface dated 1798, and the first sequel appeared
in 1893; a total of ten novels in the series were published by 1902. Another martial
arts series started with the publication of *The Tale of Romance and Heroism*, which
ran to a total of twelve installments.

twenty or even thirty installments were commonplace.[72] As to *The Three Knights* series, Shi Duo himself discreetly finished the tale with the third installment. In the late Qing period, however, the knights and the gallants were revived in alternative sequels, and by the Republican period the series comprised a total of twenty-four installments.[73]

The birth of the martial arts novel series in 1890 was, as has been noted by other scholars, intimately related on the one hand to the social changes reshaping urban readership and, on the other, to the technological and institutional developments that had begun to transform the printing industry in the last decades of the nineteenth century. Miao Huaiming, for one, has pointed out that without the introduction of modern printing presses, it would have been impossible to produce and reproduce the ten sequels totaling 528 chapters that make up the wildly successful *Cases of Judge Shi*.[74]

Yet even if the boom in martial arts series owed its impetus to modern printing techniques and new forms of organizing book production, the success of the novels rested on their ability to tap into the storytelling tradition, especially the use of cliff-hangers as a narrative device to capture audiences. Most likely, Chinese storytellers began to use spectacular cliff-hangers and sudden plot twists as early as the Song dynasty (960–1279). Evidence of actual performance is hard to come by, but Wilt Idema has convincingly argued that traces of such cliff-hang-

72. Examples include the *The Storyteller Tale of Jigong* (publication started in 1898; by 1906 there were at least three installments, with thirty-seven more to follow); and *The Cases of Judge Peng* (first novel published in 1892, with the whole series running to a total of thirty-six novels). Even though the Republican period saw a clear acceleration in the number of sequels printed, the trend of publishing sequels had already begun by the last decade of the nineteenth century.

73. In the Guangxu period, the first alternative sequel entitled *Xu Xiayi zhuan* 續俠義傳 (The continued knights and gallants) appeared. In 1905, an author writing under the pen name Xiangcaoguan zhuren 香草館主人 produced yet another sequel, *Xu Qi xia wu yi* 續七俠五義 (The continued seven knights and the five gallants). As the title shows and the author himself states, this sequel, inspired by Yu Yue's edition, seeks to replace other, inferior sequels, presumably *The Latter Five Gallants* and *The Continued Latter Five Gallants*. In the Republican period, more sequels appeared, making a total of twenty-four novels. For martial arts novel series published in the late nineteenth and early twentieth centuries, see Keulemans, "Sounds of the Novel," appendix B.

74. Miao, "Qingdai zhonghouqi chubanye de fazhan."

ers can be found in premodern performance texts. For example, the chantefables (*zhugongdiao* 諸宮調) divide each *juan* into two sections, each of which ends with a cliff-hanger, the first to create a space for collecting money from the audience halfway through the performance, and the second to bring back the audience the next day.[75] As Idema further points out, the early sixteenth-century publisher Xiong Damu 熊大木 purposefully introduced these storyteller clichés into the narrative structure of the vernacular novel, creating a literary cliché that has been followed ever since.[76] However, given that these novels were all published and sold as complete tales, the continued use of such storyteller clichés was not directly commercially motivated. The simulacrum of a storyteller voice might have incited the reader's desire to continue reading, but this desire was for turning to the next page, not purchasing the next volume. Only after 1890, when Shi Duo printed *The Latter Five Gallants* and the Chinese martial arts novel series was born, did printing press and storyteller voice combine to produce the clear ring of cold cash.

Conclusion

It has been argued that after the advent of printing, the storyteller gradually disappeared. Walter Benjamin eloquently ties the arrival of the modern printing press, the rise of the novel, and the disappearance of the storyteller together in his discussion of the short stories of Nikolai Leskov. As Benjamin writes, with more than a hint of nostalgia,

> The earliest symptom of a process whose end is the decline of storytelling is the rise of the novel at the beginning of modern times. What distinguishes the novel from the story (and from the epic in the narrower sense) is its essential dependence on the book. The dissemination of the novel became possible only with the invention of printing. What can be handed on orally, the wealth of the epic, is of a different kind from what constitutes the stock in trade of the novel.[77]

75. Idema, "Performance and Construction of the *Chu-Kung-Tiao*."
76. Idema, *Chinese Vernacular Fiction*, p. 111.
77. Benjamin, "The Storyteller," p. 87.

In China, however, the history of the printed vernacular novel developed differently. A study of the genre's development—its incorporation of the storyteller's voice, first during the late Ming and again, as shown in this chapter, during the late Qing—makes clear that at least in the initial stages, the arrival of new printing techniques did not immediately result in the disappearance of the storyteller, but rather stimulated inventive book producers to exploit the sound of the storyteller's voice for their own purposes. Indeed, even now the storyteller has not disappeared. Jin Yong 金庸 (pen name of Louis Cha 查良鏞, 1924–), the famous martial arts novelist and perhaps the most commerically successful Chinese author of all time, has on occasion likened himself to a storyteller, and his novels, first published in serialized episodes in Hong Kong newspapers during the fifties and sixties, use onomatopoeia in much the same way as did nineteenth-century tales of martial arts heroes.[78] Even more strikingly, Shan Tianfang, one of the most popular living storytellers, ends his bestselling novel version of his oral rendition of *The Three Knights and the Five Gallants* with a dramatic acoustic highlight:

> The Northern Knight raised his sword and wiped the blood traces off, saying, "Who do you want to follow, everyone?"
> "It's all the fault of this jerk making trouble. We want to go with the commander. We want to surrender to the authorities!"
> Yelling and shouting, the crowd all moved to stand on the side of Wenhua. In a second, Jun Mountain had been transformed into a sea of Song dynasty flags. Only because they recaptured Jun Mountain did they make possible a lot more exciting [*renao*] tales. If you want to know the details, please continue reading in the next installment, *Destroying the Cloud-Piercing Tower.*
> 北俠揀起寶刀, 擦淨血漿, 說道: '諸位, 你們願意跟誰?' '都怪這小子搗蛋! 我們願意跟大帥走, 願意歸降.' 眾人吵吵嚷嚷, 都站到文華一邊. 霎時間, 整個軍山, 全換成了大宋的旗號. 只因收復了軍山, 才又引出許多熱鬧故事. 欲知詳情, 請看續集 [大破沖霄樓].[79]

Even though onomatopoeia is not used, the scene presents the reader with a dramatic acoustic climax that bridges this novel and the

78. For more on Jin Yong and his use of sound, see the coda to this book.
79. Shan, *San xia wu yi*, vol. 2, chap. 85, pp. 740–41.

next installment. Prompted by brief snatches of dialogue and various snippets of anonymous shouts, the reader can imagine a chorus of voices swelling as a rebellious army surrenders to the knight and loudly proclaims its loyalty to the Song dynasty. Shan Tianfang then quickly employs the narrative crescendo to introduce the idea that many more of such exciting (*renao*) moments are to follow in his next volume of tales. More than a century after *The Latter Five Gallants* was first printed, the loud noises of the martial arts tale still call forth the liveliness of a storyteller's voice from the silence of the printed page.

CHAPTER FIVE

The Cosmopolitan Teller of Tales

Cross-Talking and the Imitation of Dialect Accents

> Urbanization and mass emigration brought together all sorts
> of languages, dialects, and idiolects previously separated by
> space and social difference. The flood of linguistic criticism
> after 1880 was part of an attempt to sort out these competing
> languages and arrange them in order of prestige.
> —Michael North, *The Dialect of Modernism*

In the 111th chapter of *The Three Knights and the Five Gallants*, the
Black Demon Fox Zhi Hua and the young knight Ding Zhaohua decide
to disguise themselves as lowly fishermen so as to infiltrate the stronghold of a rebellious outlaw. As one would expect from a literary tradition steeped in the sartorial conventions of cross-dressing, a good deal
of attention is paid to the costume makeover that allows the two heroes
to pass as a pair of lowly fishermen. Yet what strikes the reader more
than any costume change is the outrageous performance of "cross-
talking" that follows once the two heroes come to the water fortress
of the outlaw. When guards at the gate of the stronghold threaten to
shoot if the men fail to identify themselves, Zhi Hua answers not in
his own voice but instead cross-talks by affecting a strong Hubeinese
fisherman's accent:

> Hold your fire! Waddaya (*what are you*) shootin' for? Uz (*us*)'re comin'
> on invite. Us two masters 'ave bo'ath (*both*) come with fish for the lord.
> Officials don't beat those carrying gifts, do they? So waddaya shootin' for?

EPIGRAPH: North, *The Dialect of Modernism*, p. 15.

住搭拉罷, 你放麻(嗎)箭吓, 難(俺)們陳起望的, 俺當家的弟兄斗(都) 來了,
特特給你家大王送魚來了. 官兒還不打送禮的呢, 你又放箭做嘛 呢?[1]

Fooled by Zhi Hua's stellar performance of their native dialect, the two
guards take the hero to be one of their own and grant him access to the
stronghold.

The scene draws our attention for two reasons; first, its remarkable
interest in representing in print the sound of dialect speech. Regional
dialects had, of course, appeared in earlier works of fiction and had been
part of opera libretti since the earliest times.[2] However, here the late nineteenth-century *Three Knights* does not simply register dialect through the
more common techniques of syntax or lexicon. It actually attempts to
record the sound of the dialect phonetically on the printed page.

As figure 5.1, an illustration from the first printed edition of *The
Three Knights*, shows, the novel registers the sound of dialect speech by
printing certain words twice, once to register the sound of the character's accent and once to offer the reader the appropriate meaning (as well

1. *Zhonglie xiayi zhuan* (1879), chap. 111, p. 6A. The translation of a particular
Chinese dialect into English is difficult and is made even more so by the novel's
inconsistent ways of printing accents. Susan Blader's translation avoids these problems by not incorporating the novel's use of accent. I have chosen to create a set
of conventions that may not always capture the spirit of the dialect for an English
speaker but gives the reader a better sense of how accent is used in the original.
First, I follow the original text's inconsistent practice in terms of the word order of
dialect accent and standard character. This means that in some texts, dialect accent
appears before standard character, while in other texts, dialect accent appears after
standard character. Second, even though the original text does not always distinguish the second character from the regular text by printing it in a smaller font to
the side, to avoid confusion I have consistently placed the translation of that character in parentheses and italics. Third, I mark dialect accent by "miswriting" words
in the translation. Fourth, words that are very colloquial but not marked in the text
as having a distinct accent I have translated in a conspicuously "vulgar" manner,
but I have not misspelled such words. Though slight differences between the original Juzhen tang edition and the later Zhonghua shuju edition exist, I am quoting
from the more easily accessible Zhonghua shuju edition, unless the differences are
significant. See *San xia wu yi* (1996), vol. 2, chap. 111, p. 644.
2. For an overview of the issue of regional dialect in some of the most famous
vernacular novels, see Yan Jingchang, *Gudai xiaoshuo yu fangyan*. For an article on
the earliest use of dialect in opera, see West, "Shifting Spaces."

漁艔一邊一個眞是賣藝應行幹何事司何事是再不錯

的陸魯二人只得在船頭坐了依然是當家的一般水手

開船直奔水寨而來一葉小舟悠悠蕩蕩一時過了五孔

大橋卻離水寨不遠但見旌旗密佈劍戟森嚴又至切近

看時全是大竹紮縛上面敵樓下面甕門也是竹子做成

的水寨小船來至寨門只聽裡面隔着竹寨間道小船上

是何人快快說明不然就要放箭了智化挺身來至船頭

道住搭拉罷你放麻嗎箭嚇難俺們陳起墊的俺當家的

弟兄斗都來了特特給你家大王送魚來了宜兒還不打

送禮的昵你又放箭做麻昵裡面的道原來是陸大爺魯

忠烈俠義傳　第一百十一回　六

5.1 Dialect accents in *The Tale of Loyalty and Righteousness* (*The Three Knights and the Five Gallants*), chapter 111. (In *Zhong lie xia yi zhuan*, published in 1879 by the Juzhen tang. Photo courtesy of Yale University Library.)

as sound).[3] For instance, before the character *an* 俺, a personal pronoun meaning "we," itself a word already considered vulgar in tone, the text prints *nan* 難. "Both" is printed first as *dou* 斗, third tone, and then as *dou* 都, first tone. The final particle *ma* is similarly printed twice, first with the second tone as 麻, and then as the toneless 嗎. The result of the paratextual device of double printing is a remarkable sonic feat: even though faced with the silent pages of a text, the reader can imagine the sounds of Hubei dialect.

The second striking aspect of this scene is the highly self-conscious way in which it captures the sound of dialect speech as performance. After all, the scene quoted above does not simply depict a Hubeinese fisherman speaking his own dialect, but rather a clever martial arts hero *pretending* to speak in a Hubeinese accent. In fact, if we were to continue reading, we would soon note that the Black Demon Fox Zhi Hua is the *only* person speaking in Hubeinese dialect. The actual denizens of Hubei, the guards whom Zhi Hua is addressing, all speak perfect Mandarin. The attention paid to the acoustic details of dialect speech here thus does not follow the logic of mimesis, that is, the literal transcription of dialect speech onto the page in an attempt to represent reality.[4] Rather the scene follows the logic of performance, that is, the appreciation of the artistry of a person mimicking accents. The text's acoustic delight, in short, serves to highlight the act, not the object, of representation.

How do we understand the remarkable interest in recording dialect speech and its theatrical, imitative nature? The previous chapter focused on onomatopoeia in the martial arts novel; this chapter explores the

3. As a comparison of figures 5.1 and 5.2 shows, the techniques used to print dialect accents were not consistent even within a single novel. Whereas in figure 5.1 (chap. 111) the dialect accent is printed first and without any typographical distinction from the regular text, in figure 5.2 (chap. 24) (see p. 195) the dialect accent follows the standard character, is printed in a slightly smaller type, and appears slightly to the right. In the 1889 edition edited by Yu Yue, the printer seems to have failed to understand that some of the characters were used solely to register the sound of dialect, eliding some characters, keeping others, and in general creating a mess.

4. Though rendered with a great eye for acoustic detail, Zhi Hua's Hubeinese accent is not all that accurate. The pronoun *an*, for instance, is used quite widely in regional speech, but when pronounced as *nan* it is only used in three dialects: Hebei dialect, Hunan rural accent, and Chaozhou dialect, none of which correspond with the supposed local scene of action, Xiangyang in Hubei. See Xu and Miyata, *Hanyu fangyan da cidian*, vol. 4, pp. 4917–19.

novel's playful evocation of the acoustic dimensions of regional speech. This interest in imitating dialect accents represents the culmination of a developing cultural and social exploration of regional dialects. During the nineteenth century, an increasing number of novels produced in the provinces had staked their regional claims by employing their own dialects. In contrast, Beijing-produced novels such as *The Tale of Romance and Heroism*, *The Three Knights and the Five Gallants*, and *The Tale of Everlasting Blessings and Peace* reaffirmed Beijing's central position in the empire by self-consciously imitating other regional dialects. Just as the capital, functioning as the political and geographical center of the Qing state, gathered all the different regional dialects within its walls, so did the Beijing-produced novels aim to reproduce this central position for its reader by gathering a host of different dialects within its pages. The way these novels employed different dialects allowed them to stage a verbal and acoustic masquerade that produced two distinct regional identities: a fictional character whose inferior, provincial nature was told through his linguistic incompetence and regional accent, and a cosmopolitan performer/reader whose superior Beijing identity was established through his distinction from and skillful imitation of provincial speech.

To describe the method these novels use to reproduce various dialects as the source of Beijing identity, I employ the term "cross-talking" (*xiang sheng* 相聲). Drawing on an indigenous notion derived from oral storytelling, the term helps to highlight the performative aspects of printing dialect accents. In current, twenthieth-century parlance, cross-talking is solely used to describe a comic dialogue between two performers; during the nineteenth century, however, the term primarily referred to the way storytellers in marketplaces and at temple fairs would act out different personae through the imitation of variegated regional accents.[5] Hence the term cross-talking first and foremost reminds us of the early nineteenth-century storyteller performances by Shi Yukun on which *The Three Knights* is based, or of the first performances of *The Tale of Everlasting Blessings and Peace* by Jiang Zhenming and Hafuyuan. In addition this storyteller background also

5. For a brief history of the art form and its development from an acoustic form of imitation to the now familiar comic dialogue, see Wu Wenke, *Zhongguo quyi tonglun*, pp. 179–90.

helps to explain the self-consciously performative aspects of cross-talking in print: even when reproduced in printed form, the imitation of different dialects had strong oral, performative connotations. As a result, the discerning reader appreciated the text not for its accuracy in reproducing dialect accents, but for the self-conscious artifice only a connoisseur of Beijing storytelling could appreciate.

That said, despite the strong oral, storytelling connotations of the use of dialect speech in martial arts novels, the printing of regional accents was, in the end, an effect of the written language. To make this point, in this chapter I trace the cross-talking routine in these novels not only to the nineteenth-century storyteller's performance but also to a perhaps less likely textual counterpart: the Qing-dynasty scholar's philological interests in recording dialect. The best example of such a juxtaposition of vulgar storyteller performance and elite *kaozheng* scholarship is found in the first vernacular novel to print dialect mimicry, Wen Kang's *Tale of Romance and Heroism*. In this novel, dialect mimicry represents a self-conscious exploration and crossing of the boundary between orality and text, a play with the medium of sound in voice as well as in print. It is this juxtaposition of voice and print that allowed the author to create a unique, typically local and yet still elite Beijing identity. Readers and authors such as Wen Kang took pride in the mastery of the universal realm of text as embodied by philological acumen, and yet they also expressed their native, Beijing identity by showing their appreciation of the most vulgar of local storytelling practices.

The Rise of the Nineteenth-Century Dialect Novel

To understand how the seemingly playful mimicry of dialects in the late-imperial Beijing novel could carry significant sociopolitical implications, it is important to introduce the broader nineteenth-century historical trend of regionalism and the literary trend of dialect literature that accompanied this trend. As evidenced by a steady stream of scholarly publications, the nineteenth century saw a remarkable rise in the importance of regionalism and local identity in China. As noted by Stephen Platt, when we look backward from a twenty-first-century, nation-state perspective, it is sometimes easy to overlook to what degree people living in the nineteenth century did not subscribe loyalty to the Qing empire (or a future Chinese nation), but were inspired by a regional loyalty to their home province (in this case, Hunan).[6] The increase in nineteenth-century regionalism expressed itself not only through a shift in economic and political power but also through the rise of locally specific identities, explored through a variety of scholarly and literary endeavors.[7] For instance, whereas seventeenth and eighteenth-century poetry collections produced in Yangzhou had included poems produced throughout the empire by what Tobie Meyer-Fong terms a "trans-regional" elite, Yangzhou poetry collections of the nineteenth century tended to only feature poems by local Yangzhou literati.[8] Similarly, whereas Yangzhou architectural sites in the seventeenth and eighteenth century had imitated physical structures found in either Nanjing or Beijing so as to establish Yangzhou as part of a larger literati or dynastic community, the nineteenth century saw an interest in uncovering and recuperating buildings that were considered "authentically" and distinctively Yangzhou in style.[9] Nineteenth-century cultural and political forms of regionalism should, in short, be understood as closely linked, as Frederick Wakeman Jr. has shown in his work on localism and loyalty in the Jiangnan region during the early Qing dynasty.[10]

In the field of the popular vernacular novel, this historical movement towards regionalism is reflected in a shift from the military romances produced during the late eighteenth and early nineteenth centuries to the martial arts/court-case novels printed in the final decades of the nineteenth century. Although we should not read these

6. Platt, *Provincial Patriots*, pp. 1–5 and 216–23.
7. Platt, for instance, traces the regionalism of Hunan back not solely to the military exploits of the Xiang army 湘軍 lead by Zeng Guofan 曾國藩 (1811–72), but also to an earlier, rather scholarly interest in reinterpreting the writings of the seventeenth-century Ming loyalist Wang Fuzhi 王夫之 (1619–92) in a more modern, Hunanese loyalist vein. See Platt, *Provincial Patriots*, pp. 8–33.
8. Meyer-Fong, *Building Culture*. Although Meyer-Fong investigates the shift from the seventeenth century to the nineteenth century from the perspective of the city of Yangzhou, her study has clear implications for greater China.
9. See in particular Meyer-Fong's discussion of Ruan Yuan's 阮元 (1764–1849) reconstruction activities in *Building Culture*, pp. 114–27.
10. Wakeman Jr., "Localism and Loyalism."

literary explorations of empire simply as a direct reflection of political realities, we cannot help but notice how the military romances of the early nineteenth century call to mind the militarily expanding Qing empire of the eighteenth century.[11] Novels such as *Wu hu ping xi* 五虎平西 (Five tigers pacify the west; 1801), *Wu hu ping nan* 五虎平南 (Five tigers pacify the south; 1807), and *Wan hua lou* 萬花樓 (The tower of ten thousand flowers; 1808) all focus on the exploits of brave military heroes who defend and expand the borders of the empire by domesticating the unruly barbarians who live beyond the periphery of dynastic civilization. In contrast, the martial arts/court-case novels of the late Qing focus almost exclusively on the struggle between the central regime located in the capital and local uprisings by nefarious secret societies such as the Heaven and Earth Society, the White Lotus Sect, or the Eight Trigrams (*Ba gua jiao* 八卦教). Many factors contributed to the shift from military romance to martial arts/court-case fiction, and broad historical developments alone can never fully explain changes in literary trends, yet the growing interest in and apprehension of regionalism in late nineteenth-century popular vernacular novels is hard to overlook.[12]

This historical and literary shift towards regionalism in the nineteenth century found a linguistic expression in vernacular novels that explicitly used dialect to construct notions of regional identity.[13] As a

11. A literary source that reflects the politics of empire more directly can be found in the popular songs celebrating the exploits of the Qing armies, for instance the various bannerman songs associated with the Kashgar uprising led by Jahāngīr from 1826 to 1828. Though a popular version of "Huo zhuo Zhangger" 活捉張格爾 (Capturing Jahāngīr alive), a song accompanying a peepshow, is lampooned in Helüshi's "Strolling through the Huguo Temple" as outdated and clichéd, originally such popular representations clearly sought to celebrate the capture, humiliation, and execution of the rebel. For more on the history of Jahāngīr (1790–1828) and his uprising, see Millward, *Beyond the Pass*, pp. 34, 207, 213.
12. For a genre study of the popular military romances of the eighteenth and nineteenth centuries, see Hsia, "The Military Romance."
13. Although I focus on the genre of the novel, it should be noted that other local genres reflect a similar rise in regionalism. Most famously, the nineteenth century saw the demise of *kunqu* opera 昆曲 as the most important form of opera transcending regionalism. Eventually, in the twentieth century, it was to be replaced by Peking opera (*jingju* 京劇) as a new, nationally unifying form. Perhaps more important for my purposes is the flourishing of *tanci* 彈詞, which combine dialect

literary reflection of the encroaching regionalism and the decline of central power, nineteenth-century vernacular novels display an ever-increasing interest in exploring regional dialects at the expense of standardized Mandarin 官話. The most famous of these texts is undoubtedly Han Bangqing's 韓邦慶 (1856–94) novel, *Haishang hua liezhuan* 海上花列傳 (Flowers of Shanghai; 1894), a work which, as a reflection of the growing importance of Shanghai, uses Wu dialect to put the city on the map as a distinct cultural center.[14] Yet, *Flowers of Shanghai* was merely the culmination of a nineteenth-century trend towards ever more sophisticated use of dialect.[15] Fifteen years before *Flowers of Shanghai* went into print, the Shanghai publishing house Shenbao guan had already published the hilarious Wu dialect comedy *He dian* 何典 (What classic?).[16] And before *What Classic?* there were novels printed in Yangzhou dialect, most notably the novels *The Sluices of Qingfeng* and *The Tale of the Flying Cripple*, that employed the Yangzhou vernacular to reflect the "splendor" of eighteenth-century Yangzhou. Moreover, as Liu Ts'un-yen and Cynthia Brokaw have demonstrated, there are in addition a host of vernacular works printed in Guangzhou and Fujian that employ Cantonese to highlight local history and local characters.[17] We find a similar trend towards the use of local dialect as a sign of regional identity in the case of works that circulated in the province of

---

speech with a specifically local identity and which claimed an explicitly feminine reader/authorship. Indeed, the rise of the typically northern, "masculine" genre of the storyteller or *pinghua* novel in the nineteenth century can only be understood in juxtaposition with the simultaneous rise of the southern, "feminine" *tanci* text. For the most insightful exploration of the *tanci* genre, see Hu Siao-chen, *Cainü cheye wei mian.*

14. For the importance of print-cultural media in the production of Shanghai as the image of China's first modern city, see des Forges, *Mediasphere Shanghai*. For a more complete survey of Wu dialect novels, see Zhang and Liu, *Wu di fangyan xiaoshuo*.

15. Song Lihua, "Fangyan yu Ming Qing xiaoshuo."

16. For a discussion of the aesthetics and politics of the novel itself as well as those of the twentieth-century discussions surrounding its republication, see Rea, "A History of Laughter."

17. Liu Ts'un-yen, *Chinese Popular Fiction*, pp. 126–30. Liu discusses these novels in a section entitled "Dialect and Pornography," which suggests that, with a single notable exception, his opinion of these works is not particularly high. See also Brokaw, *Commerce in Culture*, pp. 318, 492–93, 505–6, and 512.

Fujian. Most famously, *Mindu bieji* 閩都別記 (A distinct record of the capital of Minnan) employs Minnan dialect to turn "wild history" into "local history."[18]

To a degree, the Beijing novels produced in the late nineteenth century partake in this broader trend of late-Qing linguistic regionalism. As I have pointed out in chapter 2, the popular martial arts tales of that era employ a variety of cultural signs to establish Beijing as a unique locale. Here, we should note that such cultural markers are matched with what has generally been recognized as a very lively Beijing vernacular.[19] For instance, Yu Pingbo 俞平伯 (1900–1990), not coincidentally the great-grandson of Yu Yue, remarks how the use of regional language in *The Three Knights and the Five Gallants* deserves proper annotation. Yet, he continues, "unfortunately my Beijing dialect is not good and my knowledge too limited, so rather than offering a smattering of scattered comments, I thought it better to simply keep my ignorance to myself."[20] Commenting on *The Tale of Romance and Heroism*, Hu Shi similarly praises its lively use of Beijing language, calling it a "textbook of Beijing vernacular." In his usual teleological manner, Hu concludes that this use of local language was part of a longer historical evolution of the novel form, stating: "All the local dialect that in the age of Cao Xueqin one did not dare [to use], was now used. Thus there are various dialogues in the *Tale of Heroism and Romance* that are even more lively than those in the *Dream of the Red Chamber*."[21] Since this early championing of the novels' use of Beijing dialect, scholars have commented here and there on the

18. *A Distinct Record of the Capital of Minnan* circulated as a hand-copied manuscript beginning from the late Jiaqing reign and was apparently a perennial crowd-pleaser in shops renting out novels. The novel is a sprawling tale in 401 chapters that recounts the history of Fujian from its mythical origins to the present. See Fu Yiling, "Qianyan."

19. The first preface to the novel by Wenzhu zhuren 問主主人 already notes the novel's plethora of "local tones" (*tuyin* 土音) and "mistaken characters" (*ezi* 訛字). However, it is not entirely clear what is meant by such phrases as "local tones." Does it refer to many different regional accents, or merely to the novel's plentiful use of the local Beijing dialect? Most twentieth-century scholars have taken the phrase simply to mean "Beijing dialect." See Wenzhu zhuren, "*Zhonglie xiayi zhuan* xu," p. 1543.

20. Yu Pingbo, "Jiao du hou ji."

21. Hu Shi, "*Ernü yingxiong zhuan* xu," p. 359.

particular Beijing dialect phrases found on their pages, while contemporary Beijing slang dictionaries invariably draw upon these novels to illustrate dialect terms.[22]

Yet even though *The Three Knights* is part of a larger historical trend that saw more and more vernacular novels published in regional languages, what sets this novel apart and marks it as a unique product of the capital Beijing is the way it gathers a host of different dialects. Other dialect novels produced in the nineteenth century explore their own dialect to stake a cultural claim separate from the imperial center of power, Beijing. Yangzhou novels such as *The Tale of the Flying Cripple* and *The Sluices of Qingfeng* are written, apart from standard vernacular, solely in Yangzhou dialect; *The Flowers of Shanghai* records the sound of Wu dialect in the speech of its courtesans. Indeed, the singular use of such dialects represents a clear effort to construct identities separate from the cultural, political, and linguistic center of Beijing. For instance, in employing Wu dialect in *The Flowers of Shanghai*, Han Bangqing is said to have been inspired by, but also to have been reacting to, the use of Beijing speech in novels produced earlier in the capital.[23] As such, the sound of Wu dialect recorded in the speech of courtesans can be seen to represent a direct, if still muted, linguistic challenge by the periphery to the center.[24] *A Distinct Record of Minnan* uses Fujianese to construct a history of Fujian. The novel, its language, and the history it produces are both unofficial and local.

In contrast, the late nineteenth-century martial arts tales produced in Beijing do not merely employ Beijing dialect—they actually gather a plethora of different dialects within their pages. This inclusion of a variety of regional languages had clear sociopolitical ramifications: whereas during the nineteenth century an increasing number of novels

---

22. For example, the scholar Guo Qinna devotes a single article to the Beijing term *daga* 打嘎 (apparently a local Beijing game involving a stick) in one particular scene in the novel. See Guo Qinna, "Shuo *daga*."

23. In his preface to the novel, Hu Shi cites the *Tuixinglu biji* 退醒廬筆記 (A record of the Tuixinglu) by a certain Sun Yusheng 孫玉聲, which recalls Han Bangqing as saying, "In writing *The Record of the Stone*, Cao Xueqin used the language of the capital. Why would you think my novel cannot use the dialect of Wu?" 曹雪芹撰《石頭記》皆操京語, 我書安見不可以操吳語? Hu Shi, "*Haishang hua liezhuan xu*," p. 367, and again on p. 382.

24. See des Forges, *Mediasphere Shanghai*, especially pp. 32–37.

produced in the provinces staked their regional claim by employing their own dialects, the Beijing-produced martial arts tales reaffirmed that city's central position in the empire by collecting and imitating other regional dialects. *The Tale of Everlasting Blessings and Peace, Part I*, for instance, has rightfully been lauded for its lively use of Beijing language, but the story was in its day actually more famous for its use of Shandong dialect spoken by the central character, the uncouth and unorthodox "Shandong Ma" 山東馬. Similarly, *The Tale of Romance and Heroism* self-consciously mirrors the sociopolitical regionalization of the nineteenth century by including in its pages colorful characters that are said to speak in local Shandong language, the Hebei dialect of country folk, or impossible-to-comprehend Jiangnan dialects. Though the bulk of these novels were still written in perfectly clear and quite standard vernacular, it is striking to what degree works such as *The Three Knights* include not only snippets of typical Beijing dialect, but also a wider heteroglossia of dialect, reproducing accented speech from Jiangsu, Zhejiang, Hubei, Shanxi, or rural Hejian.

By bringing so many different regional languages together, martial arts romances such as *The Three Knights* offered the reader a printed reflection of the way the capital was imagined as the center of a vast empire, a place where all languages come together. An early twentieth-century source, Xia Renhu's 夏仁虎 (1874–1963) *Jiu jing suo ji* 舊京瑣記 (Scattered notes on the old capital), for instance, emphasizes how the capital gathers not only all the different people found throughout the empire, but indeed all the languages these people speak:

The capital is a sea of people; it is a hybrid place that mingles people from all corners, and as a result the languages they speak are multifarious. Still, between these various languages clear borders exist. After a while you become used to the language of the bannermen, local patois, official language, so that you can differentiate them as soon as you hear them. Amongst these are also mingled Manchu and Mongolian, . . . there is also the language called Hui and a secret guild-language, which is often used by actors in their interaction to prevent others from understanding them. After the Boxer Rebellion, one or two European languages were mixed in, as well as Japanese, but these were just for laughs, and the grand men of the capital regarded these as beneath their notice.

京師人海, 各方人士雜處, 其間言龐語雜, 然亦各有界線. 旗下話, 土話, 官話, 久習者一聞而辨之. 亦間攙入滿, 蒙語 ... 又有所謂回宗語, 切口語者,

市井及倡優往往用之, 以避他人聞覺. 更子後則往往攙入 一二歐語, 日語, 資為諧笑而已, 士大夫弗屑顧也.[25]

Xia celebrates the capital as a cosmopolitan center that brings together all the different languages in the empire, if not the world. Manchu, Mongolian, Muslim Hui languages, the cant of actors, and even European and Japanese languages can be heard on the streets of cosmopolitan Beijing.

Yet even though Xia celebrates the mingling of various languages, his account reveals a strict hierarchy at the center of this linguistic melting pot. Xia begins with the language of bannermen, moves past the Hui Muslim language to continue with a secret language spoken by actors, and finally ends with foreign languages, which, of course, are only to be laughed at by the grand gentlemen of Beijing. Moreover, though Xia might celebrate the broad diversity of languages found in the capital, he also suggests that while these languages mingle, they do not mix. While describing the various languages as "multifarious," he still argues that "clear borders exist." Indeed, Xia suggests that a true cosmopolitan identity is based on the ability to distinguish between these various languages. As Xia states, the multifarious nature of the various languages may be confusing at first, but a true Beijing denizen is the person who "can differentiate them as soon as he hears them." A true Beijing identity, in short, is established not by one's ability to speak a particular language, not even if that language is the local Beijing patois. Rather, according to Xia, it is based on one's ability to recognize and appreciate the difference between all kinds of languages, dialects, and accents. Later in this chapter, I will return to this typically cosmopolitan mode of appreciating linguistic diversity. For now, however, let us return to the question of sound and explore how the printed text displays an appreciation of different languages on an acoustic level.

25. Xia, *Jiu jing suo ji*, p. 44. It is not entirely clear when *The Scattered Notes on the Old Capital* was written. Based on the events described it must have been written in the early years of the Republic. In the preface, the author himself notes how he came to the capital in 1898 and how he explicitly limits his discussion to events of the late-Qing period.

Regional Identity and Cross-Talking in
The Three Knights and the Five Gallants

Let me first turn to *The Three Knights*, in particular an episode entitled "The *Yin-yang* Mix-up."[26] The episode, which runs from chapter
23 to chapter 27, revolves primarily around a single, simple conceit. A
Shanxi merchant by the name of Qu Shen is murdered but comes back
to life in the body of a woman. In turn, Ms. Bai Yulian, the wife of a
scholar who placed first in the imperial examinations, hangs herself
to defend her chastity, but her soul is reincarnated in Qu Shen's body.
The result is a typical comedy of errors 鬧戲 where mistaken identities, physical slapstick, bad puns, and unexpected reversals of fortune
create a pleasurably loud and vociferous chaos that is untangled only
when Judge Bao finally takes the matter in hand. Recognizing how Bai
Yulian speaks Shanxi dialect and how Qu Shen uses a typical feminine
upper-class form of speech, Judge Bao unravels the dense plot of double
murders and puzzling substitutions and finally succeeds in returning
the souls to their original bodies so that once again speech matches
identity.[27]

---

26. I borrow this title from Susan Blader's translation, who in turn bases her title
on the storyteller manuscript, *The Cases of Judge Bao*. Blader, *Tales of Magistrate
Bao*, pp. 105–48.
27. Even though the episode in the novel is based on older operas, its emphasis
on the link between regional identity and speech is markedly an invention of the
later storyteller novel. In the operatic tradition, the particular episode is known
under a variety of titles, none of which suggest a strong interest in regional identity, dialect speech, or the relationship between them. Instead we find titles such
as "Qionglin yan" 瓊林宴 (The banquet in the [imperial] Qionglin Garden); "Wen
qiao nao fu" 問樵鬧府 (Questioning the wood-cutter creates a ruckus at court), also
known as "Da gun chu xiang" 打棍出箱 (Jumping out of the funeral casket while
brandishing a cudgel); "Hei lü gao zhuang" 黑驢告狀 (The black donkey lodges a
complaint), also known as "Yin yang cuo" 陰陽錯 (The mix-up of *yin* and *yang*); or
simply "Fan Zhongyu 范仲玉," which is the name of the *zhuangyuan* in the story.
As their titles suggest, the focus in these operas is not the cross-talking Shanxi
merchant, but rather the *zhuangyuan* driven berserk or, alternatively, a miraculous
claim by a donkey who brings a plea before Judge Bao. While these various themes
also appear in the novel, the interest in regional dialect in the novel seems unique
and only appears once the tale is translated into a storyteller/novel routine. See Li
Xiusheng, *Guben xiqu jumu tiyao*, p. 624.

As the plot summary above illustrates, the "*Yin-yang* Mix-up" relies on the linguistic expressions of the various characters as markers of their different identities. Gender, class, and, most significantly, regional identities are distinguished on the basis of the characters' speech. For instance, when Qu Liang, Qu Shen's brother, finds his brother's body now housed by Ms. Bai's spirit, the recognition of mistaken identities is told as follows:

> When Qu Liang heard his brother speak like a woman and moreover without a Shanxi accent, he became depressed, saying, "What's up with you! Us Shanxi folk are real men.[28] How will you face others if you're like this?"
>
> 屈良聽他哥竟是婦人的聲音, 也不是山西口氣, 不覺納悶道: "你這是怎的了呢? 咱們山西人是好朋友. 你這個光景, 以後的見人呢?"[29]

Similarly, when Zhao Hu finds Qu Shen, now in the body of the elegant Ms. Bai, we read,

> Zhao Hu heard the Old Taoist's explanation, and when he then saw how this lady might look like a woman but actually spoke like a man, and had a Shanxi accent to boot, going on about murdering someone for financial gain and what not—well, hearing this, Zhao Hu could not make any sense of it.
>
> 趙爺聽老道之言, 又見那婦人雖是女形, 卻是像男子的口氣, 而且又是山西口音, 說的都是圖財害命之言. 四爺聽了, 不甚明白.[30]

Here, Zhao Hu notes that the uncouth behavior and physical strength displayed by "the lady" do not match her feminine appearance, but most of all he is shocked to hear a male voice coming out of a "woman's" mouth. While visible markers such as bound feet and inappropriate

---

28. The phrase "hao pengyou" is northern dialect for a "real guy." Xu Shirong, *Beijing tuyu cidian*, p. 170.

29. *San xia wu yi* (1996), vol. 1, p. 152. Note that *The Three Knights* here has already dropped the typical Shanxi accent still found in its handwritten predecessor, *The Aural Record of the Dragon Diadem*. For the original phrase with a Shanxi accent, see *Longtu erlu*, vol. 1, p. 271.

30. *San xia wu yi* (1996), vol. 1, p. 154.

ritual behavior make it clear that gender boundaries have been crossed, the primary marker of crossed identities in "The *Yin-yang* Mix-up" remains linguistic. Qu Shen, despite his female body, talks like a man from the province of Shanxi, and, correspondingly, Ms. Bai Yulian, despite her male appearance, speaks like an upper-class lady married to a *zhuangyuan*.

The novel does not simply tell the reader of this mismatch of identity and speech; it actually shows the reader the dislocation of identity by having the Shanxi merchant speak in a marked northern dialect. For instance, before Qu Shen is murdered, the novel had already firmly introduced his unmistakable identity as a vulgar Shanxi merchant by registering the peculiar accent of his dialect. When Qu Shen, for instance, finds himself away from home late at night on a business trip, this is the way he introduces himself as he requests shelter for the night:

> I am on the road and it's gotten dark (*dairk*). So excuse ('*scuse*) me, could you help me find a place to put up. 'Morrow I'll reward you handsomely. 我是行路的, 因天黑(賀)了, 借光(官)兒, 尋個休兒. 明兒重禮相謝.[31]

In this passage, a variety of signs are used to mark Qu Shen's speech as regional. For instance, Qu Shen abbreviates the phrase "tomorrow" (*mingtian*) to "'morrow" (*mingr*) by dropping the *tian* and adding a typically northern "er" sound. Similarly, Qu Shen uses the phrase, "Could you help me find a place to put up?" where his word choice (*xun ge xiur* as a vulgar phrase for "find a place to put up"), grammar (the dropping of the number "yi" before *ge*), and even accent (the "er" sound added as a nominalizing suffix to the character *xiu*) combine to give a striking sense of vulgar, northern dialect speech.

Yet in order to establish the Shanxi merchant's identity as unmistakably Shanxi, rather than a more generalized northern identity, the novel goes beyond simply marking the merchant's speech as vulgar, but represents dialect accent first and foremost as an acoustic phenomenon. It does so by printing certain words twice, once to mark the meaning of the word and once to mark the actual pronunciation. Thus "dark" in Qu

31. *Zhonglie xiayi zhuan* (1879), chap. 24, p. 6B; *San xia wu yi* (1996), vol. 1, chap. 24, p. 147. I here quote the original because in the Zhonghua shuju reprint the order of appearance of standard and dialect character has been reversed.

道我誰的屈申道我是行路的因天黑賀了借光覓見尋

個休兒睍睍重禮相謝婦人道你等等又遲了半天方見

有個男子出來打著一個燈籠問道做甚嗎的屈申作個

揖道我是個走路兒的因天晚萬咧拉難以行走故此這驚

動借個休兒明兒重禮相謝男子道原來如此這有甚麼

咃請到家裡坐屈申道我還有一頭驢男子道只管拉進

來將驢子拴在東邊樹上便持燈引進來讓至屋內屈申

提了錢散子隨在後面進來一看卻是兩明一暗三間草

房屈申將散子放在炕上從新與那男子見禮那男子還

禮道茅屋草舍掌櫃的不要見笑屈申道好說好說男子

5.2 Dialect accents in *The Tale of Loyalty and Righteousness* (*The Three Knights and the Five Gallants*), chapter 24. (In *Zhong lie xia yi zhuan*, published in 1879 by the Juzhen tang. Photo courtesy of Yale University Library.)

Shen's speech is printed first as *hei* 黑 to mark the meaning, and then, off to the side, as *he* 賀 to mark his Shanxi accent. Similarly, "Excuse me" is double printed as *guang* 光 and *guan* 官. Thus whenever Qu Shen opens his mouth, the novel marks his speech by double-printed characters. Elsewhere, "even now" (*hai* 還) becomes "*ev'n now*" (*han* 含), "enter" (*jin* 進) becomes "*ent'r*" (*jing* 淨), "I" (*laozi* 老子) becomes "*Oi*" (*lezi* 樂子), "town" (*cheng* 城) becomes "*t'own*" (*chen* 沉), etc. Not only does this division between standard speech and nonstandard accent show an extreme self-consciousness on the part of the novel in terms of its use of dialect, but it also shows how, in order to distinguish Shanxi dialect from other northern dialects, the novel represents dialect first and foremost as an acoustic phenomenon.

This use of dialect speech, or what I call cross-talking, is, like cross-dressing, best understood as a performative act that involves the creation, subsequent destabilization, and final reaffirmation of different identities. Of course, in and of itself, a tale in which a man and a woman temporarily switch bodies is hardly remarkable in late-imperial Chinese vernacular literature. As testified by a steady stream of scholarly publications, late-imperial literature delighted in the confusion of mistaken identities through cross-dressing.[32] In fact, in many ways Qu Shen the uncouth Shanxi merchant acting like a demure young wife is built on the same physical humor as Lu Zhishen dressing like a young bride in chapter 5 of *The Outlaws of the Marsh* or Monkey disguising himself as the wife of Pigsy in chapter 18 of *The Journey to the West*.[33] The usual visual markers of cross-dressing, whether sartorial or physical, appear in predictably slapstick fashion. Bound feet, for instance, a standard marker of the female gender, show up as a telltale sign that prescribed

32. For instance, Zeitlin, *Historian of the Strange*; Volpp, "The Discourse on Male Marriage"; Allen, "Dressing and Undressing."

33. Historical romances and martial arts novels delight in scenes where uncouth martial heroes cross-dress as young brides as a ploy to beat up an unsuspecting, but often rapacious, groom. Tellingly, it is always the most uncouth and violent of characters—Lu Zhishen in *Outlaws of the Marsh*, or Niu Tong in *Shuo Yue quanzhuan* 說岳全傳 (The complete tale of Yue Fei; first published in 1684 or 1744)—who ends up cross-dressing. Such scenes are, if played right, a hilarious displacement from sexual dalliance to physical violence in which saucy dialogue (characters tend to address the cross-dressing Monkey or martial hero as "my darling") still has its place but is certainly subordinated to physical slapstick.

gendered identities have been crossed. For example, even after Ms. Bai Yulian has entered the vulgar, male body of Qu Shen, she still walks like a demure lady of stature: "Her two big feet took small mincing steps, less than four inches a pace, as if they were two small golden lotuses" 他兩只大腳兒, 彷彿是小小金蓮一般, 扭扭捏捏, 一步挪不了四指兒的行走.[34] In contrast, the Shanxi merchant Qu Shen, when called to take the stand before Judge Bao, "takes big strides into the hall" 大叉步兒走上堂來 and plumps down with a loud "GUDONG" 咕咚, even though he now possesses a diminutive female body with tiny bound feet.[35] Bound feet, the essential marker of female identity in late-imperial vernacular literature, here provide the opportunity for cross-gendered physical slapstick.

As is the case with cross-dressing, the fictional creation and transgression of identities in cross-talking, apart from its comic entertainment value, are associated with larger themes of political (in)stability. Scholars of premodern literature, for instance, are fond of quoting the late-imperial inhibition against actors dressing in the clothes of emperors to illustrate the serious nature of seemingly playful acts of cross-dressing.[36] A Ming anecdote by Xu Fuzuo 徐復祚 (1560–after 1630) regarding the storyteller Hu Zhong shows that cross-talking in the manner of emperors was similarly considered a potentially rebellious and anxiety-causing form of entertainment:

Yuanmei [Wang Shizhen 王世貞; 1526–90] retained a young man in his household named Hu Zhong, who was good at telling plain vernacular tales [*ping hua*]. Whenever Yuanmei was drunk, he would order him to tell stories to entertain visitors. Every time Zhong would speak of

---

34. *San xia wu yi* (1996), vol. 1, chap. 25, p. 153.
35. Ibid, p. 158. Note the use of onomatopoeias here to denote physicality.
36. The phrase, found in the Ming legal code, reads as follows: "Whenever musicians perform any kind of *zaju* or opera, they are not allowed to dress up as the various emperors and imperial consorts, loyal ministers or martyrs, or in the likeness of the sages of ages past. Those who disobey this rule shall be punished with a hundred strokes of the baton" 凡樂人搬做雜劇戲文, 不許裝扮歷代帝王后妃, 忠臣節烈, 先聖先賢像, 違者杖一百. Quoted in Hu Shiying, *Huaben xiaoshuo gailun*, p. 347. For a discussion of cross-dressing, which in this case includes vocal role-playing through song, and its implications for Ming-Qing political identities, see Tina Lu, *Persons, Roles, and Minds*.

emperors, like Minghuang,[37] Song Taizu,[38] or Wuzong[39] of our dynasty, he would refer to himself as "majesty" or use the royal "we," while addressing others in terms such as "my subjects." He made a habit of doing this, but it was only in jest. Shisu [the son of Wang Shizhen; 1566–1601] would often take Zhong to the tavern, where he would fool around with such language and everybody there would laugh out loud.

元美家有廝養名胡忠者, 善說評話. 元美酒酣, 輒命說解客頤. 忠每說明皇, 宋太祖, 我朝武宗, 輒自稱朕, 稱寡人, 稱人曰卿等, 以為常, 然直戲耳. 士騙每攜忠酒樓, 胡作此等語, 座客皆大笑.[40]

As the anecdote shows, cross-talking combines comedy with political taboo. Whenever Hu Zhong engages in a linguistic masquerade, the audience bursts out laughing. Still, it is clear that the author of the anecdote associates this kind of oral farce with rather dubious pleasures. Wang Shizhen is said to order his servant to tell these tales only when he is inebriated; Wang Shizhen's son, Shisu, takes the man to the tavern or other places of ill repute to amuse his friends. Indeed, while the author hurries to argue that Hu Zhong's impersonation of the emperor was only "in jest," there is no doubt that the use of the imperial personal pronoun by a lowly storyteller is highly inappropriate. The Ming legal code may never have explicitly forbidden such oral transgressions of the *pluralis majestatis*; however, the anecdote makes clear that crosstalking by storytellers, while common, nevertheless could be every bit as taboo as the donning of an inappropriate set of clothes by actors.

In "The *Yin-yang* Mix-up," personal pronouns similarly become the

---

37. Minghuang refers to Tang Xuanzong 唐玄宗 (685–762), the emperor famously associated with the operatic arts, his indulgence of the consort Yang Guifei 楊貴妃 (719–56), and the political instability supposedly caused by this trifectic infatuation with music, opera, and women.

38. Song Taizu 宋太祖 (927–76) was the first emperor of the Song, a famous figure in late-imperial literature because he spent much of his youth roaming the empire as a belligerent *jianghu* rogue before ascending the imperial throne later in life.

39. Wuzong is the Ming emperor Zhengde 正德 (1491–1521), an emperor associated with traveling around the empire incognito (i.e., cross-dressed) looking for romance, while forsaking his political duties in the palace. The particular list of emperors mentioned here serves to remind the reader that confusing political identities in the manner of Hu Zhong may have serious consequences. It is merely that these emperors were known to dress down, whereas Hu Zhong "talks up."

40. Xu Fuzuo, *Huadang ge cong tan, ji* 15, *juan* 5, p. 8A–B.

most succinct linguistic marker of identity, while the confusion resulting from their substitution is both pleasurably lively and potentially anarchistic. Thus, Ms. Bai Yulian calls herself "this lowly woman" 奴家 even while in the body of a man; Qu Shen, in a most vulgar manner, calls himself "Oi" 樂子, even though he looks like a woman."[41] And when Ms. Bai, in the body of Qu Shen, cries out for her "husband," the reaction of the crowd gathered round immediately brings home the comic potential of such a substitution: "Friend, you think you can still find a husband with a face like that?" 好朋友! 這個腦袋樣兒, 你還有丈夫嗎.[42] Yet even though the confusion arising from the misuse of terms of address is comically played out in the novel, it does lead to considerable confusion at court once the case is brought before the Judge. For instance, both Qu Shen and Ms. Bai Yulian fail to respond to the summons by the court attendants when they are called upon to take the stand. First, Ms. Bai, who now possesses Qu Shen's body, fails to understand that she is being addressed when the attendants shout for "Qu Shen," the result being that "Bearded Qu did not move at all" 屈鬍子他卻不動.[43] Similarly, it takes various promptings by attendants before Qu Shen takes the stand because he fails to heed the call of the judge, who addresses him as a woman. The scene is pure comedy, but it makes clear that linguistic confusion has serious consequences when authority seeks to interpellate its subject.

Though cross-talking is similar to cross-dressing in that it represents a play with markers of identity, there are, however, two important differences. First, while studies of cross-dressing focus on the crossing of gendered identities, if only to demonstrate the importance of such identities for the larger sociopolitical order, the act of cross-talking allows us to focus on the crossing of regional identities. A typical definition of the technical storytelling term *biankou* 變口, literally "changing one's mouth," bears out this emphasis on regionalism:[44]

---

41. *San xia wu yi* (1996), vol. 1, pp. 151 and 154 respectively.
42. Ibid., p. 152.
43. Ibid., p. 157.
44. Other terms seem applicable as well. For instance, *xiao xiang* 學鄉/像, literally "the imitation of regional speech," in this definition presented as southern, is probably the oldest term used for describing the imitation of accents by professional performers. See Meng Yuanlao, *Dongjing menghua lu*, p. 48.

> When, in the process of creating the likeness of characters, one uses
> dialect, the judicious imitation of the language of certain personae not
> only shows the regional background of certain characters, but also helps
> to demonstrate the social standing of the persona, his spirit, etc. . . .
> There are, for instance, yamen runners who speak Shaoxing dialect,
> traders in Beijing who speak Shanxi dialect, and pawnshop owners in
> the south who speak Huizhou dialect. In southern storytelling the shift-
> ing of one's accent is called *xiangtan* 鄉談, literally "regional speech,"
> while in the north it is called *daokou* 倒口, literally "speaking upside
> down." [45]

The encyclopedia entry demonstrates how the use of cross-talking by
storytellers is intimately related to the creation of a diverse array of
regional personalities. Such regional identities, moreover, are directly
tied to a broader imagination of social identity within a cosmopolitan
setting. Storytellers might use Shaoxing dialect to create characters
easily identifiable as Shaoxing *yamen* runners, or they might use Shanxi
dialect to create a class of Beijing traders originating from Shanxi.
Cross-talking, in other words, is not solely the fictional creation of
different distinct identities through the imitation of regional dialects.
It is the use of speech to playfully enact a complex social imaginary
that allows the listener/speaker to make sense of his urban environment by categorizing professional and class differences on the basis of
regional speech.

Second, due to its strong association with the theatrical stage, the
current scholarly discussion of cross-dressing in late-imperial literature
is often concentrated on visual and sartorial signs. In contrast, cross-
talking, precisely because it is closely associated with the oral arts of
the storyteller, allows us to expand our focus to include linguistic and
acoustic signs. This is illustrated in one of the primary sources on storytelling practices during the late-Qing and early Republican era, Lian
Kuoru's 連闊如 (1903–71) *Gathered Tales of the Jianghu*. In this exhaustive collection of anecdotes about storytellers, Lian describes the birth
of cross-talking in acoustic and regional terms:

45. Chen Fengchun, "Quyi shuogong."

Zhang Sanlu did not want to perform *bajiaogu*,[46] so he called his art *xiangsheng*. The character *xiang* refers to the face of the performer, which he uses to express joy, anger, sadness, or happiness, the use of which makes the audience smile. The character *sheng* refers to the way he uses the sound of his speech to create dimwitted characters, dumb, deaf, and blind, or to the imitation of the various accents of people from different provinces. That is the art of *xiangsheng*.

張三祿不願說八角鼓兒, 自稱其藝為相聲. 相之一字是以藝人之相貌, 形容喜怒哀樂, 使人觀而解頤. 聲之一字, 是以的[sic][47] 話聲音, 變出痴痴呆傻, 仿作聾瞎啞, 學各省人說話不同之語音. 蓋相聲之藝術.[48]

Unlike the art of cross-dressing, the art of cross-talking involves acoustic as well as visual cues. Even though the first half of the phrase refers to the facial expressions of the performer, the second half foregrounds the importance of the sound of the performer's voice. Distinctions between dumb and deaf people as well as a host of different regional identities are, as the quote makes clear, made on the basis of the sound of one's speech.

Double Printing Characters
as an Acoustic Mirror

Why does sound play such a crucial role in the scenes from *The Three Knights* involving a Shanxi merchant character? And how do we explain this unique system of printing double characters the novel invents to capture the sound of dialect? To answer these questions, we need to

---

46. *Bajiaogu* 八角鼓 is a form of performance in which the performer acts out and sings different opera character types to the accompaniment of the *bajiaogu*, an octagonal drum. Stated differently, both cross-talking and the performance of *bajiaogu* revolve around multiple characters enacted by a single performer. Zhang Sanlu is said to be the "inventor" of the *xiangsheng* act. We know little about him, but he is mentioned as a *bajiaogu* and *xiangsheng* performer in a popular *matoudiao* song from the late Qing, "Big Master Chases [his Wife] to [Nan]ding." For more on this popular series of *matoudiao*, see chap. 2.

47. Most likely this should be the character 說, "to speak."

48. Yunyouke, *Jianghu congtan*, p. 43.

understand that the mimicry of dialect is not simply the faithful recording of one single dialect. Whereas the presence of dialect in other nineteenth-century novels merely constructs a single identity, the act of cross-talking emphasizes the importance of regional accents so as to construct a double identity, that of a superior cosmopolitan versus that of an inferior provincial. Sound is crucial in the novel because it becomes the marker of distinction between these two identities. On the level of plot, this doubling of identities may be dramatized in the visual symbol of the mirror, but on the level of linguistic representation, it crucially calls for the mirage of sound. This illusion of sound, in turn, is produced by the doubling of characters on the page of the novel, the textual representation of the doubling of identities created by cross-talking.

It is tempting to argue that the emphasis on sound that marks *The Three Knights* is necessary for purely linguistic reasons. As linguists tell us, the phonetic level of distinction, as opposed to lexical or syntactical differences, plays the most crucial role when differentiating dialects. The importance of phonetics for the recording of dialect is most beautifully illustrated in the Chinese writing system, where the often striking distinction between spoken dialects simply disappears once the words are written down in characters.[49] This loss of phonetic distinction in Chinese writing helps to explain why so little dialect is found in late-imperial vernacular literature to begin with. As Patrick Hanan has noted, Chinese characters obscure the crucial phonetic level of language that allows us to tell dialects apart.[50] Indeed, we can often only identify a particular dialect in vernacular fiction by analyzing the lyrical poems that intersperse the prose because the rhyme scheme used in these poems alerts us to the particular pronunciation of a certain character.

Consequently, it is possible to argue that once Chinese vernacular literature began to explore dialect in the nineteenth century, it was inevitable that some writer would eventually invent a system similar to the

49. We should be careful not to overemphasize the "phonetic" nature of the Western alphabet and the "visual" or even "symbolic" nature of the Chinese script. After all, while the word "water" is spelled similarly throughout the United States, England, Scotland, Australia, and the Netherlands, it will be pronounced differently. For an analysis of the problem of overemphasizing the importance of the visual "nature" of the Chinese writing system, see Saussy, *The Great Walls of Discourse*, pp. 35–74.
50. Hanan, *The Chinese Vernacular Story*, p. 2.

double printing of characters found in *The Three Knights* so as to record the sound of dialect; however, this does not fully answer the question. After all, the use of double printing in *The Three Knights* is found in only a few other novels: *The Tale of Romance and Heroism*, *The Tale of Everlasting Blessings and Peace, Part 1*, and a handful of novelettes from the early twentieth century. Moreover, the emphasis on self-conscious dialect mimicry displayed through cross-talking seems unique to *The Three Knights*. Other dialect novels produced around the same time, though recognizing that it would be difficult to capture dialect speech in writing, found ways of doing so without relying on the curious meaning/pronunciation distinction employed by *The Three Knights*.

Han Bangqing's *Flowers of Shanghai*, for instance, either simply uses "dialect" characters that had long been popularized in *tanci* performance texts or employs newly invented characters to register a uniquely Wu dialect expression. As Han writes:

> As to the local dialect of Suzhou, *tanci* often use vulgar characters to record it. Since these characters have been circulating for a long time and everybody knows them, I still use them. This being a novel, there is no need to indulge in scholarly research on that part. However, there is the case of those words where there is a sound but no character. For instance, when saying "do not," Suzhou people, whenever they are pronouncing them hurriedly, will elide them. While you can still make them into the two characters "do not," this will not correspond to the spirit of the moment; moreover there is no other character that can replace them. That is why I have written the two characters "do not" together in a single frame. The reader must know that originally the character "don't" does not exist, but that they are the two characters read together as a single sound. As to those words that belong to the category where *nie* sounds like *yan*, *xia* sounds like *jia*, *nai* is *ni*, or *li* is *yi*, the reader will figure these out for himself. Here I need not burden him too much with these.
>
> 蘇州土白, 彈詞中所載多係俗字, 但通行已久, 人所共知, 故仍用之; 蓋演藝小說不必沾沾於考據也. 惟有有音而無字者, 如說勿要二字, 蘇人每急呼之, 併維一音, 若仍作勿要二字, 便不合當時神理; 又無他字可以替代, 故將勿要二字併寫一格. 閱者須知覅字本無此字, 乃合二字作一音讀也. 他若 "嗹" 音 "眼," "嗄" 音 "賈," "耐" 即 "你," "俚" 即 "伊" 之類, 閱者自能意會, 茲不多贅.[51]

51. Han Bangqing, "Liyan 例言," p. 609.

Han Bangqing shows great concern over the question of how to register dialect phrases correctly so that they "correspond to the spirit of the moment." In fact, he focuses in particular on the thorny issue of sound, noting that those characters where there is "a sound but no character" deserve special attention.[52] Yet Han does not resort to the double printing of characters to solve this problem. Rather he just invents new characters, which in this case actually reduces two characters to a single one. As to the particularities of accent, where one character pronounced in Mandarin is pronounced differently in Wu dialect, Han does replace the standard characters with others, but he does not pay too much attention to it, noting how "the reader will figure these out for himself" and how he "need not burden him too much with these." Moreover, though Han does replace certain characters to capture an accent, he does not double-print them the way *The Three Knights* does.

To understand *The Three Knights'* peculiar interest in recording the sound of an accent, it is crucial to comprehend how the double printing of characters first and foremost serves to create distinct power relations. Unlike dialect novels from other regions, the Beijing-produced *Three Knights* records the sound of a particular dialect in a way that highlights the accent of the regional speaker. Whereas other novels invent new characters to construct their particular dialect as a separate and perhaps equal language, *The Three Knights* constantly prints double characters to mark how dialect is an inferior part of a single linguistic system. To put it simply, in the novel, the Shanxi merchant speaks the same language as the other characters, but by marking his accent the novel shows how the poor fellow constantly fails to achieve true equality. The primary purpose of cross-talking, in short, is to reinscribe the distinction between cosmopolitan reader and provincial outsider.

The need for such reinscription follows, I argue, from the fear of a loss of distinction, the threat that it would become impossible to tell provincial outsider and cosmopolitan dweller apart. Indeed, the plot of "The Shanxi Merchant and the *Zhuangyuan*'s Wife" is a comic mise-en-scène that enacts the horrific idea that a low-class provincial outsider might actually take the place of a *zhuangyuan* and his wife. In *The Three Knights* the boundary that defines the Shanxi merchant as a provincial

52. Here Han draws on a long established concept in Chinese premodern linguistics and literature to describe dialect, that "there is the sound but not the character."

is, as a result, most strongly defined when he threatens to bring upper-class speech and lower-class speech together by aping the manners of his social betters. In *The Three Knights*, such moments come to the forefront most clearly when Qu Shen attempts to access a higher level of civil discourse by speaking in a more formal manner. When Qu Shen and the male head of a household introduce themselves, for instance, a series of formal bows and ritualistic salutations take place.

> Qu Shen placed his bag on the earthen bed and once again greeted the man. The man returned the greeting and said, "My humble abode is a mere grass shelter, please do not ridicule me for it."
> Qu Shen said, "That is a fine way to talk."
> The man said, "What is your honorable surname? And where does your business flourish?"
> Qu Shen said, "My surname is Qu, I am called Qu Shen (*Sheng*). I run the Prosperous (*Pros'prus*) Woodshop on the avenue (*av'nue*) next to the drum (*droim*) tower in town (*t'own*). However, I have (*'ave*) not yet requested (*rekoisted*) you for your honorable surname (*surnaim*)."
> 屈申將靫子放在炕上，重新與那男子見禮．那男子還禮，道："茅屋草舍，掌櫃的不要見笑." 屈申道："好說." 男子便道："尊姓? 在那裡發財?" 屈申道："姓屈名叫屈申(生)，在城(沉)裡鼓(故)樓大街(該)開着個興(心)隆(倫)木廠．我還(舍)沒領(客)教你老貴姓(信)."[53]

In this exchange, official phrasing and ritual exchanges are mixed in with dialect sounds to produce a grotesque disjunction. In response to the host's polite phrases such as "grass shelter" to describe his humble abode, Qu Shen responds with a heavily accented "Prosperous (*Pros'prus*) Woodshop on the avenue (*av'nue*) next to the drum (*droim*) tower in town (*t'own*)" to describe his own home. And even though Qu Shen politely bows back to his host when asking the man's name, he butchers the formal phrase "I have not yet requested your honorable surname" by pronouncing it as "I 'ave not yet rekoisted you for your honorable surnaim." Much as the Shanxi merchant would like to partake in polite, cosmopolitan discourse, his accent keeps him from ever rising above the level of an uneducated provincial incapable of pronouncing even his own name correctly.

53. *Zhonglie xiayi zhuan* (1879), chap. 24, pp. 6B–7A. *San xia wu yi* (1996), vol. 1, chap. 24, p. 147.

The imitation of speech dramatized in "The *Yin-yang* Mix-up" reflects a broader social anxiety regarding the imitation of Beijing speech by provincials. An early twentieth-century bamboo song, for instance, directly addresses the aping of cosmopolitan speech and notes how people from Beijing aggressively reinscribe the crucial difference between metropolitan Beijinger and provincial hick. The poem reads,

> The language of each province has its own characteristics;
> The clear and melodious tones of Beijing are most worthy of extolling.
> There are those who have the bad habit of putting on official airs;
> The "impure Beijing tones" really make your flesh crawl.
> 各省語言各到家.
> 都城清脆最堪誇.
> 有人習氣兼官派.
> 月白京腔真肉麻.[54]

The author, Master Youhuan 優患生, remarks on the different languages spoken in the various provinces of the empire, noting how the "clear and melodious tones" of the capital Beijing are of course the best and as such "most worthy of extolling." Not surprisingly, outsiders seek to imitate such metropolitan speech, but Beijingers, not easily foiled, quickly reinscribe the difference between themselves and their provincial cousins by coining a specific phrase "impure Beijing tones" to ridicule those who think they can fake a Beijing accent.[55]

The question is, of course, how to make oral accents, so clearly distinguished in spoken language, visible on the printed page. The novel solves this problem by visual doubling, the printing of two characters whose dissimilarities critically reflect each other and in the process produce two distinct, but related identities. Nowhere does this act of doubling become more apparent than in the final scene of "The *Yin-yang* Mix-up," the court scene in which Judge Bao restores Ms. Bai Yulian and the Shanxi merchant Qu Shen to their proper bodies (see figure 5.3). At

---

54. Youhuansheng, "Jinghua baier zhuzhici," p. 291. Youhuansheng's collection was originally published in 1909.
55. For a contemporary definition of the phrase *yue bai qiangr*, see Jia, *Beijing erhua cidian*, p. 466. Jia defines the term as "an accent that is not purely Beijing." For a more elaborate but later description of this particular phrase, see Deng, *Zengbu Yanjing xiangtu ji*, vol. 2, pp. 538–40.

5.3 An acoustic mirror in the court of Judge Bao. (In *Qi xia wu yi*, published in 1892 by the Zhenyi shuju. Photo courtesy of Fudan University Library, Rare Book Collection.)

first blush, the moment seems solely visual. After all, it involves the help
of a mirror, which, once Qu Shen and Ms. Bai peer into it, switches theirs
souls so they are once more in the appropriate body.

Yet this visual moment of doubling is preceded by an even more
telling, acoustic moment of reflection, when Judge Bao has the two
victims led to the courtroom, where, for the first time, they see one
another. The moment reads as follows:

> As soon as Bai Yulian [here in fact the Shanxi merchant] turned her head
> around and saw Qu Shen, s/he could not help but cry out, "Ey! You that
> fellow (*fella*) over there, ain't you me (*moi*)? This is mighty strange! How
> (*'ow*) did you come to occupy (*ok'apai*) my body?" . . . When on this side
> Qu Shen [here in fact the *zhuangyuan*'s wife] heard him holler, s/he in
> turn lifted his head, looked at him, and could not help but gasp, "Hey!
> That woman! Are you not me? How come you have taken my body? How
> can this be possible!?"
> 白玉蓮一回頭見了屈申, 不由的嚷道: "唔! 你這個人(仍)不是我(餓)嗎! 這
> 可雁兒孤咧, 怎(咱)的我被你站(爭)了去呢?" . . . 這邊屈申聽他亂嚷, 也就
> 抬頭瞧他, 不由的失聲道: "吓! 那婦人! 你不是我麼? 你為何站了奴家身體,
> 是何道理?"[56]

As in the slightly later mirror moment, the text at this point presents
the reader with a case of self-conscious doubling. However, not only is
this moment a tellingly visual moment where the self is reconstituted
through an exchange of gazes, it is also a moment of linguistic mirror-
ing as the lines of the two victims reflect each other word for word.
Indeed, Bai Yulian's phrase is an almost literal echo of Qu Shen's first
outcry. Whereas Qu Shen shouts "Ey," Bai Yulian shouts "Hey"; whereas
he shouts "you that fella," she shouts "that woman"; whereas he asks,
"Ain't you me," she wonders, "Are you not me?" Indeed, almost word
for word Bai Yulian's phrase is an almost literal replica of Qu Shen's
original phrase.

And yet, even though the two phrases noted above are strikingly
similar, they also diverge at crucial moments, thereby producing separate identities that follow long established dichotomies of gender and

---

56. *Longtu erlu*, vol. 1, chap. 27, p. 291. I am quoting the *Dragon Diadem* because
the novel has, at this point, elided any trace of accent.

class. Whereas Qu Shen, for instance, shouts, "That fella" 這個人, Bai Yulian shouts back, "That woman" 那婦人. Whereas Qu Shen yells that "my" body has been stolen, Ms. Bai Yulian uses the polite phrase, "This woman's body" 奴家身體. Similarly, Ms. Bai Yulian speaks in flawless standard speech with perhaps slightly upper-class markers as signs of her status as a *zhuangyuan*'s wife, while Qu Shen, the vulgar merchant from Shanxi, roars in a coarse Shanxi accent. Whereas Qu Shen shouts out a vulgar "How?" 怎, which he nicely mispronounces as "'Ow?" 咱, Bai Yulian uses a more classical phrase, "How come?" 為何. And finally, whereas Qu Shen uses the dialect phrase, "This is mighty strange" 這可雁兒孤唎, the more high-class Bai Yulian ends her speech with a typical elegant phrase, "How can this be possible?" 是何道理. The two phrases clearly reflect one another, but the distance between the two allows the reader to distinguish a marked difference.

The distinct speech patterns of Ms. Bai Yulian and Qu Shen revolve not simply around semantic markers. Also involved is a set of acoustic distinctions, which, as argued above, allow Qu Shen to speak an approximation of a standard vernacular while still constantly constructing him as the sub-species "Shanxi dialect speaker." Most obviously, the phonetic distinction is made between Bai Yulian's unaccented speech and Qu Shen's heavily marked Shanxi sound. Whereas she shouts *ren* 人 (in this case "woman"), he mispronounces the word as *reng* 仍 (here best translated as "fella"). Similarly, whereas Bai Yulian designates herself properly as *wo* 我 ("me"), Qu Shen mispronounces the word as *e* 餓 (*moi*). As such, it is Qu Shen's accent as a distinct acoustic phenomenon that marks his speech as different from Ms. Bai's more standard pronunciation.

Even more subtly, this distinction is created within the merchant's speech itself. Or more precisely, in order to register the merchant's accent in this scene, the novel has to print mirror images for certain crucial words he uses. Thus *zen* 怎 is printed next to *zan* 咱, *wo* 我 next to *e* 餓, etc. Simply put, the moment of dialect speech in the novel is externally reflected in the way the standard speech of Ms. Bai and the dialect of Qu Shen mirror each other, but this echo effect also alerts us to the fact that in the scenes involving the Shanxi merchant, standard and dialect speech are also constructed as acoustic mirror images within speech itself. By printing the Shanxi dialect of Qu Shen as an acoustic mirror, the novel constantly reminds the reader how Qu Shen is a subject of the

Qing empire, but how, within this empire, he still belongs to a linguistic sub-species. Though he might try to attain the universal civilizational ideal of standard speech, he constantly falls short because of his accent.

Finally, cross-talking introduces an identity not only for the Shanxi merchant but, even more importantly, for the supposedly superior Beijing reader. After all, if cross-talking seeks to expose the provincial who takes on the airs of a cosmopolitan Beijing native, it also crucially hides some distinctions. In particular, it allows the kind of misrecognition between Beijing dialect and standard speech that creates the impression that the language spoken in Beijing is the universal language of communication. Take, for instance, a note to the poem on "impure Beijing tones," which explains:

> Those who live in the outer provinces cannot communicate through spoken language and have to force themselves to learn the language of the capital so that they can talk. But recently, people from neighboring provinces whose language always has been communicable, each time they are in Beijing, take joy in making noise, their tongues stiff and their mouths blunt, their diction completely off. Their sounds are not clear and melodious, and they have the bad habit of putting on official airs, which makes it really unbearable to listen to. People make fun of them, calling it "impure Beijing tones."
>
> 邊省人士, 語言不通, 不得不強學京話, 以便交談. 而今日言語素通之鄰省, 凡在京者, 亦喜操之, 舌僵口鈍, 字眼不能的[sic]真, 聲音不能清脆, 惟覺習氣官派, 令人聞之難堪. 故人嘲之曰"月白京腔."[57]

The note seeks to paper over some differences that can be easily overlooked. To begin with, the official standard spoken language was Mandarin, which by the nineteenth century was close to but not really the same as the speech used in Beijing. Even more importantly, in actuality the linguistic medium of the late-imperial period that came closest to being understood throughout the empire (albeit solely by the lettered elite) was the written, not the spoken, language. Accusing the provincial outsider of mispronouncing the tones of Beijing thus serves not only to create the idea of the improper accent of the provincial outsider, but also to establish the illusion of a homogeneous Beijing accent that serves as a

---

57. Youhuansheng, "Jinghua baier zhuzhici," p. 291.

universal standard. As a result, the difference between local and imperial Beijing, between voice and text, is lost.

It is this elision between voice and text that made the late-imperial
novel so attractive to later, twentieth-century champions of the vernacular. Seeking to establish a language that would help unite China as
a modern nation, scholars could not help but be enchanted by novels
whose language seemed such a clear reflection of the ideal vernacular,
that is, a direct transcription of the spoken voice of the Chinese people
into text.[58] As the notion of "impure Beijing tones" and the example of
double printing shows, however, the process of translating voice into
text is hardly one of easy equivalence. Rather, the creation of a standard pronunciation depended on a complicated process of elision of
internal differences, an elision established through the distinction from
the provincial other. Indeed, much as martial arts romances such as
The Three Knights might seem to suggest a proto-national vernacular
form, the way they transcribed spoken voice into text did not necessarily point towards a single nation speaking in a univocal fashion.
To be sure, to paraphrase Marshall McLuhan's famous dictum on the
relationship between print culture and political identity, giving printed
form to the sound of the spoken language allowed readers "to *see* their
vernaculars for the first time, and to visualize unity and power in terms
of the vernacular bonds."[59] However, as the double printing of *The Three*

58. Hu Shi regarded dialect literature as the basis of a national language literature,
arguing that the vernacular was nothing more than the end result of hundreds of
years of evolution, the most common elements of regional literature being adapted
into a transcendent national form. As Hu Shi argued, "A few hundred years ago,
the national literature of today was nothing but dialect literature. It is only because
people in those times were willing to use dialect to create literature, indeed dared
to use dialect to create literature, that we gathered a living literature over the course
of more than a thousand years; it was the most common elements [of that dialect
literature] that gradually came to be recognized as the basis of the national literature." That said, because, as Hu Shi argued, language was a living entity that kept
developing, it was crucial for the national literature to keep drawing on regional
literature so as to preserve its vitality. See Hu Shi, "*Hai shang hua liezhuan* xu,"
pp. 380–81. See also Hu Shi, "Da Huang Jueseng jun," and "*San xia wu yi* xu," pp.
321–22.

59. McLuhan's original quote includes the term "national," and reads as follows,
"For the hot medium of print enabled men to *see* their vernaculars for the first time,
and to visualize national unity and power in terms of the vernacular bounds" (*The
Gutenberg Galaxy*, p. 138).

Knights makes clear, the identity produced through visualization of the spoken voice was not necessarily one of homogeneous national unity, but rather one that placed different and clearly hierarchized localities within a framework of universal imperial power.

The Verbal Slapstick of the Cosmopolitan Teller of Tales

The Three Knights registered the sounds of dialect mimicry because of its close links with original storytelling performances. In this section, I will explore this link between storytelling mimicry and the novel by showing how both novel and storytelling performance employ cross-talking to recreate the linguistic diversity of the capital. Novel and storyteller recreate the welter of languages found in Beijing, but they do not create all of these languages as equal. By using the notion of verbal slapstick, I will show how cross-talking employs a speech act that constantly constructs hierarchies of the languages spoken in the city, thereby creating both the figure of a bumbling provincial speaking in dialect and, in contrast, a superior cosmopolitan identity shared by the storyteller and his audience or, in the case of the novel, the implied author and his implied readers.

To understand how the mimicry of regional speech serves to create the mirror image of provincial and cosmopolitan identities, it is useful to consider the act of cross-talking as a form of verbal slapstick. As Alan Dale has shown, in many ways verbal slapstick is similar to physical slapstick. Its slips of the tongue match the slip over the banana peel. Its emphasis on breakneck tongue twisters calls keystone cop chases to mind. Punch-lines are called punch-lines for a reason.[60] Most notably, oral mimicry functions as a form of verbal slapstick because, like physical slapstick, the imitation of regional accents revolves around the simulation of clumsy fumbling while in actuality demanding an incredible amount of verbal dexterity. Shanxi merchants, Hejian prefecture peasants, and Hubeinese fishermen may be portrayed as bumbling

60. Dale, *Comedy Is a Man in Trouble*, pp. 5–6.

idiots, yet the reader realizes it actually demands a tremendous amount of verbal acuity to bring them to life on the page of the novel. It is this distinction between the character who speaks with a marked accent and the storyteller/author who cross-talks like such a character that creates the contrast between provincial and cosmopolitan spirit.

It is through slapstick that physicality and orality are linked in *The Three Knights*, something that becomes clear when we consider the way the novel embodies both forms of slapstick in heroes like Bai Yutang, Jiang Ping, and especially Zhi Hua. Their tremendous physical dexterity is matched by their skill in verbal acrobatics.[61] For instance, chapter 81 tells how the hero Zhi Hua, on a quest to steal the emperor's crown, soars over the walls of the Forbidden City, defying both the principle of gravity and imperial law in a move that beautifully captures the free spirit of knight-errantry.[62] This physical act of defiance, however, is matched by a similar act of verbal acrobatics. Indeed, before *The Three Knights* devotes two pages to describing the scene of Zhi Hua scaling walls and walking over rooftops, it first spends two full chapters on Zhi Hua engaging in an act of verbal mimicry while pretending to be a peasant from Hejian prefecture. Similarly, Bai Yutang, the Jade-Pelted Rat, may be memorable to many for the moment when he climbs the Cloud Piercing Tower towards the end of

---

61. When compared with the earlier classical Ming tale on which the novel is based, the miraculous ability at verbal mimicry possessed by the five gallants in *The Three Knights* represents a clear shift towards oral performance. The earliest version of the story of the Five Gallants, the late-Ming tale "Wu shu nao Dongjing zhuan" 五鼠閙東京傳 (Five rats create havoc in the Eastern Capital), tells of five rat creatures who use magic to transform their visual appearance so as to mimic a young examination candidate, Judge Bao, and eventually even the emperor himself. In the nineteenth-century tale, the heroes retain their "magic" ability at mimicry, but the visual transformation has been replaced by remarkable skills at oral mimicry that allow the rats to confuse unsuspecting victims and dazzle the reader. For a discussion of the earlier tale, see Ning, "Wu shu nao Dongjing," pp. 578–79.

62. Emphasizing the element of physical dexterity, Song Weijie has argued that the sheer joy of physical acrobatics has a potentially subversive edge, a notion best captured in the image of the knight-errant flying over walls. See Song Weijie, "Wan Qing xiayi gongan xiaoshuo," p. 448. For an analysis of the importance of the image of the flying martial artists in early silent-era martial arts films, see Zhang Zhen, *An Amorous History*, chap. 6.

The Three Knights.[63] Yet, tellingly, this hero first enters the novel in the disguise of a beggarly scholar who entertains the reader not through physical but instead verbal acts of acrobatics when, in the thirty-second chapter, he engages a waiter in an inn with an impossibly long list of culinary demands.

The emphasis on both verbal and physical forms of slapstick is suggestive of the origins of *The Three Knights*: the popular storytelling performances found on the streets of the Qing capital. Indeed, as I argued in chapter 2, a crucial function of the novel is to capture the sense of hustle-and-bustle and the street-carnival atmosphere that surrounded its original performance. When it comes to the representation of martial arts, for instance, many of the scenes in the novel are direct depictions of late-Qing strongman acts.[64] As to the oral element, the novel is filled with "street-language." As I showed in chapter 3, *The Three Knights* self-consciously explores vendor calls, chants used by beggars, and rhymes sung by medicine peddlers, all of which recreate the acoustic excitement of the capital's streets. The novel effectively brings the sounds of the storyteller performances of the capital's entertainment quarters to the printed page.

The verbal artistry of cross-talking represents the acoustic excitement of the capital particularly well because it highlights how a single

---

63. For a reading of the climbing of Cloud Piercing Tower which interprets the physical act of breaking and entering (*chuang* 闖) as defining the spirit of the modern martial arts novel, see David Wang, *Fin-de-Siècle Splendor*, pp. 140–45.

64. Not only are many of the martial encounters set at temple fairs, but in quite a few late nineteenth-century martial arts novels, the performance of martial arts is presented as theatrical street spectacle. Many good examples are found in *The Tale of Everlasting Blessings and Peace, Part 1*, for instance the following scene from chapter 2: "Upon this, the two took their swords and tasseled spears and left the inn. Following the avenue, they came to an empty square on the south side of the Pearl Market where they delineated a performance spot. They positioned themselves in the middle and performed a routine of leg kicks and a routine with the sword. After this they began their foot and fist routine, which was really good: their fists resembled falling stars, their gaze resembled lightning; their waists resembled a snake's coils, their legs were as if drilled into the ground. What did it look like? There is a celebratory poem as proof" 二人遂帶自己單刀, 花槍出店, 順大街到珠市口南邊空寬之所, 開了一塊場子. 當中一站, 走了一趟彈腿, 耍了一趟單刀, 然後自將拳腳拉開, 真是好; 拳似流星眼似電; 腰似蛇行腿似鑽. 怎見得? 有贊為證. Guo Guangrui, *Yongqing shengping* (1995), chap. 2, p. 7.

storyteller can reproduce the multifarious sounds of the city's crowds. A good example of this principle is found in the late nineteenth-century *zidishu* "A Cosmopolitan Teller of Tales." The *zidishu* describes the oral performance of Pockmarked Ma, a storyteller from Shuntian Prefecture (Beijing), who plies his trade on the streets of the capital. The segment in which the *zidishu* focuses explicitly on the principle of cross-talking reads as follows:

最可聽是他各樣的聲音學的好.	Best of all to listen to was the way he imitated different sounds.
尖團懲（頂）細各有其腔.	Sharp tones and round tones, thick tones and thin ones, each had its phrasing.
學老婆儿齒落唇僵半吞半吐.	When he imitated toothless old women with stiff lips, he would half swallow and half spit [the words].
學小媳婦嬌音嫩語不柔不剛.	When he imitated the petulant tones and coy words of young women, he would sound neither hard nor soft.
學醉漢呼六喝麼連架式.	When he imitated the shouting and cursing of drunkards, he would strike one pose after another.
學書生咬文呃字忒酸狂.	When he imitated scholars, their mouths full of quotations, he would be really pedantic.
學怯音句句果然像八府.	When he imitated rural slang, every word would truly sound like the Eight Prefectures.
學蠻語字字必定仿三江.	If he imitated southern speech, every word would be like those of the Three Rivers Country.
西府的鄉談他了會打.	The country speech of the Western District, he could really nail it;
惟有那山東話兒說的更強.	Only his Shandong dialect was better still.[65]

In this segment, mimicry plays an important role, but the feature of mimicry that is most crucial is the simple proliferation of characters.

65. Helüshi, "Fengliu cike," vol. 2, p. 348.

Pockmarked Ma is not described as simply imitating a single character in lifelike manner. Rather, what is truly stunning is the way the story-teller manages to move from one character to the next. Indeed, by list-ing an exhaustive array of characters—a belligerent drunk, a toothless old hag, a coquettish young woman, and a pedantic scholar—the *zidi-shu* emphasizes how the single storyteller is capable of creating a whole profusion of characters, a riot of voices.[66]

The imitation of regional accents is a crucial part of this profusion of voices because it allows the storyteller to recreate the liveliness and linguistic plurality of the capital city. This, as we will remember, was exactly the way Xia Renhu's memoir, *Scattered Notes on the Old Capital*, described Beijing, a place where all these languages come together. The *zidishu* "The Cosmopolitan Teller of Tales" shows how this sense of the capital as the gathering place of many dialects and languages is given shape in oral performance. By listing the cardinal directions (the speech of the Western Prefecture, of the Southern Region, and of Shandong Province), the *zidishu* suggests that the storyteller imitates not simply a few, but in fact *all*, of the accents to be found in the empire.

In the art of cross-talking, the storyteller employs these linguistic distinctions so as to articulate social distinctions. By emphasizing the provincial, inferior nature of the characters portrayed while displaying a tremendous linguistic acuity himself, the storyteller who engages in verbal slapstick constantly reminds his audience of the superior nature of the cosmopolitan vis-à-vis the provincial. In the end, the purpose of oral mimicry is to create a "cosmopolitan" identity that depends on the ability of the storyteller and his audience to tell the various regional

---

66. In this aspect, the storyteller's act of mimicry fundamentally differs from the actor's craft of mimicry. Whereas cross-dressing and mimicry are crucial to the liminal identity of the actor, the actor tends to merely act out a single role. The storyteller, in contrast, is celebrated for recreating an entire cast of characters within a single performance. According to the commentator "Country Fellow," the acting out of different opera roles by single storytellers came about with four famous storytellers of the late Qing: Ma Rufei 馬如飛, Zhao Xiangzhou 趙湘舟, Yao Shizhang 姚士章, and Wang Shiquan 王石泉. See Xiangxiaren, "Shuoshu xianping," pp. 201–2. As shown in the previous section, Zhang Sanlu, the reputed inventor of cross-talking, originally was a *bajiaogu* performer, an act that featured a single performer acting out all the different roles found in opera (see note 46 above).

languages apart. And, most crucially, the storyteller emphasizes the comic shortcomings of the provincial's accent so as to keep the cosmopolitan form of speech elevated above the various regional languages.

To understand how the politics of verbal slapstick work out in the novel, take, once again, the example of the Shanxi Merchant Qu Shen. In one scene, we find Qu Shen, after indulging in drink and losing track of time, attempting to hurry home. Though the theme of losing track of time is timeless, what distinguishes *The Three Knights* from earlier novels is the way this lack of self-control is mirrored in the character's speech:[67]

> The more anxious Qu Shen got, the more the donkey refused to move. So he whipped the animal left and right, cursing, "You motha fuckin' piece of shit! 'You feed an army for a thousand days to use it on a single morning.' The sun's almos' gone, and ev'n now you're still acting up (*actin' up*)!" Yet even before he had finished speaking, all of a sudden the donkey's ears pricked up and with a loud "MA" it started bellowing, its four hooves flying as it spurted forward. Qu Shen knew his donkey's ailment; the donkey must have heard another donkey braying ahead and now was giving chase. So he held onto the reins and let it run, which, after all, was better than having it "act up." The donkey ran and ran, and would you believe it, there ahead was indeed another donkey. As soon as the beast saw the other donkey, it raised its front hooves and began hopping and jumping. Qu Shen failed to stay in the saddle and came tumbling down the donkey's ass.
>
> 他越着急, 驢越不走. 左一鞭, 右一鞭, 罵道: "溻八日的臭屎蛋! '養軍千日, 用在一朝.' 老陽兒眼看着沒拉, 你含合我闌侅侅(呆呆) 呢!" 話未說完, 忽見那驢兩耳一支楞,[68] "嗎," 的一聲, 就叫起來, 四個蹄子亂窜飛跑. 屈申知道他的毛病, 必是聽見前面有驢叫喚, 他必要追. 因此攏住扯手由他跑去, 到底比闌侅侅(呆) 強. 誰知跑來跑去, 果見前面有一頭驢. 他這驢一見, 便將前蹄揚起, 連蹦帶跳. 屈申坐不住鞍心, 順着驢屁股掉將下來.[69]

67. Keith McMahon opens his study *Causality and Containment* by illustrating his notion of containment with the theme of traveling and losing track of time.
68. "支楞" is Beijing dialect, meaning "stand straight up." Gao Aijun, p. 288.
69. *Zhonglie xiayi zhuan* (1879), chap. 24, pp. 4B–5A; *San xia wu yi* (1996), vol. 1, chap. 24, p. 146. The hand-written predecessor, *The Dragon Diadem*, is a good deal more explicit and vulgar in its portrayal of the donkey's interest in the other donkey. "Qu Shen's donkey ran—, no, rushed—, to the backside of the other donkey, and without asking for permission, just hoisted its front hooves and raised itself up. On top, Qu Shen exclaimed, "Oh no, Ooh no," and failing to stay in the saddle, his two

Physical slapstick mirrors verbal slapstick so as to paint the picture of a
man thoroughly out of control. Qu Shen has lost track of time because he
has been unable to control his appetite for alcohol. Now he finds himself
on top of a donkey, which, despite the man's whipping and cursing,
refuses to obey a single command of its "master." Only when the beast
hears another donkey nearby does it start racing, at which point Qu Shen
can only desperately hold on for a moment before he is finally physically
thrown off as his donkey rears in a happy embrace with the other donkey.

Yet the scene shows more than the moral and physical lack of control
of the man. It matches these shortcomings with a similar lack of verbal
control. Dialect speech, in the novel, is not merely a different form of
speech; it is an inferior form of speech, a deviation from a proper, standard accent that speaks of a similar ability to contain oneself on the level
of moral character. The man's violent curses, for instance, mirror his
volatile temper. Even more striking, these curses themselves are mangled
because of the man's accent, changing from "Mother fucker" (*wang ba dan*
王八旦) into an almost incomprehensible *wa ba ri* 窪八日.[70] Tellingly, at
the point Qu Shen is no longer able to restrain his donkey physically, he
also loses control over the standard pronunciation as he turns the phrase
"acting up" (*nienie* 俠俠) into "*actin' up*" (*dai dai* 呆呆).

Dialect speech becomes the marker of a temper tantrum and a loss
of physical control, but, most importantly, the inability to speak properly tells of a lack of moral self-containment. This is most beautifully
demonstrated when Qu Shen appraises the donkey his own animal has
just found and is similarly seduced by its attractive looks.

---

legs went flying and he came tumbling down the donkey's ass. Fortunately he did
not fall hard, so he immediately got up and began wildly whipping the donkey, but
how could he ever hope to separate the two in that manner?" 誰知跑來跑去, 果然
前面有一頭驢; 他這驢連躓帶跑, 奔到那個驢子後面, 不容分說, 他將兩條前腿一提
便站起來了. 屈申在上面連說: '不好! 不好!' 坐不住鞍心, 兩腳一飄, 順着驢屁股就
掉下來, 幸喜沒率着. 連忙爬起, 將鞭亂打, 哪裡打得開? *Longtu erlu*, vol. 1, chap. 24,
p. 258. By linking the animal's lack of sexual control with the man's lack of physical
ability to stay in the saddle, the novel neatly suggests Qu Shen's animal-like nature.
70. *Wa* 窪 literally means "swamp," which is the way Susan Blader translates it
(Blader, p. 117). Here the word is a bastardization of *wang* 王, as attested by the
Longtu erlu where the phonetic 窪 is written next to the original 王. The word 日 is
probably a misprint for 旦 (pronounced *dan*), which is shorthand for the character
蛋 (also pronounced *dan*).

Qu Shen looked at the donkey for a while and bellowed, "Whose black donkey is this?" He shouted a couple of times, but no one responded, so he said to himself, "What a nice black donkey!" He then inspected the mouth; only four teeth, its body nice and plump; and the saddle, all new and shiny. He thought to himself, "Why don't Oi make use of the opportunity no one's here and switch this mama."

屈申看了多時, 便嚷道: "這是誰的黑驢?" 連嚷幾聲, 並無人應, 自己說道: "好一頭黑驢!" 又瞧了瞧口, 才四個牙, 臕滿肉肥, 而且鞍佲鮮明, 暗暗想道: "趁着無人, 樂子何不換他娘的."[71]

In this sequence, the novel employs layers of descending levels of speech, from regular speech to dialect slang, a descent that mirrors a moral descent. This descent into morally suspect behavior is expressed through a gradual interiorization and ever more secretive form of speech, by making the man speak ever less loudly and ever more privately. Yet even though Qu Shen ends up thinking silently to himself, it is at this moment that the sound of his dialect accent speaks the most loudly of his improper intentions. Indeed, while Qu Shen still speaks in standard speech at the beginning, he uses a marked regional accent in the end, when he says, "Why don't Oi make use of the opportunity no one's here and switch this mama." Just as when Qu Shen was berating his donkey previously, the use of a curse word, "this mama," here clearly marks a lack of emotional control. However, whereas the earlier "Motha Fucka" bespoke excessive temper, here the "mama" betrays the merchant's illegitimate desire. Finally, and most striking, is the use of the personal pronoun *laozi* 老子, a common term for an older man to refer to himself, but which the Shanxi merchant here mispronounces as *lezi* 樂子.[72] It is this regional use of speech that truly brings out the improper nature of Qu Shen's most secret thoughts and defines his true identity as fundamentally flawed. Much as the Shanxi merchant would like to hide the dubious nature of his hidden desires, his accent inevitably betrays him as a greedy, vulgar provincial whose lack of moral self-discipline is constantly marked by his inability to produce the sounds of standard speech.

71. *San xia wu yi* (1996), vol. 1, chap. 25, p. 146.
72. In Chinese literature, personal pronouns are the most common way of denoting regional speech. This is perhaps why the term is here not double-printed.

If Qu Shen's speech betrays him as a bumbling provincial, it is clear that the reader/writer consuming the text is the exact opposite. Whereas most of the time the identity of the superior reader/writer remains hidden, there are telling moments when the act of dialect slapstick is dropped and a superior cosmopolitan identity is revealed. In the scene where Qu Shen is shown to lose control, for instance, the novel moves from direct speech to description, dropping the Shanxi accent and instead using a typical Beijing word such as 支楞 to describe the donkey's ears all of a sudden "pricking up." At the same time, the novel ironically repeats Qu Shen's phrase "actin' up" 鬧捏捏, this time mimicking his accent and thereby lending the text a sense of free-indirect speech. Even more importantly, because the narrator now mimics Qu Shen's accent, the ironic distance between the original phrase and its repetition causes the Shanxi merchant's speech impediment to become even more ridiculous.

In *The Dragon Diadem*, this distinction between an inferior provincial accent and a superior Beijing way of speaking is also sometimes found in the interlineal comments that interrupt the narrative. These comments in particular demonstrate that the implied reader of the text is a cosmopolitan Beijing denizen. In one scene of *The Dragon Diadem*, for instance, Qu Shen is shown speaking his usual Shanxi accent, after which a comment using a Beijing phrase immediately ridicules the merchant for being cheap. The *Dragon Diadem* offers the following depiction of the merchant on his way home, late at night, wondering where to find a safe place to rest:

At 'dis (*this*) m'ment (*moment*), I can't enter t'own (*town*) any longer. And Oi (*I*) still have four hundr'd (*hundred*) taels of silvuh (*silver*). Wot (*what*) can I do? . . . I'd better find s'meone (*someone*)'s home to find a place to stoy (*stay*). 'Morrow, I'll bankrupt myself with one hundred or eighty cash, that'll be the safest way.

這官(光)景, 城(況)是進不了. 餓(我)還有四躉(百)蠅(銀)子, 這可咱(怎) 的 好呢? . . . 說不得只好找懷(個)仍(人)家兒借懷(個)宿兒, 明兒破產一百, 八 十的, 倒穩當.[73]

73. *Longtu erlu*, vol. 1, chap. 24, p. 259. This particular phrase is found only in the reprint and the Beijing University edition. On this point, the Beijing Normal University edition resembles the novel more closely.

The use of a Shanxi accent once again makes Qu Shen a comic figure. Yet what really is of interest is the comment that follows immediately after Qu Shen's accented moment of self-reflection. *The Dragon Diadem* shoots back with an aside to the reader:

> Truly the spirit of a Shanxi person. At a moment like this he is still calculating, thinking of "one hundred or eighty cash" as "bankrupting himself." You can tell he is extremely stingy.
>
> 真是山西人的脾氣, 到了此時, 他還打算盤, 拿着 "一百, 八十" 還說 "破產" 二字, 可見嗇刻之極![74]

This aside first demonstrates that the notion of Qu Shen being cheap is not considered merely a personal trait, but rather reflects a broader regional stereotype.[75] More importantly, the comment, which in an earlier edition of *The Dragon Diadem* must have been written as an inter-lineal aside, immediately elevates the reader to a position of authority above the text.[76] To do so, the commentary not only appropriates the

---

74. Ibid.
75. Various comments in *The Dragon Diadem* make it clear that being cheap is a typical quality of people from Shanxi. After Qu Shen fails to make a deal, for instance, an interlineal comment in the Beijing Normal University edition of *The Dragon Diadem* informs the reader, "It's not that the merchandise was not right, it is simply that Shanxi merchants like to get things cheaply" 不是行市不對, 是山西人愛買偏宜貨. *Shi da Longtu erlu*, vol. 11, chap. 24, p. 6A. Other nineteenth-century texts confirm that in late-Qing Beijing there was a widespread image of Shanxi people as uncultivated, immoral, and, most importantly, parsimonious. A good example is found in the *matoudiao* "Lao Xi piao yuan" 老西嫖冤 (Plaint by a Shanxi fellow gone whoring). This popular song depicts a poor man from Shanxi who has saved all his money by limiting his salt consumption so as to buy a few minutes of pleasure with a disfigured old prostitute. See "Lao Xi piao yuan."
76. Though the remark here is given as part of the main text, at some point this must have been an interlineal comment because throughout the episode similar dry asides regarding Qu Shen's stingy nature are offered as such. For instance, after Qu Shen offers a "handsome" reward for staying the night once he has found a shelter, an interlineal comment adds, "He must be talking about that 'hundred or eighty cash'" 就是那一百八十的重禮. This interlineal comment is only found in the *Xielong zhai* edition at Beijing University Library and is not reproduced in the 1984 typeset edition. Similarly, the earlier comment following Qu Shen's failing to reach a deal is given as an interlineal comment in the Beijing Normal University edition of the *Longtu erlu*. Miao Huaiming argues that the incorporation of an

Shanxi merchant's words by once again echoing them, restating Qu
Shen's "eighty," "one hundred," and "bankrupting," it also ends the
phrase with a typical Beijing slang-word, 齁刻, meaning "stingy."[77] It
is this contrast between the identification of the reader with a typical
Beijing phrase in the aside, and the distancing effect of a Shanxi dialect
in the character's speech, that alerts us to the fact that the implied reader
here is a typical Beijing cosmopolitan.

As shown in chapter 1, Jin Shengtan constructed a distinction
between an elite and a vulgar reader on the basis of an invisible, acoustic
distinction as early as the seventeenth century.[78] Here the brief interlineal comments in *The Dragon Diadem* demonstrate how the identity of
the implied reader has shifted from the times of Jin Shengtan's *Outlaws
of the Marsh* commentary. Whereas in Jin's seventeenth-century
commentary to the *Outlaws of the Marsh*, the reader is elevated from
the proceedings in the text on the basis of class, in *The Dragon Diadem*,
the reader is elevated on the basis of a regional Beijing identity. After
all, though Jin Shengtan might have raised the standing of the vernacular novel to new heights, he did so by writing commentaries penned in
classical Chinese. The interlineal comments and various asides found
in *The Dragon Diadem* suggest a distinctively different reader. These
comments still play a critical role by allowing the reader to distance
himself from the proceedings in the text, but the distinct Beijing accent
of some of them marks the implied reader as a streetwise denizen of
Beijing, a cosmopolitan figure who derives his identity not from his
membership in the literati class or his knowledge of Classical Chinese,
but rather from his street smarts, from being able to apprehend critically the sights and sounds of the capital Beijing.

---

interlineal comment in the text is a clear sign of a later edition, since it is unlikely
that the text would develop the other way around. As such, it is likely that the
Beijing Normal University edition predates the Beijing University edition. See
Miao, "*Longtu erlu banben kaoshu.*"

77. The phrase can be found in Song Xiaocai, *Beijing huayu cihui yi*, p. 593.
78. See in particular the discussion of fire as acoustic spectacle in *Outlaws of the
Marsh* on pp. 000–000.

Cross-Talking in Wen Kang's
Tale of Romance and Heroism

In late nineteenth-century Beijing, a true cosmopolitan identity was based not on a native ability in one single language, but instead on a carefully acquired mastery of "all" languages. The appreciation of dialect mimicry in print, I argue, follows a similar logic. Different from a straightforward transcription of the oral language that collapses the distinction between spoken and written language, it seeks to establish a cultured connoisseurship that depends on the careful mastery of both registers of language, the oral and the textual. To explore the process through which this cosmopolitan appreciation of printed orality is established, I will juxtapose the popular storytelling tradition of dialect mimicry with the scholarly appreciation of dialect accents in the philological tradition of *kaozheng* scholarship. Finally, I will focus on the Beijing martial arts novel that first brought the two together, Wen Kang's *Tale of Romance and Heroism*. As an analysis of this novel will show, its acoustic pleasure is found in a unique play with the boundaries of voice and text, allowing the author to create an identity that draws its prestige from both, and creating a reader who congratulates himself on being a connoisseur of storytelling *and* philology.

Given that so many late nineteenth-century martial arts novels proclaimed themselves to be based on popular storytelling performances, the appearance of different dialect accents in the pages of Beijing martial arts novels might at first seem merely an attempt to translate this typical cosmopolitan linguistic acumen into print. For instance, the storytellers associated with the novel *The Tale of Everlasting Blessings and Peace, Part 1*, Jiang Zhenming and Hafuyuan, were both famous for their uncanny ability to cross-talk by putting on a Shandong dialect. In the case of Jiang this reputation is not surprising; the man actually hailed from Shandong Province. Jiang, however, seems to have faithfully transmitted his accent to his disciple Hafuyuan, a bannerman-turned-Peking opera actor, turned storyteller, who was equally famous for his ability to mimic Shandong dialect.[79] In

79. For more on the storyteller Hafuyuan, see Zhang Cixi, *Renmin shoudu de Tianqiao*, pp. 122–23. See also Yunyouke, *Jianghu congtan*, p. 75.

the first printed edition of *The Tale of Everlasting Blessings and Peace, Part 1*, traces of this popular oral act can indeed still be found in the occasional snippets of double-printed dialogue spoken by its central protagonist "Shandong Ma."[80]

If in the case of *The Tale of Everlasting Blessings and Peace, Part 1*, the link between storytelling practice and printed text seems obvious, in the case of *The Three Knights* the relationship is much more tenuous. Not only are there no references to Shi Yukun ever practicing cross-talking, but the handwritten manuscripts on which *The Three Knights* is based, *The Cases of The Dragon Diadem*, do not include such imitation of dialect either. Take, for instance, the way in which the earliest textual version of the tale, the libretto *The Cases of Judge Bao*, depicts the language spoken by the Shanxi merchant Qu Shen:

> Isn't this the black donkey that I rode?
> 這不是我騎的黑驢麼?[81]

Although it is presumably the closest to an actual oral storytelling performance, this line does not employ dialect markers to signal the accent of Qu Shen's regional speech. In contrast, *The Aural Record* is filled with dialect speech and accent markers.

> Hey! Dat (*that*) blaeck (*black*) donkey is moin (*mine*).
> 唔! 這懷(個)喝(黑)驢還是餓(我)的咧.[82]

Compared to the original storyteller libretto, the later text, with its bevy of exclamations and in particular dialect markers, is remarkably loud.

---

80. The double printing of characters seems to have not been reproduced in any of the modern editions, but it can be found in the original text as photographically reproduced in the *Guben xiaoshuo ji cheng* 古本小說集成 (The collected printed classical novels). See Guo Guangrui, *Yongqing shengping qianzhuan* (1990), pp. 39 and 46 respectively. The system employed by *The Tale of Everlasting Blessings and Peace* is slightly different in that it not only offers the mispronunciation in large print following the correct character in small print, but it also adds the character 仝 *tong* (the ancient form for the character 同), meaning "same as," behind it.
81. "Yin cuo yang cha," vol. 408, p. 202.
82. *Longtu erlu*, vol. 1, chap. 26, p. 276.

Or to state it differently, the text presumably closest to the actual story-teller performance ironically appears to be the most silent.

The silence of the earliest storyteller libretto, *The Cases of Judge Bao*, however, does not necessarily mean that the storyteller Shi Yukun did not employ dialect mimicry. Like the scarcity of onomatopoeia in the storyteller's manuscript discussed in chapter 4, the absence of dialect markers may show that, as of yet, readers did not feel the need for paratextual markers of dialect to imagine the text acoustically. Locally produced by a small shop that specialized in the transcription of popular storyteller tales and opera scripts, the libretto of *The Cases of Judge Bao* was presumably read by those who were so familiar with story-telling practices, either by Shi Yukun or others, that they could imagine the dialect accent of the Shanxi merchant even without paratextual prompts. Focusing on similar markers of storyteller performance in other popular martial arts texts, Margaret Wan has made a similar point: "Serving a function analogous to punctuation, then one would expect to find them [these dialogue markers such as "he said: . . . ." (*yue* 曰)] less often in texts closely related to performance, and more often in texts that are primarily for reading."[83]

The absence of dialect speech markers in the earliest versions and their appearance in later versions thus suggests that they are not simply a direct transcription of voice into text, but rather a textual sign that needs to be invented. Moreover, this invention of a textual device geared toward writing the sound of a dialect accent seems indebted not so much to storytelling performance as to the philological interests of Qing dynasty literati, in particular the renewed interest in the two fields of phonology and dialect studies. As various scholars have pointed out, one of the major intellectual endeavors of the Qing dynasty revolved around the formulation of a set of methodologies that would allow literati to reconstruct the true meaning and true form of classical texts and thereby restore the ideal political order of the ancient sages.[84]

83. Wan, *Green Peony*, p. 137.
84. Take, for instance, the following quote by one of the first major phonology scholars of the Qing dynasty, Gu Yanwu 顧炎武 (1613–82), from the preface to one of his studies: "To summarize the ten divisions of ancient pronunciation, I prepared the *Table of Ancient Pronunciation* in two chapters. As a result, the Six Classics are now readable. . . . Heaven by preserving these writings has demonstrated that the sages will one day return and restore the pronunciation of today to the clarity and purity of ancient times." Quoted in Elman, *From Philosophy to Philology*, p. 61.

Interestingly enough, the two fields through which the meaning of classical text could be best established—the area of dialect studies and the area of phonology—had close ties to the spoken language. In pursuit of textual knowledge, a host of ever more sophisticated studies provided increasingly detailed differentiations of sound by writing down the pronunciation of various rhyme categories as well as dialect accents, thus creating a written meta-language that allowed the mapping of the spoken word.[85]

At first, nothing might seem further removed from the popular world of dialect performance in the marketplace or the printing of popular novels than the elite world of literati scholarship. However, as one scholar has intimated, the rise of dialect literature in the nineteenth century is in fact most likely related to *kaozheng* scholarship.[86] It bears remembering that many of the most famous eighteenth and nineteenth-century novels were not popular tales intended for barely literate readers, but rather works of remarkable sophistication that brought many of the literati's penchants for textual scholarship to the vernacular page. For instance, Li Ruzhen's *Flowers in the Mirror* (1828), an exemplary literati novel, includes extensive discussions about rhyme categories and scholarly lectures about interlinguistic differences.[87] This penchant for scholarly discussions of phonology is not surprising given that long before he published his novel, Li Ruzhen had already penned a work he himself would have found much more important, *Li shi yin jian* 李氏音鑒 (Master Li's mirror of rhymes; first published 1810), a comprehensive study of phonology.[88] Yet even though a work such as Li Ruzhen's *Flowers in the Mirror* thus incorporates the phonological discussions of the *kaozheng* scholars into the text, this scholarly eye for

---

85. For a brief overview of the study of rhyme categories during the Qing, see Hu, *Yinyunxue tonglun* 音韻學通論, pp. 243–75; see also Elman, *From Philosophy to Philology*, pp. 212–21. For a good overview of Qing dynasty dialect studies, see He Gengyong, *Hanyu fangyan yanjiu*, esp. chap. 6, pp. 59–83.

86. See Song Lihua, "Fangyan yu Ming Qing xiaoshuo," p. 41.

87. For good examples of such discussions of phonology, see Li Ruzhen, *Jing hua yuan*, chap. 17 and chap. 31, pp. 101–6 and 195–204 respectively. For a discussion of the way in which the novel itself reflects on the nature of language and employs the figure of a woman to do so, see Rojas, *The Naked Gaze*, pp. 54–81.

88. For one of the first discussions of Li Ruzhen's accomplishments in phonology, see Hu Shi, "*Jing hua yuan* de yinlun."

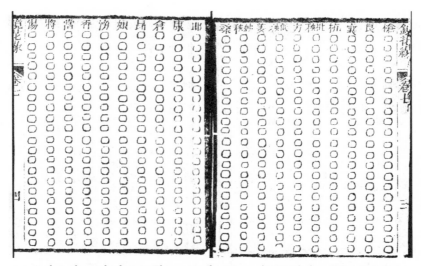

5.4 A phonological rebus in *Flowers in the Mirror*. (In Li Ruzhen, *Xiu xiang Jing hua yuan*, published in 1841 by the Jiezi yuan. Photo courtesy of Yale University Library.)

linguistic detail does not necessarily translate into literary praxis. The most striking use of the sounds of speech is found not in the conversations of the novel's cast of characters, but embedded in a complex visual table that reads like a rebus and seems directly inspired by Li's earlier, scholarly work on dialect (see figures 5.4 and 5.5).[89] Meanwhile, discussions about dialect in the novel are written in standard, quite scholarly vernacular. Indeed, as pointed out recently by Wang Songmu, some of the linguistic discussions in the novel seem to be directly lifted from the earlier work of *kaozheng* scholarship and though found in a fictional text carry with them the pedantic tone of the *kaozheng* scholar.[90]

89. As a result, historical linguists invested in reconstructing the sound of Northern *guanhua* in the eighteenth century inevitably turn to Li Ruzhen's scholarly work, which contrasts southern and northern dialect tones in detail. Yet these same linguists never turn to the author's vernacular tale.

90. Take, for instance, the similarity in diction between the following two lines, the first found in the scholarly work *Master Li's Mirror of Sound*: "One may dare to submit the question, 'Can the study of *qieyin* also be transmitted to young children?' I answer, 'I humbly submit that if you want to read books, you first have to know characters, and that if you want to know characters you first have to know

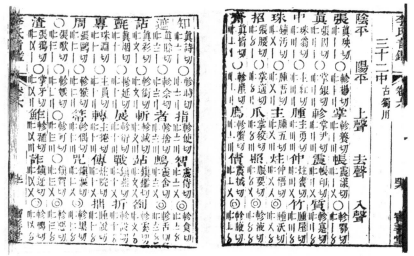

5.5 A table of dialect accents in *Master Li's Mirror of Rhymes*. (In Li Ruzhen, *Li shi yin jian*. Published in 1868 by Muxi shanfang. Photo courtesy of Yale University Library.)

In contrast, the later Beijing novel *The Tale of Romance and Heroism* not only discusses matters of dialect and rhyme categories in a scholarly manner, but it does so in a language that gives this scholarly knowledge of the spoken word a matching literary form. The result is a text that at times becomes curiously heteroglossic, playfully acting out scenes of linguistic confusion among speakers of different dialects and sociolects, all the while self-consciously juxtaposing the spoken and written language to comic effect. The novel, in short, does not elide the artificiality of either oral or textual provenance but instead consistently juxta-

---

sounds, and if you want to know sounds, you first have to practice *fanqie*, and if you want to be clear about *fanqie*, you cannot do without the initial'" 敢謂: 切音之學亦可授之童蒙乎? 對曰: 竊謂欲讀書必先識字, 欲識字必先知音, 欲知音必先翻切, 欲明翻切則非字母不可也. Li Ruzhen, *Li shi yin jian, juan* 3, p. 18A. The second line is from the novel *Flowers in the Mirror*: "The maiden in purple clothes said, 'I have heard that if you want to read books, you first have to know characters, and that if you want to know characters you first have to know sounds. If you do not first differentiate the sounds, then inarguably it looks correct but is in fact mistaken'" 紫衣女子道:「婢子聞得要讀書必先識字, 要識字必先知音。若不先將其音辨明, 一概似是而非. Li Ruzhen, *Jing hua yuan*, chap. 17, p. 101. For a fuller discussion, see Wang Songmu, "Qisheguo de bu chuan zhi mi."

poses the two, taking pleasure not in the mimetic effect of either register of language, but rather in lampooning any reader who would forget the artificiality of such mimetic effects.

Nowhere does this juxtaposition of scholarly textual and lively oral tone come to the fore more than in the scene where Wen Kang first stages a moment of cross-talking in print. The scene tells of a southern scholar, Master Cheng, who has come to his student's Beijing residence to congratulate the latter on his passing the examinations with the highest honor. When the scholar turns to the mother of the successful candidate, he congratulates her:

> After these two phrases, he tried to speak in a Beijing accent, "Dis (*this*) is cawled (*called*) 'The son ov (*of*) a good bowmaker, will be able to lea'n (*learn*) how to make a sieve; the son ov (*of*) a good foun'er (*founder*) will be able to lea'n (*learn*) how to make a fur ga'ment (*garment*).'[91] Dis (*this*) iz (*is*) all da (*the*) rezult (*result*) of your fam'ly (*family*) teaching. Wat (*what*) merit do Ai (*I*) have? I'm not worty (*worthy*), I'm not worty (*worthy*). Pleaze (*please*), let me congrittalate (*congratulate*) my shissa-ter-in-law." (The two syllables 'shissa' and 'ter' should be read aloud together according to the *qie yin*, forming the word 'sister.')

> Ta shuo le zhei liang ju, bian piezhe jingqiang shuodao, "gu(zhei) jiao zuo(zuo) 'lianggong zi(zhi) zi, bi ya(xue) wei ji; liang ya(ye) zi(zhi) zi, bi ya(xue) wei qiu.' Gu(zhei) dou si(shi) lao xiansang(sheng) ge(de) ding (ting)xun, yong(xiong)di e(he) gong zi(zhi) you? San(can) kuai(huai), san(can) kuai(huai)! Saofu nayin (er zi qieyin hedu, gai 'ren' zi ye) mianqian, ya (ye) qin(qing) huhu(hehe)!"
> 他說了這兩句, 便撇着京腔說道, "顧(這)叫胙(作) '良弓滋(之)子, 必鴨(學)為箕; 良雅(冶)滋(之)子, 必雅(學)為裘.' 顧(這)都四(是)老先桑(生)格(的)頂(庭)訓, 雍(兄)弟哦(何)功滋(之)有? 傘(慘)快(愧), 傘(慘)快(愧)! 嫂夫納銀(二字切音合讀, 蓋'人'字也)面前, 雅(也)覿(請)互互(賀賀)!"[92]

Unlike examples of vernacular writing that seek to erase the difference between voice and text, Wen Kang employs double-printing to produce both text and orality, juxtaposing elite scholarly concerns and popular

91. This is a famous phrase from the *Li ji* 禮記 (Classic of ritual), creating a juxtaposition of classical text and inappropriate pronunciation that accentuates the comedy.
92. Wen, *Ernü yingxiong zhuan* (1990), vol. 2, chap. 37, p. 876.

oral performance to create a self-consciously theatrical effect that showcases the author's linguistic expertise by foregrounding the text's artifice.
On one level, Wen Kang's use of double printing borrows from the more
popular storyteller use of "cross-talking," making fun of a southerner
who puts on pedantic airs and who, despite his quotation of classical
texts, cannot help but come across as an utter fool. Yet on another level,
Wen Kang clearly also employs scholarly textual devices to produce this
semblance of popular orality. Most notably, he adopts the *qie yin* (切音)
system used by scholars to describe the pronunciation of characters,
writing the characters "na" and "yin" and explaining that when "read
aloud together" it will produce the word for "sister" pronounced in a
typically southern way as "*nin*." Playing with textuality and orality, Wen
Kang here puts on display his linguistic skill in both philology and storyteller's practice. At the same time, he calls upon his reader to read like a
"cosmopolitan" man, to read the silent text with the eye of the philological expert and an ear for the sound of locally produced cross-talking.

Conclusion

The late nineteenth-century experiment with printing dialect mimicry
did not last; the system of double printing proved too cumbersome. As
the narrator of the 1891 novel *The Latter Five Gallants* put it, "If we were
to add the Shanxi accent to each character, you would not be able to
understand it anymore when reading, and when listening you would
simply feel confused. So we will just use *The Official Tones of Hongwu*
and be done with it" 字字綴上山西的口音, 看的反覺不明白, 聽的也覺發
亂, 倒不如還是《洪武正韻》, 倒覺爽快.[93] In the twentieth century, the
printed mimicry of dialect was used only by a now almost-forgotten
Beijing bannerman named Cai Youmei (蔡友梅; also known as Song
Youmei 宋友梅; pen name Sungong 損公; fl. 1905–20), and even he
admitted that "this mimicry is not only annoying, it is a pain" 學不但
討厭, 而且麻煩.[94]

The use of double printing characters to register the sound of dialect

---

93. *Xiao wu yi* (1993), chap. 57, p. 293.
94. Cai, "Cao erjing." Originally printed in *Xinxian ciwei zhi shiba zhong* 新鮮滋味之
十八種 (Eighteen kinds of fresh flavors), Beijing: Beijing jinhua baoshe, early republic.

speech did not disappear merely because it was "a pain." More important were the profound structural shifts that took place in the writing of vernacular novels. The northern vernacular was elevated to the status of national language and displaced the classical language in the process. The novel took over the role of poetry as the single most important genre of elite writing, as it was heralded as the genre most suited to reawaken the Chinese nation. Mimetic models of realism began to displace the self-consciously performative aspects of fictional writing. Authors who had previously anonymously dallied with the vernacular novel as acts of literati connoisseurship were either outmaneuvered by intellectuals too seriously engaged in saving the nation to engage in literary play or displaced by paid professional writers who were too invested in reaching a popular audience to indulge in obtuse linguistic games. And, as these shifts took place and a more modern notion of the individual author appeared, the central rhetorical figure of the storyteller disappeared from the pages of Chinese fiction, taking with him the lively voice that had animated dialect mimicry.

Of course, as has been argued by a variety of scholars, the shifts that took place in the twentieth-century literary scene, though real, can still be overstated. As scholars are beginning to explore genres, languages, and modes of writing that fall outside of the "May Fourth" narrative of modern Chinese literature, it is increasingly becoming clear that a variety of repressed modernities inherited from the late Qing remained irrepressibly relevant.[95] The writings of the above-mentioned Cai Youmei, arguably the most influential of the early Beijing-style novelists, present a perfect example of the continued interest in modes of writing seemingly outdated by the onset of a singular twentieth-century modernity.[96] Most notably, Cai continued the storyteller/novelist tradition that had supposedly come to an end with the arrival of the twentieth century. Writing in a lively Beijing vernacular, Cai peppered his writings with storyteller clichés and colloquial asides to his "listening audience," referring to his own writing as "storytelling" and ending his tales with the usual storyteller promise to tell a new tale the next

95. See, among others, David Wang, *Fin-de-Siècle Splendor*, pp. 21–22, 313–42.
96. For a more extensive discussion of the life and work of Cai Youmei, see Lei Xiaotong, "Jindai Beijing de Manzu xiaoshuojia."

day.[97] He explicitly acknowledged his affinity with historical storytelling practices, comparing his own novels to the tales of a nineteenth-century storyteller, Wu Futing 吳輔亭, not coincidentally the "student-brother" of Hafuyuan and likewise famous for dialect mimicry in his rendition of the tale *Everlasting Blessings and Peace*.[98]

Yet even though the writings of Cai Youmei recall the sounds of earlier vernacular fiction, they also represent a marked shift. When Cai promised to continue "telling his tale" the next day, it was when printing in a daily newspaper, *Jinhua bao* 進化報 (Progress news), a modern vernacular-style newspaper of which Cai was both co-founder and main editor. When comparing himself to storytellers of yore, Cai was writing what he called a "social novel" 社會小說, a concept that would have been meaningless to his storyteller predecessors. Though writing in a style that was unmistakably "Beijing," Cai was clearly influenced by the techniques of Shanghai novelists such as the newspaperman Bao Tianxiao 包天笑 (1875–1973). Even when using a variety of Beijing expressions, Cai was still aware that he was writing for a national audience, and though writing tongue-in-check, he still admitted that both overly vulgar and overly obscure Beijing phrases had to be avoided, or at least annotated.[99] Indeed, though he took particular pleasure in describing the old bannerman customs with great gusto, Cai admitted that these would have to be relinquished in order to create a new modern China. As to the storyteller figure central to vernacular fiction, Cai did employ the various phrases and mannerisms typical of the storyteller but added to these phrases a new, explicitly autobiographical sensibility completely foreign to the vernacular authors of the earlier era.

Cai's hybrid mode of writing, part storyteller and part journalist, part self-conscious theatricality and part observation-based realism, is also registered in the way Cai records the sounds of dialect accents. In

---

97. Cai's writing is riddled with such storyteller interruptions, but one example that nicely illustrates Beijing prejudices against people from Shanxi will suffice. In the tale of the Shanxi émigré, the Beijing doctor "After Midnight Cao," Cai offers the following aside to his "audience," "There is someone over there who says, "Why did they not go listen to the Four Happiness Opera Troupe?" Well, think about it. When a Shanxi fellow listens to opera, don't you think he will insist on listening to clapper opera instead?" Cai, "Cao erjing," p. 639.
98. See Cai, "Xiao E," vol. 2, p. 323.
99. Cai, "Kuduanyan."

his most famous novelette, the 1907 short story *Xiao E* 小額 (Xiao E), for instance, Cai Youmei includes heavily theatrical moments of Southern dialect mimicry reminiscent of Wen Kang.[100] Yet Cai also appends a rich bevy of pronunciations to his description of everyday Beijing phrases. Thus the reader learns that in old Beijing people pronounced the term "pan-fried cakes dipped in oil" (*shaobing youzha guo* 燒餅油炸果) not with a final "guo" but a "gui" (*yin gui* 音鬼), that "everybody" (*dajiahuo* 大家伙) was pronounced as "everybro" (*dajiahui* 大家會), or that the word "xun" in the phrase "nao xun le" 鬧薰了 was pronounced with a fourth tone. Indeed, as if wanting to reflect the disappearance of a society in which crucial distinctions of status were marked by a different way of enunciating one's term of address, Cai tells the reader that the honorific variant of the third-person pronoun *ta* 他 was pronounced as *tan* 貪.[101] As in the late nineteenth century, Cai here employs the double printing of characters as a way of registering the sound of a dialect accent, but as will be clear from these few examples listed here, no longer was such sound employed solely to mimic the mispronunciations of regional others. Instead, as an acoustic reflection of the ever more marginal status of the capital, characters were now double-printed to record the dying language of Beijing bannermen themselves. Perhaps even more importantly, whereas the sounds performed by the nineteenth-century storyteller persona had sought to attract attention to the artful artifice of the speaker himself, in Cai Youmei's recording of the speech of old Beijing, the sounds recorded did not necessarily perform such a theatrical function. Instead, these sounds sought to recall a disappearing world in an almost pseudo-scientific manner, ushering in new modes of direct, realist representation while borrowing a theatrical voice that now had come to represent the past.

100. For the most comprehensive discussion of this novelette, see Hatano, "Hyōron tanpen shakai shōsetsu *Shōgaku*."
101. Cai, "Xiao E," pp. 275, 286, 288, and throughout.

CHAPTER SIX

Sound and Space

The Acoustic Architecture of Wen Kang's
Tale of Romance and Heroism

> An art gallery is a room with a thousand avenues of departure,
> so that once having entered, one loses the door back to the real
> world and must go on exploring. In the same way, a descriptive
> piece of music turns the walls of the concert hall into windows,
> exposed to the country. By means of this metaphorical fenes-
> tration we break out of the confinements of the city to the free
> *paysage* beyond.{comp: note hidden footnote in epi source line}
> —R. Murray Schafer, *The Soundscape*

One of the most important narrative sequences in *The Tale of Romance
and Heroism* occurs in chapters 27 and 28 when one of the central
characters of the novel, the female knight-errant Thirteenth Sister, lays
down her identity as an unruly heroic maiden and becomes a properly
married wife. What is remarkable about this sequence is not only its
central place in Wen Kang's martial arts narrative, but also how the
transformation is accomplished through the elaborate use of acoustic cues. Note, for instance, the way the author introduces the reader
(and the bride) to the formal beginning of the wedding procession that
accomplishes Thirteenth Sister's transformation:

> Just as the women had finished putting things in order over here, they heard
> from over there "DANG" as a gong sounded, and the horns and percussion

EPIGRAPH: Schafer, *The Soundscape*, p. 104.

started playing at the same time as they prepared the wedding space.[1] Who would have thought? This girl who had charged about without ever meeting her equal had no sooner 'heard the gong sound than she became so frightened that her hands became all cold and clammy and she started calling out for her mother to hold her.

這邊才收拾完畢, 早聽那邊'當', 一聲鑼響, 喇叭號筒鼓樂齊奏的響起房來. 不想闖了個沒對兒的姑娘, 才聽得一聲鑼響, 唬了個兩手冰涼, 只叫娘拉着.[2]

The conversion of an indomitable woman warrior into a fearful young girl in this excerpt is striking, but equally striking is the loud "DANG" which prompts this transformation. This "DANG" is moreover only the first of many such acoustic cues. As we read through the pages that follow, we hear the husband arrive on his horse and the wedding attendant loudly proclaim the appropriate wedding blessings. We listen to the cart of the mother-in-law arrive as she comes to check on the bride. We are told that the "percussion music loudly rises to heaven" 鼓樂喧天 as the wedding chair arrives outside the gate of the home of the bride.[3] And throughout we hear the sounds of drums, chanting, strings, and horns as Thirteenth Sister, in her bridal chair isolated from visual contact with the outside world, is carried into the home of her future husband and into her new life as a properly wedded woman.[4]

1. The phrase *xiangfang* 響房, literally "sounding the house," refers to the use of music to drive out evil spirits in preparation for the wedding. The phrase itself, of course, nicely combines concepts of space and sound in a single verb-noun compound.
2. Wen, *Ernü yingxiong zhuan* (Ergong 尔弓 edition, 1990 rpt.), vol. 2, chap. 27, p. 592.
3. Ibid., p. 595.
4. Because all visual cues are blocked, the confines of the wedding chair help highlight the experience of acoustic cues. As a result, the acoustic liveliness (*renao*) of the wedding procession outside is not only heightened, but on the inside of the wedding chair a "silent," psychological interiority is opened up. The novel describes the way Thirteenth Sister ascends the wedding chair thus:

> The girl stepped into the palanquin. She felt how she was fully sealed off on all four sides, on the inside everything being very silent and very dark. All she heard was "GUDONG," "GUDONG," as the sound of drums shook her eardrums, and she felt how completely different this was from riding her donkey all by herself alone at night in the deep mountains and the untamed wilderness. . . . All of a sudden she thought to herself, "Aiyo! How come I

Scholars of late-imperial vernacular fiction have rightfully been intrigued by the transformation of Thirteenth Sister. From the first commentary written in 1880, scholars have remarked upon the way a "Thirteenth Sister, who used to ride alone in the far-off mountains and lonely wilds" 深山曠野單人獨騎之十三妹, can turn into "a Ms. He who burns incense and writes letters in front of the sparrow screen and behind the mandarin duck curtain" 雀屏駕帳添香著書何姑娘.[5] For scholars interested in the interaction between gender and narrative structure, the wedding sequence moreover marks a symbolic midpoint where the formal features emphasize a complementing balance of bipolar terms, male and female, martial and literati talents, action adventure and romantic tale.[6] Indeed, the way the single character of Thirteenth Sister combines early martial heroism with subsequent domestic virtue

---

did not get to see Mother as I was about to leave? There is something so very important I have to ask her."

姑娘上了轎子，只覺四圍搥蓋了個嚴密，裡邊靜悄悄的，黑暗暗的，只聽得咕咚咕咚的鼓聲振耳，覺得比那單人獨騎跨上驢兒，深山曠野黑夜微行，大是兩般風味.... 忽然想起說: "噯呀! 我怎的臨走時節也不曾見着娘? 我正有一句要緊要緊的話要問他老人家。"

Wen, *Ernü yingxiong zhuan* (Ergong 尔弓 edition, 1990 rpt.), vol. 2, chap. 27, pp. 595–96. The premodern literary use of contrastive noisy outside and psychological inside spaces clearly has been carried on in twentieth-century culture. Take, for instance, Zhang Yimou's 張藝謀 famous opening scene from *Hong gaoliang* 紅高粱 (Red sorghum; 1987), where similarly a psychological space is opened up for the female protagonist by contrasting the liveliness of the wedding procession outside with the enclosed space of the wedding chair as experienced by the bride. However, whereas in *Red Sorghum* the sequence leads to a typically twentieth-century moment of female liberation (initiated through a host of furtive glances), in *The Tale of Romance and Heroism* the purpose is the opposite, namely the subjugation of a previously untamed woman warrior. For the original, sensory-suffused scene in the novel *Hong gaoliang jiazu* 紅高粱家族 (Red sorghum), see Mo Yan, *Hong gaoliang*, pp. 37–43.

5. These lines come from a comment by Dong Xun, who not only emphasizes the transformation of Thirteenth Sister into Ms. He, but also points out that the unprecedented amount of detail in describing the wedding of the young girl functions to enable this transformation. Wen, *Ernü yingxiong zhuan* (Ergong 尔弓 edition, 1990 rpt.), vol. 2, chap. 27, p. 585.

6. Epstein, *Competing Discourses*, pp. 281–82. As Epstein points out, the way in which the text balances *yin* and *yang* seems primarily driven by a sense of aesthetic formalism as opposed to clear ideological concern.

is, of course, directly reflected in the title of the novel itself, *The Tale of Romance and Heroism.*[7]

In this chapter, I will focus on Wen Kang's novel to achieve three things. First, I will demonstrate how the meeting of bipolar elements, so often remarked upon by previous scholars, is crucially facilitated through the suggestion of sound. Sound plays an important role as a marker of these separate identities—male and female, vulgar and elite, martial and literary. Even more importantly, however, sound plays a distinctive role in the exchange and formal union of those elements. As the wedding sequence already illustrates, it is the ritual blaring of horns that announces the presence of the groom to the bride and conversely the presence of the bride to the family of the groom. And, equally crucially, it is this bevy of chanted ritual phrases, beating of drums, and playing of flutes that eventually allows a ritual and narrative progression that welds these separate identities into a single union. Simply put, from the viewpoint of sound, *The Tale of Romance and Heroism*, like the wedding sequence at the heart of it, reads like a lengthy procession of sonic prompts where diametrically opposed values and ideas are forced into dialogue and eventual synthesis.[8]

Second, I will demonstrate how the suggestion of sound allows these opposed values and ideas to be inscribed on concrete, diametrically opposed spaces, an inside and an outside. The use of spatial terms here is not solely intended in its literal sense. Space should also be understood in psychological terms as interiority and exteriority, in symbolic terms as the values of an exterior world of martial heroism (*jianghu* 江湖) and an interior world of Confucian domesticity, in gendered terms as the wife relegated to the inner chambers and the husband seeking public office, or in narrative terms as separate units of text that can be connected through

---

7. The title explores the interpenetration of two elements on the level of "romance" and "heroism," and each of these two terms is additionally composed of two interpenetrating elements. The term "romance" (*ernü* 兒女, literally "sons and daughters") consists of a male and female component, as does the term "heroism" (*yingxiong* 英雄). For an exploration of this last term and its importance for masculine identities, see Martin Huang, *Negotiating Masculinities*, chap. 5.

8. I here draw on Hu Siao-chen's recent discussion of the novel, where she characterizes the narrative as a synthesis of different values—male and female, city and countryside, Manchu and Han Chinese. See Hu Siao-chen, "Pinfan riyong yu daotong lunli," vol. 2, p. 635.

acoustic breaks.[9] Crucially, however, I argue that the term space should
also be understood quite literally. After all, as part of a wedding procession, the various acoustic prompts serve to move someone from outside
the family into the protective walls of the home. Indeed, in the wedding
sequence many of the acoustic prompts notably appear at moments when
the wedding procession arrives at a spatial boundary: the gate of the
bride's home, the moment of entrance into the palanquin, the arrival at
the groom's gate, the moment of her exit of the palanquin.[10] Simply put,
in Wen Kang's novel sound marks the simultaneous existence of separate
spaces, relationally interior and exterior, while at the same time sound
also creates a conduit between these two spaces, a path through which the
tension between inside and outside can be resolved.

Third, I will shift the discussion of the novel from a preoccupation with
gender to an examination of social hierarchy. Whereas much scholarship
to date has focused on the issue of gender and the character of Thirteenth
Sister, in this chapter I want to demonstrate how sound also introduces
two distinct social strata: the academy of the elite literati and the city
streets belonging to the popular crowd. As I will show, the juxtaposition
of elite and vulgar acoustic spaces takes the form of an extended narrative
where two literati bannermen, the patriarch An Xuehai and his son An Ji,
are forced to leave their home and face the sights and sounds outside their
sheltered study. The result is a series of often hilarious depictions where

9. It would lead too far astray to discuss the multivalent meanings of the *jianghu*,
but two main points should be made. First, the *jianghu* is a social realm that is
considered to exist outside the bounds of either family or state. This notion of
jianghu as "outside" can function on a merely spatial level, i.e., by portraying
bandits and brigands as living in a distant province of marshes, mountains, and
way-side inns. However, the *jianghu* can also simply be considered as a world that
exists everywhere throughout the Chinese empire, an alternative social space
with its own secret codes and language that novels such as *The Tale of Romance
and Heroism* reveal. Second, though the *jianghu* in (modern) martial arts fiction
is primarily associated with heroic knights and perfidious bandits, throughout
late-imperial literature street-performers, traveling hawkers, prostitutes, and the
like are also considered part of this *jianghu*.
10. The chanting of ritual phrases especially functions to mark the arrival at and
crossing of these boundaries. One term used for the wedding itself, *guomen* 過
門 (literally, "crossing the gate"), similarly highlights the crossing of boundaries.
Note how, from a narrative point of view, the break between chapters 27 and 28
falls precisely at the moment Thirteenth Sister "crosses the gate." See Wen, *Ernü
yingxiong zhuan* (Ergong 尔弓 edition, 1990 rpt.), vol. 1, chap. 27, p. 596.

the worldview of the two learned scholars constantly clashes with that of commoners outside. In the end, however, the contrast between vulgar and elite pleasures, secluded literati studio and noisy streets, is resolved by combining vulgarity (*su* 俗) and elegance (*ya* 雅), the most vocal expression of which is found in a lengthy chanted performance of a popular Taoist song. The novel itself, I argue, similarly represents a unique blend of elite literati interest and popular/vulgar entertainments by employing two narrative voices, a scholarly narrative voice embodied in the fictional author of the tale, the Leisured Gentleman of Yanbei (Yanbei xianren 燕北閒人), and an anonymous storyteller who constantly enlivens the tale with witty and vociferous asides.

Literati Interactions with the Vulgar Sounds of the Streets

Scholars including Maram Epstein, Anne Sytske Keijser, and, most recently, Haiyan Lee have argued that *The Tale of Romance and Heroism* represents a careful recalibration of the fundamental binaries that inform much of Chinese culture. In her study *Competing Discourses*, for instance, Epstein shows how the novel is divided into two symmetrical halves that seek to balance romance and heroism, masculinity and femininity, literati erudition and heroic martiality.[11] In the same vein, Anne Sytske Keijser has argued that the novel carefully combines and subverts elements any late-imperial reader would immediately recognize as major, opposing themes found in earlier vernacular novels.[12] Lee, in turn, applies a similar logic to the themes of "sentiment" and "heroism," arguing that the novel represents a culmination of a "Confucian structure of feeling" by constructing an orthodox containment of both wayward heroism and excessive sentimentalism beneath the banner of filial piety.[13]

The interaction between opposing elements in the novel takes place, however, not simply in terms of abstract values and ideals, but is also mapped out in concrete, spatial terms. Take, for instance, the depiction

11. See Epstein, *Competing Discourses*, chap. 6.
12. Keijser, "Een geschiedenis van liefde en moed."
13. See Lee, *Revolution of the Heart*, pp. 51–58.

of the male romantic lead in the novel, An Ji, the young son in a well-to-do bannerman household. As a clear critique of earlier "romantic" novels, the young protagonist of *The Tale of Romance and Heroism* is strikingly, indeed excessively, feminized.[14] However, as the following segment makes clear, this feminization of the hero literally reads as a domestication of the young man. Here is how An Ji is described in the first chapter of the novel:

> We need not even speak of such things as opera houses, restaurants, or the eastern and western temples that lay outside; of course he was never allowed to spend any time running around at those places. No, if not for a solid reason, he never even left the family's own front gate just to stand outside and look about; if, perchance, he was to visit some family member, then indoors it was the wet-nurse accompanying him and outside it was her husband accompanying him, and as a result the young master of the household had been raised to be thoroughly bashful. If he heard anyone say something that fell outside proper speech, he did not understand a word. If he saw someone act the slightest bit rash or speak with even a hint of uncouth diction, then he would get upset, calling them low-class and no good. Even if he met an outside woman with whom he was unfamiliar, he would get so embarrassed that his little face would grow bright red. In short, he was even more proper and respectable than a girl.
>
> 慢說外頭的戲館, 飯庄, 東西兩廟不肯教他混跑, 就連自己的大門, 也從不曾無故的出去站站望望. 偶然到親戚一家兒走走, 也是裡頭嬤嬤媽, 外頭嬤嬤爹的跟着. 因此上把個小爺養活得十分覥腆: 聽見人說句外話, 他都不懂; 再見人舉動野調些, 言談粗魯些, 他便有氣, 說是下流沒出息; 就連見個外來的生眼些的婦女, 也就會臊的小臉兒通紅, 竟比個女孩兒來得還尊重.[15]

As this scene shows, the novel depicts its young male romantic hero in a way that combines feminization with spatial domestication.[16]

---

14. Most notably, *The Tale of Romance and Heroism* critiques the famous eighteenth-century novel *Dream of the Red Chamber,* in which the excessively romantic protagonist, Jia Baoyu, remains firmly locked within the walls of the family compound for most of the novel's 120 chapters.
15. Wen, *Ernü yingxiong zhuan* (Ergong 尔弓 edition, 1990 rpt.), vol. 1, chap. 1, p. 10.
16. Alternatively, this passage could also be read as turning the hero into an infant. However, given that An Ji's opposite is not a grown-up who is childlike, but rather a woman who is masculine, I would argue that the narrative that follows is plot-

An Ji is not simply "more proper than a girl," like a girl he has been confined to live within the safe walls of the family compound. This juxtaposition of outside and inside worlds becomes particularly clear in the Chinese text, where spatial terms such as "outside" are repeated numerous times.[17] We are told that An Ji rarely ventures outside and that even when visiting relatives he is chaperoned by a wet-nurse or her husband. When meeting a woman from the outside, the young man blushes. Even linguistically, the notion of outside things threatening this young scholar is emphasized. We are told that words that fall "outside proper speech" are offensive to him. Most strikingly, in the first sentence of the segment, we are told that the outside world, represented by the lively but vulgar and typically urban pleasures of temple fairs, restaurants, or opera houses, lies beyond the young man's experience.[18]

In terms of plot, the spatial structure of the novel turns the gradual masculinization of the feminized hero into a narrative "outing." Stated simply, the novel opens in the An family household with father, son, and mother living happily secluded from the world in a compound in the outskirts of Beijing. The patriarch of the family, An Xuehai, unexpectedly passes the examinations and is awarded an official post in the provinces that forces him to leave his leisurely life of literati seclusion. When An Xuehai is subsequently wrongfully imprisoned,

---

ted along a binary of femininity-masculinity, the synthesis of which represents maturation. For a provocative reading that emphasizes the position of An Ji as "man-child," see McMahon, *Polygamy and Sublime Passion*, pp. 90–99.

17. Note, for instance, the phrases "outside proper speech" and "women from outside whom he had never seen before." Both of these might be overly literal translations, and phrases such as "wayward speech" and "unfamiliar women he had never seen before" might have been better, but the point here is that the feminized, upper-class, and overly protected young man is depicted in spatial terms of inside and outside. In all, the term "outside" appears four times in this passage, and a verb meaning to go out (*chuqu*) is used once.

18. In contrast with the domesticated young man, the central female lead, He Yufeng, or Thirteenth Sister, has been constructed as someone who lives outside the proper gender roles and outside the seclusion of the inner chamber. Though on the level of plot the first half of the novel thus revolves around the expulsion of the domesticated young man, the second half, in many ways, tells of the domestication of the unruly young woman who has to be brought within the fold of the household.

his son, An Ji, is in turn forced to leave the safety of the family home
so as to bring the large sum of silver needed to free his father. On the
way, An Ji meets the heroic maiden Thirteenth Sister, a young woman
whose father has been unjustly executed due to the machinations of
an extremely powerful man and who, as a result, has lived since then
outside any regular family structure in the dangerous world of the
jianghu. Thirteenth Sister saves An Ji from murderous bandits, travels
with the family back to the An family compound in Beijing, and finally
becomes a fully domesticated wife when she marries An Ji and bears
him a son. With the help of An's second wife, Thirteenth Sister turns
An Ji into a "real man" who passes the exams and becomes an official.
As this brief summary shows, the plot revolves around diametrically
constructed vectors, a vector leading outward for the feminized male
protagonist and a vector leading inward for the masculinized female
protagonist.

Thus far, scholars have primarily been interested in the second
half of this plot, the gradual domestication of Thirteenth Sister. What
interests me, however, is the way the spatial vectors implied in the
narrative not only lead to the female protagonist's domestication, but
also allow the author to construct a story where the male protagonists
are forced to face the sights and sounds associated with the outside
world. For instance, when on the road to Shandong, An Xuehai comes
to visit the kind of temple fair he would never frequent in Beijing.
There he is treated to swarms of peddlers crowding round the main
gate of the temple, the taste of yogurt sold by a street peddler, a bevy of
vulgar women questioning the scholar about their menstrual cycles,
a dry-boat performance involving a cross-dressed man, and finally a
lengthy *daoqing* 道情 performance, which the author dutifully tran-
scribes in full.[19] Similarly, the son An Ji not only comes face-to-face
with a host of murderous monks, but he is also accosted by cheap
prostitutes, forced to negotiate with clever innkeepers and listen to
debauched songs and lively big-drum performances, as well as have a
tobacco pipe thrust in his mouth. In other words, the journeys of the
two scholars, father and son, present a long list of sights and sounds
that a nineteenth-century reader, schooled in the ever-expanding

19. For more on this performance, see note 68.

guidebook literature of the age, would immediately associate with popular street life.[20]

What role does sound play in this gradual outing of the two gentlemen? First, sound simply functions as one of the many stunning phenomena the scholars face while on their long journeys. In contrast to the calm and quiet of the family compound, sound establishes the outside world as a lively and noisy place. A detailed reading of the famous chapters in the temple where An Ji is rescued by Thirteenth Sister would serve, for instance, as a perfect example of how noisy the world outside the scholar's domain can be.[21] Here, let me focus on another typical setting, a roadside inn where An Ji stays on his way to save his father and where he finds himself accosted by two prostitutes who invade his room. The author first offers a long extended visual close-up of the two ladies and then continues:

> As soon as the young master [An Ji] saw [them], he said hurriedly, "Get out immediately!" The two did not bother to answer and, without allowing themselves to be gainsaid, sat down and began playing music and singing. The young master was cowering in a corner of the room as he heard them sing something that went like, "The verdant willow is lush; I rose early and lost a single needle."[22] The young master nervously said, "I don't want to listen to that one." The one dressed in dark clothes said, "If you don't want to listen to this one, we'll sing a good one. I'll sing 'The

20. It would lead too far afield to illustrate how the various sights and sounds described in the novel are indebted to other forms of writing, but it is striking to what degree we find similar depictions of popular entertainments in nineteenth-century collections of bamboo-branch songs and guidebooks. For a discussion of these even more popular forms of urban literature, see Naquin, *Peking*, pp. 451–98.

21. Since I have already focused on the use of onomatopoeia and martial arts action in chapter 3, I will not discuss this scene here. It should be noted, however, that these chapters are not only filled with acoustic clashes of swords, they are also filled with the mimicry of voices, snippets of vulgar song, lively use of *jianghu* argot, carefully set scenes of acoustic voyeurism, and a host of other acoustic phenomena. As Patrick Hanan moreover points out, although these scenes are filled with action, much of it consists of constant and lively dialogues. See Hanan, *Chinese Fiction*, pp. 12–13.

22. I have not yet tracked down this particular song, but it might well be an actual snippet from a popular Beijing song. Its references to the "lush willows" of spring suggest sexual innuendo.

Young Couple Fights over the Quilt' for you."[23] The young master said, "I don't want to listen to any of them!"

公子一見, 連忙說: "你們快出去!" 那兩個人也不大言, 不容分說的就坐下彈唱起來. 公子一躲躲在牆角落里. 只聽他唱的甚麼 "青柳兒青, 清晨早起丟了一枚針." 公子發急道: "我不聽這個!" 那穿青的道: "你不聽這個, 咱唱個好的. 我唱個 '小兩口兒挣被窩' 你聽." 公子說: "我都不聽."[24]

The author treats the reader to a wonderful scene in which prostitutes are shown singing a few popular, lively, and quite possibly licentious tunes of the day. The brief snippets of sound suggested by songs the reader would have been well familiar with do, moreover, not solely treat the reader to a "sight" rarely seen in more exalted literary forms, they also play a clear narrative role that follows a spatial vector. In the scene, the young master An Ji's "personal" space is invaded by two prostitutes. This invasion, which combines an offensive sight, sexual overtures, and snippets of raunchy songs, represents an assault that is at the same time physical, spatial, and acoustic. The horrific effect of the two prostitutes on An Ji could not be stated more clearly when we see how, under the onslaught of their licentious songs, the young man ends up cowering in a corner of the room.

Sound, however, is more than merely one of the phenomena to be found outside one's studio. Because sound can travel through windows, over walls, and underneath doors, it uniquely functions as an element that cannot be contained outside the safe walls of one's privileged

23. Though I have not found the text for this particular song, it seems to belong to a series of similarly titled songs, including "Xiao liangkou bainian" 小兩口拜年 (The young couple offers new year's wishes), "Xiao liangkou zheng deng" 小兩口爭燈 (The young couple fights over the lamp), "Xiao liangkou duishi" 小兩口對詩 (The young couple matches poems), "Xiao liangkou nao dongfang" 小兩口鬧洞房 (The young couple enters the bridal chamber), and "Xiao liangkou bianlian" 小兩口變臉 (The young couple has a falling out). As these titles suggest, these various songs represent the couple in a variety of situations, often going tit-for-tat in quick verbal exchanges, and overall presenting the listener with the kind of lively entertainment typical of *renao*. The title of the particular song sung here, "The Young Couple Fights over the Quilt," suggests a potentially slightly more risqué topic. For a brief overview of these songs, all of them listed as brief drum-songs, see Fu Xihua, *Beijing chuantong quyi zonglu*, pp. 348–49.

24. Wen, *Ernü yingxiong zhuan* (Ergong 尔弓 edition, 1990 rpt.), vol. 1, chap. 4, p. 73.

domain. While in the inn, right before the sequence with the prostitutes, for instance, An Ji is treated to the following performance:

Before long, he heard shouting going on outside. Someone was yelling, "You wanna listen to some stories? Some episodes? How about 'Luo Cheng Sells Thread,' or 'The Fall of Shouzhou Town,' or 'Ningwu Pass,' or 'Hu Di Curses the King of the Underworld,' or 'The Old Crone Curses the Chickens,' or 'The Young Girl Curses Her Granny'?"[25] The young master said, "What manner of talking is this?" He then heard the sound of strings being plucked, "DENGLENG DENGLENG," and they walked into the courtyard. When he took a look, it turned out to be a string of blind performers. The one in front held a string instrument made of cheap wood, the one in the middle held a broken octagonal drum, and the one behind was carrying a dulcimer on his back and in his hand he clapped a pair of clappers, "DENGDONG ZHASHA," as they headed off towards the eastern wing. The young master paid no attention to them and let them make their fuss [*nao*] as they went past his window. It took a long time for he heard them go off to the north strumming their strings, where soon enough someone called them over.

不多一會, 只聽得外面嚷將起來, 他嚷的是: "聽書罷? 聽段兒罷? '羅成賣絨線兒,' '大破壽州城,' '寧武關,' '胡迪罵閻王,' '婆子罵雞,' '小大姐兒罵他姥姥'!" 公子說: "這怎麼個講法?" 跟着便聽得弦子聲兒噔楞噔楞的彈着, 走進院子來. 看了看, 原來是一溜串兒瞎子. 前面一個拿着一擔柴木弦子, 中間兒那個着個破八角鼓兒, 後頭的那個身上背着一個洋琴, 手裡打着一付扎板兒, 噔咚扎咭的就奔了東配房一帶來. 公子也不理他, 由他在窗根兒底下鬧去. 好容易聽他往北彈了去了, 早有人在那接着叫住.[26]

Once again the author treats the reader to a parade of popular song titles and sounds we associate with the vulgar streets of Beijing.[27] Yet

25. In a note, Ergong tells us these are all titles of drum-songs and tunes popular in the Daoguang 道光 (1821–50) and Xianfeng 咸豐 (1851–61) reigns. Wen, *Ernü yingxiong zhuan* (Ergong 尔弓 edition, 1990 rpt.), vol. 1, chap. 4, p. 83. For information on plays that share the same stuff-material, see Wang Senran, *Zhongguo jumu cidian*, p. 1032 ("Luo Cheng"), p. 846 ("Ningwu Pass"), and p. 918 ("Cursing the King of the Underworld").

26. Wen, *Ernü yingxiong zhuan* (Ergong 尔弓 edition, 1990 rpt.), vol. 1, chap. 4, p. 72.

27. Zhao Jingshen in fact focuses on this scene to discuss the popular "big drum" performances in Beijing, pointing out that the depiction is quite accurate. To support his argument, Zhao quotes a four-line bamboo-branch song found in Yang

the scene also shows a unique quality of sound, namely, its ability to travel from outside to inside. In the brief segment, An Ji of course looks outside, and as he does so the view confirms what the reader already knew; the voices the young man hears are from street performers who have come to the inn to sing drum-songs. Yet what is most striking about this vociferous assault is that even when An Ji turns his back and pays no attention to the men, he can hear them "parade past his window" and then "go off to the north." The source of these popular street sounds, in other words, is located safely outside, but the sounds themselves are still undeniably shown to be entering the young man's room.

As such, the liveliness that is the inn presents a true nightmare for any self-respecting young bannerman who would like to keep the sights and sounds of the street outside.[28] The long extended scene at the inn in which An Ji's "privacy" is repeatedly violated, for instance, begins as follows:

> It was just the time when the inn served breakfast, the most lively [renao] time of day. One could hear the soft tones of singing from that room, and the shouting of guess-fingers from another. The whole courtyard was filled with vendors selling snacks and odd bits and trinkets, cloth and other goods from Shandong. Hawkers were tramping in and out of the inn's rooms willy-nilly.
> 正是店裡早飯才擺上, 熱鬧兒的時候. 只聽得這屋裡淺斟低唱, 那屋裡 呼么喝六, 滿院子賣零星吃食的, 賣雜貨的, 賣山東料的, 山東布的, 各店房出來進去的亂串.[29]

Jingting's *Brief Guide to the Capital* in which a big-drum performance is depicted in similar terms. See Zhao Jingshen, "*Ernü yingxiong zhuan* zhong de dagu shiliao."

28. I do not know what role the banner identity of the An family plays in the juxtaposition of inside and outside. It is tempting to read the bannerman's attempt to keep entertainments outside of his door in light of the big wall in Beijing dividing the Manchu city in the north and the Chinese city in the south. On various occasions, the emperor was so affronted by the indulgence of bannermen in a variety of operatic and storytelling entertainments that he banished them to the southern, Han part of the city. In the novel, for instance, Deng Jiugong has to go listen to opera "outside the city at Qianmen." For some of these imperial prohibitions, see Wang Liqi, *Yuan Ming Qing sandai*, pp. 24 and 54.

29. Wen, *Ernü yingxiong zhuan* (Ergong 尔弓 edition, 1990 rpt.), vol. 1, chap. 4, p. 71.

In this scene, the inn is described as the kind of place where boundaries are crossed in the most haphazard fashion, or, as the narrator describes it, "hawkers tramping in and out of rooms willy-nilly." Yet there is not only a physical crossing of boundaries taking place. Even after retiring to his own room, An Ji can tell exactly what is going on outside his door by simply listening to "the soft tones of singing from that room and the shouting of guess-fingers from another."

The only thing that can keep out the lascivious and inappropriate sounds of the outside world turns out to be the appropriate sound of orthodox texts. Faced with the threat of boundaries being crossed, An Ji calls up his main line of defense and retreats into an act of Confucian "meditation." Cross-legged, he sits down and closes his eyes.

> Taking up the essays he had been reciting at home, he began to intone them one after the other. When he had gotten to a place where he was really pleased with his recitation, you could hear him declaiming loudly, "If you have not repaid the boundless kindness of your parents, and only have left your unfilial body, you leave your parents with an inexhaustible grief for the rest of their lives. How many months are there left in their allotted one hundred years of life? How could you bear to see the limited vitality of your parents, already further diminished by the labor of giving life and raising you . . . ?" With eyes closed, he had just come to this point in his recitation, when he felt a cold and hard thing brushing against his lips briefly, and, startled, he hurriedly opened his eyes to look.
>
> 把自家平日念過的文章，一篇篇的背誦起來. 背到那得意的地方，只聽他高聲朗誦的念道，是："罔極之深恩未報，而又徒留不肖肢體，遺父母以半生莫殫之愁. 百年之歲月幾何? 而忍吾親有限之精神，更消磨於生我劬勞之後···" 正閉著眼睛背到這裡，只覺得一個冰涼挺硬的東西，在嘴唇上咮欷了一下子，嚇了一跳，連忙睜眼一看.[30]

An Ji literally builds a wall of sound around himself, secluding his body from the rest of the world. It might be possible to argue that this seclusion is merely semantic. After all, the young man is reciting orthodox phrases from a famous examination essay which arguably has a clear-cut meaning. Yet the ultimate function of these words is dependent not simply on their meaning, but also on the loud sound of their

---

30. Wen, *Ernü yingxiong zhuan* (Ergong 尔弓 edition, 1990 rpt.), vol. 1, chap. 4, p. 71.

recitation.[31] Like a Buddhist priest reciting endless repetitions of "Emitofo," An Ji has created a sacred space of filial sound. Unfortunately, even this wall can be breached when a hawker unceremoniously attempts to stick a smoking pipe between the young man's lips, brusquely violating his mouth and physically disrupting his chanting.

In *The Tale of Romance and Heroism*, the acoustic exchange between spaces also takes the narrative form of connecting separate story segments. As Keith McMahon has shown, late-Ming vernacular tales are obsessed with inner and outer spaces, crossing of boundaries, and constructing these boundaries as links in a larger plot that is connected through constant storyteller clichés and common sayings.[32] The wall, in McMahon's argument, represents Confucian orthodoxy. Subversive elements, brief glimpses of inappropriate sexual behavior in particular, are introduced into the narrative through holes in the wall of orthodox thought.[33] Walls and holes, following McMahon's logic, combine physical, moral, spatial, and linguistic levels all at the same time, and it is precisely the overdetermined meaning of these boundaries and the crossing of such boundaries that lend vernacular tales both poignancy and forward narrative drive. Drawing on the image of the young literatus An Ji chanting orthodox phrases and the songs of courtesans piercing this wall of sound, I argue that different acoustic phenomena in *The Tale of Romance and Heroism* perform a function not unlike that which McMahon ascribes to walls and their gaps in his *Causality and Containment*.

In *The Tale of Romance and Heroism*, sound cues thus play a crucial

---

31. Zhou Zuoren in fact makes the point that the formal features (i.e., the sound) of these eight-legged essays are more important than their content, something he clearly regards negatively. As Zhou writes regarding the essay from which the lines above are culled, "The lyrics of *xipi* and *erhuang*, even *kunqu* opera tend to be neither good nor coherent. That is because they do not care about those aspects. Just like the western opera we listen to, they tend to only pay attention to the melody and do not bother with the meaning. In eight-legged essays this gives rise to a similar situation; it is perfectly legitimate to have no meaning whatsoever as long as the tune is good and the rules are obeyed. From the two examples below [i.e., the essay in question], we can discern this problem." In Zhou Zuoren, *Zhongguo xin wenxue de yuanliu*, p. 34.

32. See McMahon, *Causality and Containment*, in particular pp. 25–28.

33. Consequently, voyeurism plays a crucial role in many of these tales because it allows gazes to pass through walls. See also Liangyan Ge, "*Rou Putuan.*"

role in the gradual spatial, narrative, and ideological progression of the tale; the author cleverly manipulates sound cues to drive the male protagonist out of the safe confines of his home and the female protagonist back into the confines of Confucian patriarchy. The narrative space of the inn, with its singularly porous boundaries, functions as a particularly appropriate node for such spatial, acoustic, and narrative transitions as well as social exchanges and transformations.[34] This is not only shown in the different vignettes in which various street performers invade the young man's room and drive him to an increasingly desperate emotional state. All these preludes merely serve to prepare the young man (and the reader) for one of the major shifts in the plot where the young man finally faces his true nemesis, Thirteenth Sister, the martial heroine who eventually will become his bride. After a long, sequential buildup of narrative walls and holes, Thirteenth Sister's arrival into the narrative space is told in the following terms:

An Ji was just anxiously awaiting [the return of the donkey drivers] when outside he heard animal hooves sounding "TA TA TA TA" and he said to himself, "Good, the donkey drivers have returned." . . . Hurriedly, he left the room and stood at the bottom of the steps waiting. He heard how the hooves of the animal came closer and closer, until finally it was ridden through the entrance to the compound, and, as he looked, it was only then that he realized it wasn't the donkey drivers after all.

正在盼望，只聽得外面踏踏踏踏的一陣牲口蹄兒響，心裡說是："好了，是驢夫回來了!"... 忙忙的出了房門兒，站在台階底下等着．只聽得那牲口蹄兒的聲兒越走越近，一直的騎進穿堂門來，看了看，才知不是驢夫.[35]

In this scene, as in all the previous scenes, sound functions to create a link between inner and outer space, one segment of the plot being connected to the next. It is the sound of the hooves that drives An Ji to leave his room and venture outside. But, as it turns out, it is not the

34. For the way the inn functions in traditional storyteller tales as a narrative node, see Liangyan Ge, *Out of the Margins*, pp. 87–90. According to Ge, the idea of the inn as a place of exchange is particularly important because the novel itself can be seen as a "node" in which different registers of language meet. For another discussion of the inn in martial arts fiction, see Chen Pingyuan, "Jianghu yu xiake."
35. Wen, *Ernü yingxiong zhuan* (Ergong 尔弓 edition, 1990 rpt.), vol. 1, chap. 4, p. 74.

donkey drivers who return. Instead, it is Thirteenth Sister, the heroic maiden and An Ji's future wife who here, in striking onomatopoeic manner, rides into An Ji's life and Wen Kang's narrative.

The Tale of Romance and
Heroism *and Beijing Urban Space*

One of the most striking developments of the nineteenth-century vernacular novel is an increasing interest in depicting urban space in all its myriad complexities. Thus far, however, the nineteenth-century urban novel has been understood almost exclusively as a southern Shanghai or Yangzhou form. Alexander des Forges, for instance, has argued how the 1890s serialized novel *Flowers of Shanghai* introduces a completely new sense of space and time to offer a tale that is refracted in its many plotlines and a multifarious cast of characters.[36] In a similar manner, Patrick Hanan has argued that the new urban novel can actually be traced back to the first half of the nineteenth century. Hanan focuses on what he calls the "first Chinese 'city novel,'" Hanshang Mengren's 邗上夢人 1848 tale *Feng yue meng* 風月夢 (A dream of wind and moon), arguing that the novel is unique in Chinese vernacular fiction in offering the reader a sense of Yangzhou street life.[37]

I would argue that in Beijing as well, the liveliness of urban street life became a topic of interest to vernacular authors. *The Tale of Romance and Heroism*, by many considered the most typical Beijing novel of the nineteenth century, may serve as a perfect example.[38] As various scholars have pointed out, the novel's unparalleled use of Beijing dialect qualifies it as a "primer in Beijing dialect."[39] The author himself

36. des Forges, *Mediasphere Shanghai*, pp. 73–92.
37. Hanan, "*Fengyue Meng* and the Courtesan Novel," p. 346. For a recent essay that takes a longer historical approach to the Yangzhou novel, see Ge Yonghai, *Cong fugui zhangsheng dao fengyue fanhua.*
38. The only other novel I can think of that would rival it is *Pin hua bao jian* 品花寶鑑 (The precious mirror for evaluating flowers), Chen Sen's 陳森 (ca. 1796–ca. 1870) mid-nineteenth-century novel set in Beijing, which deals with the typically high-Qing urban delights of *kunqu* opera.
39. Hu Shi, "*Ernü yingxiong zhuan* xu," p. 357.

was a Beijing bannerman (as were the various editors and publishers involved with its printing), and the supposed "author" presented in the pages of the novel itself is moreover named the "Leisured Gentleman of Yanbei."[40] Though the official title of the novel is *The Tale of Romance and Heroism*, of the many titles the narrator suggests for the novel in the opening chapter, for our purposes one of them, *Rixia xinshu* 日下 新書 (A new tale of the capital) features rather prominently.[41] As the narrator explains, this title makes sense because the novel "tells of a case [that took place] in the best of cities, the capital" 所傳的是首善京 都一椿公案.[42] Like many other nineteenth-century novels, the tale is moreover set in the author's own dynasty, the Qing, and even though the story supposedly takes place in the final years of the Kangxi and first years of the Yongzheng reign periods, any reader would recognize the author's depictions of characters and places as veiled references to people and spaces more familiar from his own time.[43] Substantial parts

40. Yanbei is a poetic reference to Beijing.

41. As mentioned earlier, *The Tale of Romance and Heroism* is self-consciously modeled on Cao Xueqin's 曹雪芹 (ca. 1715–ca. 1763) *The Dream of the Red Chamber*. The metafictional opening chapter, with its suggestion of many different titles for the same work, is merely one of many examples of such modeling. Like Cao Xueqin's novel, *The Tale of Romance and Heroism* employs the play with what Andrew Plaks calls "bipolar complementarities." However, whereas *The Dream of the Red Chamber* creates a fictional universe primarily within the confines of the household, *The Tale of Romance and Heroism* creates a tension between domestic and public activities.

42. Wen, *Ernü yingxiong zhuan* (Ergong 尔弓 edition, 1990 rpt.), vol. 1, prologue, p. 1.

43. As the narrator tells us in chapter 1, "This tale does not tell of events as recent as the latter Tang and Five Dynasties period, nor does it relate events as ancient as the Han, Wei, and Six dynasties. Rather it is a case that is set in two reigns of our great Qing dynasty, the final years of Kangxi and the early years of Yongzheng.... In this place that is the capital, all the numberless talents under heaven are gathered. Truly it is a place where officials and their carriages fly about and carts and horses converge like the spokes on a wheel" 這部書近不說殘唐五代, 遠不講漢魏六 朝, 就是我朝大清康熙末年, 雍正初年的一椿公案.... 就這座京城地面, 聚會着天 下無數的人才. 真個是冠蓋飛揚, 車馬輻輳. Wen, *Ernü yingxiong zhuan* (Ergong 尔 弓 edition, 1990 rpt.), vol. 1, chap. 1, p. 11. This intro establishes a clear link between the novel, the fortunes of the dynasty, and the location of Beijing. For an extended discussion of the veiled references to actual historical figures who take fictional form in the novel, see Sun Kaidi, "Guanyu *Ernü yingxiong zhuan*."

of the novel are set in and around Beijing, and the tale offers quite beautifully orchestrated scenes of such typical Beijing affairs and places as
the Hanlin Academy, the theater district just outside Qianmen, and the
metropolitan examinations.

The strongly metafictional prologue that opens the novel establishes
a Beijing background for the supposed author as well as the implied
reader. The scene depicts the self-described author of the novel, "The
Leisured Gentleman of Yanbei," reading in a school room when he falls
asleep:

> Just as the Leisured Gentleman of Yanbei had fallen asleep, he left the
> study in a haze and came out to the street. There, before his eyes, he saw
> a new world full of hustle and bustle: crooked alleyways ran off on both
> sides of the street, and in them countless carts and horses converged like
> spokes on a wheel and officials in their carriages flew about; people were
> coming and going, the scene was completely lively [renao]. In the middle,
> however, there was a smooth and flat road. On it there was only an old
> bony man with short stubbly hair and a pointed head walking in front of
> him straight as a stick.
>
> 才得睡着, 便恍惚間出了書房, 來到街頭, 只見憧憧擾擾, 眼前換了一番新
> 世界: 兩旁歧途曲巷中有無數的車馬輻輳, 冠蓋飛揚, 人往人來, 十分熱
> 鬧; 當中卻有一條無偏無破蕩平大路; 這條路上只有一個瘦骨銳頭鬢髮根
> 根上指的在前面挺然值立的走了去.[44]

The Leisured Gentleman of Yanbei follows this mysterious figure
and is finally led to Heaven, where he sees the entire cast of the novel
act out an operatic performance that prophetically foreshadows the
rest of the events described in the novel. Although the metafictional
tones of the prologue are striking, what concerns us here is the way
Wen Kang suggests a Beijing setting for the novel. Not only is the
fictional author named after the capital, in the beginning of the novel
we also see him falling asleep in a school that is clearly located at the
heart of the city of Beijing. As such, the novel suggests a Beijing background for its reader as well. Just as the author dreams up his tale
from an academy somewhere in the midst of the busy city, so we can
imagine the reader, reading in his studio, dreaming of following the

44. Wen, *Ernü yingxiong zhuan* (Ergong 尔弓 edition, 1990 rpt.), vol. 1, wedge, p. 1.

author through the crowded alleyways of the capital to a grand opera set in Heaven.

Even though the opening chapter thus immediately positions author and reader as Beijing denizens in a lively Beijing city, the question remains to what degree the lively Beijing streets themselves become the interest of the novel. Like the author, the implied reader most likely belonged to the literati class, and as such many of the Beijing sights and sounds that we nowadays would regard as typically Beijing lay far beneath these men's cultured interests. The central characters in the novel, the Confucian bannerman patriarch An Xuehai and his son An Ji, both share this literati disdain for the heat and dust of the city streets. For instance, though the An family owns a luxurious compound in Beijing's Inner City, An Xuehai's father has already moved to the more quiet, secluded, and tasteful surroundings of the Western Hills because he "preferred quiet in his later years" 晚年好靜.[45] Similarly, we are told that An Xuehai spends his days in peace and in general "refuses to go into town" 不肯進城.[46] In chapter 38 it is stated even more explicitly that the usual Beijing temple fair is far beneath the elder Confucian gentleman's interests:

Even though Master An had been born and raised in Beijing and had lived there for over fifty years, he had never gone to visit any of the temple sites in the capital—not to the Eastern Mountain Temple, not to the City God Temple, not to the Temple of Caogong, nor to the Baiyun Temple, or the Fulong Temple, or the Huguo Temple.

原來安老爺雖是生長京城, 活了五十來歲, 凡是京城的東嶽廟, 城隍廟, 曹公觀, 白雲觀, 以至福隆寺, 護國寺, 這些地方, 從沒逛過.[47]

45. Wen, *Ernü yingxiong zhuan* (Ergong 尔弓 edition, 1990 rpt.), vol. 1, chap. 1, p. 13. The original family compound is said to have been bestowed by the emperor and is located at the Buliang Bridge 步量橋, right behind the northern gate of the Forbidden City.
46. Wen, *Ernü yingxiong zhuan* (Ergong 尔弓 edition, 1990 rpt.), vol. 1, chap. 1, p. 14. We are also told that An Xuehai's father moved to the Western Hills because the city compound was too large for the small number of family members. Wen Kang must have been well familiar with this part of Beijing since he himself lived not far away in the Tu'er Alley 土兒胡同. See footnote 7 by Ergong in Wen, *Ernü yingxiong zhuan* (Ergong 尔弓 edition, 1990 rpt.), vol. 1, chap. 1, pp. 24–25.
47. Wen, *Ernü yingxiong zhuan* (Ergong 尔弓 edition, 1990 rpt.), vol. 2, chap. 38, p. 917.

An Xuehai's sentiment is mirrored by at least one nineteenth-century reader. In a comment on this very passage, Dong Xun, a formidable official and influential literatus of the late nineteenth century, adds, "I am lazy by nature and must say that I follow in his footsteps" 在下腳懶, 可步後塵.[48]

Does this mean the novel is not interested in the popular sights and sounds of Beijing? Not necessarily. The novel clearly delights in depicting various street scenes. However, it does represent the lively Beijing spaces of the popular crowd as separate from those spaces that are proper to the leisured gentleman. As a result the novel does not depict the liveliness of the street directly but rather employs a mediated form of representation that deliberately creates distance between the literati world on the one hand and the dusty, noisy streets on the other. Though this distance between the world of the literatus and the world of the street is consequently tastefully widened, the result is not that the street disappears from the novel but rather that when these two worlds do meet, the shock is even stronger.

The first way in which the novel constructs a distinction between the "here" of the literati author and the "there" of popular street life is by literally emphasizing the distance between these two places. Simply put, the novelist offers a host of typically Beijing street phenomena but carefully delegates these phenomena to spaces far beyond the city walls. Rather than have the male patriarch face a crowd of vulgar revelers in Beijing, for instance, the author allows An Xuehai to leave Beijing discreetly before having him partake in the kind of lively street fair he would never have visited if it had been in the capital itself. Like so many other vernacular tales, the novel employs the motif of the journey as a distancing effect. As a result, the shock and feeling of alienation the two male characters experience can be played up and farcically overstated. At the same time, of course, the author can include a variety of vulgar street phenomena, typical of Beijing streets, but still keep them at a safe distance from the cultured reader.

Second, the novel mediates the experience of the Beijing streets through a third character.[49] The most obvious example of such self-con-

48. Ibid.
49. This technique of distancing popular street entertainments from the notion of what is considered properly Beijing is also found in other texts, which often

scious indirect experience is found in the chapter in which the heroic martial hero Deng Jiugong relates how he came to the capital and went to see opera performances just outside Qianmen. The account, which takes up a good portion of chapter 32, is arguably one of the liveliest depictions of opera performance found in vernacular literature. Yet as a whole the scene is significantly not a direct depiction of an opera performance, but rather an elaborate tale told by the character Deng Jiugong to amuse his friend An Xuehai.

The result of this mediation by Deng Jiugong allows the scholar An Xuehai to retain a bemused and tasteful distance from the Peking opera event, even though the scene is told in full color.[50] Much of this distance is merely a ruse. An Xuehai, as well as the implied reader and the author, are fully conversant with the pleasures of opera performances in Beijing. Take, for instance, the following exchange between An Xuehai and Deng Jiugong, which takes place when the scholar asks Deng Jiugong for the location of the theater:

> Master An said, "I have seen many opera houses outside the Inner City. Where did you hear the performance?"
>
> Deng Jiugong said, "Where would I have had the time to pay attention to such details? Anyway, it was in a *hutong* located in the district west of Qianmen. On the north side of the street there was a jewelry shop and in front of the theater they had placed two large baskets, and in the baskets they had piled up sunflower seeds in a big heap."
>
> 安老爺道: "我見城外頭好幾處戲園子呢, 那裡聽的?"
>
> 鄧九公道: "我也沒有那大功夫留着些閒心, 橫豎在前門西里一個胡同兒裡頭, 街北是座紅貨舖, 那園子門口兒總擺那麼倆大筐, 筐裡堆着崗尖的瓜子兒.[51]

---

emphasize the rural origins of the different performers. Most notably, the early text *The Country Bumpkin Knows Naught of the Theater* employs the device. See West, *Vaudeville and Narrative*, pp. 12–14.

50. This use of indirection is part and parcel of the way *zidishu* depict different forms of vulgar performances. See, for instance, "About Shi Yukun" and "Suiyuanle," in both of which the explicit tone of voice of the narrator visiting the performance allows an ironic distance between the performance described, the audience present, and the narrator himself.

51. Wen, *Ernü yingxiong zhuan* (Ergong 尔弓 edition, 1990 rpt.), vol. 2, chap. 32, pp. 711–12.

An Xuehai may be the kind of person who has never visited vulgar temple fairs, and similarly he is not the person who attends a rowdy Peking opera performance in the novel. As this example shows, however, even though An Xuehai might claim innocence as to the vulgar pleasures of Peking opera, he is thoroughly familiar with the area where these performances take place. Creating the character of Deng Jiugong allows the author to include lively depictions of Peking opera, while still maintaining a proper distance.

Though this form of mediation allows distance, it does not diminish the liveliness of the actual depiction of Peking opera. Deng Jiugong's supposed ignorance about Beijing, as well as his very unfamiliarity with the particulars of opera performances, only allows a more full-fledged and extended description of the actual event.[52] In the brief quote offered above, for instance, the use of Deng Jiugong as a mediator allows the author to create a pleasurable guessing game with the reader that depends on full descriptions of events without explicitly dropping any names. Consequently, the author, in the voice of Deng Jiugong, offers a description of the place, whereas otherwise simply naming it would have sufficed. As a result the reader is faced with an extremely detailed, but still distanced, depiction of a typical opera performance.[53]

To this we should add that by having a vulgar, lively character such as Deng Jiugong narrate the event, the author only enhances the liveliness of the Peking opera performance.[54] Deng Jiugong's narration takes up several pages, but let me here quote one brief segment to illustrate this point:

52. The same technique is used during the wedding scene where the incomprehension of Thirteenth Sister allows the narrator to step in and explain the various ritual proceedings.
53. For an instructive contrast, see Stephen Owen's "Place," a discussion of the high poetic tradition of depicting urban space in which continuous usage of proper names is de rigueur.
54. The comic value of Deng Jiugong's vernacular rendering of opera becomes even more obvious when compared with the more appreciative, poetic descriptions of opera found in flower registers 華譜 and the central narrative voice offered in those texts, that is, the cultivated, poetic voice of a tasteful patron. See Goldman, *Opera and the City*, pp. 17–52. Even flower registers, however, could voice the kind of sardonic criticism here voiced by Deng Jiugong. For those more critical voices, see ibid., pp. 53–58.

The opening act was "Yu Boya breaks his zither."[55] They told me the actor was particularly popular, but when I heard him wailing and hollering, causing a fuss [*nao*] for what seemed like forever, I simply couldn't stand it any longer. But then I looked at those listening to the opera: there were some who were smacking their lips, others were nodding their heads or marshalling all the air from their midriffs to shout out "Bravo!" There were even some who cocked their ears and never looked away as though they were listening to something of great importance. If you looked at them, they seemed more enraptured than those people listening to *The Classic of Poetry* or *The Classic of Ritual* you read about in books.

一開場, 唱的是 "俞伯牙摔琴," 說的是個紅腳色. 我聽他連哭帶嚷的鬧了半天, 我已經煩的受不得了. 瞧了瞧那些聽戲的, 也有砸嘴兒的, 也有點頭兒的, 還有從丹田裡運着氣往外叫好兒的, 還有幾個側着耳朵不錯眼珠兒的當一椿正經事在那裡聽的. 看他們那些樣子, 比那書上說的聞 "詩" 聞 "禮," 還聽得入神兒."[56]

The opera event is not directly depicted as a true mirror image of events. Rather, the entire scene is mediated through the voice of the hero Deng Jiugong. It is precisely this indirection that brings the depiction to life. For a few pages Deng Jiugong becomes a storyteller whose vulgar word choice, rhythmic patterning, and apt, popular, similes proffer the reader a sense of an opera performance that goes beyond mere objective depiction.[57] Simply put, it is the mediation of Deng Jiugong's voice that brings this quintessential Beijing scene to life.[58]

55. Given that the theme of this particular opera is the ideal of "appreciative listening," Deng Jiugong's "inability" to delight in the performance is particularly ironic. The opera tells of the friendship between Yu Boya and Zhong Ziqi. Zhong, it is said, was the only man capable of truly appreciating Yu's play of the zither. When Yu finds out Zhong has passed away, he plays a final tune at his friend's grave and then demonstratively breaks his zither, never to touch the instrument again. The opera was performed in the capital from at least the middle of the nineteenth century. The 1845 printing of Yang Jingting's *A Short Account of the Capital* lists the play (by the short title of *Shuaiqin*) under the Sanqing troupe and gives the name of the actor who plays Yu Boya. On the play, see Zeng, *Jingju jumu cidian*, p. 65.

56. Wen, *Ernü yingxiong zhuan* (Ergong 尔弓 edition, 1990 rpt.), vol. 2, chap. 32, p. 712.

57. As David Rolston has pointed out, various characters in the novel are explicitly compared to storytellers. See Rolston, *Traditional Chinese Fiction*, p. 307.

58. Note in particular the way in which the author combines visual gaze and acoustic patterning by having Deng Jiugong describe the crowd through a carefully

The Harmony of Street and Studio

Sounds allow the construction and linking of narrative and physical spaces. These spaces, such as the scholar's studio or the lively inn, or noises like those of the temple fair, are of course imbued with values. Most notably, these spaces are associated with elegance (*ya* 雅) and vulgarity (*su* 俗). The retreat of the scholar's studio represents the epitome of elegance, and the shouts, songs, and theatrical performances of the street represent a dusty world that is unmistakably vulgar. In these final two sections, I will suggest that Wen Kang not only presents the plot of his novel as a gradual spatial outing of the sheltered literatus, he also shows how the novel as a genre is singularly equipped to bring vulgarity and elite interests together. Though much of the fun of the novel is derived from observing how the two different worlds of literati knowledge and street entertainments collide, in the end, I argue, the author suggests that ultimately the novel can create a harmony between these two worlds.

In *The Tale of Romance and Heroism*, the two main male protagonists, father An Xuehai and son An Ji, clearly function as paragons of culture on account of their erudition. Yet, even so, the secluded life of the two scholarly gentlemen is the butt of many jokes. Similarly, even though the author does not want to uphold common prostitutes as moral exemplars, he does not reject street life outside the family compound altogether. Although common prostitutes remain far beneath the reader's appreciation, the *jianghu* characters of Thirteenth Sister and Deng

---

measured and highly rhythmic repetition. This form of a synesthetic depiction of urban crowds can be found throughout late nineteenth-century novels. A similar moment of poetic repetition can be found, for instance, in the Yangzhou novel *A Dream of Moon and Wind*, where the author offers a lengthy set-piece describing the liveliness of Yangzhou urban streets around Tianning Gate. See Hanshang mengren, *Feng yue meng*, chap. 3, pp. 14–15. There is a strong oral element to all these novelistic depictions and various forms of nineteenth-century oral performance; most notably, *zidishu* uses this form of measured and rhythmic repetition to create a sense of a crowd. For a good example, see "Pangxie duaner" 螃蟹段兒 (The eating crabs' youth book), which first describes the elaborate makeup of a Manchu woman and then tells of the effect her beauty has when she walks out onto the streets, causing a crowd to gather. See Elliot, "The 'Eating Crabs' Youth Book." For the original, see "Katuri jetere juben i bithe."

Jiugong clearly possess qualities that are of benefit to the two literati men. Rather, the novel suggests ways in which the more coarse realities found in the street can be incorporated into the life of the characters and the pages of the book. As a result, the narrative presents a constant juxtaposition of sheltered elite literati interests with more popular street entertainments, the end of which is a carefully plotted harmony of elite and vulgar sounds.

This juxtaposition is played out in a series of scenes in which the leading literati men are placed among the common people and, as a result, noisy street life is juxtaposed with elite incomprehension. We have already considered a few moments where An Ji is faced with a bevy of street characters. In this section, I will focus on a scene found in chapter 38 in which the family patriarch An Xuehai, despite his misgivings, finds himself at a crowded temple fair. The scene takes place when An Xuehai is in the city of Zhuozhou en route to Shandong, and he hears that at a local temple a phoenix has been sighted. An Xuehai at first is skeptical; he has an aversion to temple fairs. But then, realizing that since ancient times a phoenix has been considered a sign of propitious government, the patriarch decides he should investigate this omen of imperial fortune himself. As it turns out, the phoenix is a chimera, or rather, a common urban street performance that draws on visual and acoustic spectacle as well as the slippage of linguistic puns to con an unsuspecting gentleman like An Xuehai into paying a few coppers:

In the empty courtyard, there was set up a tent of worn blue cloth. From the inside, the sound of gongs and drums was rising up to heaven. Outside the tent, there stood a man shouting, "Three official coppers a person! See the phoenix spread a single wing!" When Master An heard this, he became quietly happy and hurried in. As it turned out, it was a "dry boat act." He saw a fellow in his thirties, swarthy of complexion and with stubble covering his face and cheeks. The man's head was wrapped in a turban, and he was dressed in colorful clothes. He was leaning on the boat, one hand propping up his chin, and with the other he was stretching out, all the while making all kinds of embarrassingly coquettish faces.[59] The act went on like this for some time, when once again they heard the

59. The confusion in this scene depends on the author's use of Beijing thieves' cant in which "a phoenix wing" is a standard term for the word "arm." See Chen Qi, *Zhongguo mimiyu dacidian*, p. 220.

person beating the gong shouting, "If you've finished seeing the phoenix spread its single wing, then all you gentlemen ought to see the fluttering butterflies." Only then did Master An understand that this was what was called "a phoenix spreading its single wing."

那空院子裡圈着個破藍布帳子, 裡面鑼鼓喧天. 帳子外頭一個人, 站在那裡嚷道: "撒官板兒一位! 瞧瞧這個鳳凰單展翅!" 老爺聽了, 心中暗喜, 連忙進去, 原來卻是起子跑旱船的. 只見一個三十來歲漆黑的大漢字, 一嘴巴子的黥子槎兒, 也抱了頭, 穿了彩衣, 至在那個旱船上, 一手托了腮, 把那只手單撒手兒伸了個懶腰, 臉上還作出許多百媚千嬌的醜態來. 鬧了一陣, 又聽那個打鑼的嚷道: "看完了鳳凰單展翅, 這就該着請太爺們瞧飛蝴蝶兒了." 安老爺這才明白, 原來這就叫作"鳳凰單展翅."[60]

Though set in Zhuozhou, the scene immediately calls to mind popular bamboo-branch poem descriptions of con men cheating hapless Beijing citizens. However, whereas a typical bamboo-branch song blames Beijing tricksters for confusing categories of true and false, in this scene the author focuses not so much on the perfidious nature of the tricksters as on the gullible nature of An Xuehai.[61] Admired for his in-depth knowledge of highbrow Confucian texts, An's lack of common street sense here becomes the focus of ridicule.

Most of the time, the interaction between elite and vulgar tastes is depicted as a clash between two different cultures. Linguistically, the author delights in juxtaposing elevated and more humble patterns of speech in such a manner that exalted patriarch and local town-folk constantly talk past one another. An Xuehai's visit to the temple, for instance, is the result of a miscommunication between the lodge innkeeper and the scholar. The confusion revolves around An's asking the waiter for "any traces of arcadia" 名勝, the waiter mistaking this exalted phrase as "races or arcades" 靈聖, resulting in the suggestion that the scholar should visit the fair at the Tianqi Temple. When the waiter continues and adds that at the temple fair the crowds all come to watch "sum'ting special" 希希罕兒的, it is An Xuehai's turn to be

60. Wen, *Ernü yingxiong zhuan* (Ergong 尔弓 edition, 1990 rpt.), vol. 2, chap. 38, p. 926.

61. A bamboo-branch song by the author Deshuoting 得碩亭 (fl. 1817) similarly depicts a ruse that employs a cloth confine with the promise of a miraculous monster inside. Notably Deshuoting does not reproach the viewer, but instead the perfidious performers. See Deshuoting, "Caozhu yi chuan" 草珠一串, vol. 1, p. 153.

perturbed and wonder what "sum'ting special" might mean.[62] The waiter patiently explains about the phoenix, which An Xuehai interprets in the classical sense of meaning a sign of propitious government, and the confusions and miscommunications continue from thereon. In short, the author's interest in depicting the clash between literati and popular sensibilities translates on a linguistic level into a heteroglossia of mutual incomprehension where Manchu bannermen, elite literati, burly bodyguards, and vulgar prostitutes and innkeepers all speak past one another in their own language.[63]

The constant juxtaposition of sensibilities is not only linguistic in nature. When An Xuehai visits the temple, different forms of appreciation lead to confrontations that can turn into spatial and narrative impasses. While at the temple, for instance, Master An and his entourage finally manage to gain entrance and find themselves at a major throughway: the passage with the four Heavenly Kings that leads into the temple grounds.[64] At this point, the novel begins a lengthy learned discourse between Master An and his fellow literatus companion Teacher Cheng regarding the etymological origin of the names of the four kings. In the end, the verbose discussion leads to a blockage:

62. Wen, *Ernü yingxiong zhuan* (Ergong 尔弓 edition, 1990 rpt.), vol. 1, chap. 38, p. 916. This use of "sum'ting special" occurs once again when An Xuehai is at the temple. Frustrated with the vulgarity around him, scholar An decides to engage in the most rarified of pursuits possible in a temple; he decides to read the many inscriptions found on the stelae in the garden. While gazing intently at the inscriptions, he is accosted by a group of women who insist on questioning the scholar about feminine health issues. As one of the women explains, they had come over because the scholar was gazing so intently at a stele, which convinced the women he must be looking at "sum'ting special on top" (pp. 921–22).

63. Note that in this heteroglossia the various registers of speech are rarely juxtaposed in a neutral and non-adversarial manner. Not only do people talk past one another, but there is at times a clear confrontational tone to these dialogues. Thirteenth Sister in particular excels at abusing people verbally first and physically next. For such a scene, see Wen, *Ernü yingxiong zhuan* (Ergong 尔弓 edition, 1990 rpt.), vol. 1, chap. 7, p. 139.

64. This brief scene is nicely juxtaposed with the scene that takes place at the major entrance to the temple. There, hawkers of all kinds make it impossible for the scholarly An Xuehai to enter. It is only when his servant takes the lead that the literatus is finally able to go in.

Master An only cared about investigating with his friend the origins of
[the four kings] Feng, Diao, Yu, and Shun, so the servants could only
stand and wait behind them as well;[65] in addition they were surrounded
by a group of bystanders listening in on the excitement [renao], and as a
result the main throughway past the entrance with the Four Heavenly
Guardians was all blocked up. Then they heard somebody yelling behind
them, "Move while sightseeing, will ya! Move while sightseeing, will ya!
If you insist on splitting hairs about this and that, then why don't you go
back to your own home and find a study to discuss it there! This temple
is open for all to enjoy and see something excitin' [renao]. Don't make
people complain now!" Master An immediately moved on, but Master
Cheng still insisted on asking, "What does that mean, 'see something
excitin'?"

老爺只顧合世兄一陣考據風, 調, 雨, 順, 家人們只好跟在後頭站住; 再加
上圍了一大圈子聽熱鬧兒的, 把個天王殿穿堂門兒的要路口兒給堵住了.
只聽得後面一個人嚷道: "走着逛拉! 走着逛拉! 要講究這個, 自己家園兒
裡找間學房進去! 這廟裡是個 '大家的馬兒大家騎' 的地方兒, 讓大伙兒
熱鬧熱鬧眼睛, 別招喊冤!" 老爺連忙就走. 稱相公還在那裡打聽說: "甚麼
叫做 '熱鬧眼睛'?"[66]

As shown in this brief scene, vulgar and literati appreciations of what
is worth looking at in the temple are completely at odds and constantly
threaten to collide. The learned etymological discussion drags on for
quite some time, before a vulgar voice from someone in the crowd
finally interrupts and forces the narrative to continue. Meanwhile, the
reader is treated to a form of elite-vulgar interaction that consists of an
impasse portrayed on a spatial, linguistic, and narrative level.[67]

Although scholarly and popular entertainments and interests thus
seem to be completely at odds, the author does suggest that ideally these
two worlds should be enjoyed in a harmonious manner. Such a harmony

65. These are the names of the four heavenly kings, but together they also read,
"The winds are temperate and the rains timely."
66. Wen, *Ernü yingxiong zhuan* (Ergong 尔弓 edition, 1990 rpt.), vol. 2, chap. 38,
p. 919.
67. On a larger narrative (and spatial) level, the blockage occurs when Master
An is on the way to Shandong. The scene is in many ways completely superfluous, and while various plotlines cleverly converge at this node, the main purpose
of the scenes at the temple fair of Zhuozhou is completely self-indulgent comic
spectacle. It is this kind of verbose delight of the author that made Hu Shi remark,
"Bannermen excel at talking." Hu Shi, *"Ernü yingxiong zhuan* xu," p. 357.

is presented at the conclusion of An Xuehai's trip to the temple grounds. After having been horrified by one performance after another and having failed miserably at locating a true phoenix, the scholar despondently sits down to enjoy some peace and quiet. It is at this point that he is unexpectedly treated to an exquisite *daoqing* performance of a popular Taoist ballad.[68] At first, this vulgar performance of a Taoist song is, of course, far below An Xuehai's interests. As the Beijing scholar listens more attentively, however, he is pleasantly surprised by its sophistication:

> Master An had never paid attention to opera or *tanci*, and Buddhist monks and Taoists were even less appealing to him. Add to this that this Taoist master had dolled his face up in this way. When Master An had seen it he had already become quite irritated, so he just sat there and even turned his head to look somewhere else.[69] All of a sudden, he heard the quatrain that [the performer] had begun his performance with. It was not clichéd at all, and the spoken self-introduction was not vulgar either. Master An could not help but be a little possessed by the spirit of the text, and he listened carefully for what the Taoist would sing next. He heard him sing:

> 安老爺向來於戲文, 彈詞一道本不留心, 到了和尚, 道士兩門, 更不對路,
> 何況這道士又自己弄成那等一副嘴臉! 老爺看了, 早有些不耐煩, 只管坐在
> 那裡, 卻掉轉頭來望着別處. 忽然聽他這四句開場詩, 竟不落故套, 就這段
> 科白也竟不俗, 不由得又着了點兒文字魔, 便要留心聽聽他底下唱些甚麼.
> 只聽他唱道:
> 　　鼓逢逢, 第一聲, 　　　　The drum beats 'FENG FENG,'

68. *Daoqing* is a popular form of oral performance that traces its root back to Tang dynasty songs with a Taoist content. By the Qing, however, *daoqing* had lost most of its religious connotations and was merely another form of popular song performed at temple fairs for the amusement of crowds. As in Wen Kang's novel, *daoqing* is usually performed by a single performer who sings seven-character lines to his own accompaniment with a fish-drum and rhythm stick. For a longer description of this form of oral performance, see Shanghai yishu yanjiusuo, *Zhongguo xiqu quyi cidian*, pp. 661–62. See also Li Jiarui, *Beiping suqu lue*, pp. 173–75.
69. Note that by turning his head, An's visual line is blocked and the acoustic aspect of the performance is strengthened. The strong acoustic dimension of this performance was set up earlier, when the drum-beat of the song is written out in a single onomatopoeic line: *Zha beng beng, zha beng beng, zha beng, zha beng, zha beng beng* 扎弁弁, 扎弁弁, 扎弁, 扎弁, 扎弁弁. Wen, *Ernü yingxiong zhuan* (Ergong 尔弓 edition, 1990 rpt.), vol. 2, chap. 38, p. 927.

	so goes the first sound.
莫競喧, 仔細聽.	Silence your clamor, and listen with care.
人生世上渾如夢.	In this world human existence is like a dream.
春花秋月銷磨盡.	Spring flowers and autumn moon pass till they're done,
蒼狗白雲變態中.	The Pale Dog and white clouds[70] endlessly change their shape.
游絲萬丈飄無定.	Ten thousand gossamer webs drifting in impermanence.
謅幾句盲詞瞎話.	I will make up words for the illiterate and deaf,[71]
當作他暮鼓晨鐘.	May they serve as the drum at dusk, the awakening bell at dawn.[72]

As Master An heard this, he nodded his head, thinking, "This section must be a general introduction that sums up the performance." Upon this he listened to him continue singing.

安老爺聽了, 點點頭, 心裡暗說: "他這一段, 自然要算個總起的引子了." 因又聽他往下唱道.[73]

As the performance continues, the reader is treated to an extended transcription of the song's lyrics and guided in appreciating the song through the thoughts of An Xuehai, who comments on the lyrics after each section.

The performance draws our attention because it presents the reader with a long, thirteen-stanza transcription of a popular Taoist song. This form of oral performance, much like the novel form itself, allows the author to give voice to a harmony of popular and elite tastes, oral and written pleasures. As it turns out, the Taoist's chanting follows a series of rhyme categories that, despite the vulgar setting and the simple form of

70. These are clichéd phrases referring to heavenly bodies in constant motion and thus denoting the notion of permanence found in impermanence and vice-versa.
71. Here blindness and orality are combined. *Mangci* usually refers to a kind of telling tales in musical form by blind performers.
72. The drum at dusk and the bell at dawn are used to call monks to prayer. They symbolize an appeal to enlightenment.
73. Wen, *Ernü yingxiong zhuan* (Ergong 尔弓 edition, 1990 rpt.), vol. 2, chap. 38, p. 928.

the Taoist's popular song, obey the formal rules regarding poetic rhyme categories. At the end of the performance we read how An Xuehai offers the following analysis:

> The master was just thinking to himself, "Not only are the melody and lyrics of this Taoist performance not vulgar, but when I add things up, together with the spoken intro and the final coda, this performance comes to thirteen sections. As such, it follows the ancient rhyme-categories of the twelve *she*, which, when we add the *hui* rhyme category of the lyricists, comes exactly to thirteen rhymes.[74]
> 老爺正在那裡想: "他這套 '道情' 不但聲調詞句不俗, 並且算了算, 連科白帶煞尾通共十三段, 竟是按古韻十二攝, 照詞曲家增出 '灰韻' 一韻, 合着十三轍譜成的.[75]

Although An Xuehai's quest for a phoenix has thus ended in vain, he has instead found, amid the raucous sounds and sights of the urban crowd, a form of oral performance that is worth listening to precisely because it appeals to his elite poetic sensibilities. Indeed, this mixture of popular and elite, oral and written modes of enjoyment is perfectly embodied in An Xuehai's appreciation; while listening to the song, he insists on analyzing the chanted verse in scholarly terms and, despite the acoustic form of the performance, finds himself "moved by the spirit of the text."

The Sounds of the Novel

As the final Taoist song performance shows, when vulgar street sounds and elite sensibility come together a striking harmony of sounds can arise. As such, the *daoqing* performance can be read as a metaphor for the novel as a whole. Like the *daoqing* performance, the novel aims to blend popular and literati tastes through a long and complicated

---

74. There are twelve rhymed sections in the piece, leaving out only the ninth rhyme category, 梭波.
75. Wen, *Ernü yingxiong zhuan* (Ergong 尔弓 edition, 1990 rpt.), vol. 2, chap. 38, p. 930.

interaction of vulgar and elite themes, linguistic registers, spaces, and sounds. Indeed, even though *The Tale of Romance and Heroism* is most famous for its lively depictions of martial arts heroes and street characters, we should note that the novel is in fact extremely pedantic.[76] It indulges in lengthy, abstract discussions about the classics and the proper writing of examination essays. At one point, we even see how An Xuehai lectures the progeny of four of Confucius's disciples on the correct meaning of *The Analects*.[77] As such, Wen Kang's novel represents a clear continuation of the more elevated concerns of eighteenth- and nineteenth-century novels such as Wu Jingzi's 吴敬梓 (1701–54) *Rulin waishi* 儒林外史 (The scholars) or Li Ruzhen's *Flowers in the Mirror*. Yet at the same time, the novel clearly delights in depicting the vulgar sights and sounds of the street, presenting martial heroes speaking uncouth dialect phrases and prostitutes singing debauched songs, thus offering numerous detailed depictions of lowbrow entertainments typical of Qing-dynasty Beijing.

Structurally, this blend of elegance and vulgarity comes out most clearly in the interaction between the two primary narrative voices that run throughout the text, the voice of the supposed author the Leisured Gentleman of Yanbei on the one hand, and the voice of the lively and raucous storyteller who brings the text to life through performance on the other. Neither the storyteller persona nor the metafictional device of text within a text are new developments. Yet it is remarkable to what degree the author Wen Kang plays up these two distinctively different narrative voices. For instance, when the novel ends, we as readers first see the putative author, the Leisured Gentleman of Yanbei, signing off,

76. Hu Siao-chen has stated it best when she argues that the main part of the novel uses a storyteller voice to discuss matters that have nothing to do with typical storyteller narratives. See Hu Siao-chen, "Pinfan riyong yu daotong lunli," p. 628.
77. The passage is typical in the way it allows the interpenetration of philosophical discussion and everyday life, juxtaposing listening to vulgar opera with discussing the meaning of the classics. In terms of this discussion of the classics, the passage is moreover interesting in the way it offers a philological critique of the way Song Neo-Confucian scholars such as Zhu Xi corrupted earlier texts. Ergong claims that this passage is actually a later addition since it is not found in the earliest, hand-written copy of the novel. Though this may be true, there is undoubtedly enough pedantry in the character of An Xuehai, even without his lecture to the latter-day disciples of Confucius. See Ergong, "Houji," p. 1070. Wen Kang, *Ernü yingxiong zhuan* (Ergong 尔弓 edition, 1990 rpt.), vol. 2, chap. 39, pp. 965–73.

after which the storyteller ends the tale with an additional conclusion.[78]

The strongly self-conscious use of these two distinct voices has already been discussed by various scholars, but not from the angle of sound. David Rolston, for instance, has shown how the combination of a fictitious author and an anonymous storyteller allows for a remarkably complex tale from a structural point of view.[79] Similarly, Christopher John Hamm has shown how the constant play between the various narrative voices in the novel creates a metafictional text that precludes any single authorial or ideological point of view.[80] Most recently, Patrick Hanan has once again drawn our attention to the remarkable liveliness of the storyteller voice in this novel and the unprecedented interaction that takes place between storyteller persona and fictional written text.[81] To these readings, I would simply add how the interaction between the Leisured Gentleman of Yanbei and the anonymous storyteller creates a textual and vocal binary whose interaction imbues the elegant, but silent, scholarly text with a vulgar, yet lively, storyteller voice.

This interaction leads to a variety of juxtapositions where obtuse textual knowledge and vulgar street smarts become intertwined to such a degree that it becomes hard to distinguish the two. Take, for instance, the following snippet of wisdom the storyteller offers after the scholar An Ji is faced with a *jianghu* word he does not understand. The moment occurs when An Ji offers a few hundred cash to have a heavy stone moved to block the entrance of his room so that Thirteenth Sister cannot enter. The servant in the inn informs him that *yuegan chu* 月干 楮 will be needed to cover the costs.

> This phrase the young master did not understand at all! Not only did the young master not understand it, even the listeners to this tale may well not get it. Even I, the storyteller, did not understand it [the first time around]. When this storyteller in days past heard someone tell the story of *The Tale of Romance and Heroism*, I went and looked it up in Master Yang's *Dialects*.[82] That book, however, did not contain this dialect word

---

78. See Wen, *Ernü yingxiong zhuan* (Ergong 尔弓 edition, 1990 rpt.), vol. 2, chap. 40, p. 1043.
79. See Rolston, *Traditional Chinese Fiction*, pp. 304–11.
80. Hamm, "Reading the Swordswoman's Tale."
81. See Hanan, *Chinese Fiction*, pp. 9–32.
82. Yang Xiong 揚雄 (BC 53–18 AD) was a famous *fu* poet and scholar of the Han

at all. Later I ran into someone who was familiar with the streets and markets and asked him to explain, and only he was able to provide the necessary commentary and subcommentary on it. He said, "*Yue* is used to speak of 'two,' this is because within the character *yue*, the character 'two' lies hidden.[83] *Gan* is used to speak of 'a thousand,'[84] and 'a thousand' is used to speak of 'a string of cash.' As for *gan*, it is a substitute word for 'a thousand,' and 'a string of cash' is common diction for 'a thousand.'"

這句話公子可斷斷不得明白了! 不但公子不得明白, 就是聽書的也未必得明白, 連我說書的也不得明白. 說書的當日聽人演說 "兒女英雄傳" 這樁故事的時候, 就考過揚子 "方言" 那部書, 那部書竟沒有載這句方言. 後來遇見一位市井通品, 向他請教, 他才注疏出來, 道是: "'月'之為言二也, 以月字中藏着二字也. '干'之為言千, 千之為言吊也; 干者千之替語也, 吊者千之通稱也."[85]

Rolston has rightfully pointed out how this moment represents a reference to textuality as opposed to orality.[86] Here, I merely want to briefly add how ingeniously these two categories are mixed to the point where the distinction disappears. To begin with, the term *yuegan chu* belongs to what twentieth-century dictionaries call *jianghu* language.[87] The idea that such a blatantly vulgar oral term might be found in written form in a scholarly work written close to two thousand years earlier, Yang Xiong's *Dialects*, is of course ludicrous.[88] Instead, to learn what this word means, the storyteller has to call on another reference work, a fellow fully conversant with the language of the streets (*shijing tongpin*), who subsequently provides the "necessary annotation" (*zhushu*) and

---

dynasty. His work *Fangyan* 方言 (Dialects) is the first extant work exclusively devoted to the different Chinese dialects. As part of the extensive textual scholarship done in the Qing dynasty, many scholars wrote revisions of Yang Xiong's text.
83. Within the character *yue* 月 there are two horizontal strokes that, when seen in isolation, make up the character for the number "two" 二.
84. The character "gan" (干) greatly resembles the character for a thousand (千), and it is easy to mistake one for the other.
85. Wen, *Ernü yingxiong zhuan* (Ergong 尒弓 edition, 1990 rpt.), vol. 1, chap. 4, p. 78.
86. Rolston, *Traditional Chinese Fiction*, p. 306.
87. See, for instance, Qu Yanbin, *Zhongguo miyu hanghua cidian*, p. 900.
88. Though Wen Kang plays up the distinction between textuality and orality for laughs, during the Qing dynasty scholarly works actually began to explore this area of street language. Zhai Hao's 翟灝 eighteenth-century work *Tongsu bian* 通俗編 (A compendium of popular sayings) for instance, includes the term in its extraneous category under a list of words noted as "mixed classes of the *jianghu*" 江湖雜流.

continues to speak, despite his street credentials, in the tone of Yang Xiong's scholarly work on dialect. At the end of the storyteller aside, scholarly discourse and oral street language have become fully intertwined, and the reader is allowed to enjoy both at the same time.

Most importantly, however, with this interaction between written text and storyteller voice, words on the page at times no longer seem silent. Although elite aesthetics and literati sensibilities remain, the text never becomes dull, precisely because of the storyteller's voice that causes the words to jump in acoustic profusion from the page.[89] Such is, for instance, the case at the beginning of chapter 6, where the author, in storyteller guise, continues the tale he left off in the previous chapter (not coincidentally this is the continuation of the snippet I quoted on the first page of the introduction to this book):

This chapter closely follows the previous one. The previous chapter told how the murderous monk bound young master An to a pillar in the hall, cut open his clothes and then, holding in his hand the sharp blood-sacrificial knife, stabbed at his heart. There was the sound "PU," then a "GUDONG" as someone fell over. Honored sirs listening to this story, there is no way that you could not have heard that. But I am afraid that there might be those among you who are not patient enough to pay attention to the unfolding of the plot, and who, recklessly concerned where concern is not appropriate, upon hearing this [part of the story] have begun wiping the tears from your eyes. This storyteller's fault would not be a trifling matter! Please don't be alarmed. The one who fell over was not young master An.
"How could it not be him?"
Master An was tied to the pillar in the hall. Think about it. How could he fall over with a "PUDONG"?
"Then who was it who fell over?"
It was the monk.
"So if it was the monk who toppled over, why don't you just come out and just say that the monk fell over and be done with it? Why do you have to create all this excess talk?"
This is merely the storyteller drumming up a bit of excitement.
這回書緊接上回, 不消多餘交代. 上回書表得是那凶僧把安公子綁在庭柱

89. For instance, Patrick Hanan notes that the storyteller interrupts the text over two hundred times. He concludes that the storyteller figure in *The Tale of Romance and Heroism* is probably the most individualized storyteller figure in vernacular fiction. See Hanan, *Chinese Fiction*, pp. 10–11.

上, 剝開衣服, 手執牛耳尖刀, 分心就剌. 只聽得噗的一聲, 咕咚倒了一個.
這話, 聽書的列公再沒有聽不出來的. 只怕有等不管書裡節目, 妄替古人擔
憂的, 聽到這裡, 先哭眼淚起來, 說書的罪過可也不小! 請放心, 倒的不是
安公子.怎見得不是安公子呢? 他在庭柱上綁着, 請想, 怎的會咕咚一聲倒
了呢? 然而這倒的是誰? 是和尚. 和尚倒了, 就直接痛快的說和尚倒了, 就
完了事了, 何必鬧這許多累贅呢? 這可就是說書的一點兒鼓噪.[90]

It is at moments like these that the insertion of the storyteller's voice
into a literati text and the supposed oral interaction between storyteller
and live audience allows the reader to move beyond the space where he
reads the novel. It is at moments like these that the reader can be imagined as listening to the sounds of the novel.[91]

Conclusion

In *The Tale of Romance and Heroism*, sound constructs distinctly different spaces and the worldviews associated with these spaces. At the same
time, sound functions as a conduit that allows these distinct spaces to
be connected and worldviews to be mediated. Let me conclude with
a pivotal scene from the beginning of the novel in which sound once
again is used as a conduit—this time to connect the space of Heaven
with the academy down on earth, and in turn the inside of the academy with the more popular liveliness outside. The moment occurs at
the end of the metafictional dream that has led the Leisured Gentleman
of Yanbei from a school at the heart of Beijing to the highest realm of
Heaven. It is at this point that the dream ends and the text of the novel
begins. Strikingly, it is a loud vocal cue that wakes the fictional author
from his dream and leads him back to reality:

90. Wen, *Ernü yingxiong zhuan* (Ergong 尔弓 edition, 1990 rpt.), vol. 1, chap. 6, p.
106.
91. As such, it is interesting that among the various aficionados of the text, most
notably Ergong, Sun Kaidi, and Qian Zhongshu 錢中書 (1910–98), it was the linguist
Qian Xuantong 錢玄同 (1887–1939) who delighted in chanting the text aloud to
bring out the sounds of its "pure Beijing language." See Ergong, "Houji," p. 1066.

[The Leisured Gentleman of Yanbei] saw the Heavenly Ruler shake his dragon-robe sleeves and heard the palace officials shouting, "Discharge the Ranks!"

The Leisured Gentleman of Yanbei heard a loud noise, and someone was shouting, "Grab him! Grab him! Grab him!" After this followed a huge noise of the earth splitting asunder and mountains crashing. The noise startled him so that he missed his step on the cloud under his foot. Unable to keep his balance, he came falling down, down from the edge of the clouds, when the shock from the fall woke him up. It had all been one big dream! When he opened his eyes and looked in front of him, he saw how in the courtyard there was a group of children who had skipped school and were right now playing hide and seek. Their shouts rang loudly "Grab him! Grab him! Grab him!" Before him was standing a fellow student from Xin'an[92] holding a ruler, hitting the table with it so that it rang out wildly, laughing at him: "Wake up! Wake up!"

只見天尊把龍袖一擺，殿頭官才喝得聲：「退班！」那燕北閒人耳輪中只聽得一片喧嘩，喊道："捉! 捉! 捉!" 隨着便是地坼天崩價一聲響亮. 嚇得他一步踏空雲腳，一個立足不穩，早從雲端裡落將下來，一跤跌醒，卻是一場大夢！睜開眼來看看，但見院子裡一班逃學的孩子，正在那裡捉藏耍子，口裡只嚷道："捉! 捉! 捉!" 面前卻立着合他同硯一個新安畢生，手裡拿着一方戒尺，拍的那桌子亂響，笑嘻嘻的叫道："醒來! 醒來!" [93]

In a manner reminiscent of Jia Baoyu's return from the Land of Illusion at the end of chapter 5 of *The Dream of the Red Chamber*, Wen Kang uses sound to connect dream-world with reality, heaven, and earth. It is the call of the children in the yard and the little student at the author's desk that urge him and the reader to wake up and venture outside to play.[94]

92. Xin'an might refer to a place name in Anhui. I have thus far not discovered why the author uses this particular reference.

93. Wen, *Ernü yingxiong zhuan* (Ergong 尔弓 edition, 1990 rpt.), vol. 1, wedge, p. 9.

94. In *The Dream of the Red Chamber*, Baoyu's dream ends with his crying out loudly, thus connecting his dream-space to the reality outside. In *The Tale of Romance and Heroism*, the sound from outside awakens the dreamer inside. *The Dream of the Red Chamber* further emphasizes the sense of narrative shift by placing this call right at the end of the chapter. See Keulemans, "Listening in on *The Dream of the Red Chamber*," unpublished paper. In dream literature, using sound to connect or transition between dreaming and waking states is quite common. See Zeitlin, *Historian of the Strange*, p. 190. Finally, note that, once again, misinterpretation based on a slippage of language is called upon to connect dream and reality. Fictionality is introduced through the linguistic opening that is the pun.

CODA

POW!

Our science has always desired to monitor, measure, abstract, and castrate meaning, forgetting that life is full of noise and that death alone is silent: work noise, noise of man, and noise of beast. Noise bought, sold, or prohibited. Nothing essential happens in the absence of noise.
—Attali, *Noise*, 1985

In the beginning of the first chapter of *Sishiyi pao* 四十一炮 (POW!) by Mo Yan 莫言, the hero, a hapless young man from the provinces, finds himself in an abandoned temple in front of an unorthodox Buddhist priest. As he offers his life story to the priest, he finds that his story, as well as his thoughts, are continuously interrupted by the stubborn materiality of the outside world, a world whose presence insistently makes itself known through its aromatic, visual, and, most importantly, acoustic cues:

Flies have settled on the Wise Monk's earlobes but none on his shaved head or oily face. Out in the yard, the branches of a huge gingko tree [are filled with] a chorus of birds singing; there are cat yowls ringing amid the chorus too—the cries of a pair of feral cats that sleep in a hollow of the tree and snatch the birds off its limbs. A particularly self-satisfied yowl enters the temple, followed a mere second later by the pitiful screech of a bird, and then the flapping of wings as a panicky flock takes to the sky. I don't so much smell the stench of blood as imagine it; I don't so much see the feathers fly and the blood-stained limbs as conjure up the image. The male cat is pressing its claws into its prey and trying to court favor with the tailless female. That missing tail makes her look three parts cat and

EPIGRAPH: Attali, *Noise*, p. 3.

seven parts fat rabbit. After answering the Wise Monk's questions, I wait for him to ask more.

大和尚的兩扇耳朵上，落滿了蒼蠅，但他光溜溜的頭皮上和他的油膩膩的臉上却連一只蒼蠅也沒有. 院子裡有一棵龐大的銀杏樹，樹上鳥聲一片，鳥聲裡間或響起猫叫. 那是兩只野猫，一公一母，在樹洞裡睡覺，在樹杈上捕鳥. 一聲得意的猫叫傳进小庙，接着是小鳥悽慘的叫聲，然後是群鳥驚飛的扑棱聲. 與其說我嗅到了血腥的氣味，不如說我是想到了血腥的氣味；與其說我看到了鳥羽翻飛、血染樹枝的情景，不如說我想到了這個情景. 此刻，那只公猫，用爪子按着流血的獵物，對着另外那只缺了尾巴的母猫獻媚. 那只母猫因為缺了尾巴，看上去三分像猫，七分倒像一只肥胖的兔子. 我回答完大和尚的问题，等待着他繼續問話.[1]

By the beginning of the twentieth century the rhetorical figure of the storyteller began to disappear from vernacular fiction, thus bringing an end to a mode of writing that had lasted for some three hundred years.[2] Yet, as even this brief snippet shows, the acoustic imagination originally fueled by the storyteller voice most certainly did not.[3] Here, as elsewhere in Mo Yan's fiction, images of sex and violence are conjured up not through the graphic depiction of those acts, but rather by suggesting their enigmatic acoustic traces—the onomatopoeic flutter of bird wings, the yowl of a cat, or the synaesthetic evocation of a chorus of birds.[4] Moreover, as was the case in Wen Kang's *Tale of Romance*

1. Mo Yan, *Sishiyi pao*, chap. 1, pp. 1–2; translation (with minor modifications) by Howard Goldblatt in Mo Yan, *POW!*, chap. 1, pp. 1–2. Mo Yan is the pen name of Guan Moye 管謨業 1955–, winner of the 2012 Nobel Prize for Literature.
2. The most authoritative study on the topic remains Henry Zhao's *The Uneasy Narrator*.
3. Although Mo Yan does not employ the rhetorical figure of the storyteller to infuse his fiction with sound, much of the narrative flair of *POW!* is derived from the way it presents itself as a long, oral narration. Apart from the brief snippets of interior monologue, the entire novel reads like a "confession" performed for the benefit of an attentive audience, the monk. Elsewhere Mo Yan explicitly discusses the "oral" nature of his novels as the result of his long experience of "reading with his ears," an oral mode of telling tales which directly appeals to readers' senses and imagination. That said, Mo Yan associates this oral mode of transmitting stories not with the rhetorical figure of the storyteller typical of vernacular fiction or even professional storytellers, but rather with stories told by grandfathers, grandmothers, and children. See Mo Yan, "Yong erduo yuedu."
4. To my knowledge, not much has been written about the strikingly acoustic qualities of Mo Yan's fiction. That said, in the preface to the novel *Tanxiang xing* 檀

and Heroism, Mo Yan not only shows an uncanny ear for the way in which sounds add "color" to the text, but he also displays a very similar metafictional understanding of the way in which sounds, as well as the images and smells they call forth, are in the end nothing but the willful play of the reader's imagination. After all, if Mo Yan points out that for the narrator the violent images of blood-drenched fowl are merely imaginary visions triggered by a series of acoustic cues, for the reader those acoustic cues are equally imaginary, a host of sonic impressions called forth by the silent graphs printed on the page.

Mo Yan's *POW!* may be a particularly loud example of the continued fascination with sound in Chinese fiction of the twentieth and twenty-first centuries, but clearly Mo Yan is not the only modern author to explore the possibilities of representing sound through printed text. In the critical realist fiction of an author such as Mao Dun, modernity announces its arrival into the lives of the peasantry (and of course Mao Dun's narrative itself) with the loud, disruptive onomatopoeic hooting of a steamboat barging up the Grand Canal.[5] In the more lively dramatic writings of Lao She 老舍 (pen name of Shu Qingchun 舒慶春, 1899–1966), the distance between local Beijing characters and provincial outsider is resoundingly captured in the sonic representation of a southern Kuomintang officer whose only spoken phrase in the entire scene is a consistently mispronounced "excellent/esslent" 好/蒿.[6] And even though it is easy to focus myopically on the visual qualities of the writings of the New Perceptionists, the urban modernist writers of the 1920s and 30s, it would be wrong to ignore, in between images of neon lights, visions of busy streets, and fantasies of long-legged waitresses, the lilt of a Suzhou accent, the blaring of saxophones, or the sounds of newspaper boys hawking their wares.[7]

Of course, many of these sounds are different from the sounds of the nineteenth-century martial arts novel. We cannot expect to find in nineteenth-century fiction the ringing of telephones, the screaming

---

香刑 (Sandalwood death), Mo Yan's translator, Howard Goldblatt, points out the difficulty of translating a work that is "so utterly reliant on sound, rhythm, and tone." See Goldblatt, "Translator's Note," p. ix.

5. See Mao Dun, *Chun can*, vol. 5, p. 169.

6. Lao She, "Chaguan," act 3, pp. 65–66.

7. See Shi Zhecun, *"Meiyu zhi xi,"* pp. 127 and 131 respectively; Liu Naou, "Youxi," p. 314; and Mu, "Shanghai de hubuwu," p. 190.

of car horns, or the distant churning of the industrial city Shanghai, as we do in the opening chapters of Mao Dun's *Ziye* 子夜 (Midnight).[8] Similarly, if vendor calls and acoustic advertisements are still found in the representation of the modern soundscape, they do not seem to be any longer the chosen acoustic medium for eliciting desire.[9] Instead, especially in the writing of native soil literature, snippets of folksong have become the chosen mode of depicting the acoustic lure of sexuality sublimated into narrative form.[10] The sounds of dialect speech remain a concern, but the "foreign" nature of such dialect speech is usually not captured through the double printing of characters, but rather through the abundant use of quotation marks.[11] It is beyond the scope of this conclusion to investigate how the increasing prominence of technology, the interest in folklore studies, the use of modern punctuation, or the presence of English as a new cosmopolitan language have impacted the representation of sound in modern Chinese fiction. Rather, the point is that these various modern, technological, scientific, and linguistic regimes seem to have only strengthened the use of the acoustic imagination in Chinese fiction.

8. See Mao Dun, *Ziye*, vol. 4, pp. 3–30. Note that the author explicitly comments on the way the cacophony of the city drowns out the sound of the dying patriarch; see p. 7.

9. For a short essay in which the trope of the vendor call is appropriated for the purposes of an explicitly Marxist ideology, see Mao Dun, "Mai doufu de shaozi."

10. See Shen Congwen, "Xiaoxiao." The use of folksong as narrative seduction in native soil fiction is intimately tied to the importance of the folksong movement in the 1920s and 1930s spearheaded by luminaries such as Liu Fu 劉復 (1891–1934), Gu Jiegang 顧頡剛 (1893–1980), and Wen Yiduo 聞一多 (1899–1946). Embedded in the narrative of modern short stories, these songs function to depict "tradition" and hence are usually shorn from any reference to contemporary consumer culture. Contemporary musicological accounts of the actual songs, however, show that they are often filled with references to global brand names, commodities whose function it is to elicit and express desire. For a history of the early folksong movement, see Hung, *Going to the People*, pp. 58–80.

11. Mao Dun's *Spring Silkworms*, with its abundance of dialect terms, quotation marks, and footnotes, comes to mind. In the actual performance of cross-talking as a stage act, verbal slapstick is no longer confined to the intrusion of dialect speech from China's provinces, but now also includes the mimicry of yokels attempting to speak foreign languages. For a high literary example of such practices, see Gao Xingjian's 高行健 (1940–) play *Che zhan* 車站 (Bus stop), in which a young hothead pokes fun at a student's use of English by sinicizing the sounds (p. 44).

In this regard, it is particularly striking how, despite the influence of modern media and new modes of observation, many of the narrative and ideological functions of imagined sounds have remained strikingly similar. For instance, when, in the opening chapter of Mao Dun's *Midnight*, the old patriarch Wu arrives in cosmopolitan Shanghai, the sensory delights of the city—visual, aromatic, *and* acoustic—disorient the main character, guide the reader, and map space in a way that is not all that different from how the sights and sounds of Beijing are introduced in the bannerman song translated in chapter 3, Helüshi's "Strolling through the Huguo Temple."[12] Similarly, when in Ding Ling's 丁玲 (pen name of Jiang Bingzhi 蔣冰之, 1904–86) short story "Shafei nüshi de riji" 沙菲女士的日記 (The diary of Ms. Sophie) the eponymous heroine finds herself alone in a Beijing hostel, the way in which the author emphasizes Ms. Sophie's isolation and alienation by employing the loud voices of waiters, customers, and telephone calls outside her room immediately recalls the way Wen Kang used vendor calls, snippets of songs, and loud rambunctious voices to sketch the disorientation of Young Master An in a small roadside inn in *The Tale of Romance and Heroism* (chapter 6).[13] And, even though the twentieth century supposedly introduced a univocal national language whose parameters were distinctly different from the late-imperial imagination of language and dialect discussed in chapter 5, the sound of dialect speech still tellingly differentiates provincial other from self-doubting cosmopolitan self, as is the case in Lu Xun's famous use of the character *zha* 猹.[14]

What changed, in short, was not the use of sound in printed text per se, but rather the way the twentieth century introduced new ways of imagining the voice of enunciation that brought these sounds to life.

12. See Mao Dun, *Ziye*, pp. 9–16.
13. Ding Ling, "Shafei nüshi de riji," vol. 2, p. 47.
14. Lu Xun, "Guxiang," p. 61. Lu Xun later explained his famous use of this character. Though modern editions append such scholarly comments as footnotes, as opposed to inserting them as *pingdian* comment as in Wen Kang's novel, the remark neatly shows how the representation of dialect in text remained an affair of the interaction between local speech and scholarly erudition even after the fall of the Qing dynasty. As Lu Xun explained, "I invented the character '*zha*' on the basis of the sound of the speech of the people in the countryside; it should be pronounced as *zha*." Ibid, p. 68.

Most notably, as new Western modes of observation became increasingly prominent in nineteenth- and early twentieth-century China, the self-consciously fictional mode of voicing vernacular narrative through the rhetorical figure of the storyteller was displaced by the (supposedly) unmediated representation typical of realist writing.[15] Such a modern mode of realist writing is easily conflated with a purely visual imagination. Yet, as the examples quoted above make clear, acoustic cues played a crucial role in the canon of modern realist writings of Mao Dun and Lao She. In addition, and perhaps equally important to the invention of a realist mode of acoustic expression, was the shift from a singular, if anonymous, storyteller voice to the unanimous, collective voice of the people itself.[16] Though most readily imagined as voices coming together in actual song or chanted poetry, as theorized by Xiaobing Tang and John Crespi, in fiction such an acoustic imagination of the crowd could easily find its way into the printed imagination of revolutionary martyrs singing *The Internationale* or the roar of an undifferentiated peasant mob.[17] Moreover, if realism highlighted an "invisible" voice and revolutionary writing emphasized a collective voice, in contrast authors such as Lu Xun excelled in imagining sounds through a highly individualized, lyrical voice.[18] Finally, in contrast with the humanist acoustic imagination of Lu Xun, we can suggest a technologized acoustic imagination beginning to take shape in modern Chinese literature, an imagination that marshals the technologies of film, telephone, loudspeakers,

15. des Forges, "From Source Texts to 'Reality Observed.'"
16. For the way in which this collective voice is imagined in the chanting of poetry, see Crespi, *Voices in Revolution*, pp. 18–42, and throughout. For the way such a collective voice is given visual form, see Xiaobing Tang, "Echoes of *Roar China!*"
17. See Ding Ling, "Mou ye," and "Shui," in *Ding Ling xuan ji*, vol. 2, pp. 326–32 and 287–325 respectively. For a discussion of the way the anonymous voices of the masses erupt as an (acoustic) sign of collectivity, see Anderson, *The Limits of Realism*, pp. 184–87.
18. Such is the case, for instance, in Lu Xun's short story "Zhufu" 祝福 (New Year's sacrifice). This story is beautifully book-ended by the sounds of New Year's firecrackers. These sounds, however, are clearly mediated by the narrator's consciousness; it is his presence that transforms the joyous communal sounds of New Year's firecrackers into a horrific acoustic evocation of a primitive mob mentality. See Lu Xun, "Zhufu," pp. 132 and 148.

or the Internet as a way of capturing the modern and postmodern experience of sound in print.[19]

Although the modern Chinese literary acoustic imagination is hence characterized by a host of alternative "voices," it is important to emphasize that the storyteller figure of the premodern period did not disappear altogether, either. As David Wang has noted, in the writings of a canonical Beijing author such as Lao She we can still discern the rhetorical figure of the storyteller.[20] It is merely that, for an author so consciously torn between a desire for a modern mode of temporal progress on the one hand and a nostalgia for the fragmentary traces of the past on the other, this lively voice of the "past" has to be balanced with a more rational, twentieth-century narrative voice. Not surprisingly, Lao She's traditional Beijing soundscapes are inevitably represented with a good deal of distance, the infectious nature of their lively sounds carefully inoculated by a heavy dose of bitter irony.[21]

Tellingly, one of the best representatives of the use of sound in modern fiction, as well as the continued use of the storyteller voice, is found within the genre of martial arts fiction itself, most notably in the works of its most famous author, Jin Yong. As scholars such as Liu Zaifu, Xiaofei Tian, and Tuo Li have noted, Jin Yong has long embraced premodern literary forms as a way of evoking a continuous Chinese

19. Here I am not referring to the way in which an individual, humanist spirit is marshaled by juxtaposing it with the acoustic image of mass rallies broadcast through loudspeakers (as is the case, for instance, in Mo Yan's novel *Shengsi pilao* 生死疲勞 [Life and death are wearing me out]). Rather I am more interested in the way modern technology comes to inform the actual (visual) and acoustic shape of literary texts. Good examples are found in the way concrete poetry has developed from Chen Li's 陳黎 (pen name of Chen Yingwen 陳膺文; 1954–) "Zhanzheng jiaoxiang qu" 戰爭交響曲 (War symphony) to the even more experimental works of Yao Dajuin 姚大鈞, whose work increasingly employs the (interactive) technology of the Internet to shape the acoustic (and visual) experience of the "text." See Michelle Yeh, "'There are No Camels in the Koran'"; Hockx, *Internet Literature in China*, chap. 4. For a good study of the way such modern technologies have shaped Japanese fiction, see Yasar, *Electrified Voices*.
20. See David Wang, "Storytelling Context in Chinese Fiction."
21. For a good example, see the famous final chapter of *Luotuo Xiangzi* 駱駝祥子 (Rickshaw), which is filled with the sights and sounds of Beijing in spring, but only as a way of criticizing such outdated sensory pleasures. Lao She, *Luotuo Xiangzi*, pp. 249–58.

cultural tradition that crosses the modern/premodern boundary.[22] This use of premodern literary forms is not limited to some snippets of classical poetry or some of the generic elements of the late-imperial *zhanghui* 章回 novel, but also includes a variety of specific features usually associated with the rhetorical figure of the storyteller. Jin Yong typically begins his works of fiction with a preamble that introduces the main topic of the work as a whole.[23] Similarly, the classical poems with which Jin Yong so often commences his novels recall the opening poems of vernacular fiction, just as his way of explaining such poems harkens back to the way the storyteller in late-imperial vernacular fiction would explain such poems to his "listeners." Moreover Jin Yong, at least in the original versions of his works, employs typical storyteller phrases such as, "Let's not talk about this in detail, but instead talk about . . ." 不必細表, 單表 . . . .[24] Jin Yong himself, of course, is well aware of his debt to vernacular fiction and the rhetorical figure of the storyteller. In fact, he has explicitly cast his own authorial persona in the image of the late-imperial storyteller. In his rewrite of the novel *Shediao yingxiong zhuan* 射雕英雄傳 (Eagle-shooting heroes), for instance, Jin Yong incorporated a storyteller performance of the *huaben* 話本 tale, "Virtuous Third Sister Ye" 葉三姐節烈記, and, when explaining this use of a storyteller tale as intro (*yinzi* 引子), stated he had done so to honor the storyteller origins of Chinese fiction.[25]

22. Liu Zaifu, "Jin Yong"; Tuo Li, "The Language of Jin Yong's Writing"; Xiaofei Tian, "The Ship in a Bottle."

23. The first chapter of *Lu ding ji* 鹿鼎記 (The deer and the cauldron), for instance, opens with a lengthy historical discussion mouthed by three prominent scholars of the early Qing period, Huang Zongxi 黃宗羲 (1610–95), Gu Yanwu, and Lü Liuliang 呂留良 (1629–83). Meanwhile the main tale is not launched until the beginning of chapter 2.

24. Jin Yong, *She diao yingxiong zhuan* (1960–69?), vol. 1, chap. 1, p. 6. Note that this phrase, as well as other typically vernacular elements—long lists of imperial successions, clichéd four-character phrases describing the heat of battle—are only found in the early editions of the novel, not in the later revised edition first published in 1977. Indeed, it is quite ironic that the more Jin Yong self-consciously emphasized his literary linkages to the past, the more these telltale signs of the storyteller manner disappeared. For a brief discussion of the way Jin Yong elided such storyteller phrases, see Lin Baochun, *Jiegou Jin Yong*, p. 212.

25. See Jin Yong, *She diao yingxiong zhuan* (2003), vol. 1, chap. 1, pp. 7–14. For Jin Yong's explanation of the use of the storyteller, see Jin Yong, "Houji," vol. 4, p. 1620.

Jin Yong's evocation of traditional modes of telling a tale fuel an acoustic imagination that is strikingly similar to the late-imperial literary soundscapes I have explored in the body of this book. The second chapter of his final novel, *The Deer and the Cauldron,* for instance, opens with an extended soundscape of seventeenth-century Yangzhou, in particular its infamous pleasure quarters, "the Chiming Jade Ward." After situating his tale acoustically with the "sounds of musical instruments and laughter spilling forth" and "the sounds of people playing guess fingers and chanting drunken balladry," Jin Yong then introduces the first stirrings of plot with "a sudden chorus of five or six men shouting" and a gate being kicked in with a strikingly loud "PENG."[26] Before long, this is a martial arts novel after all; the reader finds himself amid broken furniture, heroic action, and a sundry assortment of cries and onomatopoeia. This is how Jin Yong brought the episode to its raucous climax when it was first published in its original, serialized format on November 7, 1968, in the Hong Kong newspaper *Mingbao* 明報:

From the room [next door] the heavy clashing of blades was heard, "PINGPING PANGPANG." The tall salt smuggler was using a whip made of steel, and every time the sound "KECICI" was heard another piece of furniture was smashed to pieces. The House of Vernal Pleasures was one of the four main brothels of the Ward of Chiming Jade, and each room had been exquisitely laid out with rosewood tables and oak wood beds. As the sounds "PINGPING KECI" kept ringing forth, the brothel owner's fat face became increasingly distraught. Soon the bawd was mouthing a pained series of heartfelt prayers to the Buddha.

   All the while the four salt smugglers kept yelling and screaming. The guest in the room, however, remained perfectly quiet. In the main courtyard, the others had all carefully kept their distance, afraid of getting caught in the cross-fire. They heard how the clashing of the blades became increasingly frantic until, all of a sudden, there was a single piercing scream.

只聽得房中乒乒乓乓, 兵刀相交之聲大作. 那身材魁梧的鹽梟所用兵刃乃是一條竹節鋼鞭, 每聽得喀喇喇一聲響, 便是一件傢俬打得粉碎. 那麗春院乃鳴玉坊中四大院子之一, 每一間房中都是擺設得極為考究, 梨花木的桌子, 紅木的床. 乒乒喀喇之聲不絕, 老鴇臉上肥肉直抖, 口中念佛, 心痛不絕.

26. Jin Yong, *Lu ding ji*, vol. 1, chap. 2, pp. 47–48. For a full translation, see Cha, *The Deer and the Cauldron*, vol. 1, chap. 2, p. 51.

那四名鹽梟不斷吆喝呼叫，房中那客人卻是默不作聲. 廳堂上眾人都是站得遠遠地，唯恐遭上池魚之殃，但聽得兵刃碰撞之聲越來越快，忽然有人長聲慘呼. [27]

In the nineteenth century, savvy storytellers, authors, and publishers exploited a wide variety of sounds for artistic and economic purposes. Jin Yong's similarly ingenious use of onomatopoeia and exclamations aptly illustrates how the (commercial) attraction of such acoustic delights continued well into the twentieth century. Jin Yong, after all, made his name and fortune by publishing his novels in installments, his daily adventures of heroic martial men enthralling readers throughout the 1950s and '60s.[28] Tellingly, the episode from *The Deer and the Cauldron* of November 8 ends with an acoustic cliff-hanger, a series of onomato-poeic bursts followed by a single piercing scream that leaves the reader both excited and wondering: who is it exactly that has just been struck a fatal blow?

Some might suggest that the sounds of the nineteenth-century martial arts novel and its storyteller persona belong to a different, less technologically-mediated world. As the opening scenes from Jin Yong's *Deer and the Cauldron* and Mo Yan's *POW!* suggest, however, the sounds of the novel are still eminently on display in our modern age. It has been the aim of this study to call attention to the evanescent pleasures as well as the purposeful profits produced by these sounds rising from the page.

27. Jin Yong, "Lu ding ji," p. 6; Cha, *The Deer and the Cauldron*, vol. 1, chap. 1, pp. 55–56.
28. For a study of the interaction between commercial newspaper publishing and Jin Yong's serialized novels, see Hamm, *Paper Swordsmen*, pp. 51–55, 114–37, and throughout.

Bibliography

Chinese and Japanese Language Sources

Aying 阿英. "Guanyu Shi Yukun" 關於石玉昆 (About Shi Yukun). In *Xiaoshuo er tan* 小說二談 (Second collection of chats about novels), pp. 89–92. Shanghai: Gudian wenxue chubanshe, 1958.

Bao gongan guci 包公案鼓詞 (A drumsong of the cases of Judge Bao). Microfilm reprint edition. *Che wangfu quben* 車王府曲本 (Che prince household collection libretti). Microfilm reprint edition, reel 32–33. Beijing: Zhonghua quanguo tushuguan wenxian suowei zhongxin, 1994.

Boyin 伯寅. "*Xu xiao wu yi xu*" 續小五義序 (Introduction to *The continued latter five gallants*). In Ding Xigen, *Zhongguo lidai xiaoshuo xuba ji*, vol. 3, pp. 1556–57.

Cai Youmei 蔡友梅. "Cao erjing" 曹二更 (After midnight Cao). In *Qing mo min chu xiaoshuo shuxi: jing shi juan* 清末民初小說書系: 警世卷 (A series of novels from the late Qing and early Republic: admonishing the world), edited by Yu Runqi 于潤琦, pp. 626–72. Beijing: Zhongguo wenlian chuban gongsi, 1997.

———. "Kuduanyan" 庫緞眼 (The snob). In *Qing mo min chu xiaoshuo shuxi: jing shi juan* 清末民初小說書系: 警世卷 (A series of novels from the late Qing and early Republic: admonishing the world), edited by Yu Runqi 于潤琦, pp. 510–46. Beijing: Zhongguo wenlian chuban gongsi, 1997.

———. "Xiao E" 小額 (Xiao E). In *Zhongguo jindai wenxue yanjiu*. 2 vols. First edition 1907. Guangzhou: Guangdong renmin chubanshe, 1983–85.

Caixiang jushi 採香居士. "*Xu Peng gongan xu*" 續彭公案序 (Preface to *The continued cases of Judge Peng*). In Ding Xigen, *Zhongguo lidai xiaoshuo xuba ji*, vol. 3, pp. 1616–17.

———. "*Xu Peng gongan you xu*" 續彭公案又序 (Another preface to *The continued cases of Judge Peng*). In Ding Xigen, *Zhongguo lidai xiaoshuo xuba ji*, vol. 3, p. 1618.

Cao Yibing 曹亦冰. *Xiayi gongan xiaoshuo shi* 俠義公案小說史 (A history of novels of adventure and detection). Hangzhou: Zhejiang guji chubanshe, 1998.

Chang Renchun 常人春. *Lao Beijing de fengqing* 老北京的風情 (Customs of old Beijing). Beijing: Beijing chubanshe, 2001.

Chanmeng anzhu 懺夢庵主. "*Yingxiong xiao ba yi zhuiyan*" 英雄小八義贅言 (Some superfluous words [to introduce] *The heroic latter eight gallants*). In Ding Xigen, *Zhongguo lidai xiaoshuo xuba ji*, vol. 4, pp. 1569–70.

Chen Fengchun 陳逢春. "Quyi shuogong" 曲藝說功 (The oral craft of *qu yi*).
    In *Zhongguo dabaikequanshu: xiqu, yishu* 中國大百科全書: 戲曲, 曲藝 (The
    great encyclopedia of China: opera, oral performance), edited by Zhongguo
    dabaikequanshu chubanshe bianjibu 中國大百科全書出版社編輯部, pp. 321–
    25. Beijing: Zhongguo da baikequanshu chubanshe, 1983.
Chen Jinzhao 陳錦釗. "Zidishu zhi ticai yu laiyuan jiqi zonghe yanjiu" 子弟書
    之題才與來源及其綜合研究 (The content and sources of *Zidishu* and their
    comprehensive research). Phd diss., Zhengzhi daxue, 1977.
———. "Shipaishu de tizhi: jianlun xiancun *qingshishan de banben deng*" 石派書
    的體製—兼論現存《青石山》的版本等 (The form of the Shi-style storyteller
    manuscripts: a discussion of the extant editions of *Blackrock Mountain* and
    other things). In *Di san jie tong su wen xue yu yazheng wenxue yantaohui
    lunwen ji* 第三屆通俗文學與雅正文學全國學樹研討會論文集 (Collection of
    papers from the third congress on popular and refined literature), pp. 389–407.
    Taipei: Zhongxin daxue, 2002.
Chen Pingyuan 陳平原. *Qiangu wenren xiake meng: wuxia xiaoshuo leixing
    yanjiu* 千古文人俠客夢: 武俠小說類型研究 (The literati's chivalric dreams:
    narrative models of Chinese knight-errant literature). Taipei: Maita, 1995.
———. "Jianghu yu xiake" 江湖與俠客 (The *jianghu* and the knight-errant). In
    Chen Pingyuan zixuanji 陳平原自選集 (Essays selected by Chen Pingyuan),
    pp. 158–84. Guilin: Guangxi shifan daxue chubanshe, 1997.
Chen Qi 陳崎, ed. *Zhongguo mimiyu dacidian* 中國秘密語大辭典 (A grand
    dictionary of Chinese secret languages). Shanghai: Hanyu dacidian
    chubanshe, 2002.
Chen Qiaoyi 陳橋驛. *Zhongguo ducheng cidian* 中國都城辭典 (A dictionary of
    China's capitals). Nanchang: Jiangxi jiaoyu chubanshe, 1999.
Chen Tao 陳濤. *Bao gong xi yanjiu* 包公系研究 (Research on Judge Bao opera).
    Beijing: Renmin chubanshe, 2011.
Chen Wenliang 陳文良, ed. *Beijing chuantong wenhua bianlan* 北京傳統文化便覽
    (A guide to traditional Beijing culture). Beijing: Beijing Yanshan chubanshe,
    1992.
Chen Ying 陳穎. *Zhongguo yingxiong xiayi xiaoshuo tongshi* 中國英雄俠義小說
    通史 (A complete history of the Chinese novel of heroic and chivalric justice).
    Nanjing: Jiangsu jiaoyu chubanshe, 1998.
Cheng Junbao 陳君保. "Bu *hong lou meng*" 補紅樓夢 (The addition to *The dream
    of the red chamber*). In *Zhongguo gudai xiaoshuo baikequanshu* 中國古代小說
    百科全書 (The encyclopedia of Chinese ancient novels), edited by Liu Shide 劉
    世德, p. 19. Beijing: Zhongguo dabaike quanshu chubanshe, 1993.
Chong Yi 崇彝. *Dao Xian yilai chaoye zaji* 道咸以來朝野雜記 (Miscellaneous
    notes on the court and the people in the Daoguang and Xianfeng reigns).
    Reprint edition. Beijing: Beijing guji chubanshe, 1982.
Cui Yunhua 崔蘊華. *Shuzhai yu shufang zhi jian: Qing dai zidishu yanjiu* 書齋
    與書坊之間: 清代子弟書研究 (Between studio and print-shop: research in
    zidishu of the Qing dynasty). Beijing: Beijing daxue chubanshe, 2005.
———. "Cong shuochang dao xiaoshuo: xiayi gongan wenxue de liubian yanjiu"
    從說唱到小說: 俠義公案文學的流變研究 (From prosimetric tale to novel:

research on the development of martial arts literature. In *Mingqing xiaoshuo yanjiu* 3 (2008): 43–53.

Daiyusheng 待余生 (Zhuang Yingtang 庄蔭棠). *Yanshi jibi* 燕市積弊 (The collected ills of Beijing). Oldest extant edition 1909. In Daiyusheng 待余生 and Nilüguoke 逆旅過客, *Yanshi jibi, Dushi congtan* 燕市積弊，都市叢談 (The collected ills of the capital, The collected chats on the capital), edited and annotated by Zhang Rongqi 張榮起, pp. 1–107. Beijing: Beijing guji chubanshe, 1995.

Deng Yunxiang 鄧雲鄉. *Zengbu Yanjing xiangtu ji* 增補燕京鄉土記 (Expanded record of the region of Beijing). 2 vols. Beijing: Zhonghua shuju, 1998.

Deshuoting 得碩亭. "Caozhu yi chuan" 草珠一串 (A string of local pearls). First published in 1817. In *Zhonghua zhuzhici* 中華竹枝詞 (Bamboo branch songs of China), edited by Lei Mengshui 雷夢水 et al. 6 vols. Beijing: Beijing guji chubanshe, 1996. Vol. 1, pp. 141–58.

Ding Ling 丁玲. "Shafei nüshi de riji" 沙菲女士的日記 (The diary of Ms. Sophie). In *Ding Ling xuanji* 丁玲選集 (Selected writings of Ding Ling). 3 vols. Chengdu: Sichuan renmin chubanshe, 1984. Vol. 2, pp. 46–89.

———. "Shui" 水 (Water). In *Ding Ling xuan ji* 丁玲選集 (Selected works by Ding Ling). 3 vols. Chengdu: Sichuan renmin chubanshe, 1984. Vol. 2, pp. 287–325.

———. "Mou ye" 某夜 (A certain night). In *Ding Ling xuan ji* 丁玲選集 (Selected works by Ding Ling). 3 vols. Chengdu: Sichuan renmin chubanshe, 1984. Vol. 2, pp. 326–32.

Ding Xigen 丁錫根, ed. *Zhongguo lidai xiaoshuo xuba ji* 中國歷代小說序跋集 (A collection of prefatory material to Chinese novels through the dynasties). 3 vols. Beijing: Renmin wenxue chubanshe, 1996.

Dongxuanzhuren 東軒主人. "Kouji ji" 口技記 (A record of ventriloquism). In *Yu Chu xu zhi* 虞初續志 (A continued record of Yu Chu), compiled by Zheng Shuruo 鄭澍若, *juan* 7, pp. 23–25. Photographic reprint of the late Qing edition by Guangzhi shuju. Shanghai: Shanghai shudian, 1986.

"Dou gen" 逗哏 (Having a laugh). In *Beijing qiren yishu: Chaqu* 北京旗人藝術：岔曲 (The art of Beijing bannermen: short songs), edited by Jin Qiping 金啟平 and Zhang Xuekai 章學楷, p. 37. Beijing: Beijing shifan daxue chubanshe, 2007.

Ergong 尔弓. "Houji" 後記 (Postface). In Wen Kang 文康, *Ernü yingxiong zhuan* 兒女英雄傳 (The tale of romance and heroism), edited, punctuated, and annotated by Ergong, pp. 1049–77. First edition 1878. 2 vols. Ji'nan: Qi Lu shushe, 1990.

Feng Menglong 馮夢龍. *Jingshi tongyan* 警世通言 (Stories to caution the world), edited by Li Tianyi 李田意. Photographic reprint edition. 2 vols. Taipei: Shijie shuju, 1958.

Fengmi daoren 風迷道人. "*Xiao wu yi* ban" 小五義辨 (Authentication of *The latter five gallants*). In Ding Xigen, *Zhongguo lidai xiaoshuo xuba ji*, vol. 3, pp. 1554–55.

Fu Xihua 傅惜華. "Baiben Zhang xiqu shuji kaolue" 百本張戲曲書籍考略 (A study of the opera libretti of Baiben Zhang). In *Zhongguo jindai chubanshiliao er bian* 中國近代出版史料二編 (Second collection of historical material on Chinese publishing in the modern era), edited by Zhang Jinglu 張靜廬, pp. 317–29. Shanghai: Qunlian chubanshe, 1954.

———. *Beijing chuantong quyi zonglu* 北京傳統曲藝總錄 (A complete list of the traditional popular performance libretti of Beijing). Shanghai: Zhonghua shuju, 1962.

Fu Yiling 傅衣凌. "Qianyan" 前言 (Preface). In *Mindu bieji* 閩都別記 (A distinct record of the capital of Minnan). 2 vols. Fuzhou: Fujian renmin chubanshe, 1987. Vol. 1, pp. 1–4.

Ganban paizi kuaishu chaqu matoudiao geyang qumu 趕板牌子快書岔曲馬頭調各樣曲目 (A catalogue of songs: ganban, paizi, kuaishu, chaqu, matoudiao, and others). 1877.

Gao Aijun 高艾軍 and Fu Min 傅民, eds. *Beijinghua ciyu* 北京話詞語 (A dictionary of Beijing speech). Beijing: Beijing daxue chubanshe, 2001.

Gao Xingjian 高行健. *Che zhan* 車站 (Bus stop). Taipei: Lianhe wenxue, 2001.

Ge Yonghai 葛永海. *Cong fugui zhangsheng dao fengyue fanhua: gudai Yangzhou xiaoshuo de lishi liubian* 從富貴長生到風月繁華: 古代陽州小說的歷史流變 (The development from wealth and fortune to the splendor of wind and moon: the historical transformation of ancient Yangzhou novels). In *Ming Qing xiaoshuo yanjiu* 71.1 (2004): 4–21.

Gu Qiyin 顧啟音. "Qianyan" 前言 (Preface). In Guo Xiaoting 郭小亭, *Pingyan Jigong zhuan* 評演濟公傳 (The storyteller tale of Jigong), edited by Zhu Qing 竺青. Preface 1898 (first part), 1900 (second part); reprint edition. 2 vols. Beijing: Zhonghua shuju, 2001. Vol. 1, pp. 1–10.

Guang Dedong 關得棟. "Shiyin 'Qing Menggu Che wangfu cangquben' xu" 石印'清蒙古車王府藏曲本'序 (An introduction to the lithographically printed "Libretti of the collection of the Qing-dynasty household of the Prince of Che"). In *Che wangfu quben yanjiu* 車王府曲本研究 (Research on the libretti of the household of the Prince of Che), edited by Liu Liemao 劉烈茂 and Guo Jingrui 郭精銳, pp. 481–85.

———, and Zhou Zhongming 周中明. "Xu" 序 (Preface). In *Zidishu congchao* 子弟書叢鈔 (A collection of *zidishu*), vol. 1, pp. 1–18.

———, eds. *Zidishu congchao* 子弟書叢鈔 (A collection of *zidishu*). 2 vols. Shanghai: Shanghai guji chubanshe, 1984.

"Guo Dong'er" 郭棟兒 (Guo Dong'er). In *Qing Che wangfu chaocang quben: zidishu ji* 清車王府鈔藏曲本: 子弟書集 (The handwritten libretti of the Qing-dynasty household of the Prince of Che: the collected *zidishu*), edited by Liu Liemao 劉烈茂 and Guo Jingrui 郭精銳, vol. 2, pp. 338–39.

Guo Guangrui 郭廣瑞. *Yongqing shengping qianzhuan* 永慶昇平前傳 (The tale of everlasting blessings and peace part 1). Beijing: Baowen tang, 1892.

———. *Yongqing shengping qianzhuan* 永慶昇平前傳 (The tale of everlasting blessings and peace, part 1), annotated and edited by Ergong 尔弓. First edition 1892; reprint edition. Wuhan: Jing Chu shushe, 1988.

———. *Yongqing shengping quanzhuan* 永慶昇平全傳 (The complete tale of everlasting blessings and peace). First edition 1892–94; Photographic reprint edition. Vol. 87 in *Guben xiaoshuo jicheng [di er pi]* 古本小説集成 [第二批] (The collection of ancient Chinese novels [second series]). Shanghai: Shanghai guji chubanshe, 1990.

———. *"Yongqing shengping* xu"《永慶昇平》序 (Preface to *The tale of everlasting blessings and peace*). In Ding Xigen, *Zhongguo lidai xiaoshuo xuba ji*, vol. 3, p. 1561.

Guo Qinna 郭芹納. "Shuo daga" 説打嘠 (About *daga*). In *Zhongguo yuwen* 244.1 (1995): 34.

Guo Xiaoting 郭小亭. *Pingyan Jigong zhuan* 評演濟公傳 (The storyteller tale of Jigong), edited by Zhu Qing 竺青. Preface 1898 (first part), 1900 (second part); reprint edition. 2 vols. Beijing: Zhonghua shuju, 2001.

Han Bangqing 韓邦慶. *Haishang hua liezhuan* 海上花列傳 (Flowers of Shanghai). Reprint edition. Taipei: Wenhua tushu gongsi, 1993.

———. "Liyan" 例言 (Editorial principles). In *Haishang hua liezhuan* 海上花列傳 (Flowers of Shanghai), pp. 609–10. Reprint edition. Taipei: Wenhua tushu gongsi, 1993.

Han Youli 韓又黎. *Dumen zhuiyu* 都門贅語 (Superfluous words from the capital), edited by Wu Dongshan 吳東山. Beijing: Zhuoguishanfang, 1880.

Hanshang mengren 邗上夢人. *Feng yue meng* 風月夢 (Feng yue meng). Reprint edition; original 1848 preface. Beijing: Beijing daxue chubanshe, 1990.

Hatano Tarō 波多野太郎. "Hyōron tanpen shakai shōsetsu Shōgaku" 評論短篇社會小説小額 (A discussion of the social novel *Xiao E*). In *Eiin tanpen shakai shōsetsu Shōgaku: Tsuketari Hyōron tanpen shakai shōsetsu Shōgaku: Chugoku shōsetsushi kenkyū* 影印短篇社會小説小額: 附評論短篇社會小説小額—中國小説史研究 (A photographic reprint of the social novel Xiao E: including A discussion of the social novel Xiao E"), pp. 1–22. Yokohama: Yokohama shiritsu daigaku, 1968.

He Gengyong 何耿鏞. *Hanyu fangyan yanjiu xiaoshi* 漢語方言研究小史 (A brief history of research on Chinese dialects). Taiyuan: Shanxi renmin chubanshe, 1984.

Helüshi 鶴侶氏 (Yigeng 奕賡). "Fengliu cike" 風流詞客 (The cosmopolitan teller of tales). In *Qing Che wangfu chaocang quben: zidishu ji* 清車王府鈔藏曲本: 子弟書集 (The collection of handwritten libretti of the Qing-dynasty household of Prince Che: the collected *zidishu*), edited by Liu Liemao 劉烈茂 and Guo Jingrui 郭精銳, vol. 2, pp. 346–50.

———. "Guang Huguo si" 逛護國寺 (Strolling through the Huguo Temple). In *Qing Che wangfu chaocang quben: zidishu ji* 清車王府鈔藏曲本: 子弟書集 (The collection of handwritten libretti of the Qing-dynasty household of Prince Che: the collected *zidishu*), edited by Liu Liemao 劉烈茂 and Guo Jingrui 郭精銳, vol. 2, pp. 327–30.

Hou Zhongyi 侯忠義. *San xia wu yi xilie xiaoshuo* 三俠五義系列小説 (The three knights and five gallants novel series). Shenyang: Liaoning jiaoyu chubanshe, 1992.

Hu Anshun 胡安順. *Yinyunxue tonglun* 音韻學通論 (A comprehensive discussion of rhyme). Reprint edition; first edition 2002. Beijing: Zhonghua shuju, 2003.

Hu Shi 胡適. "Da Huang Jueseng jun 'Zhezhong de wenxue gexin lun'" 答黃覺僧君《折衷的文學革新論》(Responding to Huang Jueseng's "A compromised argument for literary innovation"). In *Hu Shi wenji* 胡適文集 (Collected writings by Hu Shi), edited by Ouyang Zhesheng 歐陽哲生. 12 vols. Beijing: Beijing daxue chubanshe, 1998. Vol. 2, pp. 89–93.

———. *Guoyu wenxue shi* 國語文學史 (A history of vernacular literature). Hefei: Anhui jiaoyu chubanshe, 1999.

———. "*Ernü yingxiong zhuan* xu" 《兒女英雄傳》序 (Preface to *The tale of romance and heroism*). In *Zhongguo zhanghui xiaoshuo kaozheng* 中國章回小說考證 (A study of the Chinese zhanghui novel), pp. 345–62. Hefei: Anhui jiaoyu chubanshe, 1999.

———. "*Haishang hua liezhuan* xu" 《海上花列傳》序 (Preface to *The flowers of Shanghai*). In *Zhongguo zhanghui xiaoshuo kaozheng* 中國章回小說考證 (A study of the Chinese zhanghui novel), pp. 365–88. Hefei: Anhui jiaoyu chubanshe, 1999.

———. "*Jing hua yuan* de yinlun" 《鏡花緣》的引論 (An introductory discussion to *Flowers in the Mirror*). In *Zhongguo zhanghui xiaoshuo kaozheng* 中國章回小說考證 (A study of the Chinese zhanghui novel), pp. 391–423. Hefei: Anhui jiaoyu chubanshe, 1999.

———. "*San xia wu yi* xu" 《三俠五義》序 (Preface to *The three knights and the five gallants*). In *Zhongguo zhanghui xiaoshuo kaozheng* 中國章回小說考證 (A study of the Chinese zhanghui novel), pp. 293–323. Hefei: Anhui jiaoyu chubanshe, 1999.

———. *Baihua wenxue shi* 白話文學史 (A history of vernacular literature). Tianjin: Baihua wenyi chubanshe, 2002.

Hu Shiying 胡士瑩. *Huaben xiaoshuo gailun* 話本小說概論 (A general discussion of the storyteller novel). Taipei: Danqing tushu, 1983.

Hu Siao-chen 胡曉真. *Cainü cheye wei mian: jindai zhongguo nüxing xushi wenxue de xingqu* 才女徹夜未眠: 近代中國女性敘事文學的興趣 (Burning the midnight oil: the rise of female narrative in early modern China). Taipei: Maita, 2003.

———. "Pinfan riyong yu daotong lunli—lun *Ernü yingxiong zhuan*" 蘋蘩日用與道統倫理——論《兒女英雄傳》(Everyday life and Confucian orthodox ethics—about *The tale of romance and heroism*)." In *Ming Qing wenxue yu sixiang zhong zhi zhuti yishi yu shehui—wenxue pian* 明清文學與思想中之主題意識與社會—文學篇 (Subjectivity and society in Ming Qing literature and thought—literature), edited by Wang Ayling 王瓊玲. 2 vols. Taipei: Institute of Chinese Literature and Philosophy, 2004. Vol. 2, pp. 589–638.

Huang Shizhong 黃仕忠. "Chewangfu chaocang zidishu zuozhe kao" 車王府鈔藏子弟書作者考 (An investigation of the authors of *zidishu* in the Household of the Prince of Che). In *Che wangfu quben yanjiu* 車王府曲本研究 (Research on the libretti of the Household of the Prince of Che), edited by Liu Liemao 劉烈茂 and Guo Jingrui 郭精銳, pp. 413–57.

Jia Caizhu 賈采珠, ed. *Beijing erhua cidian* 北京兒話詞典 (A dictionary of Beijing children's speech). Beijing: Yuwen chubanshe, 1991.

Jiang Kun 姜昆 and Ni Zhongzhi 倪鍾之, eds. *Zhongguo quyi tongshi* 中國曲藝通始 (A comprehensive history of China's oral performance arts). Beijing: Renmin wenxue chubanshe, 2005.

Jiangsu sheng shehuikexueyuan Ming Qing xiaoshuo yanjiu zhongxin wenxue yanjiusuo 江苏省社会科学院明清小说研究中心文学研究所. *Zhongguo tongsu xiaoshuo zongmu tiyao* 中國通俗小說總目提要 (A comprehensive summary of contents of the Chinese popular novel). Beijing: Zhongguo wenlian chubanshe, 1991.

Jiangsu sheng zhengxie wenshi ziliao weiyuanhui 江蘇省政協文史資料委員會 and Taishou shi zhengxie wenshi ziliao weiyuanhui 泰州市政協文史資料委員會, eds. *Pinghua zongshi Liu Jingting* 評話宗師柳敬亭 (The first master of storytelling Liu Jingting). Nanjing: Jiangsu wenshi ziliao, 1995.

Jin Mingqiu 金明求. *Song Yuan Ming huaben xiaoshuo ruhua zhi xushi yanjiu* 宋元明話本小說入話之敘事研究 (A narratological investigation of the introductory tale of the Song, Yuan, Ming storyteller novel). Taipei: Da'an chubanshe, 2009.

Jin Qiping 金啟平 and Zhang Xuekai 章學楷, eds. *Beijing qiren yishu: Chaqu* 北京旗人藝術: 岔曲 (The art of Beijing bannermen: short songs). Beijing: Beijing shifan daxue chubanshe, 2007.

Jin Shengtan 金聖嘆. *Du di wu caizi shufa* 讀第五才子書法 (How to read *The fifth book of genius*). In *Shuihuzhuan huiping ben*, pp. 15–22.

Jin Wenjing 金文京. "Yu Yue de wenyi guan" 俞樾的文藝觀 (The literary views of Yu Yue). In Chen Pingyuan 陳平原, Wang Dewei 王德威, and Shang Wei 商偉, eds. *Wan Ming yu wan Qing: lishi chuancheng yu wenhua chuanxin* 晚明與晚清: 歷史傳承與文化創新 (The late Ming and the late Qing: historical dynamics and cultural renewal), pp. 579–93. Changsha: Hubei jiaoyu chubanshe, 2002.

Jin Yong 金庸. *She diao yingxiong zhuan* 射雕英雄傳 (The eagle-shooting heroes). 9 vols. Kowloon: Cheung Hing Book Co., 1960–69?

———. "Lu ding ji 鹿鼎記 (The deer and the cauldron)." In *Mingpao*, November 7, 1968. p. 6.

———. *Lu ding ji* 鹿鼎記 (The deer and the cauldron). 5 vols. Taipei: Yuanjing chubanshi, 1981.

———. "Houji" 後記 (Postscript). In *Shediao yingxiong zhuan* 射雕英雄傳 (The eagle-shooting heroes). 4 vols. 3rd edition. Taipei: Yuanliu chubanshe, 2003. Vol. 4, pp. 1619–23.

———. *She diao yingxiong zhuan* 射雕英雄傳 (The eagle-shooting heroes). 4 vols. 3rd edition. Taipei: Yuanliu chubanshe, 2003.

———. *Jujuan tang Li, Baibeng Zhang suo chao zaqu* 聚卷堂李, 百本張所抄雜曲 (Catalogs from the Jujuan tang of Li and Baiben Zhang). Manuscript. 9 vols.

Kang Baocheng 康保成. "Zidishu zuozhe 'Helü shi' shengping, jiashi kaolüe" 子弟書作者'鶴侶氏'生平, 家世考略 (A brief study of the life and family of the author of *zidishu*, master He Lü). In *Che wangfu quben yanjiu* 車王府曲本研究

(Research on the libretti of the household of the Prince of Che), edited by Liu Liemao 劉烈茂 and Guo Jingrui 郭精鋭, pp. 458–80.

Kang Laixin 康來新. *Wan Qing xiaoshuo lilun yanjiu* 晚清小說理論研究 (A study of late-Qing theories of the novel). Taipei: Da'an chubanshe, 1986.

"Katuri jetere juben i bithe, *pangxie duan'er*" 螃蟹段兒 (Eating crabs *zidishu*). In *Zidishu congchao* 子弟書叢鈔 (A collection of *zidishu*), edited by Guang Dedong 關德棟 and Zhou Zhongming 周中明, vol. 2, pp. 771–87.

Kenryū keijō zenzu kaisetsu sakuin 乾隆京城全圖解說, 考引 (The Qianlong-era complete map of the capital with explanation, index). Beijing: Kōain Kahoku Renrakubu Seimukyoku Chōsajo, 1940.

"Kuo danainai zhen guang Xiding" 闊大奶奶真逛西頂 (The grand dame truly tours Xiding). In *Zhongyang yanjiu yuan lishi yuyan yanjiusuo suocang su qu* 中央研究院歷史語言研究所所藏俗曲 (Popular songs collected in the Research Institute of Historical Philology of the Academia Sinica), reel 307. Microfilm reprint edition. Ithaca, NY: Cornell University, 1970–1979?.

"Kuo daye zhui Ding" 闊大爺追丁 (A wealthy master chases [his wife] to [Ximen] ding). In *Zhongyang yanjiu yuan lishi yuyan yanjiusuo suocang su qu* 中央研究院歷史語言研究所所藏俗曲 (Popular songs collected in the Research Institute of Historical Philology of the Academia Sineca), reel 307. Microfilm reprint edition. Ithaca, NY: Cornell University, 1970–79?.

Lan Shaohua 蘭少華 and Lu Shulun 陸樹侖. "Qianyan" 前言 (Preface). In *Xu xiao wu yi* 續小五義 (The latter five gallants), pp. 1–4. Shanghai: Shanghai guji chubanshe, 1993.

Lanling xiaoxiaosheng 蘭陵笑笑生. *Jin ping mei cihua* 金瓶梅詞話 (The tale of Jin Ping Mei). Preface dated 1618; facsimile reprint edition. 5 vols. Tokyo: Daian, 1963.

———. *Mengmeiguan jiaoben Jin ping mei cihua* 夢梅館校本金瓶梅詞話 (The Mengmeiguan edited edition of *Jin Ping Mei cihua*), edited and annotated by Mei Jie 梅節. Reprint edition. 3 vols. Taipei: Liren, 2007.

Lao She 老舍. "Chaguan" 茶館 (Tea-house). In *Chaguan, Longxugou* 茶館, 龍須溝 (Tea-house, Dragon Beard Ditch), pp. 1–66. Beijing: Renmin wenxue chubanshe, 1994.

———. *Luotuo Xiangzi* 駱駝祥子 (Rickshaw). Taipei: Liren shuju, 1998.

"Lao xi piao yuan" 老西嫖冤 (Complaint by a Shanxi fellow gone whoring). In *Zhongyang yanjiu yuan lishi yuyan yanjiusuo suocang su qu* 中央研究院歷史語言研究所所藏俗曲 (Popular songs collected in the Research Institute of Historical Philology of the Academia Sinica), reel 306. Microfilm reprint edition. Ithaca, NY: Cornell University, 1970–79?.

Lei Xiaotong 雷曉彤. "Jindai Beijing de Manzu xiaoshuojia Cai Youmei" 近代北京的滿族小說家蔡友梅 (Cai Youmei, a modern Manchu novelist from Beijing). In *Manzu yanjiu* (2005.4): 108–16.

"[Leshan tang] zidi, dagu shu mulu" [樂善堂] 子弟大鼓書目錄 (A catalogue of *zidishu* and drumsong libretti [of the Leshan tang]). In *Zhongyang yanjiu yuan lishi yuyan yanjiusuo suocang su qu* 中央研究院歷史語言研究所所藏俗曲 (Popular songs collected in the Research Institute of Historical Philology of the Academia Sinica), edited by Zhongyang yanjiu yuan Lishi yuyan yanjiusuo

中央研究院歷史語言研究所, reel 21. Microfilm reprint edition. Ithaca, NY: Cornell University, 1970–1979?.

Li Dou 李斗. *Yangzhou huafang lu* 揚州畫舫錄 (Record of the painted boats of Yangzhou). Annotated by Yang Jialuo 楊家駱. Preface 1795; reprint edition. Taipei: Shijie shuju, 1999.

Li Jiarui 李家瑞. *Beiping suqu lüe* 北平俗曲略 (An overview of popular Beijing songs). First edition 1932; reprint edition. Taipei: Wenshizhe chubanshe, 1974.

———. "Cong Shi Yukun de 'Longtu gongan' shuodao 'San xia wu yi'" 從石玉昆的 '龍圖公案' 說到 '三俠五義' (From Shi Yukun's *Cases of the Dragon Diadem* to *The three knights and the five gallants*). In *Li Jiarui xiansheng tongsu wenxue lunwen ji* 李家瑞先生通俗文學論文集 (Collected essays by Li Jiarui about popular literature), edited by Wang Qiugui 王秋桂, pp. 17–23. Taipei: Xuesheng shuju, 1982.

———. *Li Jiarui xiansheng tongsu wenxue lunwen ji* 李家瑞先生通俗文學論文集 (Collected essays by Li Jiarui about popular literature). Edited by Wang Qiugui 王秋桂. Taipei: Xuesheng shuju, 1982.

———. "Qingdai Beijing mantou pu zulin changben de gaikuang" 清代北京饅頭鋪租賃唱本的概況 (The circumstances of Mantou shops selling and renting *changben* during the Qing). In *Li Jiarui xiansheng tongsu wenji* 李家瑞先生通俗文學論文集 (Collected essays by Li Jiarui about popular literature), edited by Wang Qiugui 王秋桂, pp. 161–64. Taipei: Xuesheng shuju, 1982.

Li Luke 李路珂, Wang Nan 王南, Hu Jiezhong 胡介中, Li Jing 李菁, eds. *Beijing gu jianzhu ditu, shang* 北京古建筑地圖, 上 (The historical architectural map of Beijing, part 1). Beijing: Qinghua daxue chubanshe, 2009.

Li Rong 李榮, ed. *Taiyuan fangyan cidian* 太原方言詞典 (A dictionary of Taiyuan dialect). Nanjing: Jiangsu jiaoyu chubanshe, 1994.

Li Ruzhen 李汝珍. *Li shi yin jian* 李氏音鑒 (Master Li's mirror of rhymes). First edition 1810; reprint edition 1868. Muxi shanfang.

———. *Jing hua yuan* 鏡花緣 (Flowers in the mirror). First edition 1828; reprint edition. 2 vols. Shanghai: Shanghai guji chubanshe, 1990.

Li Xiusheng 李修生. *Guben xiqu jumu tiyao* 古本戲曲劇目提要 (Summaries of pre-modern operas). Beijing: Wenhua yishu chubanshe, 1997.

Li Yonghu 李永祜. "Jiaodian houji" 校點後記 (Some comments after editing). In Tanmeng daoren 貪夢道人 et al., *Peng gongan quanzhuan* 彭公安全傳 (The complete cases of Judge Peng). Annotated by Li Yonghu 李永祜, Li Wenling 李文苓, and Wei Shuidong 魏水東. Reprint edition. 4 Vols. Beijing: Qunzhong chubanshe, 2001. Vol. 4, pp. 330–34.

Li Yu 李豫 et al., eds. *Zhongguo guci zongmu* 中國鼓詞總目. Taiyuan: Shanxi guji chubanshe, 2006.

———. "*Zhongguo guci zongmu* bianzhuan fenduan yiju ji lilun tantao" 《中國鼓詞總目》編撰分斷依据及理論探討 (The foundation and a theoretical inquiry of the categorization of the compilation *A complete list of Chinese drum songs*). In Li Yu 李豫 et al., eds. *Zhongguo guci zong mu* 中國鼓詞總目 (A complete list of Chinese drum songs), pp. 1–50. Taiyuan: Shanxi guji chubanshe, 2006.

Li Zhen 李貞. *Ernü yingxiong zhuan de wenxue yuyan yanjiu* 《兒女英雄傳》的文學語言研究 (A study of the literary language of *A tale of romance and heroism*). Hangzhou: Zhejiang daxue chubanshe, 2011.

Li Zhengquan 李正權, ed. *Zhongguo mimian shipin dadian* 中國米麵食品大典 (The great dictionary of Chinese staples and food). Qingdao: Qingdao chubanshe, 1997.

Liang Qichao 梁啟超. "Lun xiaoshuo yu qunzhi zhi guanxi" 論小說與群治之關係 (On the relationship between fiction and the government of the people). In *Zhongguo jindai wenlun xuan* 中國近代文論選 (Selected Chinese essays on literary theory of the modern age), vol. 1, pp. 157–61. Beijing: Renmin chubanshe, 1962.

Lin Baochun 林寶淳. *Jiegou Jin Yong* 解構金庸 (Deconstructing Jin Yong). Taipei: Yuanliu chubanshe, 2000.

Lin Tieya 林鐵. "Qiu sheng xu" 秋聲序 (Preface to *Autumn sounds*). In *Yu Chu xin zhi* 虞初新志 (A new record of Yu Chu), edited and commentated by Zhang Chao 張潮, pp. 10–11. Shijiazhuang: Hebei renmin chubanshe, 1985.

Liu gongan 劉公案 (The cases of Judge Liu). Edited by Yan Qi 燕琦. Beijing: Renmin wenxue chubanshe, 1990.

Liu Liemao 劉烈茂 and Guo Jingrui 郭精銳, eds. *Qing Che wangfu chaocang quben: zidishu ji* 清車王府鈔藏曲本: 子弟書集 (The handwritten libretti of the Qing dynasty household of the Prince of Che collection: the collected *zidishu*). 2 vols. Nanjing: Jiangsu guji chubanshe, 1993.

———. *Che wangfu quben yanjiu* 車王府曲本研究 (Research on the libretti of the household of the Prince of Che). Guangzhou: Guangdong renmin chubanshe, 2000.

Liu Naou 劉吶鷗. "Youxi" 遊戲 (Games). In *Shanghaide hubuwu: Xin ganjue pai xiaoshuo xuan* 上海的狐步舞:新感覺派小說選 (Shanghai foxtrot: selected stories of the New Perceptionists), selected and edited by Leo Lee 李歐梵, pp. 313–21. Taipei: Yunchen wenhua shiye gufen youxian gongxi, 2001.

Liu Shide 劉世德, ed. *Zhongguo gudai xiaoshuo baikequanshu* 中國古代小說百科全書 (The encyclopedia of Chinese ancient novels). Beijing: Zhongguo dabaike quanshu chubanshe, 1993.

Liu Xiaomeng 劉小萌. *Qingdai Beijing qiren shehui* 清代北京旗人社會 (Bannerman society in Qing dynasty Beijing). Beijing: Zhongguo shehui kexue chubanshe, 2008.

Liu Yinbo 劉蔭柏. *Zhongguo wuxia xiaoshuo shi (gudai bufen)* 中國武俠小說史 (古代部分) (A history of the Chinese martial-arts novel [the premodern era]). Shijiazhuang: Huashan wenyi chubanshe, 1992.

Longtu erlu 龍圖耳錄 (Aural record of the Dragon Diadem). Annotated by Fu Xihua 傅惜華. Manuscript Xielan zhai 謝藍齋: reprint edition. 2 vols. Shanghai: Shanghai guji chubanshe, 1981.

Loujiang deguhuanshi zhuren 婁江得古歡室主人. "Pingyan Jigong zhuan xu" 評演濟公傳序 (Preface to *The storyteller tale of Jigong*). In Guo Xiaoting 郭小亭, *Pingyan Jigong zhuan* 評演濟公傳 (The storyteller tale of Jigong), edited by Zhu Qing 竺青. Preface 1898 (first part), 1900 (second part); reprint edition. 2 vols. Beijing: Zhonghua shuju, 2001. Vol. 1, p. 11.

Lu Decai 魯德才. *Lu Decai shuo Bao gongan* 魯德才說包公案. Beijing: Zhonghua shuju, 2008.

Lu Xun 魯迅. "Guxiang" 故鄉 (My old hometown). In *Lu Xun xuanji* 魯迅選集 (Selected writings by Lu Xun). 4 vols. Chengdu: Sichuan renmin chubanshe, 1983. Vol. 1, pp. 58–68.

———. "Zhufu" 祝福 (The new year's sacrifice). In *Lu Xun xuanji* 魯迅選集 (Selected writings by Lu Xun). 2 vols. Chengdu: Sichuan renmin chubanshe, 1983. Vol. 2, pp. 132–50.

———. *Xiaoshuo jiu wen chao* 小說舊聞抄 (Writings on things I heard long ago on novels). Ji'nan: Qi Lu shushe, 1997.

———. *Zhongguo xiaoshuo shilüe* 中國小說史略 (A brief history of Chinese fiction). Reprint edition. Shanghai: Shanghai guji chubanshe, 1998.

Luo Liqun 羅立群. *Zhongguo wuxia xiaoshuo shi* 中國武俠小說史 (History of the Chinese martial arts novel). Shenyang: Liaoning renmin chubanshe, 1990.

Luo Xiongfei 羅雄飛. "Lun Yu Yue zai wan Qing xueshushishang de diwei" 論俞樾在晚清學術史上的地位 (Yu Yue's position in the history of late Qing scholarship). In *Suzhou daxue xuebao* 1 (2007): 99–104.

Mao Dun 茅盾. *Ziye* 子夜 (Midnight). Vol. 4 in the series *Mao Dun quan ji* 茅盾全集 (The complete works of Mao Dun). 72 vols. Beijing: Renmin wenxue chubanshe, 1984.

———. "Fengjian de xiaoshimin wenyi" 封建的小市民文藝 (On the feudal literary art of the urban petty bourgeoisie). Originally published in *Dongfang zazhi* 東方雜誌 33.3 (Feb. 1, 1933). Republished in *Mao Dun quan ji* 茅盾全集 (The complete works of Mao Dun). 38 volumes. Beijing: Renmin wenxue chubanshe, 1991. Vol. 19, pp. 368–72.

———. *Chun can* 春蠶 (Spring silkworms). In *Mao Dun xiaoshuo xuanji* 茅盾小說選集 (Selected fiction by Mao Dun). 5 vols. Chengdu: Sichuan wenyi chubanshe, 1994. Vol. 5, pp. 167–88.

———. "Mai doufu de shaozi" 賣豆腐的哨子 (The whistle of the *doufu* peddler)." In *Mao Dun xuan ji* 茅盾選集 (Selected works of Mao Dun). 3 vols. Beijing: Renmin wenxue chubanshe, 1997. Vol. 3, pp. 15–16.

Meng Yuanlao 孟元老, et al. *Dongjing menghua lu (wai si zhong)* 東京夢華錄(外四種) (A record of a Hua dream of the Eastern Capital [and four other works]). Reprint edition. Taipei: Dali chubanshe, 1980.

Miao Huaiming 苗懷明. "*Xiao wu yi, Xu xiao wu yi* de kanxingzhe Shi Duo ji qi Wenguang lou shufang" 小五義, 續小五義的刊行者石鐸及其文光樓書坊 (Shi Duo, the publisher of *The latter five gallants* and *The continued latter five gallants* and his Wenguang publishing house). In *Bianji xuekan* 6 (1995): 96–97.

———. "*Longtu erlu* banben kaoshu"《龍圖耳錄》版本考述 (An investigation of the editions of *The aural record of the Dragon Diadem*). In *Wenjiao ziliao* 文教資料 6 (1995): 108–14.

———. "*San xia wu yi* de chengshu guocheng"《三俠五義》的成書過程 (The process through which *The three knights and the five gallants* became a book). In *Gudian wenxue zhishi* 66.3 (1996): 76–79.

———. "Qingdai zhonghouqi chubanye de fazhan yu Qingdai gongan wudai xiaoshuo de fanrong 清代中後期出版業的發展與清代公案俠義小說的繁榮

(The development of the publishing industry in the mid- and late Qing and the blossoming of the Qing-dynasty martial-arts novel). In *Bianji xuekan* 2 (1997): 109–13.

———. "*San xia wu yi* chengshu xinkao" 三俠五義成書新考 (A new investigation of the way *The three knights* became a book). In *Ming Qing xiaoshuo yanjiu* 3 (1998): 209–24.

———. "Wan Qing gongan xia'yi xi shulüe" 晚清公案俠義戲書略 (A brief discussion of late-Qing martial-arts operas). *Yishu baijia* 3 (2000): 27–31.

Mindu bieji 閩都別記 (A distinct record of the capital of Minnan). 2 vols. Fujian renmin chubanshe, 1987.

Mo Yan 莫言. *Sishiyi pao* 四十一炮 (POW!). Shenyang: Chunfeng wenyi chubanshe, 2003.

———. "Yong erduo yuedu" 用耳朵閱讀 (Reading with your ears). In *Yong erduo yuedu* 用耳朵閱讀 (Reading with your ears), pp. 55–59. Beijing: Zuojia chubanshe, 2012.

———. *Hong gaoliang jiazu* 紅高粱家族 (Red sorghum). Shanghai: Shanghai wenyi chubanshe, 2012.

Mu Shiying 穆時英. *Shanghai de hubuwu-yige duanpian* 上海的狐步舞——一個斷片 (Shanghai foxtrot; a fragment). In *Shanghaide hubuwu Xin ganjue pai xiaoshuo xuan* 上海狐步舞: 新感覺派小說選 (Shanghai foxtrot: selected stories of the New Perceptionists), selected and edited by Leo Lee 李歐梵, pp. 184–96. Taipei: Yunchen wenhua shiye gufen youxian gongxi, 2001.

"Nanqing gong qing shou" 南清宮慶壽 (The birthday celebration in the Nanqing Palace). In *Zhongyang yanjiuyuan lishi yuyan yanjiusuo cang su wenxue congkan* 中央研究院歷史語言研究所藏俗文學叢刊 (Folk literature: materials in the collection of the Institute of History and Philology), edited by Zhongyang yanjiuyuan lishi yuyan yanjiusuo suwenxue congkan bianji xiaozu 中央研究院歷史語言研究所俗文學叢刊編輯小組. Photographic reprint edition. 500 vols. Taipei: Zhongyang yanjiuyuan lishi yuyan yanjiusuo and Xinwenfeng chuban gufen youxian gongsi, 2005. Vol. 407, pp. 1–150.

Ning Jiayu 寧稼雨. "Wu shu nao Dongjing zhuan" 五鼠鬧東京傳 (The tale of the five rats creating havoc in the Eastern Capital). In *Zhongguo gudai xiaoshuo baikequanshu* 中國古代小說百科全書 (The encyclopedia of Chinese ancient novels), edited by Liu Shide 劉世德, pp. 578–79. Beijing: Zhongguo dabaike quanshu chubanshe, 1993.

"Qi li cun" 七里村 (Seven-mile village). In *Zhongyang yanjiuyuan lishi yuyan yanjiusuo cang su wenxue congkan* 中央研究院歷史語言研究所藏俗文學叢刊 (Folk literature: materials in the collection of the Institute of History and Philology), edited by Zhongyang yanjiuyuan lishi yuyan yanjiusuo suwenxue congkan bianji xiaozu 中央研究院歷史語言研究所俗文學叢刊編輯小組. Photographic reprint edition. 500 vols. Taipei: Zhongyang yanjiuyuan lishi yuyan yanjiusuo and Xinwenfeng chuban gufen youxian gongsi, 2005. Vol. 405, c. 1, pp. 1–191.

Qi xia wu yi 七俠五義 (The seven knights and the five gallants). Edited by Yu Yue
俞樾. First edition 1890, reprint edition. In *Guben xiaoshuo jicheng* 古本小說
集成 (The collection of ancient Chinese novels). 2 vols. Shanghai: Shanghai
guji chubanshe, 1990.

Qing neiwufu cang jingcheng quan tu 清內務府藏京城全圖 (The Qing Imperial
Household Agency's complete map of the capital). 1750. Held in the Palace
Museum, Peking. Reprinted edition.

Qiu Jiang 仇江. "Che wangfu quben chaocang guci de tese" 車王府曲本抄藏
鼓詞的特色 (The characteristics of the preserved drum-song manuscripts
among the libretti of the collection of the household of the Prince of Che).
In *Che wangfu quben yanjiu* 車王府曲本研究 (Research on the libretti of the
household of the Prince of Che), edited by Liu Liemao 劉烈茂 and Guo Jingrui
郭精銳, pp. 235–59.

Qu Yanbin 曲彥斌, ed. *Zhongguo miyu hanghua cidian* 中國密語行話詞典 (A
dictionary of Chinese secret languages and guild speech). Beijing: Shumu
wenxian chubanshe, 1994.

Rongyu tang Shuihu zhuan 容與堂水滸傳 (The Rongyutang edition of *The
outlaws of the marsh*). 2 vols. Shanghai: Shanghai guji chubanshe, 1988.

San guo yan yi huiping ben 三國演義會評本 (The romance of the three kingdoms
with collected commentaries). Edited and compiled by Chen Xizhong 陳曦鍾,
Song Xiangrui 宋祥瑞, and Lu Yuchuan 魯玉川. 2 vols. Beijing: Beijing daxue
chubanshe, 1998.

San xia wu yi 三俠五義 (The three knights and the five gallants). Punctuated
by Yu Pingbo 俞平伯. First edition 1878; reprint edition. Shanghai: Yadong
tushuguan, 1925.

San xia wu yi 三俠五義 (The three knights and the five gallants). First edition
1878; reprint edition. Taipei: Zhiyang chubanshe, 1993.

San xia wu yi 三俠五義 (The three knights and the five gallants). Annotated
and punctuated by Wang Jun 王軍. First edition 1878; reprint edition. 2 vols.
Beijing: Zhonghua shuju, 1996.

San xia wu yi guci 三俠五義鼓詞 (The three knights and the five gallants drum
song). In *Che wangfu quben* 車王府曲本 (Che prince household collection
libretti), reel 33–34. Microfilm reprint edition. Beijing: Zhonghua quanguo
tushuguan wenxian suowei zhongxin, 1994.

San xia wu yi xi 三俠五義戲 (The three knights and the five gallants opera). In
Che wangfu quben 車王府曲本 (Che prince household collection libretti). reel
123–25. Microfilm reprint edition. Beijing: Zhonghua quanguo tushuguan
wenxian suowei zhongxin, 1994.

Shan Tianfang 單田芳. *San xia wu yi* 三俠五義 (The three knights and the five
gallants). 2 vols. Beijing: Qunzhong chubanshe, 1998.

Shanghai yishu yanjiusuo 上海藝術研究所 and Zhongguo xijujia shanghai fenhui
中國戲劇家上海分會, eds. *Zhongguo xiqu quyi cidian* 中國戲曲曲藝辭典 (A
dictionary of Chinese opera and oral performing arts). Shanghai: Shanghai
cishu chubanshe, 1981.

Shen Congwen 沈從文. "Xiaoxiao" 蕭蕭 (Xiaoxiao). In *Shen Congwen xiaoshuo xuan* 沈從文小說選 (Selected fiction by Shen Congwen), pp. 88–104. Changsha: Hunan renmin wenxue chubanshe, 1981.

Shi An 石菴. "Chankongshi suibi" 懺空室隨筆 (The spontaneous jottings of the Chankong Hall). Originally published in *Yangzijiang xiaoshuo bao* 揚子江 小說報 1.1 (1909). Republished in *Wan qing wenxue congchao: xiaoshuo xiqu yanjiu juan* 晚清文學叢抄: 小說戲曲研究卷 (Collected writings on literature of the late Qing: opera and fiction), edited by Aying 阿英, pp. 440–44. Beijing: Zhonghua shuju, 1960.

Shi da Longtu erlu 師大龍圖耳錄 (The Beijing Normal Teachers University edition of *The aural record of the Dragon Diadem*).

Shi Duo 石鐸 (The Master of the Wenguanglou 文光樓主人). "*Xiao wu yi* xu" 小五義序 (Preface to *The latter five gallants*). In Ding Xigen, *Zhongguo lidai xiaoshuo xuba ji*, vol. 3, pp. 1552–53.

Shi gong quan an 施公全案 (The complete cases of Judge Shi). 2 vols. Nanjing: Jiangsu guji chubanshe, 1994.

Shi gongan 施公案 (The cases of Judge Shi). 3 vols. Beijing: Baowen tang, 1982.

Shi Qu 石渠. *Kuiqingju shilu* 葵青居詩錄 (A record of poetry from the Kuiqing Studio). In *Congshu jicheng chubian* 叢書集成初編 (The collected collectanae, first series) Vol. 2347. Beijing: Zhonghua shu ju, 1985.

"Shi Yukun" 石玉昆 (Shi Yukun). In *Zidishu congchao* 子弟書叢鈔 (A collection of *zidishu*), edited by Guang Dedong 關德棟 and Zhou Zhongming 周中明, vol. 2, pp. 734–37.

Shi yun shu chaoben Bao gongan 石韻書抄本包公案 (Shi rhyme scheme manuscript of *The cases of Judge Bao*). In *Gu gong zhenben congkan* 故宮珍 本叢刊 (The gathered rare books of the Palace Museum). Haikou: Hainan chubanshe, 2000. Vol. 702.

Shi Zhecun 施蟄存. "Meiyu zhi xi" 梅雨之夕 (One evening in the rainy season). In *Shi Zhecun daibiao zuo* 施蟄存代表作 (Representative works of Shi Zhecun), pp. 121–32. Beijing: Huaxia chubanshe, 1998.

Shuihu zhuan huiping ben 水滸傳會評本 (The outlaws of the marsh with collected commentaries). Edited and compiled by Chen Xizhong 陳曦鐘, Hou Zhongyi 侯忠義, and Lu Yuchuan 魯玉川. 2 vols. Beijing: Beijing daxue chubanshe, 1998.

Song Kefu 宋克夫. "Zheng xu *Xiao wu yi* zuozhe kaolun" 正續《小五義》作者考 論 (An investigation into the author of the preface to the sequel *The latter five gallants*). In *Wenxian* 3 (1997): 75–85.

Song Lihua 宋莉華. "Fangyan yu Ming Qing xiaoshuo jiqi chuanbo 方言與明 清小說及其傳播 (Dialect, its relationship with the Ming/Qing novel and its transmission). *Ming Qing xiaoshuo yanjiu* 4 (1999): 36–50.

Song Weijie 宋偉杰. "Wan Qing xiayi gongan xiaoshuo de shenti xiangxiang: jiedu *San xia wu yi*" 晚清俠義公案小說的身體想象: 解讀《三俠五義》(The imagination of the body in the late-Qing martial-arts novel: Reading *The three knights and the five gallants*). In *Wan Ming yu wan Qing: lishi chuancheng yu wenhua chuanxin* 晚明與晚清: 歷史傳承與文化創新 (The late Ming and the late Qing: historical dynamics and cultural renewal), edited by Chen Pingyuan 陳平原, Wang Dewei 王德威, and Shang Wei 商偉, pp. 441–51. Changsha: Hubei jiaoyu chubanshe, 2002.

Song Xiaocai 宋孝才, ed. *Beijing huayu cihui yi* 北京話語詞匯譯 (A collection of Beijing dialect phrases). Beijing: Beijing yuyan xueyuan chubanshe, 1987.

"Suiyuanle" 隨緣樂 (Suiyuanle). In *Zidishu congchao* 子弟書叢鈔 (A collection of *zidishu*), edited by Guang Dedong 關德棟 and Zhou Zhongming 周中明. 2 vols. Shanghai: Shanghai guji chubanshe, 1984. Vol. 2, pp. 738–41.

Sun Kaidi 孫楷第. *Zhongguo tongsu xiaoshuo shumu* 中國通俗小說書目 (A list of Chinese popular novels). Beijing: Renmin wenxue chubanshe, 1982.

———. "Guanyu *Ernü yingxiong zhuan*" 關於兒女英雄傳 (About *The tale of romance and heroism*). In *Zhongguo jindai wenxue lunwen ji* 中國近代文學論文集 (1919–1949): 小說卷 (A collection of essays on modern Chinese literature [1919–1949]: fiction), edited by Wang Junnian 王俊年, pp. 255–68. Beijing: Zhongguo shehui kexue chubanshe, 1988.

Sun Shoupeng 孫壽彭. "*Peng gongan xu*" 彭公案序 (Preface to *The cases of Judge Peng*). In Ding Xigen, *Zhongguo lidai xiaoshuo xuba ji*, vol. 3, p. 1616.

Tanmeng daoren 貪夢道人 (Yao Yidian 楊挹殿). *Peng gongan* 彭公案 (The cases of Judge Peng). 1st edition. Beijing: Jinwen tang, 1892.

———. *Peng gongan* 彭公案 (The cases of Judge Peng). First edition 1892; reprint edition. Vol. 1 in *Peng gongan quan zhuan* 彭公案全傳 (The complete cases of Judge Peng), annotated by Li Yonghu 李永祐, Li Wenling 李文苓, and Wei Shuidong 魏水東. 4 vols. Beijing: Qunzhong chubanshe, 2001.

Tanmeng daoren 貪夢道人 et al. *Peng gongan quanzhuan* 彭公案全傳 (The complete cases of Judge Peng. 4 vols. Beijing: Qunzhong chubanshe, 2001.

Tsien Tsuen-hsuin 錢存訓. *Zhongguo shuji, zhimo ji yinshua shi lunwen ji* 中國書籍、紙墨及印刷史論文集 (A collection of essays on Chinese books, paper, ink, and printing). Hong Kong: The Chinese University of Hong Kong, 1992.

Wang Bin 王彬 and Xu Xiushan 徐秀珊, eds. *Beijing diming cidian* 北京地名辭典 (A dictionary of Beijing place names). Beijing: Zhongguo wenlian chubanshe, 2001.

Wang Jiaju 王稼句. *Sanbai liushi hang tu ji* 三百六十行圖集 (A collection of pictures of the 360 occupations). 2 vols. Suzhou: Guwuxuan chubanshe, 2002.

Wang Jingshou 王景壽, Wang Jue 王決, and Zeng Huijie 曾蕙杰. *Zhongguo pingshu yishu lun* 中國評書藝術論 (A theory of the art of Chinese storytelling). Beijing: Jingji ribao chubanshe, 1997.

Wang Junnian 王俊年, ed. *Zhongguo jindai wenxue lunwen ji: xiaoshuo juan* 中國近代文學論文集 (1919–1949): 小說卷 (A collection of essays on modern Chinese literature [1919–1949]: fiction). Beijing: Zhongguo shehui kexue chubanshe, 1988.

Wang Liqi 王利器. *Yuan Ming Qing sandai jinhui xiaoshuo xiqu shiliao* 元明清三代禁毀小說戲曲史料 (Historical material regarding banned novels and operas of the Yuan, Ming and Qing dynasties). Shanghai: Shanghai gujie chuanshe, 1981.

Wang Qingyuan 王清原, Mou Renlong 牟仁隆, and Han Xifeng 韓錫鋒. *Xiaoshuo shufang lu* 小說書坊錄 (A list of bookstores selling novels). Beijing: Beijing tushuguan chubanshe, 2002.

Wang Senran 王森然. *Zhongguo jumu cidian* 中國劇目辭典 (A dictionary of Chinese opera titles). Shijiazhuang: Hebei jiaoyu chubanshe, 1997.

Wang Songmu 王松木. "Qisheguo de bu chuan zhi mi—cong *Lishi yinjian*, *Jinghuayuan* fansi dangqian Hanyu yinyue xue de chuanbo" 歧舌國的不傳之密--從《李氏音鑑》、《鏡花緣》反思當前漢語音韻學的傳播 (The secret of the Forked-Tongue Kingdom: An examination of the circulation of Chinese phonology based on *Lishi yinjian* and *Jinghuayuan*). In *Hanxue yanjiu* 26.1 (2008): 231–60.

Wenguang zhuren 文光主人. "Preface to *The latter tale of the cases of Judge Shi*" 施公案後傳序. In Ding Xigen, *Zhongguo lidai xiaoshuo xuba ji*, vol. 3, pp. 1612–13.

Wen Kang 文康. *Ernü yingxiong zhuan* 兒女英雄傳 (The tale of romance and heroism). Republished edition, 2 vols. Taipei: He luo tushu chubanshe, 1980.

———. *Ernü yingxiong zhuan* 兒女英雄傳 (The tale of romance and heroism). Photographic reprint edition. Vols. 104–7 in *Guben xiaoshuo jicheng* 古本小說集成 (The collection of ancient Chinese novels). Shanghai: Shanghai guji chubanshe, 1990.

———. *Ernü yingxiong zhuan* 兒女英雄傳 (The tale of romance and heroism). Edited, punctuated, and annotated by Ergong 尔弓. First edition 1878; reprint edition. 2 vols. Ji'nan: Qi Lu shushe, 1990.

———. *Huitu Ernü yingxiong zhuan* 繪圖兒女英雄傳 (The illustrated tale of romance and heroism). Shanghai: Saoye shanfang, Guangxu period (1875–1906).

Wenzhu zhuren 問竹主人. "*Zhonglie xia'yi zhuan* xu" 忠烈俠義傳序 (Preface to *The tale of loyalty and knightly righteousness*). In Ding Xigen, *Zhongguo lidai xiaoshuo xuba ji*, vol. 3, pp. 1542–43.

Wu Wenke 吳文科. *Zhongguo quyi tonglun* 中國曲藝通論 (A survey of China's folk musical theater). Taiyan: Shanxi jiaoyu chubanshe, 2002.

Wu Yinghua 吳英華 and Wu Shaoying 吳紹英. "You guan 'San xia wu yi' zuozhe de yi shou kegui de shi" 有關'三俠五義'作者的一首可貴的詩 (An important poem about the author of *The three knights and the five gallants*). In *Zhongguo jindai wenxue lunwen ji: xiaoshuo zhuan* 中國近代文學論文集: 小說傳 (A collection of essays on modern Chinese literature: fiction), pp. 90–93. Beijing: Zhongguo shehui kexue chubanshe, 1983.

Xia Renhu 夏仁虎. *Jiu jing suo ji* 舊京瑣記 (Scattered notes on the old capital). Beijing: Guji chubanshe, 1986.

Xiangxiaren 鄉下人 (Country fellow). "Shuoshu xianping" 說書閒評 (Some idle comments on storytelling). First published in *Xiaoshuo bawang* 57 (1919); reprinted in *Suzhou pingtan jiuwen chao* 蘇州評彈舊聞鈔 (A collection of old anecdotes regarding storytelling in Suzhou), edited by Zhou Liang 周良, pp. 201–2. Huaiyin: Jiangsu sheng renmin chubanshe, 1983.

Xiao wu yi 小五義 (The latter five gallants). Photographic reprint of the 1896 edition. Shanghai: Shanghai guji chubanshe, 1990.

Xiao wu yi 小五義 (The latter five gallants). First edition 1890; reprint edition. Punctuated by Lu Shulun 陸樹侖 and Zhu Shaohua 竺少華. Shanghai: Shanghai guji chubanshe, 1993.

Xiuxiang qixia wuyi 繡像七俠五義 (The illustrated seven knights and the five gallants). Edited by Yu Yue 俞樾. Shanghai: Zhenyi shuju, 1892.

Xu Baohua 許寶華 and Miyata Ichirō 宮田一郎, eds. *Hanyu fangyan da cidian* 漢語方言大辭典 (The great dictionary of Chinese dialects). 5 vols. Beijing: Zhonghua shuju, 1999.

Xu Fuzuo 徐復祚 (b. 1560–after 1630). *Huadang ge cong tan* 花當閣叢談 (The collected chats of the Huadan Lodge). In *Collected Transcriptions of the Jieyue Mountain Lodge* 借月山房彙鈔, edited by Zhang Haipeng 張海鵬. Shanghai: Boguzhai, 1920.

Xu Shirong 徐世榮. *Beijing tuyu cidian* 北京土語辭典 (A dictionary of Beijing dialect). Beijing: Beijing chubanshe, 1990.

Xu xiao wu yi 續小五義 (The continued latter five gallants). Beijing: Renmin wenxue chubanshe, 2001.

Yan Jingchang 顏景常. *Gudai xiaoshuo yu fangyan* 古代小說與方言 (Premodern novels and dialect). Shenyang: Liaoning jiaoyu chubanshe, 1992.

Yang Dingjian 楊定見. "*Shuihu zhuan* xiaoyin" 水滸傳小引 (Brief introduction to *The Outlaws*). In *Shuihu zhuan huiping ben* 水滸傳會評本 (The outlaws of the marsh with collected commentaries), vol. 1, pp. 29–30.

Yang Jingting 楊靜亭. *Dumen jilüe* 都門紀略 (A short account of the capital). First edition 1845; 1910 reprint edition. Vol. 716–17 in *Jindai Zhongguo shiliao congkan* 近代中國史料叢刊 (Gathered publications of historical material of modern China). Taipei: Wenhai chubanshe, 1971.

Yang Jingting and Li Jingshan 李靜山. *Zengbu dumen jilüe* 增補都門紀略 (The expanded brief guide to the capital). Beijing: 1879.

Ye Hongsheng 葉洪生. *Lun jian: Wuxia xiaoshuo tanyi lu* 論劍: 武俠小說談藝錄 (Discussing swords: A record of chats about the aesthetics of martial arts fiction). Shanghai: Xuelin chubanshe, 1997.

Ye Zihao 葉子豪. "*Quan xu Peng gongan* xu" 全續彭公案序 (Preface to *The complete continued cases of Judge Peng*). In Ding Xigen, *Zhongguo lidai xiaoshuo xuba ji*,vol. 3, pp. 1618–19.

"Yin cuo yang cha" 陰錯陽差 (The *yin-yang* mix-up). In *Zhongyang yanjiuyuan lishi yuyan yanjiusuo cang su wenxue congkan* 中央研究院歷史語言研究所藏俗文學叢刊 (Folk literature: materials in the collection of the Institute of History and Philology), edited by Zhongyang yanjiuyuan lishi yuyan yanjiusuo suwenxue congkan bianji xiaozu 中央研究院歷史 語言研究所俗文學叢刊編輯小組. Photographic reprint edition. 500 vols. Taipei: Zhongyang yanjiuyuan lishi yuyan yanjiusuo and Xinwenfeng chuban gufen youxian gongsi, 2005. Vol. 408, c. 1, pp. 193–221.

Youhuansheng 優患生. "Jinghua baier zhuzhici" 京華百二竹枝詞 (One-hundred-twenty bamboo branch songs of splendid Beijing). In *Zhonghua zhuzhici* 中華竹枝詞 (Bamboo branch songs of China), edited by Lei Mengshui 雷夢水 et al. 6 vols. Beijing: Beijing guji chubanshe, 1996. Vol. 1, pp. 273–97.

Yu Pingbo 俞平伯. "Jiao du hou ji" 校讀後記 (Some comments after editing the novel). In *San xia wu yi* 三俠五義 (Three knights and the five gallants), pp. 1–10. Reprinted edition. Shanghai: Yadong tushuguan, 1925.

Yu Shengting 于盛庭. "Shi Yukun ji qi zhushu chengshu" 石玉昆及其著述成書 (Shi Yukun and the composition of his book). In *Ming Qing xiaoshuo yanjiu* 8.2 (1998): 145–57.

Yu Yue 俞樾. *Chaxiang shi congchao* 茶香室叢抄 (Gathered writings from the Chaxiang Studio). Punctuated by Zhen Fan 貞凡, Gu Xin 顧馨, and Xu Minxia 徐敏霞. 4 vols. Beijing: Zhonghua shuju, 1995.

———. "*Chongbian qixia wuyi zhuan* xu" 重編《七俠五義》傳序 (Preface to *The reedited edition of the seven knights and five gallants*). In Ding Xigen, *Zhongguo lidai xiaoshuo xuba ji*, vol. 3, pp. 1544–45.

Yuan Jin 袁進. *Jindai wenxue de tupo* 近代文學的突圍 (The breakthrough of modern literature). Shanghai: Renmin chubanshe, 2001.

Yunyouke 雲游客 (Lian Kuoru 連闊如). *Jianghu congtan* 江湖叢談 (Gathered tales of the *jianghu*). First edition 1936; photographic reprinted edition. Shanghai: Shanghai wenyi chubanshe, 1991.

Zeng Bairong 曾白融, ed. *Jingju jumu cidian* 京劇劇目辭典 (A dictionary of Chinese opera titles). Beijing: Zhongguo xiju chubanshe, 1989.

"Zha Junheng" 鍘君恆. In *Zhongyang yanjiuyuan lishi yuyan yanjiusuo cang su wenxue congkan* 中央研究院歷史語言研究所藏俗文學叢刊 (Folk literature: materials in the collection of the Institute of History and Philology), edited by Zhongyang yanjiuyuan lishi yuyan yanjiusuo suwenxue congkan bianji xiaozu 中央研究院歷史語言研究所俗文學叢刊編輯小組. Photographic reprint edition. 500 vols. Taipei: Zhongyang yanjiuyuan lishi yuyan yanjiusuo and Xinwenfeng chuban gufen youxian gongsi, 2005. Vol. 408, c. 1, pp. 407–35.

Zhang Bing 張兵. *Wen Kang yu 'Ernü yingxiong zhuan'* 文康與《兒女英雄傳》 (Wen Kang and *The tale of romance and heroism*). Shenyang: Liaoning chubanshe, 1993.

Zhang Chao 張潮. *Yu Chu xin zhi* 虞初新志 (A new record of Yu Chu). Shijiazhuang: Hebei renmin chubanshe, 1985.

Zhang Cixi 張次溪. *Renmin shoudu de Tianqiao* 人民首都的天橋 (Tianqiao, capital of the people). First edition 1951; reprint edition. Beijing: Zhongguo quyi chubanshe, 1988.

Zhang Dai 張岱. "Liu Mazi shuoshu" 柳麻子說書 (The storytelling of Pockmarked Liu). In *Pinghua zongshi Liu Jingting* 評話宗師柳敬亭 (The first master of storytelling, Liu Jingting), edited by Jiangsu sheng zhengxie wenshi ziliao weiyuanhui 江蘇省政協文史資料委員會 and Taizhou shi zhengxie wenshi ziliao weiyuanhui 泰州市政協文史資料委員會, p. 35. Nanjing: Jiangsu wenshi ziliao, 1995.

———. "Liu Jingting shuoshu" 柳敬亭說書 (The storytelling of Liu Jingting). In *Tao'an meng yi; Xihu meng xun* 陶庵夢憶；西湖夢尋 (Tao'an's dream memories; remembrances of dreams of West Lake), pp. 81–82. Shanghai: Shanghai guji chubanshe, 2001.

Zhang Huaijiu 張懷久 and Liu Chongyi 劉崇義, eds. *Wu di fangyan xiaoshuo* 吳
地方言小説 (Dialect novels from the Wu region). Nanjing: Nanjing daxue
chubanshe, 1997.

Zhang Jinglu 張靜廬, ed. *Zhongguo jindai chubanshiliao er bian* 中國近代出版史
料二編 (Second collection of historical material on Chinese publishing in the
modern era). Shanghai: Qunlian chubanshe, 1954.

Zhang Lianming 張廉明. "Chazi huoshao" 叉子火燒 (Fork-fried fritters). In
Zhongguo mimian shipin dadian 中國米麵食品大典 (The great dictionary of
Chinese staples and food), edited by Li Zhengquan 李正權, p. 14. Qingdao:
Qingdao chubanshe, 1997.

Zhang Shijun 張世君. Hong lou meng *de kongjian xushi* 紅樓夢的空間敘事 (The
narration of space in *Dream of the Red Chamber*). Beijing: Zhongguo shehe
kexue chubanshe, 1999.

Zhao Jingshen 趙景深. "*Ernü yingxiong zhuan* zhong de dagu shiliao" '兒女英
雄傳'中的大鼓史料 (Historical material on *dagu* in *The tale of romance and
heroism*). In Wen Kang 文康, *Ernü yingxiong zhuan* 兒女雄傳 (The tale
of romance and heroism). Republished edition, 2 vols. Taipei: He luo tushu
chubanshe, 1980. Vol. 2, pp. 983–84.

Zheng Yuyu 鄭毓瑜. "Lianlei, fengsong yu shiyu tiyan de chuanyi—cong *Qi fa* de
yuanji xiaoneng tanqi" 連類, 諷誦與嗜欲體驗的傳譯—從《七發》的療疾效
能談起 (Correlative thinking, recitation and the realization of desire in early
Han *fu*). In *Qinghua xuebao* 36.2 (2006): 399–425.

Zheng Zhenduo 鄭振鐸, ed. *Shuihu quan zhuan* 水滸全傳 (The complete outlaws
of the marsh). Beijing: Renmin wenxue chubanshe, 1954.

Zhongguo dabaikequanshu chubanshe bianjibu 中國大百科全書出版社編輯部,
ed. *Zhongguo dabaikequanshu: xiqu, yishu* 中國大百科全書: 戲曲, 曲藝 (The
great encyclopedia of China: opera, oral performance). Beijing: Zhongguo
dabaikequanshu chubanshe, 1983.

Zhongguo yishu yanjiuyuan yinyue yanjiusuo bianjibu 中國藝術研究院音樂研
究所編輯部, ed. *Zhongguo yinyue cidian* 中國音樂詞典 (An encyclopedia of
Chinese music). Beijing: Renmin yinyue chubanshe, 2000.

Zhonglie xiao wu yi zhuan 忠烈小五義傳 (The continued tale of the latter five
gallants). Beijing: Wenguanglou, 1890.

Zhonglie xiayi zhuan 忠烈俠義傳 (The tale of loyalty and knightly righteousness).
Beijing: Juzhen tang, 1879.

Zhonglie xiayi zhuan 忠烈俠義傳 (The tale of loyal heroes and knightly gallants).
Annotated and punctuated by Wang Jun 王軍. First edition 1878; reprint
edition. 2 vols. Beijing: Zhonghua shuju, 1996.

Zhonglie xiayi zhuan: xu xiao wu yi 忠烈俠義傳: 續小五義 (The tale of loyal
heroes and knightly gallants: the continued latter five gallants). Edited and
punctuated by Wang Shu 王述. First edition 1891; reprint edition. Beijing:
Renmin wenxue chubanshe, 2001.

Zhongyang yanjiuyuan yuyan yanjiusuo suwenxue congkan bianji xiaozu 中央
研究院語言研究所俗文學叢刊編輯小組. "Shuochang lei Shipai shu zongmu"
説唱類石派書總目 (The comprehensive table of contents of Shi style libretti

in the prosometric literature section). In *Zhongyang yanjiuyuan lishi yuyan yanjiusuo cang su wenxue congkan* 中央研究院歷史語言研究所藏俗文學叢刊 (Folk literature: materials in the collection of the Institute of History and Philology), edited by Zhongyang yanjiuyuan lishi yuyan yanjiusuo suwenxue congkan bianji xiaozu 中央研究院歷史語言研究所俗文學叢刊編輯小組. Photographic reprint edition. 500 vols. Taipei: Zhongyang yanjiuyuan lishi yuyan yanjiusuo and Xinwenfeng chuban gufen youxian gongsi, 2005. Vol. 401, pp. 1–4.

Zhou Zuoren 周作人. *Zhongguo xin wenxue de yuanliu* 中國新文學的源流 (The origins and development of China's new literature). Changsha: Yue Lu Shushe chubanshe, 1989.

English and Other European Language Sources

Allen, Joseph. "Dressing and Undressing the Chinese Woman Warrior." *Positions* 4.2 (1996): 343–79.

Altenberger, Roland. "Is It Clothes That Make the Man? Cross-dressing, Gender, and Sex in Pre-twentieth Century Zhu Yingtai Lore." *Asian Folklore Studies* 64.2 (2005): 165–205.

———. *The Sword or the Needle: The Female Knight-errant* (xia) *in Traditional Chinese Narrative.* Bern: Peter Lang, 2009.

Anderson, Marston. *The Limits of Realism: Chinese Fiction in the Revolutionary Period.* Berkeley: University of California Press, 1990.

Attali, Jacques. *Noise: The Political Economy of Music.* Translated by Brian Massumi. Minneapolis: University of Minnesota Press, 1999.

Balzer, Richard. *Peepshows: A Visual History.* New York: Harry N. Abrams, 1998.

Barthes, Roland. "The Reality Effect." In *French Literary Theory Today: A Reader*, translated by Richard Howard and edited by Tzvetan Todorov, pp. 11–17. Cambridge: Cambridge University Press, 1982.

Bausinger, Herman. *Folk Culture in a World of Technology.* Translated by Elke Dettmer. Bloomington and Indianapolis: Indiana University Press, 1990.

Behr, Wolfgang, and Bernhard Führer. "Einführende Notizen zum Lesen mit besonderer Berücksichtiggung der Frühzeit." In *Aspekte des Lesens in China in Vergangheit und Gegenwart*, edited by Bernard Führer, pp. 1–43. Bochum: Projekt Verlag, 2005.

Benjamin, Walter. "The Storyteller: Reflections on the Works of Nikolai Leskov." In *Illuminations: Essays and Reflections,* edited by Hannah Arendt and translated by Harry Zohn, pp. 83–110. New York: Schocken Books, 1968.

Birch, Cyril. "Some Formal Characteristics of the Hua-pen Story." *Bulletin of the School of Oriental and African Studies* 17.2 (1955): 346–64.

———. *Studies in Chinese Literary Genres.* Berkeley: University of California Press, 1974.

Birrell, Anne. *Games Poets Play: Readings in Medieval Chinese Poetry*. Cambridge: McGuinness Chinese Monographs, 2004.

Blader, Susan. "A Critical Study of *San-hsia wu-yi* and its relationship to the 'Lung-t'u kung-an' Song-book." PhD diss., University of Pennsylvania, 1977.

———. "*San-hsia wu-yi* and its link to Oral Literature." *CHINOPERL* 8 (1978): 9–38.

———. "Introduction." In *Tales of Magistrate Bao and His Valiant Lieutenants*, translated by Susan Blader, pp. i–xlvi. Hong Kong: Chinese University Press, 1998.

———, trans. *Tales of Magistrate Bao and His Valiant Lieutenants*. Hong Kong: Chinese University Press, 1998.

Børdahl, Vibeke, and Jette Ross. *Chinese Storytellers: Life and Art in the Yangzhou Tradition*. Boston: Cheng & Tsui, 2002.

———, and Margaret B. Wan, eds. *The Interplay of the Oral and the Written in Chinese Popular Literature*. Singapore: NIAS Press, 2010.

Brogan, T.V.F. "Iconicity." In *The New Princeton Encyclopedia of Poetry and Poetics*, edited by Alex Preminger and T.V.F. Brogan, p. 552. Princeton: Princeton University Press, 1993.

———. "Onomatopoeia." In *The New Princeton Encyclopedia of Poetry and Poetics*, edited by Alex Preminger and T.V.F. Brogan, pp. 860–63. Princeton: Princeton University Press, 1993.

Brokaw, Cynthia J. *Commerce in Culture: The Sibao Book Trade in the Qing and Republican Periods*. Cambridge, MA: Harvard University Asia Center, 2007.

Brook, Timothy. *The Confusions of Pleasure: Commerce and Culture in Ming China*. Berkeley: University of California Press, 1998.

Brooks, Peter. *Reading for the Plot: Design and Invention in Narrative*. New York: Alfred A. Knopf, 1984.

Cha, Louis. *The Deer and the Cauldron, the First Book*. Translated and edited by John Minford. Oxford: Oxford University Press, 1997.

Chang, Kang-I Sun. "The Device of the Mask in the Poetry of Wu Wei-yeh (1609–1671)." In *The Power of Culture: Studies in Chinese Cultural History*. edited by Willard J. Peterson, Andrew H. Plaks, and Ying-shih Yü, pp. 247–74. Hong Kong: The Chinese University Press, 1994.

Chartier, Roger. "Gutenberg Revisited from the East." *Late Imperial China* 17.1 (June 1996): 1–9.

Chau, Adam. *Miraculous Response: Doing Popular Religion in Contemporary China*. Stanford: Stanford University Press, 2008.

Chia, Lucille. *Printing for Profit: The Commercial Publishers of Jianyang, Fujian (11th–17th Centuries)*. Cambridge, MA: Harvard University Asia Center, 2002.

Chion, Michel. *Audio-Vision: Sound on Screen*. Edited and translated by Claudia Gorbman. New York: Columbia University Press, 1994.

———. *The Voice in Cinema*. Translated by Claudia Gorbman. New York: Columbia University Press, 1999.

Chiu, Suet Ying. "Cultural Hybridity in Manchu Bannermen Tales (*Zidishu*)." PhD diss., University of California at Los Angeles, 2007.

Chou, Chih-p'ing. *Yüan Hung-tao and the Kung-an School*. Cambridge: Cambridge University Press, 1988.

Chow Kai-wing. "Writing for Success: Printing, Examinations, and Intellectual Change in Late Ming China." *Late Imperial China* 17.1 (June 1996): 120–57.

Chow, Rey. *The Protestant Ethnic & The Spirit of Capitalism*. New York: Columbia University Press, 2002.

Clunas, Craig. *Pictures and Visuality in Early Modern China*. Princeton: Princeton University Press, 1997.

———. *Empire of Great Brightness: Visual and Material Cultures of Ming China, 1368–1644*. Honolulu: University of Hawaii Press, 2007.

Corbin, Alain. *Village Bells: Sound and Meaning in the Nineteenth-century French Countryside*. Translated by Martin Thom. New York: Columbia University Press, 1998.

Crary, Jonathan. *Suspension of Perceptions: Attention, Spectacle, and Modern Culture*. London and Cambridge, MA: MIT Press, 1999.

Crespi, John. *Voices in Revolution: Poetry and the Auditory Imagination in Modern China*. Honolulu: University of Hawai'i Press, 2007.

Crossley, Pamela Kyle. *Orphan Warriors: Three Manchu Generations and the End of the Qing World*. Princeton: Princeton University Press, 1990.

Dale, Alan. *Comedy Is a Man in Trouble: Slapstick in American Movies*. Minneapolis: University of Minnesota Press, 2000.

Davies, Bronwyn, and Rom Harre. "Positioning: The Discursive Production of Selves." *Journal for the Theory of Social Behavior* 20 (1990): 43–63.

Debord, Guy. *Society of the Spectacle*. Translated by Ken Knabb. Oakland: AK Press, 2004.

des Forges, Alexander. "From Source Texts to 'Reality Observed': The Creation of the 'Author' in Nineteenth-Century Chinese Vernacular Fiction." *Chinese Literature: Essays, Articles, Reviews* 22 (2000): 64–87.

———. *Mediasphere Shanghai: The Aesthetics of Cultural Production*. Honolulu: University of Hawaii Press, 2007.

Ding Naifei. *Obscene Things: Sexual Politics in* Jin Ping Mei. Durham and London: Duke University Press, 2002.

Eberhard, Wolfram. "Notes on Chinese Storytellers." *Fabula* 11 (1970): 1–31.

Elliott, Mark C. "The 'Eating Crabs' Youth Book." In *Under Confucian Eyes: Writings on Gender in Chinese History*, edited by Susan Mann and Yu-yin Cheng, pp. 262–81. Berkeley: University of California Press, 2001.

———. *The Manchu Way: The Eight Banners and Ethnic Identity in Late Imperial China*. Stanford: Stanford University Press, 2001.

Elman, Benjamin. *From Philosophy to Philology: Intellectual and Social Aspects of Change in Late Imperial China*. Cambridge, MA: Harvard University Press, 1990.

———. "Naval Warfare and the Refraction of China's Self—Strengthening Reforms into Scientific and Technological Failure, 1860–1895." *Zhongguo xueshu* 4.3 (2003): 130–72.

Eoyang, Eugene. "The Immediate Audience: Oral Narration in Chinese Fiction." In *Critical Essays on Chinese Literature*, edited by William H. Nienhauser, Jr., pp. 43–57. Hong Kong: The Chinese University of Hong Kong, 1976.

Epstein, Maram. *Competing Discourses: Orthodoxy, Authenticity, and Engendered Meanings in Late Imperial Chinese Fiction*. Cambridge, MA: Harvard University Asia Center, 2001.

Fan, Victor Ho Lok. "Football Meets Opium: A Topological Study of Political Violence, Sovereignty, and Cinema Archaeology between 'England' and 'China.'" PhD diss., Yale University, 2010.

Feng Menglong. *Stories to Caution the World, A Ming Dynasty Collection, Vol. 2*. Translated by Shuhui Yang and Yunqin Yang. Seattle: University of Washington Press, 2005.

Folkenflik, Robert. "The Heirs of Watt." *Eighteenth Century Studies* 25.2 (Winter 1991–92): 203–17.

France, Rose. "The Speaking Author: 'Skaz' in Mikhail Zoshechenko's *Sentimental Tales*." In *Orality, Literacy, and Modern Media*, edited by Dietrich Scheunemann, pp. 62–76. Columbia, SC: Camden House, 1996.

Ge, Liangyan. "*Rou Putuan*: Voyeurism, Exhibitionism, and the 'Examination Complex.'" *Chinese Literature: Essays, Articles, Reviews* 20 (Dec. 1988): 127–52.

———. *Out of the Margins: The Rise of Chinese Vernacular Fiction*. Honolulu: University of Hawaii Press, 2001.

Goh, Meow Hui. *Sound and Sight: Poetry and Courtier Culture in the Yongming Era (483–493)*. Stanford: Stanford University Press, 2011.

Goldblatt, Howard. "Translator's Note." In Mo Yan, *Sandalwood Death: A Novel*, pp. ix–x. Norman: University of Oklahoma Press, 2013.

Goldman, Andrea S. "The Nun Who Wouldn't Be: Representations of Female Desire in Two Performance Genres of 'Si Fan.'" *Late Imperial China* 22.1 (June 2001): 71–138.

———. *Opera in the City: Theatrical Performance and Urbanite Aesthetics 1770–1900*. PhD diss, University of California ar Berkeley, 2005.

Granet, Marcel. *Fêtes et chansons anciennes de la Chine*. Paris: Bibliothèque de l'école des hautes études, 1919.

Hamm, John Christopher. "Reading the Swordswoman's Tale: Shisanmei and *Ernü Yingxiong Zhuan*." *T'oung Pao* LXXXIV (1998): 328–55.

———. "Wu-hsia Hsiao-shuo." In *The Indiana Companion to Traditional Chinese Literature (Volume 2)*, edited and compiled by William H. Nienhauser, Jr., pp. 188–92. Bloomington and Indianapolis: Indiana University Press, 1998.

———. *Paper Swordsmen: Jin Yong and the Modern Chinese Martial Arts Novel*. Honolulu: University of Hawaii Press, 2005.

Hanan, Patrick. *The Chinese Short Story: Studies in Dating, Authorship, and Composition*. Cambridge, MA: Harvard University Press, 1973.

———. "The Making of the *Pearl-sewn Shirt* and *The Courtesan's Jewel Box*." *Harvard Journal of Asiatic Studies* 33 (June 1973): 124–53.

————. "The Nature of Ling Meng-Ch'u's Fiction." In *Chinese Narrative: Critical and Theoretical Essays*, edited by Andrew H. Plaks, pp. 85–114. Princeton: Princeton University Press, 1977.

————. *The Chinese Vernacular Story*. Cambridge, MA: Harvard University Press, 1981.

————. "*Fengyue Meng* and the Courtesan Novel." *Harvard Journal of Asiatic Studies* 58.2 (1998): 345–72.

————. *Chinese Fiction of the Nineteenth and Early Twentieth Centuries*. New York: Columbia University Press, 2004.

He Yuming. "Difficulties of Performance: The Musical Career of Xu Wei's *The Mad Drummer*." *Harvard Journal of Asiatic Studies* 68.2 (December 2008): 77–114.

Hegel, Robert. *Reading Illustrated Fiction in Late Imperial China*. Stanford: Stanford University Press, 1998.

Hockx, Michel. *Internet Literature in China*. New York: Columbia University Press, forthcoming.

Hsia, C. T. *The Classic Chinese Novel: A Critical Introduction*. Ithaca, NY: Cornell University Press, 1968.

————. "The Military Romance: A Genre of Chinese Fiction." In *Studies in Chinese Literary Genres*, edited by Cyril Birch, pp. 339–90. Berkeley: University of California Press, 1974.

Hu Siao-chen. "In the Name of Correctness: Ding Yaokang's *Xu Jin Ping Mei* as a Reading of *Jin Ping Mei*." In *Snakes' Legs: Sequels, Continuations, Rewritings, and Chinese Fiction*, edited by Martin Huang, pp. 75–97. Honolulu: University of Hawaii Press, 2004.

Huang, Martin. *Literati and Self-Re/Presentation: Autobiographical Sensibility in the Eighteenth-Century Chinese Novel*. Stanford: Stanford University Press, 1995.

————. *Snakes' Legs: Sequels, Continuations, Rewritings, and Chinese Fiction*. Honolulu: University of Hawaii Press, 2004.

————. *Negotiating Masculinities in Late-imperial China*. Honolulu: University of Hawaii Press, 2006.

Hummel, Arthur W., ed. *Eminent Chinese of the Ch'ing Period*. 2 vols. Washington: U.S. Government Printing Office, 1943–44.

Hung, Chang-Tai. *Going to the People: Chinese Intellectuals and Folk Literature: 1918–1937*. Cambridge, MA: Harvard University Press, 1985.

Idema, Wilt. *Chinese Vernacular Fiction: The Formative Period*. Leiden: Brill, 1974.

————. "Performance and Construction of the *Chu-Kung-Tiao*." *Journal of Oriental Studies* 16.1 (1978): 63–78.

Idema, Wilt, and Beata Grant. *The Red Brush: Writing Women of Imperial China*. Cambridge, MA: Harvard University Asia Center, 2004.

Idema, Wilt, and Lloyd Haft. *Chinese Letterkunde—Inleiding, Historisch Overzicht en Bibliografieen* (Chinese literature—introduction, historical overview, and bibliographies). Utrecht: Het Spectrum, 1985.

Jahandarie, Khosrow. *Spoken and Written Discourse: A Multi-Disciplinary Perspective.* Stamford, CT: Ablex Publishing Corporation, 1999.

Jajdelska, Elspeth. *Silent Reading and the Birth of the Narrator.* Toronto: University of Toronto Press, 2007.

Jin Shengtan. "Jin Shengtan on *How to Read the Shuihu zhuan.*" Translated by John C. Y. Wang. In *How to Read the Chinese Novel,* edited by David Rolston. Princeton: Princeton University Press, 1990.

Johnson, Dale. *A Glossary of Words and Phrases in the Oral Performing and Dramatic Literature of the Jin, Yuan, and Ming.* Ann Arbor: Center for Chinese Studies, 2000.

Kafalas, Philip A. *In Limpid Dream: Nostalgia and Zhang Dai's Reminiscences of the Ming.* Norwalk, CT: Signature Books, 2007.

Karlitz, Catherine. *The Rhetoric of the* Chin p'ing mei. Bloomington: Indiana University Press, 1986.

Keijser, Anne Sytske. "Een geschiedenis van liefde en moed: Een stichtelijk avontuur" (A history of love and courage: an orthodox adventure). In *Op Avontuur! Aspecten van avonturenverhalen in Oost en West* (Adventure! aspects of adventure tales in east and west), edited by S. Houppermans, W. L. Idema, and R. Kruk, pp. 173–85. Zutphen: Walburg pers, 1998.

Kern, Martin. "*Shi jing* Songs as Performance Texts: A Case Study of 'Chu ci' ('Thorny Caltrop')." *Early China* 25 (2000): 49–111.

———. "Western Han Aesthetics and the Genesis of the *Fu.*" In *Harvard Journal of Asiatic Studies* 63.2 (December 2003): 383–437.

Keulemans, Pieter C. A. "Sounds of the Novel: Storytelling, Print-Culture, and Martial Arts Fiction in Nineteenth-Century Beijing." PhD diss., University of Chicago, 2004.

———. "Listening in on *The Dream of the Red Chamber*: Overhearing, Hearsay, and the Vernacular Architecture of Narrative, Space, and Subjectivity." Paper presented at the annual meeting of the Association for Asian Studies, Atlanta, 2008.

Korda, Natasha. "Gender at Work in the Cries of London." In *Oral Traditions and Gender in Early Modern Literary Texts,* edited by Mary Ellen Lamb and Karen Bamford, pp. 117–38. Aldershot: Ashgate, 2008.

Laing, Ellen Johnson. *Selling Happiness: Calendar Posters and Visual Culture in Early-Twentieth-Century Shanghai.* Honolulu: University of Hawaii Press, 2004.

Lam, Ling Hon. "The Matriarch's Private Ear: Performance, Reading, Censorship, and the Fabrication of Interiority in *The Story of the Stone.*" *Harvard Journal of Asiatic Studies* (December 2005): 357–415.

Lee, Haiyan. *Revolution of the Heart: A Genealogy of Love in China, 1900–1950.* Stanford: Stanford University Press, 2007.

Li, Han. "News, History, and 'Fiction on Current Events': Novels on Suppressing the Chuang Rebellion." In *Ming Studies* 66 (September 2012): 56–75.

Li, Tuo. "The Language of Jin Yong's Writing: A New Direction in the Development of Modern Chinese." In *The Jin Yong Phenomenon: Chinese Martial Arts Fiction and Modern Chinese Literary History*, edited by Ann Huss and Liu Jianmei, pp. 39–53. Translated by John Christopher Hamm. Youngstown, NY: Cambria Press, 2007.

Li, Wai-yee. *Enchantment and Disenchantment: Love and Illusion in Chinese Literature*. Princeton: Princeton University Press, 1993.

———. *The Readability of the Past in Early Chinese Historiography*. Cambridge, MA: Harvard University Asia Center, 2007.

Li Yu. "Learning to Read in Late-imperial China." In *Studies on Asia*, series 2, 1.1 (Fall 2004): 7–28.

Liang Qichao. "On the Relationship between Fiction and the Government of the People." Translated by Gek Nai Cheng. In *Modern Chinese Literary Thought: Writings on Literature, 1893–1945*, edited by Kirk Denton, pp. 74–81. Stanford: Stanford University Press, 1996.

Link, Perry. *Mandarin Ducks and Butterflies: Popular Fiction in Early Twentieth-Century Chinese Cities*. Berkeley: University of California Press, 1981.

Liu, James. *The Chinese Knight-errant*. London: Routledge and Kegan Paul, 1967.

Liu, Lydia H. *Translingual Practice: Literature, National Culture, and Translated Modernity—China, 1900–1937*. Stanford: Stanford University Press, 1995.

———. "Robinson Crusoe's Earthenware Pot." *Critical Inquiry* 86 (Summer 1999): 728–57.

Liu, Petrus. *Stateless Subjects: Chinese Martial Arts Literature and Postcolonial History*. Ithaca, NY: East Asia Program, Cornell University, 2011.

Liu Ts'un-yen. *Chinese Popular Fiction in Two London Libraries*. Hong Kong: Lung Men Bookstore, 1967.

Liu, Zaifu. "Jin Yong and Twentieth-Century Chinese Literature." In *The Jin Yong Phenomenon: Chinese Martial Arts Fiction and Modern Chinese Literary History*, edited by Ann Huss and Jianmei Liu, pp. 23–37. Translated by Kristof Van den Troost and Ann Huss. Youngstown, NY: Cambria Press, 2007.

Lord, Albert B. *The Singer of Tales*. Cambridge, MA: Harvard University Press, 1960.

Lu, Tina. *Persons, Roles, and Minds: Identity in* Peony Pavilion *and* Peach Blossom Fan. Stanford: Stanford University Press, 2001.

———. *Accidental Incest, Filial Cannibalism and Other Peculiar Encounters in Late Imperial Chinese Literature*. Cambridge, MA: Harvard University Asia Center, 2009.

Lu Xun. *A Brief History of Chinese Fiction*. Translated by Yang Xianyi and Gladys Yang. Beijing: Foreign Language Press, 1959.

Lyotard, Jean-Francois. *Discours/Figure*. Cambridge: Cambridge University Press, 1996.

Mair, Victor H., ed. *The Columbia Anthology of Traditional Chinese Literature*. New York: Columbia University Press, 1994.

Maspero, Henri. *China in Antiquity*. Translated by Frank A. Kierman, Jr. Amherst: University of Massachusetts Press, 1978.

McDaniel, Laura Andrews. "Jumping the Dragon Gate: Social Mobility among Storytellers in Shanghai, 1849–1949." PhD diss., Yale University, 1997.

McLaren, Anne. "Ming Audiences and Vernacular Hermeneutics: The Uses of *The Romance of the Three Kingdoms.*" *T'oung Pao* 81.1–3 (1995): 51–80.

———. *Chinese Popular Culture and Ming Chantefables.* Leiden: Brill, 1998.

———. "Constructing New Reading Publics in Late Ming China." In *Printing and Book Culture in Late Imperial China*, edited by Cynthia J. Brokaw, pp. 152–83. Berkeley: University of California Press, 2005.

McLuhan, Marshall. *The Gutenberg Galaxy: The Making of Typographic Man.* Toronto: University of Toronto Press, 1965.

McMahon, Keith. *Causality and Containment in Seventeenth-Century Chinese Fiction.* Leiden: Brill, 1988.

———. *Misers, Shrews, and Polygamists: Sexuality and Male-Female Relations in Eighteenth-century Chinese Fiction.* Durham: Duke University Press, 1995.

———. *Polygamy and Sublime Passion: Sexuality in China on the Verge of Modernity.* Honolulu: University of Hawaii Press, 2010.

Meng Yue. "The Invention of Shanghai: Cultural Passages and Their Transformation, 1860–1920." PhD diss., University of California at Los Angeles, 2000.

———. *Shanghai and the Edges of Empires.* Minneapolis: University of Minnesota Press, 2006.

Metz, Christian. "Aural Objects." In *Film Sound: Theory and Practice*, edited by Elisabeth Weis and John Belton, pp. 154–61. New York: Columbia University Press, 1985.

Meyer, Jeffrey F. "Rural Villages and Buddhist Monasteries: Contrasting Spatial Orientations in China." *Arch.& Comport./Arch. & Behav.* 9.2 (1993): 227–83.

Meyer-Fong, Tobie S. *Building Culture in Early Qing Yangzhou.* Stanford: Stanford University Press, 2003.

———. "Gathering in a Ruined City: Metaphor, Practice and Recovery in Post-Taiping Yangzhou." In *Lifestyle and Entertainment in Yangzhou*, edited by Lucie B. Olivová and Vibeke Børdahl, pp. 37–61. Copenhagen: NIAS Press, 2009.

Millward, James A. *Beyond the Pass: Economy, Ethnicity, and Empire in Qing Central Asia, 1759–1864.* Stanford: Stanford University Press, 1998.

Mo Yan. *POW!* Translated by Howard Goldblatt. London: Seagull Books, 2012.

Naquin, Susan. *Peking: Temples and City Life, 1400–1900.* Berkeley: University of California Press, 2000.

North, Michael. *The Dialect of Modernism: Race, Language and Twentieth-century Literature.* Oxford: Oxford University Press, 1994.

Ong, Walter. *Orality and Literacy: The Technologizing of the Word.* London: Methuen, 1982.

Owen, Stephen. *Remembrances: The Experience of the Past in Classical Chinese Literature.* Cambridge, MA: Harvard University Press, 1986.

———. "Place: Meditation on the Past at Chin-ling." In *Harvard Journal of Asiatic Studies* 49.2 (December 1990): 417–57.

Pettegree, Andrew. *The Book in the Renaissance*. New Haven: Yale University Press, 2010.

Picker, John M. *Victorian Soundscapes*. Oxford: Oxford University Press, 2003.

Plaks, Andrew H. *Four Masterworks of the Ming: Ssu ta ch'i shu*. Princeton: Princeton University Press, 1987.

Platt, Stephen R. *Provincial Patriots: The Hunanese and Modern China*. Cambridge, MA: Harvard University Press, 2007.

Preminger, Alex, and Terry V. F. Brogan, eds. *The New Princeton Encyclopedia of Poetry and Poetics*. Princeton: Princeton University Press, 1993.

Rankin, Mary Backus. *Elite Activism and Political Transformation in China: Zhejiang Province, 1865–1911*. Stanford: Stanford University Press, 1986.

Rea, Christopher Gordon. *A History of Laughter: Comic Culture in Early Twentieth-Century China*. PhD diss., Columbia University, 2008.

Reed, Christoper A. "Gutenberg in Shanghai: Mechanized Printing, Modern Publishing, and Their Effects on the City, 1876–1937." PhD diss., University of California at Berkeley, 1996.

———. *Gutenberg in Shanghai: Chinese Print Capitalism 1876–1937*. Vancouver: University of British Columbia Press, 2004.

Roddy, Stephen J. *Literati Identity and its Fictional Representations in Late Imperial China*. Stanford: Stanford University Press, 1998.

Rojas, Carlos. *The Naked Gaze: Reflections on Chinese Modernity*. Cambridge, MA: Harvard University Press, 2009.

Rolston, David. "Appendix 2: The Authenticity of the Li Chih Commentaries on the *Shui-hu chuan* and Other Novels Treated in this Volume." In *How to Read the Chinese Novel*, edited by David Rolston, pp. 356–63. Princeton: Princeton University Press, 1990.

Traditional Chinese Fiction and Fiction Commentary: Reading and Writing Between the Lines. Stanford: Stanford University Press, 1997.

———, ed. *How to Read the Chinese Novel*. Princeton: Princeton University Press, 1990.

Roy, David. "Introduction." In *The Plum in the Golden Vase or, Chin P'ing Mei: Vol. 1, The Gathering*, translated by David Roy, pp. xvii–xlviii. Princeton: Princeton University Press, 1993.

———, trans. *The Plum in the Golden Vase or, Chin P'ing Mei: Vol. 1, The Gathering*. Princeton: Princeton University Press, 1993.

Saussy, Haun. *The Great Walls of Discourse and Other Adventures in Cultural China*. Cambridge, MA: Harvard University Asia Center, 2001.

———. " 'Ritual Separates, Music Unites': Why Musical Hermeneutics Matters." In *Recarving the Dragon: Understanding Chinese Poetics*, edited by Olga Lomova. Prague: Charles University, 2003.

Schaberg, David. "'Virtue's Sound Shining': On Images of Sound." Paper presented at "Representing Things: Visuality and Materiality in East Asia," held at Yale University, April 23, 2009.

Schafer, R. Murray. *The Soundscape: Our Sonic Environment and the Tuning of the World*. Revised edition. Rochester, VT: Destiny Books, 1994.

Schwartz, Vanessa. *Spectacular Realities: Early Mass Culture in Fin-de-Siècle Paris*. Berkeley: University of California Press, 1998.

Shahar, Meir. *Crazy Ji: Chinese Religion and Popular Culture*. Cambridge, MA: Harvard University Press, 1998.

Shang Wei. "'Jin Ping Mei' and Late Ming Print Culture." In Zeitlin, Liu, and Widmer, *Writing and Materiality in China*, pp. 187–238. Cambridge, MA: Harvard University Asia Center, 2003.

———. "The Making of the Everyday World: *Jin Ping Mei cihua* and Encyclopedias for Daily Use." In *Dynastic Crisis and Cultural Innovation: From the Late Ming to the Late Qing and Beyond*, edited by David Der-wei Wang and Shang Wei, pp. 63–92. Cambridge, MA: Harvard University Press, 2005.

Sieber, Patricia. "Seeing the World through *Xianqing ouji* (1671): Visuality, Performance and Narratives of Modernity." *Modern Chinese Literature and Culture* 12.2 (2000): 1–41.

Silverman, Kaja. *The Acoustic Mirror: The Female Voice in Psychoanalysis and Cinema*. Bloomington: Indiana University Press, 1988.

Smith, Bruce R. *The Acoustic World of Early Modern England: Attending the O-Factor*. Chicago: University of Chicago Press, 1999.

Spence, Jonathan. *Return to Dragon Mountain: Memories of a Late Ming Man*. New York: Viking, 2007.

St. André, James. "Getting Down off a Tiger Isn't Easy: Editing Wuxia Fiction, 1870–1900." Paper delivered at the annual meeting of the Association for Asian Studies, Washington D.C., March 1998.

Starr, Chloë. *Red-light Novels of the Late Qing*. Leiden: Brill, 2007.

Stevens, Kate. "Peking Drumsinging." PhD diss., Harvard University, 1973.

Tang, Xiaobing. "Echoes of *Roar China!* On Vision and Voice in Modern Chinese Art." In *positions* 16.2 (Fall 2008): 467–94.

Tian, Xiaofei. "The Ship in a Bottle: The Construction of an Imaginary China in Jin Yong's Fiction." In *The Jin Yong Phenomenon: Chinese Martial Arts Fiction and Modern Chinese Literary History*, edited by Ann Huss and Jianmei Liu, pp. 219–40. Youngstown, NY: Cambria Press, 2007.

Todorov, Tzvetan, ed. *French Literary Theory Today: A Reader*. Translated by Richard Howard. Cambridge: Cambridge University Press, 1982.

Vallette-Hémery, Martine. *Yuan Hungdao (1568–1610): Théorie et Pratique Littéraire*. Paris: Presses Universitaires de France, 1982.

Volpp, Sophie. "The Discourse on Male Marriage: Li Yu's 'A Male Mencius's Mother.'" *positions* 2.1 (1994): 113–32.

———. "The Gift of a Python Robe: The Circulation of Objects in *Jin Ping Mei*." *Harvard Journal of Asiatic Studies* 65.1 (June 2005): 133–58.

Wakeman Jr., Frederic. "Localism and Loyalism during the Ch'ing Conquest of Kiangnan: The Tragedy of Chiang-yin." In *Conflict and Control in Late Imperial China*, edited by Frederic Wakeman Jr. and Carolyn Grant, pp. 43–85. Berkeley: University of California Press, 1975.

Wakeman Jr., Frederic, and Carolyn Grant, eds. *Conflict and Control in Late Imperial China*. Berkeley: University of California Press, 1975.

Wan, Margaret Baptist. Green Peony *and the Rise of the Martial Arts Novel*. Albany: State University of New York Press, 2009.

———. "Local Fiction of the Yangzhou Region: *Qingfengzha*." In *Lifestyle and Entertainment in Yangzhou*, edited by Lucie Olivova and Vibeke Børdahl, pp. 177–204. Copenhagen: Nordic Institute of Asian Studies Press, 2009.

———. "The Drum Ballad *Cases of Judge Liu*: A Window on the Form in the Early Nineteenth Century." In *China and Around: Mythology, Folklore, Literature*, edited by I. S. Smirnov, pp. 237–50. Moscow: Russian State University for the Humanities, 2010.

Wang, C. H. *The Bell and the Drum*: Shih Ching *as Formulaic Poetry in an Oral Tradition*. Berkeley: University of California Press, 1974.

Wang, David. "Storytelling Context in Chinese Fiction: A Preliminary Examination of It as a Mode of Narrative Discourse." *Tamkang Review* XV (Autumn 1984): 133–50.

———. *Fin-de-Siècle Splendor: Repressed Modernities of Late Qing fiction, 1849–1911*. Stanford: Stanford University Press, 1997.

Wang, Di. "The Rhythm of the City: Everyday Chengdu in Nineteenth-century Bamboo Branch Poetry." *Late Imperial China* 24.1 (June 2003): 33–78.

Wang, Jing. *The Story of Stone: Intertextuality, Ancient Chinese Stone Lore, and the Stone Symbolism in* Dream of the Red Chamber, Water Margin, *and* Journey to the West. Durham, NC: Duke University Press, 1992.

Wang, John C. Y. *Chin Sheng-t'an*. New York: Twayne Publishers, 1972.

———. "How to Read *The Fifth Book of Genius*." In *How to Read the Chinese Novel*, edited by David L. Rolston, pp. 131–45. Princeton: Princeton University Press, 1990.

Watt, Ian. *The Rise of the Novel: Studies in Defoe, Richardson, and Fielding*. Berkeley: University of California Press, 1957.

West, Stephen H. *Vaudeville and Narrative: Aspects of Chin Theater*. Wiesbaden: Franz Steiner Verlag, 1977.

———. "Playing with Food: Performance, Food, and the Aesthetics of Artificiality in the Sung and Yuan." *Harvard Journal of Asiatic Studies* 57.1 (1997): 67–106.

———. "Look at the Finger, Not Where it is Pointing." In *Ways with Words: Writing about Reading Texts from Early China*, edited by Pauline Yu et al., pp. 71–78. Berkeley: University of California Press, 2000.

———. "Crossing Over: Huizong in the Afterglow, or the Deaths of a Troubling Emperor." In *Emperor Huizong and Late Northern Song China: The Politics of Culture and the Culture of Politics*, edited by Patricia Buckley Ebrey and Maggie Bickford, pp. 565–608. Cambridge, MA: Harvard University Asia Center, 2006.

———. "Shifting Spaces: Local Dialect in *A Playboy from a Noble House Opts for the Wrong Career*." *Xiju yanjiu* 1 (2008): 83–108.

Widmer, Ellen. *The Margins of Utopia*: Shui-hu hou-chuan *and the Literature of Ming Loyalsim*. Cambridge, MA: Harvard University Asia Center, 1987.

———. "*Honglou meng ying* and its Publisher, Juzhen Tang of Beijing." *Late Imperial China* 23.2 (December 2002): 33–52.

———. *The Beauty and the Book: Women and Fiction in Nineteenth-Century China*. Cambridge, MA: Harvard University Asia Center, 2006.

Wright, Mary. *The Last Stand of Chinese Conservatism: The T'ung-chih Restoration, 1862–1874*. Stanford: Stanford University Press, 1962.

Wu Hung. "The Hong Kong Clock—Public Time-Telling and Political Time/Space." *Public Culture* 9.3 (1997): 329–54.

Yang, Shuhui. *Appropriation and Representation: Feng Menglong and the Chinese Vernacular Story*. Ann Arbor: Center for Chinese Studies, University of Michigan, 1998.

Yasar, Kerim. *Electrified Voices: Auditory Technology and Culture in Prewar Japan*. Forthcoming.

Yeh, Catherine Vance. *Shanghai Love: Courtesans, Intellectuals, and Entertainment Culture, 1850–1910*. Seattle: University of Washington Press, 2006.

———. "Creating the Urban Beauty: The Shanghai Courtesan in Late Qing Illustrations." In Zeitlin, Liu, and Widmer, *Writing and Materiality in China*, pp. 397–447. Cambridge, MA: Harvard University Asia Center, 2003.

Yeh, Michelle. " 'There are No Camels in the Koran'—What is Modern about Modern Chinese Poetry?" In *New Perspectives on Contemporary Chinese Poetry*, edited by Christopher Lupke, pp. 9–26. New York: Palgrave Macmillan, 2007.

Yu, Anthony. *Rereading the Stone: Desire and the Making of Fiction in* Dream of the Red Chamber. Princeton: Princeton University Press, 1997.

Yung, Sai-shing. "From Exorcism to Connoisseurship: Aural Experiences in Late-Ming Drama." Paper presented at "Sounds Chinese: Performance, Commodification, and Interpretation," National University of Singapore, December 15–17, 2008.

Zeitlin, Judith. *Historian of the Strange: Pu Songling and the Chinese Classical Tale*. Stanford: Stanford University Press, 1993.

———. *The Phantom Heroine: Ghosts and Gender in Seventeenth-Century Chinese Literature*. Honolulu: University of Hawaii Press, 2007.

———, and Lydia Liu, eds., with Ellen Widmer. *Writing and Materiality in China: Essays in Honor of Patrick Hanan*. Cambridge, MA: Harvard University Asia Center, 2003.

Zhang Zhen. *An Amorous History of the Silver Screen: Shanghai Cinema, 1896–1937*. Chicago: University of Chicago Press, 2005.

Zhao, Henry. *The Uneasy Narrator: Chinese Fiction from the Traditional to the Modern*. Oxford: Oxford University Press, 1995.

Zhou, Zuyan. "Carnivalization in *The Journey to the West*: Cultural Dialogism in Fictional Festivity." *Chinese Literature: Essays, Articles, Reviews* 16 (December 1994): 69–92.

Index

Page numbers in italics refer to figures

Harvard East Asian Monographs
(titles now in print)